THE SOCIAL CONSTRUCTION
OF SWEDISH NEUTRALITY

Manchester University Press

New Approaches to Conflict Analysis

Series editor: Peter Lawler, Senior Lecturer in International Relations, Department of Government, University of Manchester

Until recently, the study of conflict and conflict resolution remained comparatively immune to broad developments in social and political theory. When the changing nature and locus of large-scale conflict in the post-Cold War era is also taken into account, the case for a reconsideration of the fundamentals of conflict analysis and conflict resolution becomes all the more stark.

New Approaches to Conflict Analysis promotes the development of new theoretical insights and their application to concrete cases of large-scale conflict, broadly defined. The series intends not to ignore established approaches to conflict analysis and conflict resolution, but to contribute to the reconstruction of the field through a dialogue between orthodoxy and its contemporary critics. Equally, the series reflects the contemporary porosity of intellectual borderlines rather than simply perpetuating rigid boundaries around the study of conflict and peace. *New Approaches to Conflict Analysis* seeks to uphold the normative commitment of the field's founders yet also recognises that the moral impulse to research is properly part of its subject matter. To these ends, the series is comprised of the highest quality work of scholars drawn from throughout the international academic community, and from a wide range of disciplines within the social sciences.

PUBLISHED

Eşref Aksu
The United Nations, intra-state peacekeeping and normative change

M. Anne Brown
Human rights and the borders of suffering: the promotion of human rights in international politics

Lorraine Elliott and Graeme Cheeseman (eds)
Forces for good: cosmopolitan militaries in the twenty-first century

Richard Jackson
Writing the war on terrorism: language, politics and counter-terrorism

Tami Amanda Jacoby and Brent Sasley (eds)
Redefining security in the Middle East

Jan Koehler and Christoph Zürcher (eds)
Potentials of disorder

Helena Lindholm Schulz
Reconstruction of Palestinian nationalism: between revolution and statehood

David Bruce MacDonald
Balkan holocausts? Serbian and Croatian victim-centred propaganda and the war in Yugoslavia

Jennifer Milliken
The social construction of the Korean War

Ami Pedahzur
The Israeli response to Jewish extremism and violence: defending democracy

Maria Stern
Naming insecurity – constructing identity: 'Mayan-women' in Guatemala on the eve of 'peace'

Virginia Tilley
The one state solution: A breakthrough for peace in the israeli-palestinian deadlock

Tarja Väyrynen
Culture and international conflict resolution: a critical analysis of the work of John Burton

The social construction of Swedish neutrality

Challenges to Swedish identity and sovereignty

CHRISTINE AGIUS

Manchester University Press
MANCHESTER AND NEW YORK

distributed exclusively in the USA by Palgrave

Copyright © Christine Agius 2006

The right of Christine Agius to be identified as the author of this work has been asserted by her in accordance with the Copyright, Designs and Patents Act 1988.

Published by Manchester University Press
Oxford Road, Manchester M13 9NR, UK
and Room 400, 175 Fifth Avenue, New York, NY 10010, USA
www.manchesteruniversitypress.co.uk

Distributed in the United States exclusively by
Palgrave Macmillan, 175 Fifth Avenue,
New York, NY 10010, USA

Distributed in Canada exclusively by
UBC Press, University of British Columbia, 2029 West Mall,
Vancouver, BC, Canada V6T 1Z2

British Library Cataloguing-in-Publication Data is available

Library of Congress Cataloging-in-Publication Data is available

ISBN 978 0 7190 7153 9 paperback

First published by Manchester University Press in hardback 2006

This paperback edition first published 2012

The publisher has no responsibility for the persistence or accuracy of URLs for any external or third-party internet websites referred to in this book, and does not guarantee that any content on such websites is, or will remain, accurate or appropriate.

Printed by Lightning Source

CONTENTS

Abbreviations and acronyms — *page* vi
Acknowledgements — ix

	Introduction	1
1	Writing neutrality: from the Peloponnesian War to the Cold War	10
2	Neutrality 'is what states make of it': rethinking neutrality through constructivism	32
3	Neutrality as a Social Democratic project: tracing the origins of Swedish neutrality, 1814–1945	60
4	Sweden's post-war neutrality doctrine: active internationalism and 'credible neutrality'	90
5	The crisis in Swedish Social Democracy: paving the path for a new identity	120
6	A new Swedish identity? Bildt, Europe and neutrality in the post-Cold War era	142
7	Into Europe with the SAP: Sweden as an EU member state	165
8	The 'war on terror' and globalisation: implications for neutrality and sovereignty	188
	Conclusion: The failure of neutrality?	206

Bibliography — 210
Index — 247

ABBREVIATIONS AND ACRONYMS

ANC	African National Congress
CCP	Common Commercial Policy
CDU	Christian Democratic Union (Germany)
CSU	Christian Social Union (Germany)
CESDP	Common European Security and Defence Policy
CFSP	Common Foreign and Security Policy
CSCE	Conference on Security and Cooperation in Europe
CJTF	Combined Joint Task Forces
CoCom	Coordination Committee on Multilateral Export Controls
COMECON	Council for Mutual Economic Assistance
CTBT	Comprehensive Test Ban Treaty
CTBTO	Comprehensive Nuclear Test Ban Treaty Organisation
DDR	Deutsche Demokratische Republik (East Germany)
EAPC	Euro-Atlantic Partnership Council
ECB	European Central Bank
ECJ	European Court of Justice
ECSC	European Coal and Steel Community
ECU	European Currency Unit
EDC	European Defence Community
EEA	European Economic Area
EEC	European Economic Community
EFTA	European Free Trade Association
EMU	Economic and Monetary Union
ENDC	Eighteen Nation Disarmament Commission (UN)
EP	European Parliament
EPC	European Political Cooperation
ERRF	European Rapid Reaction Force
ESDI	European Security and Defence Identity
ESDP	European Security and Defence Policy
ESF	European Social Fund

Abbreviations and acronyms

ETUC	European Trade Union Confederation
FDP	Free Democratic Party (Germany)
FPÖ	Freuheitliche Partei Österreichs (Austrian Freedom Party)
GATT	General Agreement on Tariffs and Trade
GDP	Gross Domestic Product
GNI	Gross National Income
GNP	Gross National Product
IFOR	Implementation Forces
IGC	Intergovernmental Conference
IMF	International Monetary Fund
INF	Intermediate Range Nuclear Forces
IR	International Relations
IUI	Industriens Utredningsinstitut (Research Institute of Industrial Economics, Sweden)
KD	Kristdemokraterna (Christian Democrats, Sweden)
KFOR	Kosovo Implementation Force
LMB	Labour Market Board
LN	Lega Nord (Northern League, Italy)
LO	Landsorganisationen Sverige (Swedish Trade Union Confederation)
MEP	Member of the European Parliament
MP	Member of Parliament
MFA	Ministry of Foreign Affairs
MPLA	Movement for the Popular Liberation of Angola
NACC	North Atlantic Cooperation Council
NATO	North Atlantic Treaty Organisation
NIB	Nämnden för internationellt bistånd (Committee for International Assistance, Sweden)
NIEO	New International Economic Order
NGO	Non-Governmental Organisation
N+N	Neutral and Non-Aligned
NORDCAPS	Nordic Coordinated Arrangement for Military Peace Support
NORDEK	Nordic Economic Community
NPT	Non-Proliferation Treaty
NSC	National Security Council
NWFZ	Nuclear Weapon-Free Zone
ODA	Overseas development assistance
OECD	Organisation for Economic Cooperation and Development
OPEC	Organisation of Petroleum Exporting Countries
OSCE	Organisation for Security and Cooperation in Europe
ÖVP	Österreichs Volkspartei (Austrian People's Party)
PAIGC	African Party for the Independence of Guinea and Cape Verde

Abbreviations and acronyms

PANA	Peace and Neutrality Alliance (Ireland)
PARP	Planning and Review Process
PES	Party of European Socialists
PFP	Partnership for Peace
PLO	Palestinian Liberation Organisation
PTBT	Partial Test Ban Treaty
PTK	Privattjänstmänna-kartellen (salaried employees in private industry, Sweden)
QMV	Qualified Majority Voting
RRF	Rapid Reaction Force
SACO	Sveriges Akademikers Centralorganisation (Swedish Confederation of Professional Associations)
SAF	Svenska Arbetsgivareföreningen (Swedish Employers' Association)
SALT	Strategic Arms Limitation Talks
SAP	Socialdemokratiska arbetarepartiet (The Social Democratic Party of Sweden)
SDU	Scandinavian Defence Union
SEA	Single European Act
SEK	Swedish Krona
SFOR	Stabilisation Forces
SI	Sveriges Industriförbundet (Swedish Association of Industries)
SIDA	Swedish International Development Authority
SPÖ	Sozialistische Partei Österreichs (Austrian Socialist Party)
SNS	Studieförbundet Näringsliv och Samhälle (Centre for Business and Policy Studies, Sweden)
SSBN	Ballistic Missile Nuclear Submarine
START	Strategic Arms Reduction Treaty
SWAPO	South West Africa People's Organisation
TCO	Tjänstemännens Centralorganisationen (Central Organisation of Salaried Employees, Sweden)
TFCMA	Treaty of Friendship, Cooperation and Mutual Assistance
UNCED	United Nations Conference on Environment and Development
UNEF	United Nations Emergency Force
UNICEF	United Nations Children's Emergency Fund
UNIDO	United Nations Industrial Development Organisation
UNIFIL	United Nations Interim Force in Lebanon
USSR	Union of Soviet Socialist Republics
VF	Verkstadsföreningen (Association of Engineering Industries, Sweden)
WEAG	Western European Armaments Group
WEU	Western European Union

ACKNOWLEDGEMENTS

My interest in neutral states began many years back as part of my research on European foreign and security policy. I was fascinated by the negativity surrounding the concept of neutrality and surprised by the gendered language employed in the discourse on neutral states (which unfortunately this book could not cover in the detail it deserves – a future project perhaps). I was able to investigate neutrality (and particularly Swedish neutrality) in my doctoral studies at the University of Manchester, and as far as acknowledgements go, it is here I must begin.

My thanks and gratitude go first and foremost to Peter Lawler, who convinced me to come to Manchester to undertake my PhD in what was then known as the Department of Government. Peter helped to mould my ideas about neutrality and international relations and has been a crucial source of support through the writing of the PhD and the book itself. Quite simply, I would not have been able to articulate my ideas in the same way had he not been part of the picture. Aside from his professionalism, interest and commitment to my project, he has also been a good friend and has constantly provided support and wise advice, despite his taste in music.

I have been extremely fortunate to have had the intellectual support of a number of rather impressive individuals, who also contributed to the shape of this book in their own ways. The following people deserve more than just to have their name in a list, but list I must: Annika Bergman, Véronique Pin-Fat, Simon Bulmer, Martin Burch, David Farrell, Jill Lovecy, Rorden Wilkinson, Paul Cammack, Elisa Roller, Clive Archer, Peter Wilkin, Cindy Weber, Mick Dillon, Richard Devetak, Sarah Beresford, Mark Lacy, Anne-Maree Farrell, Richard Whitaker, Liz Carter, Peter Stafford, Neville Wylie, Thomas Johansson, Annette Nilsson, Les Holmes, and Derek McDougall. At Salford, I have had wonderful support from Jocelyn Evans, Steve Fielding, Gideon Baker, John Garrard, Kathryn Allan, Jim Newell, and Cristina Chiva (with extra thanks to Cristina for help with proofreading). I would also like to express my thanks to the people who permitted me to interview them in the course of my research in Sweden. I could not have asked for better interviewees, who were so open and generous with their knowledge, and gave me insights into Swedish politics and neutrality of which I would have otherwise been ignorant. I was also fortunate enough to enjoy a brief research visit to the Copenhagen Peace Research Institute (COPRI) which provided me with a great deal of documentation on neutrality. The support and patience I have

Acknowlegements

received from Tony Mason and Manchester University Press has been excellent and has made the experience of publishing a book for the first time a pleasure.

Friends and family have provided me with an incredible amount of support over the years. Of those back home in Melbourne, I must first thank my mum and my sister, Simone, and my friends, Silvia Superina, Louisa di Pietro, Sonia Rocco, Louise Clarke, Lilian Topic and Toni Milone. My aunty Georgina and uncle George in Malta also provided support. At risk of creating another list of people who deserve mention, I would also like to thank Nikie Marston, Mark Perkins, Julia Houston, Imogen Bowers, Anna Fielder, Luqman Hayes, Michelle Weightman, Lucy Peake and Sarah Wixey. All of these people have given me the time to discuss my ideas, and their friendship and support has been invaluable. My final thanks are reserved for my husband, Joe Mechan, and Steven Patrick Morrissey and The Smiths.

Introduction

> The very men that have their eyes perfectly open to what they are rushing into, let the thing called disgrace, by the mere influence of a seductive name, lead them on to a point at which they become so enslaved by the phrase as in fact to fall wilfully into hopeless disaster, and incur disgrace more disgraceful as the companion of error, than when it comes as the result of misfortune. This, if you are well advised, you will guard against ... when you have the choice given you between war and security, will you be so blinded as to choose the worse. (Parting words of the Athenians to the Melians, Thucydides, 1951: 336)

> There can be no neutrality. (George W. Bush, BBC, 11/03/02)

FROM THE Peloponnesian War to the 'war on terrorism', neutrality has been depicted as an unrealistic and unacceptable security stance. It is commonly regarded as the security choice of small and weak states, a position that is synonymous with self-interested isolationism. Neutral states are largely seen as inconsequential and peripheral actors in the international system, responding to, rather than shaping the world. Subsequently, neutrality has been of little interest to security studies and International Relations (IR) theory, which casts its gaze to the more exciting topics of war, power and alliances. For many, the time of neutrality has passed, and in a world characterised by international cooperation, globalisation and security threats that affect all, neutrality is seen as a legacy of the Cold War which should be consigned to the dustbin of history. Yet neutrality persists.

In a little over a decade, there have been three serious exogenous challenges to neutrality. The end of the Cold War presents the first challenge to neutrality in the 1990s. With nothing to be neutral between, neutral states were simply urged to abandon this outdated security posture in exchange for greater cooperation in security matters. The end of bipolarity opened up new avenues for theorising security[1] but it was assumed that neutrality would become invalid because the nature of the international system had changed. But with no discernable enemy to fight, neutral states adopted a cautious attitude and resisted change to their policy.

Second, European integration became another source of pressure, as Finland, Austria and Sweden became member states of the European Union (EU) in 1995. These three neutrals joined the EU at a time when the Union began to accelerate its plans to establish a European Security and Defence Policy (ESDP) which many regarded as incompatible with neutrality. It is at this juncture that a shift occurs in the policies of neutral states as they attempt to fit in with the norms and values of the EU.

Finally, the events of September 11, 2001 have ushered in a new era in international relations. The terrorist attacks, and the subsequent 'war on terrorism' have been presented as a challenge that extinguishes any claims towards a neutral stance. For the Bush administration, international terrorism provides the twenty-first century with 'an enemy of ruthless ambition, unconstrained by law or morality ... The terror that targeted New York and Washington could next strike any center of civilization. Against such an enemy, there is no immunity, and there can be no neutrality.' (Bush, 2002) This appears to be a compelling argument for edging out neutrality because the enemy is not a state, the traditional referent for neutrality. Furthermore, the 'war on terrorism' is located on a moral and 'civilising' plane where 'no country has the luxury of remaining on the sidelines'. (Powell, 2002) Security cooperation is divided between those who are 'with us or against us'. (CNN, 06/11/01) For Europe's 'military non-aligned' states,[2] the viability of maintaining a non-aligned stance has resulted in the loosening or revision of neutrality. Within this debate, little attention is paid to how neutrality may be adapted to deal with new security concerns. The focus is how neutrality is problematic in relation to new circles of cooperation and new threats. But this still does not answer the question of why neutrality cannot be accommodated in today's security architecture.

The problem of neutrality: a survey of the literature on neutral states

That neutrality is regarded as an obsolete practice and idea in the current age is a consequence of a number of factors. A survey of the literature on neutrality, however, reveals a deeper problem of neglect and narrow inquiry, which should be addressed. If mainstream understanding of neutrality is dismissive, it is so for good reason – neutrality has largely been a neglected subject. Most studies on neutrality can be located in the fields of law and history, with the focus leaning heavily towards legal definitions and the formal rights and responsibilities of neutral states (Grant-Bailey, 1944; Henkin et al., 1987; Jessup and Deák, 1935; Leonard, 1988). Historical texts on the subject of neu-

Introduction

trality largely read as shameful war stories, with the bulk of the literature examining how belligerents violate neutral rights, or how neutrals fail to fulfil their obligations.[3] These writings do not reveal a great deal about neutrality *per se*. More importantly, they manage the task of divorcing neutrality from politics: what is obtained from these texts is a chronological exercise in history and law, of comparisons between different types of neutralities. In this sense, much of the traditional literature is concerned with categorising permanent neutral states (where neutrality is maintained during peace and war[4]) and traditional neutrality (which is engaged when war erupts[5]), or explaining similar phenomena such as non-alignment[6] and neutralisation.[7] There is little concern, however, with focusing on how neutral states *interpret and employ* their neutrality, or differentiating between what Stern (1991: 43) calls 'positive' ('interactionist' or activist) and 'negative' (isolationist) neutrality.

Modern accounts of neutrality in the Cold War era likewise view the subject through selective categories. In much of the writing, neutrality is treated as a twentieth-century phenomenon, with little reference made to the existence of neutrality before the Cold War. Here the literature is devoted to comparative case studies of neutral states and their military doctrines and capabilities, or examining superpower pressure on neutral states or the role of neutrals in the balance of power, with emphasis on the limits and constraints on neutral states (Divine, 1962; Kruzel and Haltzel, 1989; Neuhold and Thalberg, 1984; Sundelius, 1987). Much of the tone implies that by virtue of their aversion to military alliances, neutrals are therefore subject to the uncertainties of the anarchic international system. Belligerent states find it too tempting to pre-emptively attack a neutral state, as their weak position implies that another belligerent would do the same. Studies of pressures on or violations of neutral rights assume that neutrality is a weak stance unless backed up by force. For Handel, neutrality is a doctrine of 'defence nihilism' and neutrals invite belligerent aggression through their minimal military defence postures (1981: 175). Due to geography, resources and non-participation in military alliances, neutrals are investigated only insofar as they do not 'fit' within the international system or are 'small and weak states' with few options. Ultimately, neutrality is broadly regarded as unwise statecraft, which perhaps explains why neutrality does not merit strong academic attention.

When it comes to IR theory, neutrality is absent. Neutrality predates key concepts such as the state, sovereignty and anarchy but is largely sidelined in theorising. There has been little in the way of empirical research on neutrality that engages with IR theory and moves away from chronological analysis (Hakovirta, 1988: 1-2). Only traditional idealism (Wilsonian internationalism) and realism have commented on neutrality, but neutrality remains of marginal interest to both, given the nature of their own projects and investigations. Traditional idealism, with its universalist assumptions and emphasis on collective security, encouraged the view that the neutral state lacked integrity (for refusing to fight wars or for profiting from war without 'getting their hands dirty'). Realism oscillates between rejecting neutral states (because they are not power maximisers) and tacitly accepting neutrals (due to their 'balancing' role in the anarchic international system). Thus, a reliance on realist or idealist approaches provides only a limited analytical framework for understanding neutrality.

Yet what underlines this neglect of neutrality is the notion of aberration. Neutral states are not part of the system of friends and enemies that characterise international political relations (Morgenthau, 1958, 1993; Ross, 1989). Consequently, they are seen as 'pawns' or 'objects' (Joenniemi, 1988). Realism neglected the issue of neutrality because it did not readily conform, in all senses, to the maxim that states will 'act alike' in the anarchic international system. Connected to this premise is also an assumption about the 'correct' uses of sovereignty. Much of the literature on neutrality is critical of the way in which neutral states interpret sovereignty to mean the right *not* to use war as an instrument of policy. Hence, neutral states are studied as aberrations. The aberration is both political and moral. Neutrality is equated with self-interested isolationism, a stance that is not compatible with peace or notions of justice (Raymond, 1997: 124), with the neutral state cast as the cynical actor, gaining from war without incurring sacrifice. Swiss author Friedrich Dürrenmatt summed it up bluntly when he said that Swiss neutrality 'makes me think of a virgin who earns her living in a bordello but wants to remain chaste'. (*The European*, 24–30/12/93) Immorality has become firmly entwined in the discourse on neutrality, yet this goes virtually unnoticed in most analyses. These largely negative connotations have shaped the mainstream understanding of neutrality and have relegated neutrality to a category of research which is not only underdeveloped but also disengaged from contemporary IR theory and writing.

Current writing on neutrality

In the post-Cold War era, the writing on neutrality has not moved on from these assumptions and categorisations. Whilst the end of bipolarity has opened up numerous avenues of research for academics, the question of neutrality has faded into the background. Written off as obsolete, neutrality is still seen as a hindrance to closer forms of security cooperation between states. Post-Cold War literature has concentrated on how neutrals are to shed this now 'meaningless label' and begin to engage in 'constructive' policies and forms of cooperation, especially on questions of European security and the 'war on terrorism' (Cox and MacGinty, 1996; Laursen, 1997; Ojanen, 2000a,

Introduction

2002; Ojanen, et al, 2000). This repeats the above cycle of discussing neutrality as problematic in relation to other questions, such as the international system, regional cooperation and the new security agenda.

Only a very small amount of the literature has proposed that neutrality may be a viable alternative, or offers something positive to security (Albrecht et al., 1988; Binter, 1989, 1992; Joenniemi, 1988, 1989b, 1993). The literature on neutrality as an alternative to alliance membership and as a different approach to peace and security is sparse.[8] Some scholars have considered how neutrality is still relevant for post-Cold War security (Bebler, 1992; Binter, 1989, 1992; Joenniemi, 1993; Windsor, 1989), or that neutrality is part of embedded 'national identity' (Browning, 1999; Bukovansky, 1997; Goetschel, 1999; Goldmann, 1994; Malmborg, 2001), but this makes up a minority of the literature. Rather than mine this vein, the attachment to identity is pitched against the more important demands of interdependence and new 'realities' in the international system. There has been a distinctive debate which has clouded any potential work that may conceptualise neutrality as something other than an 'idiosyncratic' policy (Joenniemi, 1993: 293). As a result, the normative nature of neutrality remains underdeveloped. The notion of neutrality in rhetoric and practice has been misused and abused, according to Andrén (1991: 69) and there is a need to clarify the debate on neutrality, rethink some core assumptions and address alternative interpretations.

Rethinking neutrality

This book proposes to rethink the mainstream conceptualisation of neutrality through a social constructivist methodology. Briefly, constructivism is concerned with the impact of ideas as well as material factors, and focuses on how the interests and identities of actors are flexible, or a result of certain historical processes. By focusing on what constitutes identity, interests and action, constructivism provides a broader picture of neutrality, highlighting how neutrality is an important part of the identity of the nation-state that practises it. In the words of the former Finnish President, Urho Kekkonen, 'there are as many kinds of neutrality as there are neutral states'. (Kekkonen [1967], 1970: 199) Neutrality differs in definition and practice between states, but this research draws upon a common normative thread that is consistent, but often overlooked: that neutrality has played an important role in the internal and external *identity* of the nation-state. Foreign and security policy is an expression of a particular set of norms or values that says something about the nation-state, both internally and externally. Therefore, the broad aim of this research is to locate neutrality as a component of what constitutes nation-state *identity and actions*.

Swedish neutrality

I examine the link between neutrality and identity, and neutrality and the uses of sovereignty, through a constructivist account of Swedish neutrality. Swedish neutrality is adopted as the case study because its neutrality is unique for a number of reasons. First, in the current climate of debate about neutrality, the main argument against neutrality is that it is a product of the Cold War era, which is now over. Yet Sweden has been a neutral state for almost two hundred years. Its neutrality did not originate in the context of bipolarity. Thus, it has a deeper lineage than neutral states such as Finland and Austria, whose neutrality has essentially been a product of the post-war era. Rather than a *realpolitik* choice after military defeat, the origins of Swedish neutrality contain some deeply normative foundations, which are related to domestic politics and state-building.

Second, Swedish neutrality, I argue, is closely tied to the hegemonic role of the Social Democratic Party (SAP) in Swedish politics and society. The Social Democratic vision of society permeated not only social and political life in Sweden, but also provided a particular ideology that underlined the core policies of the welfare state, active internationalism and the Swedish Model. Social Democratic norms and values have become entrenched over a number of decades, and as such, even conservative elements within Swedish politics generally accepted these core Social Democratic 'institutions', such as consensus and policy reform. The Social Democratic idea of society remains bound up in concepts of solidarity, consensus and universalism, which contained a deeper resonance or spoke of something universal to all Swedes. Neutrality was part of this understanding of collective self, and thus not wholly derived from external understandings of the anarchic international system.

Third, Sweden practised an active brand of neutrality. Far from isolationist, Swedish neutrality was the platform from which to export core Social Democratic norms and values to the international level. This is evidenced in an active neutrality policy that embraced solidarity with the Third World, development cooperation, mediation, peacekeeping, initiatives such as disarmament and non-proliferation, active UN involvement and criticism of the superpowers during the Cold War. Sweden's attachment to ideas of progressivism in its social, economic and political history has formed the basis for Sweden's unique use of its neutrality. Neutrality complemented Sweden's strong internationalist profile.

Swedish neutrality demands closer attention due to what I claim is the *embedded* nature of its foreign and security policy. Under the constructivist lens, it is possible to explore the ideas connected to the development of Swedish neutrality and to reveal its more normative content. Constructivism

Introduction

contains a number of strands stretching from rationalist to reflectivist varieties and the examination of Swedish neutrality put forward in this book takes into account the importance of discourse, historicity, collective meanings, and metaphor and myth, which have been powerful tools in the shaping of Swedish neutrality. The ideas of the *folkhem* ('the Peoples' Home'), solidarity and universalism were potent metaphors which were tied to Swedish neutrality as much as they were to Swedish society, economics and politics. The explanation of neutrality as the policy of weak and small states is not the only account of neutrality. The story is far more complex, reflecting endogenous factors that reveal a different story of how the nation-state imagines itself and responds to the outside environment. Neutrality is part of the package of Swedish political life and its particular worldview. The embedded nature of Swedish neutrality is tied up with collective meanings and values that have constructed the Swedish nation-state, and efforts to abandon neutrality remain a difficult and sensitive subject. Neutrality still enjoys widespread support within Sweden, primarily because it has a strong connection to Swedish identity.[9]

Interests and identities are, however, susceptible to change, and this book also investigates how Swedish neutrality is being reconstituted, particularly since the 1990s. Now an EU member state, Sweden has reconsidered the uses of neutrality in the context of interdependence and new security threats. Although resisting the lure of military alliances, Sweden now participates in the Common Foreign and Security Policy (CFSP) and cooperates with NATO in the context of the Euro-Atlantic Partnership Council (EAPC), the Western European Armaments Group (WEAG), and Partnership for Peace (PFP). In February 2002, the Swedish government produced a new formulation of Swedish security policy, which is the sharpest signal yet of a new interpretation of Swedish neutrality and opens up the possibility for its eventual abandonment in the future. A little over a decade ago, such a scenario would have been unimaginable. Clearly, neutrality has turned 'into a different political animal' (Andrén, 1991: 67); one, which many would claim, may soon become extinct.

Whilst exogenous sources can easily be identified to explain the shift in Swedish neutrality, there are also endogenous sources that must be accounted for. Globalisation and EU membership, along with an altered international security environment, will undoubtedly influence how a state formulates and conducts its foreign and security policy. Nonetheless, there have been efforts to recast Sweden as a different type of state. The challenge to neutrality is part of this desire to etch out a new 'normalised' Sweden now that it is part of the EU. Much of the collective meanings that constructed the modern Swedish state alongside the development of neutrality are now under question. Thus, the debate on neutrality is a reflection of the contested ideas of Sweden's place in European and international politics.

This book commences with a study of the conceptualisation of neutrality from the Peloponnesian War up to the end of the Cold War, and then, in Chapter 2, goes on to rethink some of the central assumptions surrounding neutrality through a constructivist lens. Chapter 3 applies the constructivist approach by examining the origins of Swedish neutrality and progresses on to Chapter 4 to explain how neutrality became embedded in Swedish identity as part of Social Democratic hegemony. Chapter 5 explores how the established institutions of Social Democracy underwent 'crises' which then opened the path to a re-evaluation of Swedish identity and neutrality in the 1990s, which is discussed in Chapter 6. In Chapter 7, Sweden's membership of the EU is examined in reference to shifts in neutrality, and the broader question of neutrality in the current age is returned to in Chapter 8.

NOTES

1 On new thinking about security in the post-Cold War setting, see Baldwin, 1995; Booth, 1991; George, 1996; Krause and Williams, 1997; Lipschutz, 1995, and in particular, the writings of Buzan and Waever and the Copenhagen School on securitisation. The debate about the challenge to power politics persists, nonetheless (see Mearsheimer, 1990; Walt, 1997, and in the context of US policy since September 11, Gray, 2002).

2 Since the end of the Cold War, many neutral states have distanced themselves from the label of neutrality by referring to their security policy as 'militarily non-aligned'. In some cases, such as the Finnish, a technical change in the foundation of their neutrality has prompted a new description, but for others, the shift in labels has had more to do with attempts to shake off Cold War baggage about neutrality. This is discussed further in Chapter 2.

3 On this, see Divine, 1962; Ogley, 1970; Ørvik, 1953. In the case of Sweden, see Hägglöf, 1960; Hedin, 1943; Hopper, 1945; Joesten, 1945; Tunander, 1999.

4 Permanent neutrals often have a treaty base for their status, with Switzerland often cited as the key example due to its neutrality gaining recognition under the Congress of Vienna in 1815 (see Ogley, 1970: 3; Ørvik, 1953: 28).

5 Usually, this form of neutrality – such as Swedish neutrality – is not codified and can be shed at any time. Some writers use the term 'classical neutrality' to denote 'traditional neutrality' and at times there appears to be loose usage of the terms. For instance, Ross defines classical neutrality as being 'limited to a legal, contractual relationship between the neutrals and the belligerents, commencing at the outbreak of hostilities and remaining in effect only for the duration of the conflict; neutrality ceases to have effect when hostilities end'. (1989: 7)

6 Non-alignment, broadly associated with the Cold War nuclear age and the North–South debate, differs from neutrality in that it is not a legal position or concept. Non-alignment was a way to circumvent reliance on or estrangement from the superpowers. For neutrality, the distinction between war and peace is more central to its doctrine (Lyon, 1963: 20; Martin, 1962).

7 Neutralisation is the label given to exogenous forms of neutrality, where the neutral status of a country is initiated by another state or through international agreement, such as that of Belgium (1839), Luxembourg (1867), Austria (1955), and Laos

Introduction

(1962). Neutralisation, however, is a contentious and sensitive label, as it implies an imposed condition.

8 Some of the more progressive commentators have bemoaned the 'lack of a comprehensive theory of neutrality' (Albrecht et al., 1988; Joenniemi, 1988). From the standpoint of this book, which examines how neutrality is *socially constructed*, an enveloping 'theory' of neutrality may locate some neutrals into inaccurate categories. See also Carlsnaes (1993) on observations about the difficulty of comparing neutral states.

9 Identity is an ambiguous concept: a nation-state has a number of identities. References to a 'Swedish identity' throughout this book will refer to the Social Democratic idea or vision of society.

1

Writing neutrality: from the Peloponnesian War to the Cold War

> But what is neutrality? I don't understand it. It means nothing. (Gustavus Adolphus to George Frederick, Elector of Brandenburg, cited in Politis, 1935: 13)

NEUTRALITY STANDS AS one of the most under-represented concepts in international political relations. Despite containing a deeper lineage than concepts such as 'sovereignty' or the 'state', neutrality has largely been conceptualised as a problematic adjunct to more serious academic questions, such as war and power. As such, neutrality has a limited presence in IR literature. And although neutrality is given attention in historical, legal and religious texts, the story of neutrality is a largely negative one. The general perception of neutral states is that they are weak and insignificant, and neutrality is depicted as the policy of isolationism and self-interest, an unrealistic posture, lacking in morality and integrity.

By exploring the history, interpretations and meanings accorded to neutrality, found in references as early as Thucydides' account of the Peloponnesian War, one finds that the validity of neutrality has been consistently challenged. Neutrality does not sit comfortably between war and peace. It is commonly regarded as a state of limbo (Politis, 1935: 3), a policy of indecision. Much of the contextualisation of neutrality has not permitted the possibility of examining and developing various underlying themes implicit in the concept, due to its inconsistent and negative legacy.

The purpose of this chapter is to examine the way in which neutrality has been conceptualised throughout key points in history, and how the meanings and associations connected to neutrality have become established. Beginning with the Melian Dialogue, it explores how neutrality was pitched against the realities of power and empire. Just war theory and legal philosophy also found neutrality problematic, solidifying the problems of morals and action. The rise of the Westphalian state and the development of international law provided some space for neutrality in the context of sovereignty, but neutrality faced harsh tests during conflicts of the twentieth century. This chapter also examines how mainstream IR theory neglected the concept of neutrality during this period. This prepares the ground for Chapter 2, which then rethinks this depiction of neutrality, and opens up the question of neutrality in the present age, with particular reference to increased interdependence and the changing nature of sovereignty.

Setting the precedent: the Peloponnesian War and the question of neutrality

Thucydides' account of the Peloponnesian War provides one of the earliest written records of neutrality. The Melian Dialogue of 416 BC recounts the events surrounding the neutral status of Melos, which was politically and legally linked to Sparta, but wished to remain neutral during the hostilities between Sparta and Athens. The Athenians refuse to submit to the Melian plea for neutrality because to do so would be a sign of weakness: 'the fact that you are islanders and weaker than others rendering it all the more important that you should not succeed in baffling the masters of the sea'. (Thucydides, 1951: 332) The Athenians, concerned with power and empire, provide the justification that 'the strong do what they can and the weak suffer what they must'. (Thucydides, 1951: 331) The Melian Dialogue provides important insights into how neutrality was conceptualised in terms of power politics. Independence can only be guaranteed through strength, and those who are weak cannot afford to make claims to be impartial. However, the Athenians do not leave it at that, and in their parting words chastise the Melians for choosing the path of neutrality rather than seeking security through alliance. For the Athenians, the Melians are short-sighted in their desire to be neutral – for the Athenians, the promise of neutrality is an 'extravagant' and foolish pursuit: 'Hope, danger's comforter, may be indulged in by those who have abundant resources, if not without loss at all events without ruin; but its nature is to be extravagant, and those who go so far as to put their all upon the venture see it in its true colours only when they are ruined.' (Thucydides, 1951: 333) And that they do, as their refusal to submit to the Athenians results in the Melos massacre.

At this particular point in history, there was no room for the uninvolved. Ancient Greece was a cultural–religious association or entity, not a legal–political one. It contained a geographical area and cultural unity, but did not exist as a single political state; rather it was constructed from city-states. The *polis* (the city-state political communities) did not have equal rights and obligations. Hence there was no concept of equal sovereignty among units (Jackson, 1997: 37).[1] There were allies or enemies, and neutrality was not readily permissible, even though it had a presence in ancient times (Raymond 1997: 138). Although 'abstention' was common in Greek warfare, accounts of such were made in passing and more attention was paid to the occasional cases of 'unexpected neutrality' (Bauslaugh, 1991: xxi). The concept and practice of neutrality lacked a vocabulary: no word for 'neutrality' existed during antiquity.[2] Instead, terms such as *intermediaries, friends, tranquillity* or *abstention* were employed to denote non-participation in war, and words such as *truces, peace,* and *friendship* were used in the same manner for maritime relations (Politis, 1935: 4). Thucydides employed different descriptions, such as 'those standing aloof from both sides' or 'those who were allies of neither side'. Herodotus combined the two in his phrase 'standing aloof in the middle'. (Bauslaugh, 1991: xx) Furthermore, diplomacy between city-states at this time was more complex than a demarcation of 'friends' or 'enemies'. Modern terms, such as 'truce', 'treaty' or similar legal phrasings, were not signifiers of a particular description that we understand today (Bauslaugh, 1991: 4–7).

Realists claim Thucydides as their founding father and in this regard perhaps the most important lesson of the Melian Dialogue is that the stance of the Athenians prescribes to a natural rule, a *timeless wisdom*, that the powerful will subdue the weak: 'it is not as if we were the first to make this law, or to act upon it when made; we found it existing before us, and shall leave it to exist for ever after us; all we do is to make use of it, knowing that you and everybody else, having the same power as we have, would do the same as we do.' (Thucydides, 1951: 334) It is this lesson which has not only shaped realist discourse but has also constructed the parameters of definition and association when it comes to the question of neutrality. The Athenians are able to discipline the Melians not simply for their choice in rejecting alliance, but because their stance contradicted the 'timeless wisdom' of strong over weak. Modern interpretations of neutrality, as will be demonstrated later in this chapter, return to this formulation, noticeably in the way neutrality is dealt with as the policy of small and weak states which obstructs the necessities of war.

There appears to be a large gap in the literature on neutrality since the Melian Dialogue. During the Middle Ages, religious and imperial unity meant there was little room for neutrality (Politis, 1935: 11). The Crusades (1085–1270) were a moral commitment; to pursue the right not to participate in such wars, especially on a legal footing, was an act of castration from the order itself. To be neutral was to reject the establishment (Rubin, 1988: 14). The connection between religion and neutrality as a negative relationship is a common theme. Dante's *Inferno* depicts neutrals as 'wretched spirits ... Whose lives knew neither praise nor infamy ... who against God rebelled not, nor to Him were faithful, but to self alone were true'. (Aligheri, 1996: 22) Among Christian nations, an injustice against one was considered an injustice against all. Efforts to unite Christendom against the enemies of God made neutrality impossible, particularly since the papal bull of 1500, which ordered peace and unity among Christians under threat of excommunication (Jessup and Deák, 1935: 7).

Likewise, in feudal times, 'private wars' were linked to feudal obligations, and rulers could not remain neutral. Again there was scant distinction between public and private feuds, making the practice of neutrality difficult (Brown, 1997: 67–9; Jessup and Deák, 1935: 5–6). Reprisals, according to Rubin (1988: 16) were 'available to equals on the feudal scale at all levels'. Throughout the thirteenth and fourteenth centuries, neutrality was decided on an *ad hoc* basis, resulting in bilateral treaties, such as the 1408 French royal decree where the King of France declared neutrality in the struggle between the Popes of Rome and Avignon (Karsh, 1988: 14). Dynastic bonds also linked together Europe's monarchy, providing little option to be neutral (Malmborg, 2001: 24). Machiavelli (1995: 71–2) was also unsympathetic to the proclamations of neutrality, believing that those who followed this path would essentially be ruined by it: 'It is always the case that the one who is not your friend will request your neutrality, and the one that is your friend will request your armed support. Princes who are irresolute usually follow the way of neutrality in order to escape immediate danger, and usually they come to grief.' In legal philosophy, natural law was the order of the day, and for Dominican professor Francisco de Vitoria, the question of neutrality bore little weight where Christian unity was concerned (Politis, 1935: 6).

This legacy does not reveal a great deal about neutrality *per se*. Rather, neutrality is depicted as a challenge to other concepts, such as power between weak and strong states, questions of religious loyalty and the demarcation between enemy and ally. There was nothing noble to be found in being neutral. Neutrality was seen as trickery and indecision. More importantly, it was regarded with suspicion because it signalled a refusal to defend certain values that held the unit or community together. Abstaining from choosing between friend and foe, refusing to fight religious wars, the neutral was cast as the self-interested outsider. Connected to such powerful themes, there was no solid defence or basis for such a stance; passivity was not an acceptable option (Politis, 1935: 6–7). Neutrality was mainly viewed as unwise statecraft and a failure to participate in honourable duty.

As such, no firm rules existed about the role and place of neutrality. In the fifteenth century, maritime trade expanded and became more competitive. As attempts were made to claim sovereignty over the seas, neutral trade became a legal issue embroiled in 'the difficulties resulting from an anarchic situation'. (Jessup and Deák, 1935: 11) The Court of Maritime Trade of Barcelona initiated the first legal codification of neutral rights. The *Consolato del Mare* (1494), influenced by customary law, became the common law of the Mediterranean, and set out the first restrictions on neutral trade and property rights. The rule of the *Consolato* spared neutral ships and goods from capture: neutral goods seized aboard an enemy ship had to be returned, and all enemy goods aboard neutral ships could be seized by the belligerents (Politis, 1935:

13; Ross, 1989: 4). Rulings on neutrality were not made in the spirit of neutral rights but more as a regulatory device to ensure the continuation of trading patterns. The growth of international trade was the catalyst for the development of international law, which was to significantly affect neutrality (Henkin et al., 1987: xxxv). The following section explores the influence of the 'just war' doctrine and how it affected certain notions about neutral rights and obligations.

Legal philosophy, just war, and the rise of the state

During the sixteenth century, the shift to a system of separate, sovereign states was under way with the decline of the Papacy and the medieval unity of Christendom. The Reformation weakened the power of the Church and by the seventeenth century, commerce and trade began to bypass religious domination. Such changes prompted important shifts in legal philosophy, which began to address matters of *international* relations, and brought the question of the neutral state into a different context.

Central to the doctrine of just war is whether war can be waged in the first place (*jus ad bellum*) and the conduct of that war (*jus in bello*). International law attempted to formulate rulings regarding war, but legal philosophy found it difficult to reconcile the just war thesis with neutrality. If an 'injustice can morally require a military response', then neutrality was illegal. However, having a legal basis for war also meant that neutrality was acceptable: 'Those who lack the standing, the just cause, object or intention have no moral or legal basis for participating in the armed struggle. Neutrality for them would not be a right but an obligation.' (Rubin, 1988: 14) It is with Grotius that the question of sovereignty over the seas arose, which was to have an important impact upon neutral trade and rights. Grotius supported the 1609 principle of the freedom of the seas (*Mare Librum*), because of Dutch interests as a rising maritime and colonial power against England, Spain and Portugal (Henkin et al., 1987: xxxvii).

Grotius made small reference to neutrality in one chapter of his three-volume work *De Jure Belli ac Pacis* (*The Law of War and Peace*, 1625). Grotius established two principles guiding the conduct of neutral countries. The first stipulated that the neutral (or the *medii* – those between war and peace) must not assist an 'unjust' cause, nor harm a 'just' one (Ørvik, 1953: 11). The second principle focused on the question of determining the justness of the cause – if the neutral could not decide, each party must be treated equally.[3] These principles were included in the first formal codification of *jus ad bellum* and became established in 1653, when first cited by a French Prize Court (Ross, 1989: 4). At this time, there was no protection against belligerent violation of neutral territory, which would later become a key aspect of modern neutrality. Grotius still privileged a just war over the right to exercise neutrality (Walzer, 1992: 246). Grotius held that there was no reason for war to end; only to be controlled (Grotius, 1957: 21; Holmes, 1989: 153). Since the development of neutral rights and responsibilities emerged at a time when 'the solidifying norms of territorial sovereignty were applied more easily to land than to the high seas', the state of maritime law relating to neutral rights was not readily accepted by some belligerents (Bukovansky, 1997: 220).

With the Treaty of Westphalia (1648), the political and geographical map of Europe altered, and power shifted from the Church to the state. The emergence of the state altered the legal characteristics of entities or 'juristic persons' who were the subjects (Holmes, 1989: 152). During this time, legal philosophy was shifting from the natural law foundation to positive law, which emerged with the rise of the state. This had important implications for the status of neutrality. In a state of nature (the Hobbesian interpretation of the state of war), morals did not dictate how states behaved toward each other. From this premise, states could not judge each other morally (Holmes, 1989: 157). Therefore much of the moral undertone attached to the question of neutrality lost its force.

Eighteenth-century positivists, such as Emmerich de Vattel, focused on the question of the neutral state's impartiality. Before Vattel, some of the groundwork had already been laid by other positivist writers such as Samuel Pufendorf, who agreed with the just war thesis but warned of the dangers of permitting neutral states to decide if a cause was just or not. Cornelius von Bynkershoek, in *Quaestiones Juris Publici* (1737), claimed that since neutrals were *non hostis* ('of neither party') in war, they must therefore be impartial and could refuse the passage of troops to any belligerent waging war for an unjust cause (Ross, 1989: 5). Although neutrality was beginning to receive serious attention in legal philosophy, the rights of belligerents still bore stronger weight compared to the rights of neutrals, and if a war was considered just, then neutral rights became questionable or redundant (as argued by jurists Lormier and Westlake, and Wolff). Bynkershoek appealed for restraint by belligerents regarding the violation of neutral territory, but this was not impenetrable 'in the heat of action' (*dum fervet opus*) (Politis, 1935: 22 and 37; Walzer, 1992: 236).

In the climate of sovereign states, neutrals began to take a less passive view of their role and rights. Just at it was a state's right to wage war in order to protect its national interests and security, so too was it considered the right of a state to abstain from war if that suited its national interest and security. What little rights neutrals had, however, were still regularly violated, leading to the creation of armed neutrality leagues such as those of Sweden and Denmark in 1691, in order to protect neutral commerce.[4] The First League of Armed Neutrality formed in 1780 in response to British intervention in neutral shipping during the US War of Independence. Initially limited to Denmark, Sweden and Russia (later joined by the Netherlands, Portugal, Prussia, Austria and the Kingdom of the Two Sicilies), the First League protected neutral commerce and had the effect of localising war (Ross, 1989: 6). By the time of the Napoleonic Wars, the opportunity for unprecedented warfare grew. It was difficult for states to practise neutrality at this time since central Europe was divided into weak states. There was little uniformity and neutrality was practised in an *ad hoc* manner (Lyon, 1963: 17; Ørvik, 1953: 16–17 and 25). In 1800, the Second League of Armed Neutrality formed, paving the path for the extension of neutral rights and obligations in the nineteenth century and forming the precedent for armed neutrality in the twentieth century (Karsh, 1988: 16–17; Ross, 1989: 6–7).

In the post-Napoleonic period, the international system was a more congenial environment for neutrals – no bloc structure had emerged and wars were limited. This 'golden age' of diplomacy and international law characterised Europe from 1815 until 1914 (Morgenthau, 1958: 191). The moderately stable balance of power in the nineteenth century produced a new development for neutrality. In order to localise conflict and limit the 'theatres of war', some states and provinces were neutralised. The great powers at the Congress of Vienna (1815) acknowledged the right of a state to practise neutrality as a strategic policy which signalled 'a recognition that a neutral status during a war was legally justifiable, as was belligerency'. (Karsh, 1988: 18; Ørvik, 1953: 32) Further rules developed that worked in the interests of the neutral state, such as the Declaration of Paris (1856) which protected neutral trade (a concern of the Leagues of Armed Neutrality) and served as a precursor to the developments outlined in the following section.

The Hague Conventions, the First World War, and neutrality

The Hague Conventions (1899 and 1907), which regulated aspects of land and naval warfare, are commonly regarded as the first embodiment of neutral rights and duties under positivist international law. They stipulated that neutrals had to defend their territory from violation (stressing armed neutrality); neutrals could not supply belligerents with war material, loans or aid; and impartiality had to be practised between belligerents.[5] Much of the moral undertone that overshadowed the question of neutral rights in the past had now diminished; war was 'seen simply as a state of affairs'.[6] For neutrals, however, the stable balance of power that existed at the time appeared to provide the basis for neutrality (Ross, 1989: 10; see also Lindell and Persson, 1986: 80–2). The rights of neutral states, although given legal substance, were still juxtaposed against the rights of those states who used force to secure their national interests.

Writing neutrality

The First World War became the litmus test for the sustainability of neutrality in the new setting of sovereign nation-states. It was a test that neutrality failed, mostly due to the abuses of neutral rights by belligerent states securing their own national interests. To many, geography, the 'necessities of war', and the harsh realities of power politics justified the violation of neutrality. According to Morgenthau (1958: 190), for belligerents, the situation was simple: 'The belligerents look at the existence, the interests, and the "rights" of neutrals only from one angle: in what way are they likely to influence the outcome of the war?' Therefore, whether a neutral was successful in avoiding war or invasion depended largely on the benevolence of the belligerent. The most famous example was the 'rape' of Belgium, whose neutrality was guaranteed by the five great powers of the Concert of Europe under the Treaty of 1839, but lasted no longer than one week at the outset of WWI (Ogley, 1970: 75 and 400). Mirroring the Melian Debate, the breach of Belgian neutrality was deemed necessary by Germany in order to conduct its offensive against France (Andrén, 1991: 69). Norway's neutrality was violated without it even entering the war. German submarines succeeded in sinking almost half of Norway's merchant shipping fleet. Norway was reliant upon food imports and raw materials for industrial production and shipping was its main source of income.

Another negative turn for neutrality came in 1917, when the US, neutral since 1793,[7] abandoned its neutrality to enter WWI. Three years earlier, Wilson declared: 'Every man who really loves America will act and speak in the true spirit of neutrality, which is the spirit of impartiality and fairness and friendliness to all concerned.' (1914) Three years later, Wilson turned harshly on the use and purpose of neutrality:

> Armed neutrality is ineffectual enough at best; in such circumstances and in the face of such pretensions it is worse than ineffectual: it is likely only to produce what it was meant to prevent ... Neutrality is no longer feasible or desirable where the peace of the world is involved and the freedom of its peoples ... We have seen the last of neutrality in such circumstances. (Wilson, 1917)

Although developments of the seventeenth century saw a positivist view of neutrality gain ground (in that neutrality was as permissible as war in the international system), the natural law view of neutrality as immoral still contained resonance. Amoral neutrality became the key tone of neutrality debates, particularly in the US after it abandoned neutrality, and would persist in the inter-war period.

The League of Nations and the 'harmony of the peace'

The idealism of the inter-war years marked a different phase for neutral states. The establishment of the League of Nations in 1919 embodied, according to realists such as E. H. Carr, the ideals of utopianism as a way to manage the anarchical nature of the international system. Idealism of the type associated with Woodrow Wilson's Fourteen Points sought to counter anarchic international relations through the 'harmony of the peace' and the belief that was in the interests of all to pursue justice (Wilson [1918], 1994: 18).

Through the League of Nations, rule of law would settle disputes between nations and reduce the occurrence of war. There was a firm belief that states ought to act morally and collective security formed a strong part of the idealist doctrine. There was also dissatisfaction with the lack of democracy in foreign affairs. Wilsonian idealism encompassed the view that human nature was not static and that 'politics could be made to conform to an ethical standard'. (Wilson, 1998: 9) War was considered to be the result of the balance of power, imperfect institutions, international anarchy, prejudice and nationalism. The way to peace was through democracy, international law and organisations, open diplomacy, disarmament, arbitration and mediation, collective security and cooperation, leading to a world government (Long, 1991: 294; Nicholson, 1998: 66).

Much of this thinking has its roots in Kant's notion of an international cosmopolitan moral order within which states were moral agents and ought to act morally.[8] With Kant there existed 'prohibitive laws' that if abided by, removed the possibility of conflict between states and established a genuine or perpetual peace. Kant likewise held that states had the right to abstain from war; neutrality was part of the *rights to peace*. Thus, Kant's ideas for peace were more ambitious than those of earlier legal philosophers such as Grotius, Pufendorf and Vattel (the 'sorry comforters' (Kant [1795], 1996: 170 and 105)), who still permitted the phenomenon of a just war. Idealism tried to translate 'democratic rationalism' to the international arena (Carr, 1946: 23 and 28), with the assumption that if all nations were democratic, war would not occur (Brown, 1997: 23). In this sense, Kant's ideas contain deeper relevance for the ambition to establish a League of Nations; reason condemns the right to war, and peace is a duty to be fulfilled by a pacific federation, guaranteeing the freedom of states, leading to an international state ([1795] 1996: 93–105).

Most European neutral states were drawn to the new diplomacy as a way to maintain peaceful coexistence. Sweden, along with many other neutrals, was prepared to embrace the opportunity to establish a peaceful international order based on the rule of law in favour of neutrality (discussed further in Chapter 3). Switzerland joined the League but with stipulations that its neutrality be recognised and that it was exempt from participation in military sanctions. For many neutral states, it was seen as the solution to the dilemma of the small state caught up in the anarchic international environment.

It soon became clear that through the League of Nations, a 'harmony of interests' would be a difficult objective to attain. The Great Powers formed the permanent majority on the Council of the League. For Carr (1946: 53), the peace settlement of 1919 and the League of Nations served to protect the *status quo* for the victorious and the 'harmony of interests' doctrine was a moral device used by a privileged group to maintain a dominant position. It is no coincidence that it was established by the victors under the premise that 'peace is indivisible' and that war could no longer be tolerated as a legitimate instrument of policy (Ogley, 1970: 5). The demands of collective security also meant that neutrality came under question. The Covenant of the League of Nations (1924) stipulated that members must mutually defend one another (Article 10) and that war against one was considered war against all. In this sense, some of the founding ideas behind the League have their basis in the just war doctrine. Sanctions under Article 16 also proved to be a difficult request for neutrals to abide by. The idea of sanctions implied different treatment of belligerents, depending on their cause and which was the aggressor state. Where The Hague Convention granted neutral states rights, the Covenant appeared to make them invalid in the context of collective security. The League of Nations Council in 1920 did not consider neutrality to be compatible with the common principles of the Covenant (Ross, 1989: 17; see also Morgenthau, 1958: 192). Churchill ([1936], 1974: 5796) likewise, was against the principle of neutrality in the League, claiming 'the doctrine of absolute neutrality as between right and wrong is inconsistent with the Covenant of the League of Nations, which represents the moral principle in human relations'. The ideals of international cooperation appeared to challenge neutrality, and the general belief was that neutrality was an outdated formula for conflict resolution. Under the new internationalism, neutrality was seen to be in conflict with the 'harmony of interests'.

Since the League of Nations did not include the US[9] and the USSR, and Germany and Japan participated at different stages, Karsh observes that there was little choice but to accept the neutral status of some of its members. States still possessed the freedom to pursue an independent foreign policy; in the case of Swiss involvement, sanctions did not always have to be adopted. Hence, there was a stark difference between the ideals behind collective cooperation and the actual practice of it, and the implications of this revealed the uncommon ground between the states in the League and the premise on which it was based.[10]

The problem of neutrality remained relatively untested in the League of Nations until 1935 when Italy invaded Ethiopia. All neutrals, except Switzerland, participated in sanctions directed by the League. However, it failed to produce the desired effect. Seven neutrals (Denmark, Finland, Holland, Sweden, Switzerland, Norway and Spain) issued a joint declaration in July 1936 which nullified their obligation to Article 16. There appeared to be a deep concern that the great powers in the League were pursuing unilateral, not international interests. The neutrals further distanced themselves from the collective security stipulation through the Declaration of Copenhagen (1938), whereby Finland, Denmark, Norway, Sweden, Belgium, Holland and Luxembourg declared Article 16 to be without legal basis (Karsh, 1988: 114).

Despite the failure of the League of Nations, hopes for a collective security arrangement were not quelled. Roosevelt, in his Quarantine Speech of 1937, spoke of the need to restore international morality and fight the 'disease' of war. Isolationism, he claimed, made the path for solidarity in the modern world a difficult one (Roosevelt, 1937). Despite the lack of success the League encountered, many neutral states were still interested in being involved in such an arrangement. Switzerland retracted back to traditional neutrality but for many neutrals, cooperation of an international nature was not abandoned. Salmon notes that efforts towards Scandinavian cooperation were pursued during the First World War, but such hopes were dampened due to British suspicion and American reluctance to take part, forcing neutrality, in a sense, down the path of isolationism.[11] Roosevelt had in mind the internationalist project, based on international law and morals. Commitment to idealism was strong enough to drown out arguments for neutrality as a possible way to peace. In announcing a war against the 'disease' of war, he in effect set the parameters for discussion and placed neutrality as akin to lawlessness and immorality.

It is here that a distinction can be made between small states and major powers in terms of internationalism. Neutral states revealed a positive attitude towards efforts to eliminate war as a method of resolving conflict between states, and most were willing to surrender the neutral path if internationalism could successfully work. However, there appear to be different understandings of 'internationalism' between the small and major powers. For the large powers, the idea of internationalism under the League of Nations essentially secured their post-war status and provided a platform for certain ideals and values, which were expected to be universalised. For smaller states, the opportunity was unity and an attempt at a meaningful peace through respect for law and arbitration. For this, neutrality would have easily been abandoned. The failure of these hopes led to a 'resurrection' of neutrality according to Morgenthau (1939: 476); collective solutions to international disharmony were tarnished as the power relations within the League became apparent, and neutral states reverted to their established security stances.

The Second World War and the realist interpretation of neutrality

The failure of the League of Nations brought a different conceptualisation of world politics to the forefront, which was to dominate international relations theory up until the early 1980s. For Carr, the problem with idealism was its concern with 'teleology over analysis'. 'Absolute' or 'universal' principles reflected national policy based on national interest and did not work in practice. The 'shared interests' spoken of were those of the *status quo* powers. Carr (1946: 80–7) regarded the harmony of the peace doctrine as a 'moral device' (recalling Machiavelli's maxim that morality is a product of power) employed by dominant groups to preserve their position. Carr's critique of idealism laid the accusation that idealism could not explain world events (such as Manchuria, Abyssinia, the failure of the League and the descent into WWII). Realism on the other hand, could explain such events and could also predict patterns and prescribe actions (Wilson, 1998: 6).

For traditional or classic realists, a state-centric account of the world was a more appropriate way to explain what *is* rather than what *should be*. Idealism's emphasis on the *laissez-faire* school of economic thought underlined this contradiction, which served the interests of the economically strong. The focus on eliminating war overlooked the underlying basis for it, which was the unequal distribution of power in the international system. Idealists such as Hobson sought to overcome the balance of power through collective arrangements amongst units. For realists, the balance of power was the ordering mechanism in the absence of an overriding authority (Long, 1991: 292–3). States are the main actors, pursuing their own interests defined in terms of power. Classical realists such as Morgenthau, Carr and early Waltz (*Man, the State and War*, 1954) acknowledge power politics as a key characteristic of humanity. Morgenthau's principles of political realism state that politics is governed by objective laws that are founded on human nature, and that interest is defined in terms of power. A rational foreign policy is a sound foreign policy. Power is not a fixed category, however, and Morgenthau recognises that what determines political action (power and interests) is dependent upon the political and cultural environment of the time (Morgenthau, 1993: 4–14). The central tenet of Morgenthau's *Politics Among Nations* is that states are 'power maximisers', existing in the anarchic world where states are forced to be self-sufficient if they are to survive. For Waltz, the causes of war were to be found in the three 'images': in human behaviour, the state, and the international system. All three images are linked to nature, and there exists no harmony in anarchy. So long as an overriding authority is absent, the state will act 'according to the dictates of its own reason or desire'. (1954: 159)

The premise of no authority higher than the state in the international system presented a new set of dilemmas for neutral states. In the realist equation, neutrals were essentially prey to the balance of power. Within the confines of the liberal perspective of international relations, neutral states invested hopes of some form of collective cooperation which might remove the need for neutrality. Realist ideas about the nature of international political life drew a sharper distinction between relations between belligerents and neutrals. For Morgenthau, neutrality was a 'negative status' for two reasons – first, it depends on the existence of war (no neutrality without war as the context) and second, the rights and obligations of the neutral depend to a large extent on the belligerent. The belligerent will wish to prevent the neutral from siding with its enemy. Morgenthau (1958: 189) saw neutrality and war as related concepts, with the rights and obligations of the neutral stemming from a 'balance of interests' between the neutral and the belligerent. Morgenthau, however, balances these provisions for neutrality with some wage of risk – the belligerent's only interest is to win war – and violations of neutral rights were regarded by belligerents as less important than its war goals. A neutral, on the other hand, must contend with the desire to stay out of war and the pursuit of its national interest with regard to other states.

That neutrality was so openly violated during WWII is easily explained through the realist account, which contains echoes of the reasoning related to the Melians by the Athenians centuries before. Might is right, and the small and weak state will not stand as an obstacle to the stronger power securing its interests. A case in point was Churchill's attempts to cease the passage of iron ore to Germany through Norwegian territorial waters. Churchill's plan was considered by some as an illegal act against a neutral country, and 'would constitute a crime as bad as any that the Germans had committed elsewhere'.[12] For Churchill, however, this was a *causa justa*, invoking a Grotian sense of the primacy of belligerent rights over those of the neutral – thereby echoing the Wilsonian line in 1917 that neutrality was not morally feasible. For Churchill, 'Small nations must not tie our hands when we are fighting for their rights and freedom ... Humanity, rather than legality, must be our guide.' (Churchill, cited in Walzer, 1992: 245) By the end of WWII, only five neutral states remained in Europe: Sweden, Switzerland, Ireland, Portugal and Spain. Of the remaining neutrals, their status remained intact due to the fortunes of geography; Ireland was behind Allied lines, and Spain and Portugal, Ogley argues, were situated where the power of the blocs were relatively balanced. Sweden and Switzerland survived on their diplomatic skills and their usefulness to the belligerents. The reason for the demise of neutrality in Belgium, Norway, Denmark, Luxembourg and the Netherlands was due to their exposure to both sides and their inability to resist belligerent pressure (Ogley, 1970: 17–18).

The experiences of the Second World War did little to provoke a different understanding of the neutral state. Neutrality was not regarded as a viable or moral policy – for the dominant realist view of state relations, neutrality had simply nothing to do with morals, and its viability was questioned in most circumstances, underscoring another theme inherited from the Melian dialogue – that neutrality was a foolish or short-sighted policy. It was easily violated by a belligerent and worse still, neutral states were seen to be favouring one belligerent over another at various stages during the war; therefore their commitment to neutrality was questionable and could hardly be respected. This 'internal violation' (where the neutral does not act impartially) and 'external violation' (from a belligerent) (Karsh, 1988: 23–5) has dominated the post-war assessment of neutrality and cast neutrals in a dubious light. The neutral state increasingly gained the label of the cunning actor, playing off both sides to its own advantage. Sweden was regarded in negative terms by Western politicians and academics because it was seen to have favoured Germany at the start of the war (through its concessions to Hitler, such as trade in iron ore and the passage of German troops) and the Allies towards the end, as their position grew stronger (see Chapter 3). Switzerland, faced with the threat of German domination, acquiesced to the German demand for a blackout in November 1940, which aided Germany and hindered navigation for Allied bombing efforts over Italy. Although neutrals were largely criticised for their actions, Karsh comments that distinctions must be made between the political and the legal failure of neutrality. External violation denotes the political failure of neutrality. Internal violations are a different matter. If the purpose of neutrality is to retain independence and sovereignty, to protect territorial integrity, then neutrality is not breached (1988: 26).

For some observers, this may appear to be the apologists' view. However, realism does concur on this point. The neutral state acts in its own interests – be it protection of its sovereignty, avoidance of military entanglements or simply isolationism – and the state acting in its own interests is acceptable to the realist doctrine. Morgenthau (1958: 198) regarded neutrals almost in the same category as belligerents, since all nations 'would act in the face of war according to their interests as they saw them, to intervene or to remain neutral as they saw fit'. Here realism reveals a dual approach to neutrality. On the one hand, neutrality is an uncomfortable phenomenon. The neutral state does not seek to define its interests in terms of power. It withdraws from the system of allies and enemies and refuses to use force to attain its objectives or to join alliances. Yet on the other hand, neutrality is permissible and has a role to play in the international system. For Morgenthau, neutrality is 'a function of the balance of power'. In the anarchic system, the balance of power determines how states behave internationally. Indeed, this view held currency amongst many practitioners, such as the Swedish ambassador to Britain in 1960, H. Gunnar Hägglöf (1960: 160–3): 'I have underlined repeatedly that small states can pursue a policy of neutrality with some chance of success only if there exists some sort of balance of power between belligerents.' In his opinion, Swedish neutrality survived not because of its intrinsic principles or strength, but rather because 'Herr Hitler was otherwise occupied'.

Just as alliances are also a necessary function of the balance of power, there appears to be a tension between participation and non-participation. For some, the law of neutrality mirrors the balance of power and encourages 'non-participation as a function of "balancing"'. (Morgenthau, 1993: 197) Different interpretations locate neutrals as either a necessary element of or a nuisance to the balance of power in the international system; necessary because they do play a role within the anarchic system. Neutral states act as mediators and aim to limit war; their presence and actions balance the stronger elements. For Cox and MacGinty (1996: 128), this is reversed, and 'the neutrals' integrity actually came to be guaranteed by a balance of power, rather than the neutral policies themselves'.

In IR theory, the realist account of neutrality dominates our understanding; the research agendas of other areas have been largely silent about neutrality. Realism's explanation of neutrality, nonetheless, has become entrenched; it remains *the* only way to explain neutral behaviour. Väyrynen (1989a: 124) claims that after WWII, neutrality was consigned to the balance of power, and decades beyond this it is still difficult to untangle common associations of neutrality with that of power politics and the balance of power. Broadly, Schindler (1991) claims that from 1945, neutrality lost its significance in international law; many viewed The Hague rules as outdated. Neutrality was absent as a subject in university courses and programmes and was increasingly viewed as irrelevant because of the UN Charter, economic interdependence, the rise of new types of warfare, and increasing ideological cleavages.

The United Nations, the Cold War, and neutrality

The experience of the League of Nations behind them, some neutrals were wary of plans to create international organisations. The foundation of the UN created difficulties for neutral states. The UN Charter gave the Security Council the power to apply diplomatic, economic and military sanctions to an offending state, whether it was a member of the UN or not (Ogley, 1970: 18–20). Unlike the League of Nations, the UN appeared to be a more binding organisation, and concerns were raised in neutral states as to whether neutrality could be maintained.

Although neutrals were ready to participate in the League, they became more reserved where the UN was concerned. Some saw it as a chance to practise active neutrality, but others decided against involvement. For instance, Switzerland preferred to provide sites for mediation and participate in peacekeeping without the UN umbrella. With the end of colonialism in many countries, new nations emerged on the global scene. In this sense, the UN soon became a useful sounding board, witnessed in the creation of some groupings, such as the Neutral and Non-Aligned (N+N) Group. Some neutrals also used the UN to put forward a more active policy of neutrality and to illustrate the uses of a neutral in a conflict situation. Other neutrals did not use the UN platform to promote such interests. Austria has been considered 'non-controversial'; its voting patterns in the UN General Assembly have been rather 'safe', preferring to adopt a pro-Western stance or a 'balanced' position (Bitzinger, 1991: 284). Regardless of the potential coercive aspects of the UN, the involvement of the neutrals in this organisation became vitally important. With the onset of the Cold War, the UN would provide a legitimate forum for neutrals to play a useful role in the bipolar setting, namely through its 'good offices' of providing neutral sites for the superpowers to meet and negotiate.

The advent of the Cold War posed a new challenge to those neutral states that survived WWII. The extent to which neutrality was tolerated in the bloc structure varied from suspicion to accommodation, depending on the intensity of the conflict. In the early years of the Cold War, both superpowers were uneasy about these states that had no interest in bloc politics (Gasteyger, 1989: 30). The Cold War, with its emphasis on power politics, the balance of power, the security dilemma and defining international relations as based on bipolarity and collective security arrangements did not accommodate neutrality easily. Neutral states were subject to superpower pressure to choose sides politically, economically and militarily. The US in particular placed economic pressure on neutrals such as Sweden and forms of regionalism or cooperation between neutral states (such as plans for a Scandinavian defence union, discussed further in Chapter 4) were regarded with suspicion.

The US was more troubled about neutrality and neutralism than its Soviet counterpart. The Truman era, with its doctrine of containment, saw a concern about neutral states succumbing to Soviet pressure. According to Ruddy, this position began to shift towards an uneasy accommodation of neutrals as a 'third option' as the Cold War took shape. The Eisenhower administration nonetheless exhibited conflicting views of neutral states. Eisenhower accepted neutrality as a legitimate option and sought to have political and economic relations with the European neutrals in the hope of keeping them ideologically on side. A National Security Council (NSC) report of 1955 distinguished between *neutrality as a government policy* and *neutralism as attitudes and psychological tendencies*. The latter was undesirable, and the NSC report expressed hostility to forms of 'quasi-neutralism' (a disinclination to cooperate with US objectives indicating openness to Soviet exploitation) (Ruddy, 2000: 68–70). Nonetheless, in the era of McCarthyism, the US stance that was most noted came not from Eisenhower but from his Secretary of State, John Foster Dulles. In his 1956 speech on NATO to Iowa State College, Dulles declared that neutrality 'pretends that a nation can best gain safety for itself by being indifferent to the fate of others. This has increasingly become an obsolete conception, and, except under very exceptional circumstances, it is an immoral and shortsighted conception.' (Dulles, 1956: 549)

In the late 1940s–mid 1950s, the Soviet Union was concerned about neutral states becoming part of the Western camp, particularly because many were liberal democracies and Western in ideological orientation. Although not as critical or suspicious as the USA, the USSR likewise kept a firm eye on neutral states. Morgenthau claims that such 'totalitarian' regimes as the USSR were equally hostile to neutrality:

> To nations that consider themselves the repositories of universal truths which it is their historic mission to bring to the rest of humanity, the impartial aloofness of the neutrals becomes intolerable indifference ... In the contest between truth and falsehood, good and evil, neutrality appears to the crusading nations tantamount to passive hostility to be fought by all means fair or foul. (Morgenthau, 1958: 199)

Whereas the US regarded countries wishing to remain out of its sphere with suspicion, the Soviet Union was somewhat more amicable towards those that showed no desire to join the Western alliance, despite ideological preferences. There existed concern that Eastern Europe might be lured by the idea of neutrality, but simultaneously there was an effort to turn neutrality to the advantage of the USSR (Hakovirta, 1987a: 270; 1987b; Kruzel, 1989a: 136). Concern with Western expansion and European and Western economic integration gave way to a different attitude in the 1960s. The USSR came to regard the neutral and non-aligned states as important players in its notion of a 'world peace front', linking neutrality with disarmament and peaceful coexistence, in the hope of a wider neutralisation of Western Europe. Khrushchev proposed towards this end a neutral zone across Europe which would separate the Warsaw Pact and NATO[13] and Moscow supported the establishment of nuclear-free zones in Scandinavia, the Baltic, the Balkans and the Adriatic region. There were also appeals to Denmark and Norway to adopt the neutral stances of Finland and Sweden.

The more receptive attitude of the Soviet Union did not detract from certain pressures that it placed on neutral countries such as Finland. Finnish neutrality was established under the terms of the Treaty of Friendship, Cooperation and Mutual Assistance (TFCMA) (1948–92) with its Soviet neighbour. The USSR was concerned over the rise of German power in the Baltic, the Berlin crisis and the inclusion of northern NATO members into the NATO command structure (Joint Baltic Command) (Karsh, 1986a: 272–4). Fearing an attack by Germany through Finnish territory, the TFCMA placed limits on the size of the Finnish armed forces and ruled out Finland joining a military alliance. Finland was placed in a difficult position – regarded as a buffer state by the USSR (Karsh, 1986b), it maintained a delicate balance of independence in economic and domestic policy – until, of course, developments were seen to work against Soviet interests, as evidenced by the 'Night Frost' incident of 1958, and the 1961 'Note Crisis'.[14]

Writing neutrality

The USSR also regarded Austrian neutrality with suspicion. The USSR wanted Austria to practise a similar brand of neutrality as the Swiss (except Switzerland has no limits on the types of armaments it can possess; Austria does in the State Treaty) (Arnold, 1989: 389; Ogley, 1970: 183). The USSR was also concerned about the 'German question' and the legacy of *Anschluß*, which had become entwined with Austrian national identity. With the end of the Austro-Hungarian Empire in 1918, there was widespread belief that Austria could not survive without a strong link to Germany. The idea of the *Anschluß* existed well before Hitler; Otto Bauer, the then State Secretary for Foreign Affairs, wanted to pursue a policy 'aiming at unification with Germany'. (Hinteregger, 1989: 271–3) The *Anschluß* in 1938 ended the sovereignty of Austria but the question remained after the war whether Austria was a willing participant in Hitler's campaign or a victim of it. In the decade before the State Treaty, the Austrian government opted for the latter explanation (or the 'occupation theory', by which Austria was not a subject of international law and lost its ability to act when the *Anschluß* occurred). This explains the former USSR's resistance to Austrian membership of the European Community (EC). Since Germany was a strong partner in the EC, it would have been considered an '*Anschluss* through the back door'. (Neuhold, 1996: 5–8) A change in policy came when Khrushchev gained support in the Politburo and managed to separate the issues of Austrian independence and the German question. According to Thalberg, the USA was more supportive of Austrian neutrality as a way to keep Austria intact as a political unit (1989: 237–8). Thus, superpower concerns and insecurities were reflected in their treatment of the neutral states.

By the late 1970s, neo-realist explanations began to hold weight. For Waltz, international politics could best be understood as a system with defined and separate structures. Systemic constraints on states (or units) created similar foreign policy behaviour: 'Despite cultural and other differences, similar structures produce similar effects.' (1979: 88) Therefore, the conditions of international politics could not be solely gleaned from the internal features of the state.[15] Waltz regarded anarchy as a condition for the cause of war; since there is no overarching authority in the international system, there is nothing to prevent war from occurring. The balance of power in this configuration is also important. The sovereignty of states does not provide an automatic guarantee that they can do as they please, or will not be affected by others. The state will decide for itself how it will respond to internal and external phenomena, but constraints exist; states are similar in the tasks they face, but not in their abilities to perform them: 'the differences are of capability, not of function'. (Waltz, 1979: 96)

This applied to 'non-conformists' in the international system as well. In terms of neutral states, these units would have to behave in a particular way in order to maintain their survival and secure their interests. Lessons from WWI meant that in order for neutrality to be respected and not violated, defence (armed neutrality) took on a strong accent in their security policy doctrines. Sweden and Switzerland, after WWII, increased their conventional defence forces, despite accusations of double standards (Karsh, 1988; Sundelius, 1987). However, in the nuclear age, the conventional defences of armed neutral states appeared worthless in the face of the potential of nuclear destruction. In the late 1970s, the position of neutral states became even more tenuous. The Carter Doctrine and NATO's dual track decision of 1979 (to modernise its theatre nuclear forces whilst at the same time participating in arms control efforts to avoid deploying Cruise and Pershing II missiles) increased superpower tension (Kremenyuk, 1984). The deployment of NATO's Intermediate Range Nuclear Forces (INF) systems in Western Europe, and the advent of cruise missiles, which were capable of transgressing neutral airspace, forced the European neutrals to concede that armed neutrality was perhaps not enough to guard against a nuclear attack. The sale and transfer of military technology also created tensions between the US and some neutral states (Dörfer, 1987: 183–7 and 190–5).

The Cold War years did open up a new avenue for neutrals, nonetheless. Through the UN, neutral states increasingly became more active and outspoken on superpower behaviour and the role of the small state in the international arena. Given the significance of nuclear weaponry and the potential for mass destruction, some neutral states engaged in dialogue and served as the 'moral voice' in the international sphere against this. Some neutral states were more active in this respect than others, notably Sweden. The Palme Doctrine of 1974 (which asserted the right of small states to resist superpower influence) serves as an example of efforts by neutrals in particular to disassociate from Cold War practices. Sundelius notes that the Nordic neutrals were not satisfied with shifting their foreign policies in order to accommodate the international scene and attempted to 'directly promote international systemic change'. (1987: 1 and 6) In this case, it can be argued that the assumptions of the realist and neo-realist camp remain incomplete – small states, despite their capabilities, can articulate some level of change, using international organisations such as the UN and the Conference on Security and Cooperation in Europe (CSCE).[16] The obvious example of this is the Scandinavian neutrals, particularly Sweden and Finland in their efforts towards disarmament and non-proliferation. The Reagan Government did not support initiatives such as nuclear-free zones, the Comprehensive Test Ban Treaty (CTBT), and the SALT II ratification, as these initiatives were seen to undermine NATO's credibility and encourage neutralism.

Despite the pressures on neutral states during the Cold War, within this setting neutrality gained some form of acceptance. Superpower suspicion of neutrals meant 'ideology did not long prevail over interest'. (Waltz, 1979: 172) Neutrals had a specific role to play in relation to the bipolar setting and the opportunity for neutrality to develop as a concept or foreign policy tool was bracketed in these terms. The post-WWII environment has characterised our understanding of neutrality in the twentieth century in a number of ways. It is at this point in time that a more active form of neutrality developed. Neutrals began to make the distinction between being a part of the international system and actively promoting change in the international system through international bodies.

Conclusion: constructions of neutrality

The development of neutrality from the Peloponnesian War to the Cold War has been influenced by a number of ideas concerning the international system and the state, resulting in a one-dimensional treatment of neutrality. Different international settings affected the acceptance (or not) of neutrality in different ways. A sketchy picture of neutrality thus unfolds; the Peloponnesian War revealed that neutrality was conceived in terms of power relations. During the Middle Ages, religion was a strong force uniting units in the international system and neutrality was regarded as an affront to Christian unity. Some legal rulings arose to adjudicate maritime relations with regard to neutral states, yet this was largely underdeveloped at the time. With the decline of the papacy and the rise of the sovereign state, neutrality found some rights and obligations in international law. The 'just war' thesis marked the content of neutral rights and obligations. The Hague rulings provided the most solid provision of rules on neutrality, yet the events of the First World War saw neutrality 'fail the test' and become abandoned by a number of practitioners. Attempts to create a 'harmony of the peace' via international organisation did little to cater for neutral states, which reverted back to neutral policies as a way to negotiate the anarchical international system. The Second World War left five neutral European states on the map, which faced an enormous amount of pressure by belligerents. The Cold War years permitted a role for the neutral states in the bipolar balance of power, yet again neutrality was regarded as a suspicious phenomenon, as neutrals refused to 'take sides'.

The pivotal point in examining the history of neutrality is to show that neutrality has been conceptualised as a state's response to exogenous phenomena. There is little consideration of the domestic sources of neutrality. The dominant understanding of neutrality has been conditioned by how great powers (belligerents) have come to regard them: 'The credibility and respectability of neutrality ultimately exists as images of neutrality and neutral states, these images being held by interested actors, including the neutral states themselves and the foreign-policy actors in their domestic envi-

The social construction of Swedish neutrality

ronments.' (Hakovirta, 1988: 27) From the point of view of mainstream International Relations theory, the neutral state predominantly responds to the anarchic international system, and there is little in the way of investigating the endogenous roots of neutrality. These images of the neutral state have not altered; in fact, the reason why neutrality is seen as anachronistic today has its foundation in how it has been understood in the past and the associations that have accompanied its development and interpretation.

In the following chapter, the neutral state is examined in the context of the post-Cold War setting. As the international system faced dramatic shifts, a number of challenges and opportunities arose for neutral states. Chapter 2 investigates the implications of the end of bipolarity, the rise of new international norms and the impact of cooperation and globalisation for the neutral state, moving on to alternative and different interpretations of neutrality that have been obscured in IR theory. However, it the is constructivist account which provides a more meaningful interpretation of neutrality and its place in contemporary International Relations, and through this approach, it is possible to unpack some truth claims about neutrality and the neutral state.

NOTES

1 Despite the neutrality of Melos, wealthy individuals made private donations to Sparta (Cartledge, 1986: 12). Thus, the neutrality of Melos is disputed to some degree, although the notion of separation of state and civil society during this era was not comparable to our contemporary understanding of such.
2 This seems to be disputed in the literature. Rhee claims that no term existed for 'neutrality' until the mid-sixteenth century (1912). However, Jackson points to a 1954 publication by H. Nicolson, *The Evolution of Diplomatic Method*, which claims that the Ancient Greeks did have a concept of neutrality that translated as 'to stay quiet'. (Jackson, 1997: 37)
3 There existed stipulations for the neutral in a situation of *jus in bello*. At times, discrimination was made between 'benevolent neutrality', 'absolute neutrality' and 'qualified neutrality' (for clarification of the distinction between such terms, see Grant-Bailey, 1944: 6). However, these nuanced definitions of neutrality were secondary to the primary decision of which side was the more *just* (Tooke, 1965: 231).
4 Malmborg cites an earlier example of Holland and Lübeck in 1613 (2001: 30).
5 The Hague Convention V, [1907] 1994: 134–43. According to Malmborg, the Conventions signalled an important separation of the civil and military spheres, a reflection of the liberal age. Should citizens or private companies of a neutral state provide a belligerent with materials, this was not considered a breach of international law (Malmborg, 2001: 124). When Washington proclaimed neutrality for the US in 1793, the duty of abstention was clearly defined. Aiding a belligerent, or providing indirect aid, was a criminal offence (Politis, 1935: 18).
6 According to Louis Renault, professor of law and France's main representative at the Hague Conferences of 1899 and 1907 (cited in Best, 1983: 6).
7 The United States wanted to protect and free up commerce and the Revolutionary War was propelled by a desire to be free of interference from Europe (Rhee, 1912: 14). Although this appears to be the general impression, one author tells a different

8   account, claiming that Wilson's 'benevolent' neutrality was unbalanced (see Buehrig, 1950).
8   For Kant, international morality must be premised on the categorical imperative (to treat others as having value in themselves, and to act in accordance with principles that are valid for all other actors). Reason guides action, which is motivated by duty, and this is the correct action to take. Such a path should become universalised, a maxim which the agent should strive towards. Kant held that the idea of a perpetual peace ought to be pursued even if the goal seemed unattainable (see Donaldson, 1992).
9   When the Treaty of Versailles (1919) came before the Senate, there was opposition by supporters of neutrality to Article 10, particularly its notion of peace by force. This was construed to mean the protection of the *status quo* and the use of economic and military sanctions went directly against the League's promise of territorial integrity and political independence. Wilson refused to compromise on Article 10, and thus failed to attain sufficient support for the passage of the Treaty, resulting in its defeat (Divine, 1962: 2).
10 For instance, in 1921, the Allies put forward a joint declaration of neutrality during the Greco-Turkish war. Certain Latin American countries asserted their neutrality in 1933 during the Chaco war between Bolivia and Paraguay (Karsh, 1988: 110–11).
11 Along with Scandinavia, Greece, Spain and the Netherlands were also interested in collaboration (Salmon, 1993: 122–3). After withdrawal from the League of Nations, there were some attempts at 'regional isolationism', for instance the Scandinavian Rules of Neutrality (1938) and the Convention of the Baltic States (1938). Those nations wishing to remain out of WWII also debated a 'Third Europe', using collective action to protect their neutrality. Interestingly, Morgenthau writes that for this to succeed there had to be a 'community of interests transcending the mere negative desire to stay out of the next general war' and comparable power projection to potential belligerents (both of which were lacking) (1958: 198).
12 Commander-in-Chief Lord Beatty (cited in Walzer, 1992: 245). Lord Halifax was also opposed. Churchill's plan was not taken seriously until it was realised that Sweden would not desist from supplying Germany. After the Altmark incident in February 1940, Hitler invaded Norway (Karsh, 1988: 102–3).
13 This was to include Finland, Sweden, Switzerland and Austria and could possibly encompass the two Germanies (Lukas, 1992: 60).
14 The 'Night Frost' crisis (so named by Khrushchev in his reference to frosty relations between Finland and the USSR) refers to Soviet pressure on Kekkonen to remove the Social Democrat Karl-August Fagerholm, who had formed a minority cabinet. The 'Note Crisis' again concerned Finnish domestic politics, with the USSR displeased with Social Democrat Olavi Honka's coalition. The USSR threatened to put the TFCMA into use (implying military intervention). Pressure from the USSR also meant that Finland refrained from joining the Nordic Economic Community project (NORDEK) and did not become a full member of the European Free Trade Association (EFTA) until 1986. Karsh, however notes that Soviet actions may not have stemmed from a desire to control Finnish domestic politics, but rather sprang from security concerns of the USSR, particularly with regard to Germany and other external developments (Karsh, 1986a: 273).
15 It must be noted, however, that Waltz's perspective has been misconstrued on a number of occasions. One common assumption is that Waltz separates the domestic from the international. There can be no understanding of 'international politics without understanding something about the domestic character'. (Waltz, interviewed by Halliday and Rosenberg, 1998: 397)
16 Renamed the Organisation for Security and Cooperation in Europe (OSCE) in 1995.

2

Neutrality 'is what states make of it': rethinking neutrality through constructivism

NEUTRALITY HAS ONLY enjoyed attention as a problematic category of international political life. On the whole, this seems rather unsurprising. The story of neutrality garners little interest when measured against more exciting topics such as war, 'the stuff of great drama'. (Spielberg, 1998) In the history of nations, the dominant stories that capture the imagination are those that tell of how the nation defined itself in battle. There are no such stories about neutral states. This chapter is concerned with the established story of neutrality and how it is possible to rethink mainstream assumptions about the neutral state and 'break out of the categories that have determined the discourse on neutrality'. (Binter, 1992: 213) Here I explore alternative interpretations of neutrality and examine through a constructivist methodology the key assumptions and characteristics that have become attached to neutrality. By focussing on ideas about identity and norms, rather than purely material factors and legal descriptions, this chapter aims to rethink neutrality from a political rather than purely legal or materialist approach, which has dominated the conceptualisation of neutrality (Väyrynen, 1989a: 122).

Where the previous chapter covered the Peloponnesian War to the Cold War era, this chapter moves on to consider the position of neutrality in the post-Cold War international system of the 1990s. Many academics and practitioners have argued that neutrality no longer has a role to play because it is equated with state-centric isolationism that is counterproductive to addressing the myriad of security issues that have arisen since the end of bipolarity. Yet neutrality did not simply fade away as expected. In order to understand why some neutral states have found it difficult to shed neutrality in the post-Cold War era, it is important to rethink neutrality in a way that goes beyond the label of isolationism or the policy of small or weak states that suffer the cruelties of geography. Neutrality has become embedded into a set of specific accounts of the nation-state, which reflects certain notions about the self and other. Furthermore, neutrality has become a key reference point in determining what makes up the nation-state and how it responds to other actors in the international environment. Therefore, the aim is to investigate the endogenous sources of neutrality, rather than simply the exogenous. Through the lenses of social constructivism, this chapter explores alternative readings of neutrality as a concept and a practice, and takes into account issues of identity and state-building, providing a richer understanding of why neutrality is so entrenched in certain countries against the mainstream logic that neutrality is now outdated. Armed with new approaches to neutrality, the groundwork is then laid for an examination of Swedish neutrality through constructivist lenses in Chapter 3.

The end of the Cold War and neutrality in the 1990s

The demise of East–West tensions in the late 1980s represented a break with many long-held assumptions and understandings about international political relations. The certainty that bipolarity provided for international relations gave way to *uncertainty* and new ways of thinking about the international system and the concept of anarchy. Subsequently, the nature of state relations underwent revision. No longer regarded as a bounded entity, academics identified new challenges to the state in the post-Cold War setting, as interdependence began to characterise state relations in an era of globalisation (Barkin and Cronin, 1994; Keohane, 1989). Non-state actors gained prominence in scholarly work, increasing the challenge to the idea of the state as the only important actor in international relations (Risse-Kappen, 1995). The development of international or transnational institutions, such as the European Union, indicated a post-sovereign turn, as the EU progressed in terms of security and defence cooperation, and began serious moves towards a common currency and an active global role.

In the realm of security, the separation of 'high' and 'low' politics blurred, and military strength and capabilities were no longer the key arbiters of state power. Indeed, in the post-Cold War climate, the concept and practice of security faced new realities and priorities. The Warsaw Pact dissolved in 1991 and NATO reconfigured its rationale and doctrine under the Strategic Concept to adapt to the new security environment (discussed further in Chapter 6). Security became a porous concept, and encouraged new theories and approaches, spurred on by the end of bipolarity, but also by 'new wars' (Kaldor, 1999), and new forms of insecurity. Conflicts in the 1990s were characterised by ethnic and civil violence, witnessed in the Balkans, and intervention on humanitarian grounds signalled a shift in the nature of war and conflict. The new threats that gained prominence in the 1990s went beyond military security to include terrorism, trans-border crime, immigration, environmental degradation, economic security, human rights, and ethnic tension.

Since the end of the Cold War, the broad claim in International Relations theory is that traditional understandings of power politics are being challenged or modified. For Barkin and Cronin (1994: 125) 'the end of the cold war has seen a reaction against realpolitik and against noninterference in the domestic affairs of other states, and for the role of the West in promoting its political and economic ideals internationally. This has led to a change in both the discourse concerning legitimacy in foreign affairs and the conduct of foreign affairs.' According to Luke 'realist discourses and designs for world order are decaying'. (1993: 230; see also Vasquez, 1997) Neo-realism's failure to predict the largely peaceful end of the Cold War raised serious challenges to its orthodoxy. For George, the realist tradition was 'exposed as a politico-philosophical emperor at best only scantily clad'. (George, 1996: 33; see also Baldwin, 1995; Lebow, 1994; Sørensen, 1998) Some were quick to explain the changes as the triumph of western liberalism, or 'the liberal *idea*' (original emphasis), content that democracy and market capitalism had won the ideological battle (Fukuyama, 1992: 45). Laclau (1994: 1) equated the end of the Cold War with the end of ideologies, whilst Huntington (1993) predicted a clash of civilisations, whereby conflict would be based on cultural and religious differences. Some realists predicted a more turbulent world with the loss of bipolarity (Mearsheimer, 1990) and kept faith in realism's resonance (Walt, 1997). The significance of this challenge to realism was that alternative theories and ideas were given more purchase in academic debate. The discipline of IR and security studies subsequently widened beyond the dominance of realist, neo-realist and rationalist paradigms. Thus, the end of the Cold War not only produced a different international setting, it also forced a reconsideration of *how* international phenomena are understood. Despite the promise of new directions and debates in IR theory, nonetheless neutrality continued to be viewed in terms that reflected the old intellectual order rather than the new.

Post-Cold War, post-neutral?

With such changes to the international system and its conceptualisation, it seems as though some intellectual space may open up in terms of recasting a unique role for neutrals in this setting. Neutral states themselves were at least optimistic that their status could perhaps provide an alternative approach to dealing with the wider range of security threats that now occupied the security agenda. Neutrality was briefly considered as an option for some Eastern European countries as they emerged from the shadow of the former Soviet Union (Bitzinger, 1991). Some suggested that neutrals had a role to play that

NATO members could not (Windsor, 1989: 9) and would contribute to stability (Bebler, 1992). Some were even hopeful that there would be 'a renaissance of the *status* of neutrality'. (Binter, 1992: 213, original emphasis) Sweden in particular glimpsed an opportunity to project neutrality as a valuable posture to deal with the new security situation. As Huldt (1995: 155) explains, 'it was a strategy useful not only for the Swedes but also for others'. Many neutral states expected that their experience in mediation and peacekeeping could contribute towards conflict resolution in the emerging post-Cold War order, where nothing seemed certain. Sweden's Prime Minister, Ingvar Carlsson, stated in 1990 that Swedish neutrality

> contributes to stability and détente in our part of the world and, at the same time, constitutes the basis of our efforts at the international level to achieve peace and solidarity. This policy of neutrality is a great asset, especially in times of unpredictability and great change. This policy will be pursued purposefully and consistently. (Carlsson, 1990: 2–3)

Where Sweden saw neutrality as a positive status in uncertain times, the post-Cold War climate signalled uncertainty over the purpose of neutrality in other quarters. The Non-Alignment Movement, meeting in Accra in 1991, announced at the opening session of its colloquium on neutrality and non-alignment: 'Whereas neutrality as non-participation in a given armed conflict remains certainly an option in the future, permanent neutrality as a lasting policy needs re-thinking and may have to be adjusted to changing circumstances in Europe and worldwide.' (Mediterranean Academy of Diplomatic Studies, 1991) The setting which accommodated neutrality was now widely perceived to have disappeared (Gärtner, 1996: 608–9). There was nothing to be neutral between. Despite the widening of the security agenda, neutrality was not widely considered a viable option for dealing with new security issues. In fact, to many, the end of the Cold War signalled the end of neutrality. In an era of increased cooperation and the breakdown of ideological divisions, neutrality, to most, represented the past. As many perceived neutrality to be based on sovereignty and independent foreign and security policies (those who primarily understood neutrality through realism), such a stance is now unattainable in an interdependent world, where notions of sovereignty (and particularly 'state') are becoming increasingly blurred. Cox and MacGinty did not mince words when it came to their prediction of neutrality's fate in the post-Cold War era:

> It is unlikely that the sacred cow will make it into the next millennium in anything like its present form. The sacred cow has not been defeated – it has been deprived of that honour. There will be no ritual slaughter of neutrality by a superior method of organising a state's defence and security. Instead, the beast's demise will be somewhat less glorious; death by irrelevance. (Cox and MacGinty, 1996: 122–3)

Neutral states came under pressure to finally drop their Cold War legacy and approach security problems in a cooperative way. In the past neutrality was considered to be an alternative to alliance membership but now 'neutrality has disappeared *de facto* from the official security discourse'. (Goetschel, 1999: 115) One of the most telling signs could be found in the simple re-labelling of policy from 'neutrality' to 'militarily non-aligned', which became something of a trend amongst the West European neutrals in the post-Cold War setting. With the EU adding flesh to the bones of its fledgling CFSP, a neutral stance was seen as something of an anomaly, out of step with the developments in – and an obstacle to – European security cooperation. Instead of being pushed to the periphery, neutrality was widely considered to be part of an era that was now over.[1]

Rethinking the mainstream understanding of neutrality

The reasons why neutrality is deemed anachronistic today relate to the way it has been conceptualised in the past. The mainstream conception of neutrality, as outlined in the previous chapter, has depicted neutrality as an immoral and selfish stance in international politics. From a moral perspective – largely taking its cue from religious teachings – the neutral state is analogous to the disinterested passer-by who does nothing to assist a troubled neighbour. In times where religion guided action, the neutral state was compared to, or imagined as akin to, the individual. The philosopher Christian Wolff argued that nations, like individuals, must assist each other and that abstention was not always lawful (Politis, 1935: 37). Galiani, in *De' Doveri de' Principi Neutrali* (1782), provided the first distinction between individual and state morality at a time when sovereignty began to reshape international politics. Galiani observed that while individuals were obliged to assist each other, the same could not be claimed of states. The task of the neutral state was to protect its citizens; providing assistance to other states was a secondary consideration. Nonetheless, such order of priorities earned neutral states the label of 'passivity and disinterestedness which came to characterize neutrality in the nineteenth century'. (Ross, 1989: 6) Thus, 'with its individualist connotations', Joenniemi (1988: 54) claims that neutrality 'has occasioned little understanding other than as a form of abstentionism'.

Despite the rise of the sovereign state, neutrality was still a confusing category, tangled up in previous definitions and assumptions. The legacy of the realist tradition, nonetheless, provides the base for understanding the neutral state in the international system. However, realism is limited in its perspective and conceptualisation of neutrality. It fails to adequately elaborate how the *idea* of neutrality does not fit neatly into its worldview. This is clear from realism's dual approach to the question of the neutral state. On the one hand, neutrality was an undesirable stance in international relations, because neutral states did not adhere to specific power maxims, mainly due to their rejection of war and their refusal to partake in balancing and alliances. Yet realists afforded neutrals uneasy accommodation in the international system, in terms of both practice ('good offices') and recognition that neutral states did what other states would do – act in their own interests. This dualism in the realist approach to the neutral state raises some important questions about how neutrality has come to be understood. The following section explores how realist interpretations of the neutral state remain limited, particularly in light of a more critical examination of how neutrality subverts some of the most central themes of realist orthodoxy, that of sovereignty and the nature of how states act internationally and interpret their interests.

The problem with neutrality: subverting the norms of sovereignty and state

Realism's problematic relationship with the subject of neutrality is based upon a narrowly defined understanding of sovereignty and the role of the state in the anarchic international system. For realists, sovereignty is an institution that has been interpreted in a singular manner. Beyond mutual recognition and non-interference, sovereignty is an essential feature of the anarchic international system and permits states within that system to pursue national interests and security. The meaning of sovereignty was related to the internal and external realm, but in the external environment, sovereignty created a situation of anarchy, as states competed for their national interests in the absence of an overarching authority.

For Jackson, sovereignty as an institution represents 'a basic element of the grammar of politics'. (1999: 9) If the institution of sovereignty is a grammar, as Jackson claims, then the rules of grammar have been set by realism. Neutral states accept sovereignty as a vital component to state survival, but choose to guard their sovereignty by refusing to wage war. Before the institutionalisation and legitimation of sovereign rights, neutrality was difficult to uphold. Neutral rights were easily violated because they relied on belligerents respecting them. Thus, sovereignty afforded little comfort where unequal power was an issue, recalling the justification of the Athenians in the Melian Dialogue that 'might is right'. Early on, neutral states learnt that in order to protect their neutrality and sovereignty, armed neutrality or bilateral treaties with other states were necessary. Möttölä (1989: 224) even suggests that 'the only type of neutrality policy that gets recognised from the West is armed neutrality'. Thus there exists a tension between the idealist underpinnings of neutrality and the realities required to maintain a neutral stance:

> Neutrality was something of a double strategy. On the one hand it belonged to the repertoire of state formation as a weapon against various transnational structures

> ... neutrality also reflected, in certain aspects, an internationalist-idealist tradition as well as a number of ethical and moral considerations ... Neutrality was a critical concept with great peace potential. The understanding of neutrality has ... narrowed down, become standardised and militarised too. (Joenniemi, 1989b: 176)

The discourse and practice surrounding the concept of sovereignty and the state was defined in a way that excluded the acceptance of neutrality. Realism's key problem with the concept of neutrality is that it regards neutrality as a *misuse* of sovereignty. Sovereignty should mark clear boundaries of inside/out. However, in the case of active neutrality, the effort to resolve conflict by means other than military represents an inversion of the practice of sovereignty, or what realism understands to be the *correct* use of sovereignty. The Clausewitzian notion of war as an instrument of policy was deeply connected to the anarchic international system, and was commonly accepted as the way states obtained their objectives. Thus to be neutral was to invert one of the key intentions of what sovereignty promised. For realists, neutrality confuses the established understanding of the uses of sovereignty in the refusal to engage sovereignty according to realist maxims. Neutral states do not seek to enhance their security through the normal processes, nor do they engage in war as an extension of policy. For classical realists, the national interest remains the sole occupation of the state, and this is normally interpreted in terms of obtaining security in an insecure world.[2]

But as Shapiro (1992: 462) points out, the Clausewitzian idea was also a 'process within which subjects are producing and reproducing themselves'. Realist conceptions of the balance of power and the arms race that ensued encouraged neutrals to adopt a militaristic stance. The assumption of capabilities applies to neutrals as well. Belgian neutrality 'failed', for example, not only because the guarantee provided by the great powers proved worthless, but also because Belgium did not have the material capabilities to defend itself against invasion. According to Joenniemi, the emphasis on armed neutrality reflects an ideology of the security/warfare state. Yet neutral states *had* to be armed in order to protect their sovereignty in the anarchical international setting. Neutrality was employed by some countries to protect trade, or as part of nation-state formation, curtailing potential societal divisions or as a way to guard against interference from other states. Joenniemi is correct in pointing out that the emphasis on militarism distracts from a more normative appreciation of the peace potential of neutrality. For Joenniemi (1989b: 180), the dominant understanding of neutrality is weak, 'produced culturally in conflict between the ideology and interests of the security/warfare state on the one hand, and those of civil society on the other'. This reduced the notion of neutrality to that of a categorisation of the neutral as acting in a realist fashion, responding to the 'realities' of the anarchic international environment.

Neutrality 'is what states make of it'

Two different interpretations are at work here; that of the neutral and the non-neutral. This is a vital point to earmark when assessing how neutral states adopt a different approach to exogenous and endogenous phenomena. For the non-neutral, the best way for a neutral state to maintain its neutrality is through armed neutrality. For many realists, neutrality was an unrealistic posture to adopt in the first place. Yet for neutrals, their stance contains a different meaning:

> In manifesting this apparently idealistic behaviour, the neutral states are behaving very realistically. Their best hope for long-term survival is to elevate the status of neutrality, to promote an international mindset that makes it inconceivable for a great power to abuse a neutral state. Their idealism is the most realistic policy they could adopt. (Kruzel, 1989b: 310)

Taking up this last point, neutrality, by its very nature, thus subverted the idea of the anarchic international realm where states would use force to secure their interests. As Dougherty and Pfaltzgraff (1981: 9) contend, some states 'focus on power in an inverted manner, seeking security through non-involvement, isolation, neutrality, appeasement, or the acceptance of a dependent buffer or satellite status'. From the realist perspective, neutral states do not conform to the accepted reading of the state in the international system, and reinterpret sovereignty in a manner that marginalises them from international politics. Although many writers will state that the condition of anarchy gives birth to the status of neutrality (Ogley, 1970; Politis, 1935), it also works against that structure. Neutrality by its very nature is deviant to the anarchic international system. It *responds* to its environment by refusing to be co-opted into a bloc arrangement. Neutrality becomes the tool to protect sovereignty.

If one considers the ideals behind neutrality as being something more than maximising security via non-participation based on geography, resources or otherwise, then an alternative reading can be produced; neutrality can be seen to have its own rhetoric and neutrals 'were able to present their neutrality in universalist terms'. (Salmon, 1993: 120) To expand Salmon's comment, the existence of neutrality, no matter how widely disputed or regarded as 'immoral', became acceptable due to its inclusion in international law. The rhetoric of neutrality is state-based and centres on the protection of state sovereignty, not by waging war but by remaining outside of conflict. As such, it develops its own reasoning, language and rhetoric and can be presented as an alternative that contains a wider significance for obtaining peace. Of course, it can be argued that neutrals did play a particular role in the anarchic system, namely through other avenues such as peacekeeping, mediation, and 'good offices'. But as Väyrynen points out, neutral states '*circumvent* the existing international constraints by seeking alternative policies'. (1989b: 53, original emphasis) Since one of the purposes of the sovereign state is to obtain 'security', neutral states complied with this idea, but through different means. Bodin recognised this strategy in neutrality as a useful one: 'he who remains neutral often finds means to reconcile enemies, and so remains himself everyone's friend, and receives honours and rewards at the hands of both parties. If all princes were aligned against one another in hostile camps, who could compose their differences?'[3] Neutrality pursues sovereignty, but not in the framework of alliances, thereby divorcing itself from the bipolar system and assigning neutrality to 'a kind of deviant behaviour' that does not 'play the tune of balance of power policies'. (Albrecht et al., 1988: 1)

Rethinking sovereignty

As Camilleri and Falk (1992: 11) rightly comment, sovereignty is not a 'fact' but rather a concept or claim about how political power should be exercised. It contains different meanings, such as the national interest, independence, and security, and complies with a notion of strength both internally and externally (in relation to imposing its will on its citizens and securing its objectives in the international system). Sovereignty remains a product of historical, economic, and social conditions, or, as Barkin and Cronin (1994: 109) state, 'sovereignty is a social construct, and like all social institutions its location is subject to changing interpretations'. Like juridical ideas and institutions, 'there is nothing about it that is natural, inevitable or immutable'. (Jackson, 1999: 10) For Bartelson (1995: 14), sovereignty has long been an uncontested idea, and as such it has 'soak[ed] up a multitude of meanings through its various functions'.

The notion of sovereignty can be applied to different circumstances, for instance, in the manner in which Britain employed sovereignty as a principle to distance itself from Latin Christendom, and then later as an argument towards decolonisation (Jackson, 1999: 10). Likewise, claims or demands for sovereignty can be invoked at opportune moments in political history, or at times when concepts like sovereignty are in a state of vacillation. For instance, EU member states trade off sovereignty with the understanding that 'they cannot effectively pursue their interests or concerns within the traditional framework of sovereignty'. (Jackson, 1999: 4) Yet the ideal of sovereignty is invoked when such forms of cooperation are presented as a threat, for instance, the Danish referenda with regard to the EU, first on the Maastricht Treaty, and second, on the question of EMU. Thus, the ideal of sovereignty is far from over in the present age, as Werner and de Wilde (2001: 284) note: 'The most passionate defences of the idea of state sovereignty can be found in times when the freedom and independence of states is believed to be at stake.'

On the relationship between sovereignty and neutrality, there are also nuances that demand greater attention. For instance, in some cases, neutrality facilitates sovereignty, and *vice versa*: 'Whereas in countries like Sweden and Switzerland neutrality is an expression of sovereignty, in Austria and Finland such a policy has become an instrument *for* sovereignty.' (Bitzinger, 1991: 283, original emphasis)

What troubles critics of neutrality the most is the assumption that neutral states cling to certain ideas about the state and sovereignty that are losing their saliency. In the post-Cold War era, the institution of sovereignty has been subjected to a series of challenges, where post-modernity is equated with a post-sovereign world (Jackson, 1999: 4). In IR theory and international law, there exist two positions on the nature of sovereignty, with one pole claiming its obsolescence and another continuing to view the practice of sovereignty as thriving in the new era (Goetschel, 2000: 270; Werner and de Wilde, 2001: 283). In an age of globalisation and interdependence, the saliency of sovereignty is said to be slipping in favour of new forms of cooperation that transcend the state and new norms in international relations that lay serious challenge to the sovereign rights of nations. Neutrality is still equated with isolationism and an unwillingness to participate in the 'common good' or a common vision of international society.

Although neutrality was accommodated in the anarchic system and the balance of power, its very actions and responses to that system constructed a different set of meanings that conflicted with the dominant ones (that states are power maximisers, that security is conceived in militaristic terms). The use of neutrality also confronts certain assumptions about the likely behaviour of weak or small states – that they are bound to bandwagon or form alliances with stronger states in order to secure their interests. History does not always support this claim. Melos did not bandwagon with Athens during the Peloponnesian War; Belgium did not join Germany in 1914 despite France and Britain reneging on commitments to guarantee Belgian neutrality; and Finland resisted Russia during the Winter War (1939–40) (Labs, 1992: 386). The success or failure of policy in such instances does not address the point that states may *not* act according to the logic of the anarchic international system. Neutrality in the case of Melos and Belgium was violated, and Finland lost the Winter War, but these states did not adhere to the expectation that they would join an alliance. The focus on neutral states has been confined to the realist vision of anarchy and bipolarity, and exogenous factors are assumed to determine not only a state's decision to adopt neutrality but entirely shape it as well. The following section aims to rethink neutrality through social constructivism, to uncover the endogenous and normative features of neutrality as a concept and a practice.

The constructivist approach

Social constructivism has rapidly situated itself in the field of IR theory as a sociological approach that occupies the 'middle ground' between rationalism and reflectivism (Reus-Smit, 1996; Ruggie, 1998; Smith, 1999: 638). Unlike realism or liberalism, constructivism is not primarily concerned with material factors. It is concerned with the impact of ideas and focuses on how interests and identities of nation-states are flexible or a result of certain historical processes (Adler, 1997a: 322–3).

According to Wendt (1999: 1), constructivism contains two broad tenets: first, that 'structures of human association are determined primarily by shared ideas rather than material forces' and second, that 'the identities and interests of purposive actors are constructed by these shared ideas rather than given by nature'. Constructivism focuses on how actors are socially constructed, and how ideas matter (Wendt, 1999: 7). Constructivism posits that identity is part of a historical process of interaction which consolidates practices and beliefs, creating norms, which in turn determine action. The foundational premise of constructivism holds that people act towards objects and other actors based on the meanings that the objects have for them. How this form of identity is created and sustained depends on a number of factors. Collective meanings, norms and culture play a role, but for some constructivists (such as Wendt), identity and action are sufficiently explained through these variables. This form of constructivism, or what Reus-Smit calls 'third image'[4] constructivism, provides some explanation of the social construction of actors.

However, in order to explore identity, social structures, and institutions more intersubjectively, 'fourth image' constructivism allows for a more historicist analysis. This 'thick' rather than 'thin' variety of constructivism takes into account the importance of discourse, language and historicity (Dessler, 1999: 124). Examining neutrality through these lenses brings in the more interpretive perspectives, and to this I add metaphor and myth, which have played a substantial role in shaping public attachment to Swedish neutrality, the focus of this book. Thus, collective meanings, norms, culture, language, and metaphor and myth will be the components through which Swedish neutrality is re-examined.

Collective meanings make up the structures that dictate actions (Wendt, 1992: 397) but collective meanings require more than simply shared notions of knowledge and understanding. In this manner, norms and culture take on an important role in the formation of collective meanings. Norms are the 'collective expectations about proper behaviour for a given identity'. (Jepperson et al., 1996: 54) Systems of meaning define how actors interpret their material environment and the social identities of actors shape their interests and actions (Reus-Smit, 1996: 8). For Katzenstein (1996: 6), culture is the set of evaluative standards that produce norms and values. Culture 'is a system of signs, or ideas, or objects that is widely if not completely shared by a social group'. It defines the limits of thought within social groups and creates forms of solidarity (Stromberg, 1986: 5). Norms define identity, but as Finnemore and Sikkink (1998: 896) elaborate: 'Norms do not appear out of thin air; they are actively built by agents having strong notions about appropriate behaviour or desirable behaviour in their community.' Cognitive 'frames' are forged, usually against norms that are already established. Finnemore and Sikkink illustrate this in their work on women's suffrage, and how this confronted ideas about women and the appropriate role for women: 'New norms never enter a normative vacuum but instead emerge in a highly contested normative space where they must compete with other norms and perceptions of interest.' Norms then 'cascade and become institutionalised'. (1998: 897 and 896–902)

As Wendt (1992: 399) explains, the processes of institutionalisation see new identities and interests become 'internalised', producing norms. Institutions are 'cognitive entities' that exist with collective identities and meanings – they reinforce each other and cannot be separated. Adler calls this 'cognitive evolution' because social facts become established and influential. Social reality, therefore, is reproduced through the interaction of agents and structures, or what Checkel (1999) refers to as 'mutual constitution'. Cognitive evolution takes into account 'history and historicity': 'at any point in time and place of a historical process, institutional or social facts may be socially constructed by collective understandings of the physical and the social world'. These social facts are processed and subsequently subject to change (Adler, 1997a: 339).

Adler appears to borrow this reasoning from Berger and Luckmann, who make the claim that institutions must be understood through the 'historical processes' which produce them; institutions are not *given*: 'Institutions further imply historicity and control. Reciprocal typifications of actions are built up in the course of a shared history.' (Berger and Luckmann, 1971: 72) Historicity generally refers to the historical nature of social phenomena, but Touraine (1988: 41) adopts a wider interpretation, linking historicity to culture: 'Historicity is not a set of values solidly established at the centre of society; rather it represents a set of instruments, of cultural orientations, through which social practices are constituted, and thus one can say it is a set of investments.' Touraine's concept of historicity relies on the idea of 'self-production'[5] of society by social agency (Delanty, 1997: 118). Historicity is vital to the production of a culture and is a 'set of cultural, cognitive, economic, and ethical models by means of which a collectivity sets up relations with its environment'. (Touraine, 1988: 40) The consolidation of collective meanings becomes influential in identity formation and behaviour. The behaviour of states is not simply the result of exogenous forces. States will respond to phenomena differently because of domestic and international constraints, historically built up understandings of self and other, and the meanings attributed to these internal and external factors. The behaviour of the nation-state is conditioned by norms, values and practices that have been historically established, contested, embedded, and understood to be part of self-definition or identity.

Even amongst neutral states (which do not wholly conform to the expectations of the realist premise), behaviour differs. Norms connected to neutrality differ between neutral states because of the historical experiences and interactions of those states. Switzerland, for instance, uses its neutrality quite differently to Sweden. This is because neutrality is not merely a posture adopted out of convenience or shrewdness – it reflects the historical experiences of nation-state formation, culture and practices which are built up over a period of time.

For neutrality, the implications of the constructivist approach reveal how dominant perceptions of neutrals became so defining. Neutrality was understood primarily by what it was not. The pursuit of sovereignty and national interests in the anarchic international system differed between neutrals and non-neutrals. The norms that guided non-neutrals gave a different reading of the state's role in the anarchical arena. States largely understood each other as power maximisers. In order to secure the state and maintain sovereignty, war was sometimes a necessity. For neutrals, a different understanding emerged, that of securing sovereignty by abstaining from war. Sovereignty essentially held the same currency, but the way to obtain it was through different means.

Rather than assume that structure conditions state behaviour, actors *create* the structure through their interests and the influence of their norms. Wendt challenged the assumption of anarchy as the overarching condition of the international system. For Wendt, *anarchy is what states make of it*. A different conception of anarchy emerges to reveal how identities are intersubjectively constructed, which produces a particular set of meanings and identities that inform action (Wendt, 1992). The realist conception of national interest is inferred from the anarchic international system, but 'this cannot help us to explain the adoption by a state of particular policies over alternative means for achieving security. That is, it cannot tell us about the historically contingent content of the national interest as identified and pursued by state officials.' (Weldes, 1996: 278) For Weldes, national interests 'are social constructions created as meaningful objects out of the intersubjective and culturally established meanings with which the world, particularly the international system and the place of the state in it, is understood'. (1996: 280)

Neutrality 'is what states make of it'

Neutrality, when reconsidered through constructivist lenses, thus invites further questions that go beyond the external realm and the balance of power. Through a constructivist account, variables such as identity, interests, history, processes, institutions and actions are pieced together and included in a new type of analysis. As well as taking on board material explanations or external determinants, constructivism widens the scope to consider the role of language, rhetoric, culture, norms and interactions of an internal and external nature. Quite simply, interests cannot be pursued without a particular identity, and 'The identities, interests and behaviour of political agents are socially constructed by collective meaning, interpretations and assumptions about the world.' (Adler, 1997a: 324) For instance, Irish neutrality, according to Tonra, has been related to a number of key social and political phenomena, such as narratives of independence and contested notions about the nation, defining self against other (2000: 11). Here I argue that neutrality has played a substantive part in constructing nation-state identity and actions, both internally and externally. For many neutral states, neutrality has been closely tied to issues of identity and has provided the foundation to pursue other aspects of nation-state building and international participation. Foreign and security policy is essentially reflective of the internal identity of the nation-state. A neutral state responds differently to the anarchical international system than a non-neutral state.

Nevertheless, identities and interests are not static. For Adler, the social identities of nation-states are comprised of a mixture of causal and normative understandings and practices, and identities and interests alter and 'converge' (1997b: 252). Ideational structures, according to Copeland, have a constitutive rather than a regulative effect on actors, and through interaction, a process of socialisation occurs (2000: 190). The identity of a nation-state is not fixed, nor is it singular. 'Nations, like individuals, tend to formulate their policy in accordance with both their unique historical experience and their idiosyncratic traits.' (Karsh, 1988: 137) For instance, Britain is not simply a European middle power. It has a colonial past, a monarchy, a particular brand of democracy, and a market economy. It is a nuclear power, a member of the UN, the EU and other international organisations. Yet it is the internal aspects which filter, read and interpret how Britain acts in the world. Britain regards *itself* as distinct because of its tradition, culture and history. As Wallace (1991: 66) states: 'Nationhood and national identity represent necessary myths which underpin foreign policy.' Britain's problematic relationship with the EC is a case in point. The UK joined the EC late, and largely for economic reasons. As such, 'it bred a sense of being "off-side" in a game that had been framed for other players'. (Wallace, 1997: 678) Geographically, the UK was separated from the continent, and regarded itself as detached from continental politics and the broader visions of European unity, and preferred its

Commonwealth links. Membership of the EC was a pragmatic, not a symbolic choice and there has been a failure 'to embed the discourse of integration as a virtuous objective'. (Wallace, 1997: 677–8) Britain's relationship with its European counterparts in the EU differs to its 'special relationship' with the USA, arguably for reasons of identity, as Blair (2000) indicates: 'It is about bonds of kinship and history. It is about a shared language and most of all it is about shared values.' Its relationship with the US is symbolically more important because it is conceived on the basis of a shared identity. Yet Britain, through its membership in the EU, does have a specific set of relations with other European countries. This interaction has prompted a shift in self-understanding, has been the subject of wide media debate, and has been deeply tied to the question of British identity. This process of interaction with other actors has signalled a significant shift in Britain's approach to Europe and to its own internal sense of identity (as seen in the Blair Government's more open approach to the European question). National interests can shift and are not static.

Likewise, *within* the nation-state, there are regional differences which vary for a number of reasons. Comparing states such as Italy, Switzerland and Britain reveals such nuances. For Italy, the regional divisions produce a different response by the nation towards cooperation in organisations such as the EU. The Italian commitment to European integration is regarded by Laffan as 'the desire to contain a weak state with a weak government in a wider and more stable framework. The European edifice was central to the search for regime maintenance in Italy.' (1994; see also Radaelli and Bruni, 1998) The perceived cultural and historical differences between the Italian north and south are finding expression in new identities that these regional groupings forge, particularly from the dominance of the Northern League (*Lega Nord* – LN), which formed in 1991. For the LN, identity is regionally based – the divide between *il Nord* and *il Sud* is based on culture, language, history and economics – and the LN identifies more closely with its neighbours across the border than it does with its southern counterparts, which it regards as corrupt (Lega Nord, 1996; 2000). The LN has built its political project on an 'invented' geographical area – Padania[6] – which has never existed as an administrative or political unit, but has the accompanying myths and symbols one would normally attribute to the creation of an identity-based unit (Giordano, 2000: 446–7). The LN has indicated that it prefers a Europe of the Regions, which would work towards the dissolution of the power of the nation-state.[7] Increased fragmentation is not only restricted to the example of Italy, and this phenomenon appears to be present across Europe. The EU is increasingly becoming the focal point for regional groups, either in terms of opposition to, or as an avenue for, furthering their causes. Where right-wing groups are generally opposed to European integration, fearing a European super-state, new nationalist and separatist groups embrace the EU, citing how Scotland is seeking direct representation on the EU Council of Ministers and increased representation on the EU Committee of the Regions (Newell, 1994).

For Switzerland, on the other hand, membership of the EU could produce a divisive effect and identities within the unit could come apart. Although the French-speaking majority is in favour of EU membership, the German-speaking sector fears a loss of identity to Germany in the EU.[8] On a similar level, neutrality in Switzerland secures the nation-state. Membership of the EU might harm Switzerland's federal system, which has maintained the four linguistic communities that occupy the nation-state. The German-speaking population of Switzerland largely fear that '*Schweizerdeutsch*', the unwritten language of the Swiss Germans, would be wiped out by EU membership (*The European*, 24–30/12/93). On the other hand, language can be seen as a bargaining tool. During the accession negotiations for EU membership, Sweden announced that it would forego EU official documents being translated into Swedish, as a vast majority of Swedes understand English, French or German. Likewise, the Maltese took the same approach in their effort to become 'acceptable' for a favourable Commission opinion on the suitability of their membership application (House of Lords, 1993: 23). Similarly, Iver B. Neumann makes the point that language is an important 'marker' of identity.[9] Language is an important cultural signifier and the more radical variants of constructivism grants it status because it is regarded, as Sapir claims, as a 'guide to "social reality"'. Language 'shapes the entire "world picture" of the population whose native language it is'. (Collin, 1997: 80) For Berger and Luckmann, language 'provides the fundamental superimposition of logic on the objectivated social world'. (1971: 82) The world and social phenomena are comprehended through language, which makes shared experiences 'available to all within the linguistic community, thus becoming both the basis and the instrument of the collective stock of knowledge'. (1971: 85–6)

Constructivism can therefore also be interpretive in its methodology. It employs narratives and histories in order to unveil collective meanings, the identities of actors and the 'substance of political interests' (Adler, 1997a: 335). In the case of Sweden, *metaphor* and *myth* play an important political and societal role. The image of the *folkhem*, for instance, has developed into a myth, part of the collective understanding of society in Sweden. Myths can also change in their significance and meaning. Until recently, the welfare state and Swedish neutrality were labelled unassailable myths in that they were broadly accepted into the fabric of politics, culture and society in Sweden. Nonetheless, neutrality and the welfare state now stand as contested myths in that their presence and relevance for Swedish society today is deemed less powerful or more questionable. Constructivist literature has only timidly handled the possibilities of myth[10] and metaphor but much remains to be explained and elaborated in terms of how myth and metaphor occupy a powerful place in terms of identity construction and alteration. Metaphor and myth combine to create powerful rhetorical tools to create the mental imagery of collective identities and ideas, and 'although metaphors can sometimes serve as literary ornamentation, more importantly they have the potential rhetorically to influence the formation of beliefs and guides to action'. (Sarbin, 2003: 149) The meaning attached to the idea of the *folkhem* and 'solidarity' became key Social Democratic symbols. These symbols became so concrete that they infused the Social Democratic project with almost unquestionable authority. Neutrality has been so entrenched among Swedes that the current critical debate about neutrality is seen to be breaking some 'taboo' area. All of these factors work towards providing a more complete picture of neutrality. Metaphor and myth are vital elements of constructing identity and transmitting ideas. Wendt (1992: 402) speaks of this when he talks of the state's conception of 'self' as being incomplete without an idea about the 'other'; the 'raw material' which constructs states 'is created by domestic society before states enter the constitutive process of international society'. Berger and Luckmann (1971: 48) contend that myths inform 'the reality of everyday life, sometimes in a very decisive way'. For Brzozowska (2003: 51), 'myths are built by many "blocks" of various interlocked symbolic propositions'. Metaphor provides the discursive imagery to convey ideas about self and other, articulating ideas about identity and reinforcing this identity on numerous levels. In the following section, I commence with a different account of how neutrality has been constitutive of nation-state internal identity and interests.

Neutrality 'is what states make of it'

Since constructivism places importance on ideas and identity, the focus shifts from material and rationalist approaches to understanding neutrality as constitutive of identity and ideas that differ. However, not all neutral states act alike, and this section explores how neutral states interpret and employ their neutrality in different ways. If neutrality is an issue of identity, then identities differ according to historicity, culture and norms. The realist understanding of the neutral state assumes that states arrive at a neutral position because they are weak and opt for isolationism. The core of the assumption here is that neutral states act out their neutrality in the same way because as units in the anarchic international system, they share certain attributes (small and weak states, a preference for isolationism, and so on). However, as Wendt claims, institutions such as anarchy and the security dilemma are results of practice, and therefore we must dig deeper in questioning the determinism of these institutions. Anarchy does not explain why there is an absence of inter-state wars: 'It stretches credulity to think that the peace between Norway and Sweden, or the United States and Canada, or Nigeria and Benin are all due to material balancing.' (Wendt, 1995: 77–8) Applying this logic to the case of neutral states raises an important issue in the underlying conceptualisation of neutrality based on realist grounds. Not all states act the same, and thus, not all neutral states have a common foundation for their neutrality.

For states that are 'neutralised', or whose neutrality derives from exogenous events or sources, neutrality appears 'imposed'. Even if neutrality is not endogenous, the neutralised state may subscribe to it, sometimes in exchange for other arrangements, such as autonomy and sovereignty in the case of Austria. Austria's sovereignty was restored when it became a neutralised state in 1955,[11] 'the political price Austria had to pay' (Neuhold, 1994a: 27) to regain autonomy after WWII. Despite the common suggestion that Austria was 'neutralised' by the USSR and the USA, Austrian neutrality was based on a consensus reached by Austrian politicians (Bruno Kreisky, Julius Raab, Leopold Fige and Adolf Schärf). Raab (Chancellor between 1953 and 1961), in his declaration to parliament in 1955, made it clear that Austria was not ideologically neutral (Thalberg, 1989: 234–6) and that Austria accepted neutrality 'voluntarily' as a sovereign state[12] (Arnold, 1989: 388; Hinteregger, 1989: 274). Hence, neutralisation can develop into an endogenous or internalised variety (Carlsnaes, 1993: 13).

In the Finnish case, neutrality permitted the country to avoid the category of a Soviet 'satellite' and formed the basis of relations with the former USSR in the period after 1948. The term 'Finlandisation' has commonly been used by the West to imply that Finland was a satellite state of the USSR. Its neutrality pact with the former Soviet Union was seen to denote Finnish submissiveness to its neighbour in foreign and domestic policy. For Mouritzen, Finland adapted its internal and external policy to the interests of the USSR: what he calls 'adaptive acquiescence', which 'implies conscious, voluntary, and continuous infringements on the regime's values'. (1988: 5) The label of 'Finlandisation' has been a sensitive one for the Finns.[13] Finland's foremost diplomat and neutrality expert, Max Jakobson, argued that Finland could not be compared with Eastern Europe (1962: 196–8). The Helsinki–Moscow relationship was more open compared to the USSR's relations with its satellites. Finland was able to maintain a pluralistic and democratic political system and its economy was capitalist/Western, as were Finnish culture and public attitudes.[14] The label of Finlandisation was intended to capture this meaning, rather than imply subservience.

Hakovirta (1988: 18) claims that norms surrounding neutrality are built upon three foundations: the first pertains to the 'laws' of neutrality. From this basis, patterns of behaviour become established (for instance, duties and obligations under the laws of neutrality), leading to a process of 'customisation'.

Finally, norms are produced and substantiated by a combination of the first two foundations. It is the 'customisation' that Hakovirta speaks of that requires special interest, and it is important to focus on the way in which neutrality has been 'customised' by the nation-state that practises it to reflect its own values, domestic institutions and norms.

Rationalist approaches to the idea of the neutral state disguise interpretations and explanations of neutrality that go beyond measurable observations. The question of interests and identities in the formation of neutrality policy do not enter into the debate. It is a matter of cause and effect. Taken this way, it is not difficult to recognise the problems that metatheories such as realism had when it came to dealing with neutral states. With its assumptions about the state and the nature of anarchy, on the one hand it would appear rational for small and weak states to adopt neutrality to protect their national interests. On the other hand, however, the *act* of neutrality excluded neutrals to a large degree. Neutrals were seen as 'non-players' or on the periphery of where the 'action' was happening – that is, within the spheres of interest and the system of 'enemies and allies' that characterised the Cold War era. There was little consideration of how ideologies and identities within the nation-state play a role in the construction of foreign and security policy. For Ireland, neutrality has been a way to maintain a distance from the UK and not become embroiled in British and American conflicts (Fanning, 1996; Keatinge, 1987: 76). Austrian neutrality was a means to not only obtain sovereignty but also to form a separate identity from that of Germany (Missiroli, 1994: 6). Attention must also be paid to how neutral states define their own policies.

What becomes clear when looking at the differing interpretations of neutrality is that the concept itself contains dualisms. Some interpretations place neutrality as a part of the balance of power, protecting the *status quo.* Joenniemi (1993: 296) claims that during the Cold War years and the concentration on armed neutrality, this was certainly the case. Others look to neutrality as an alternative security policy with a significant peace potential. The reason for this can primarily be explained by the fact that neutrality means different things to different countries: 'All the neutrals tend to stress their individual features rather than those that are common to them all.' (Joenniemi, 1988: 54) For some, it is a means to an end, for others, it is a way of staying out of war. Either way, neutrality signified a different idea about conflict and peace; but in the world of power politics, this is not always possible. For the former Austrian statesman Bruno Kreisky (1959: 269), 'The big power conflict is supposed to leave practically no room for small states to manoeuvre and advance their own concepts of international policy.' For some countries, neutrality serves as a binding factor, holding the internal community together. Neutrality has always been an elastic concept, with differing roles and forms (Binter, 1992: 213). There are positive and negative connotations. Albrecht et al. (1988) see dominant interpretations creating neutrals as 'objects rather than subjects' since neutrals do not comply with 'rational' ways of obtaining security (see also Masker, 1995: 10). Neutrality, to borrow Wendt's phrase, 'is what states make of it'. There are passive and active brands of neutrality, and neutrals play out their policies in different ways. In the 1980s, debate amongst neutrality theorists identified two types of neutral state: the 'neutrality realists' and the 'neutrality idealists'. The former type accepts the anarchic international system, whereas the latter rejects it and seeks alternative avenues rather than war for conflict resolution (Kruzel, 1989b: 298–9). The way a country uses its neutrality should reveal more about the internal character of the nation-state rather than the external environment. Small states do not act in the same way as larger states because of the policy realms they grant importance to and the resources they possess. Joenniemi states that the link between small/weak states and neutrality should no longer be a defining categorisation: 'The concept is relative rather than absolute and should not be treated ... as a measurable property.' (*Eagle Street*, 1998) Defining small and weak states is a difficult process. By what category do we assign this definition? Military strength? Population, territorial size, economy or resources? Academics are in disagreement over this term. For Keohane, states should be defined on the basis of their influence in the international system (Handel, 1981: 21). In order to deduce nation-state action, variables such as internal historical, political and social development are equally important parts of the picture.

For countries such as Sweden, nation-state building took precedence in the years after its warrior-state phase. When Sweden lost the Åland Islands to Finland through a League of Nations ruling, and when Norway withdrew from its union with Sweden, Sweden was in a position to reclaim these territories, but refused. Sweden was more interested in good relations with Norway and abided by the League's ruling because of its adherence to the rule of law. According to Väyrynen (1989b: 53–6), due to the inequalities in the international system, small states will promote 'economic development, national security and foreign policy influence'. The neutral in this sense can be a 'force of change'. During the Cold War, the 'good offices' role of the neutrals was accommodated because of the 'stabilising' role it played in the bipolar system. Change was to be incremental, not sudden. Neutral states did not alter the international system but aimed to reform it, by advocating multilateral rather than unilateral cooperation. Yet these attempts were constantly challenged by the superpowers. Kremenyuk claimed that the USA attempted to discredit neutral initiatives for European security by employing negative images of neutrality (such as the Finlandisation rhetoric so prevalent in the 1960s) (1984: 97–100). This emphasis on the ability (or inability) of neutral states to deter belligerents distracts from an examination of the different forms of cooperation that neutrals employ (multilateralism, mediation, peacekeeping). Thus, an inherently alternative approach to international affairs begins to emerge. Neutrality can be regarded as a rejection of the balance of power system (Joenniemi, 1989a: 55) and the ideas of power politics. Or, as Galtung has noted, neutrality is equally meaningful in a bipolar, unipolar or multipolar world 'as a policy of military non-participation' (Binter, 1992: 214). This provides an alternative reading of the external determinants of neutrality, but this still does not instruct us in a clear way as to how neutrality becomes entrenched in nation-state identity.

Prevailing discourses about security also contribute to the formation of identity and interests, shaping beliefs and thereby establishing accepted norms and behaviour (Price and Reus-Smit, 1998: 259; Walt, 1997). As Katzenstein comments, security interests are defined by actors who respond to cultural references and factors: 'Interests are constructed through a process of social interaction.' (1996: 2) For instance, early US neutrality was more related to general ideas and discourse about republicanism rather than isolationism.[15] If, as realist and neo-realist explanations would have us believe, US neutrality was a means to isolation, then the US could have adopted a different position (relying on agrarian self-sufficiency and avoidance of war and trade with Europe) (Bukovansky, 1997: 213). Yet the US pushed for neutral rights because trade was linked to Jefferson's commitment to the view that wealth would improve the status of the republic. Jefferson's worldview was rooted in an eighteenth-century mercantilist pattern of interstate relations. Trade was of utmost importance and US foreign policy was underpinned by the desire to secure trade routes and maintain its status as a neutral power (Sofka, 1997: 520). Bukovansky (1997) notes that maritime law in the eighteenth century was still no guarantee for the protection of neutral trade and US naval power was no match against Britain. As Sofka claims: 'A small neutral power lacking a credible naval force could base its claims on little more than the sanctity of treaties and enlightened notions of free trade.' (1997: 523) Realist explanations do not appear to suffice in this case. If the US were a small or weak state, it would have done better to bandwagon rather than become an advocate for the extension of neutral rights. Furthermore, Wilson's speech of 1914 reveals more about a nation trying to maintain internal unity:

> Such divisions amongst us would be fatal to our peace of mind and might seriously stand in the way of the proper performance of our duty as the one great nation at peace, the one people holding itself ready to play a part of impartial mediation and speak the counsels of peace and accommodation, not as a partisan, but as a friend. (Wilson, 1914)

When the Treaty of Versailles came before the US Senate in 1919 (just two years after Wilson abandoned neutrality to enter WWI), there was a deep divide between the 'new internationalists' who supported collective security, and the traditionalists who supported neutrality. For the latter, war was seen as inevitable; hence, neutrality remained the best option in the anarchic international environment (Divine, 1962: 7–21). Supporters of neutrality were wary of plans to try to create peace by force. Furthermore, initiatives such as the Kellogg-Briand Pact (1928) that called for 'the renunciation of war as an instrument of national policy' were regarded as unrealistic and unenforceable; it did not aim to abolish war as an institution (Politis, 1935: 8 and 57–9). For Borchard (of the Yale Law School) the complexities of international relations could not be altered by 'a stroke of the pen'. He defended neutrality as a progressive idea, considering it 'the greatest gift that God has put in the hands of the American people'. (Borchard, cited in Divine, 1962: 23) The idea of neutrality in the US was strongly wedded to ideas of independence, but was also held as an ideal itself in an anarchic international system:

> Most nations, and especially small nations, owe their existence to the fact that they were legally privileged to remain neutral when other nations lost their heads ... The instinct of self-preservation and the necessity of limiting the area and the destructive effects of war are the source and justification of the doctrine of neutrality. It is humanitarian in its purpose and effects. It is a peace-preserving institution – one of the beneficent achievements of a long struggle with barbarism. Its abandonment, in the name of a supposed universal 'peace', would be likely to spell universal chaos. (Borchard, 1933: 523)

Likewise, Swiss neutrality emerged out of related circumstances. For Switzerland, neutrality serves to bind the different groups that constitute the nation-state. Economic dependence on exports and poor economic conditions saw the rise of the mercenary service, whose soldiers fought the wars of other powers. At times Swiss mercenaries were fighting each other, leading to the development of an 'embryonic neutrality policy ... directed towards the outside world'. (Freymond, 1990: 178–9) Underlying the formal arrangements of Swiss neutrality, however, is a deeper domestic or internal explanation. Switzerland, divided into cantons and housing different cultures, uses neutrality as a point of consensus in order to keep the internal homogenous and bound. Hence neutrality is understood in terms of the state and not due to ethical considerations (leading to some criticism of it being isolationist in its neutrality).

There exists a linkage between Swiss democracy, federalism and neutrality. As Freymond (1990: 178) notes: 'To put it schematically: direct democracy is the political organisation of the basic communities; federalism relates to the manner of managing intercommunal or intercantonal relations; and neutrality constitutes the foundation on which the external relations of this intercommunal system are built.' Switzerland was built on a network of treaties, and the potential for division was strong. Internal and external threats inspired a system of collective security amongst the cantons dating back to the thirteenth century. Freymond claims that collective security was the foundation of the confederation, but neutrality was more directed towards potential internal conflict: 'It was an internal "institution", the attitude expected of a canton which was not a party to a conflict between other cantons.' (1990: 176–80) This was then turned towards outward threats, whereby the cantons united and employed the tools of mediation, neutrality, arbitration and law, which now constitute a large part of Swiss policy to date. As early as the sixteenth century, Switzerland renounced military involvement outside its borders. When the Swedish army (under King Gustavus Adolpus) entered southern Germany during the Thirty Years War (1618–48), the Protestant sections of the confederation refused to join a Swedish military alliance as this would have harmed the sense of community that had developed with its Catholic confederates (Widmer, 1989: 23). Neutrality was the tool that held together the cantons in the face of the Reformation and other divisions.

Therefore, Adler's idea of 'cognitive evolution' would explain to some extent how certain neutrality norms came into existence. With the defeat of small and weak neutral countries by larger, more aggressive powers, a lesson (albeit external to some) was learned. However, for an active neutral such as Sweden, there is a combination of external and internal influences on the norms that develop around its neutrality. Armed neutrality underwrites a 'credible' neutrality policy. A state is deterred from attacking Sweden because it is hoped that the costs will be perceived to outweigh the action. This protects and secures neutrality, which is then used on the international scene in a variety of ways, be it as a mediator encouraging peace or in order to export its values and ideas on a number of different subjects. The application of these norms rested with the states. Neutral states could be active or passive, have strong or weak defence, participate in international organisations or not. Norms and identity are linked; norms prescribe behaviour for national policy-making elites and nations and 'underlying norms at one level may shape specific norms at another level'. (Klowert and Legro, 1996: 466 and 452) The active neutrality practised by Sweden, for example, does not exist in a vacuum. It derives from domestic sources and informs policy choices on the international front (seen in its development aid policy and its criticism of superpower behaviour in the UN and support for small states).

The treatment of the state in constructivism makes a clear break from monist understandings of it as a territorially-defined sovereign unit that has coercive powers over the population it contains. Constructivism also calls into question the neo-realist understanding of the state. For neo-realists, theories about the state are systemic: 'Structures encourage certain behaviors and penalize those who do not respond to the encouragement.' (Waltz, 1979:

106) Anarchy is the organising principle of the system, and the anarchic international system conditions or socialises units (states) into similar behaviour. This is essentially an outside-in approach – explanations occur at the systemic level and causality runs from system to unit. This immutability thesis of realism – that structures are given and unchangeable – exists because there is a division of the internal and the external. Mainstream international relations theory has largely treated the state as a given entity, its boundaries and content determined and inflexible to change. Yet the state is not simply *given*. For Devetak, the project of the state is an ongoing one, always 'constituting and reconstituting itself' (Devetak, 1995: 19–21). Machiavelli talked of constituting and reconstituting *a particular type of state*, one which was constantly on guard against external threat (Machiavelli, 1995). For Bartelson, the attributes of the state are the end result of structural context or historical process. The 'state' is a discursive fact (Bartelson, 1998: 305).

Hence, the idea and the meaning of the state in the post-Cold War era is open to debate. As such, notions connected with the state, for instance, national identity and national interests, are also affected by the current state of thought in international political theory. Whereas until recently the 'home' or the image of the 'home' has derived from the nation-state, this imagery is now being recast in terms of transnational or regional security communities, or 'cognitive regions'. 'Social epistemes' (the collective knowledge people share about themselves and others – i.e. intersubjective meanings) are under reconstruction. These 'regional systems of meanings' have the ability to 'institutionalise commonalities' or sub-national commonalities. Shared knowledge amongst groups and individuals with an authoritative claim to policy (such as nuclear arms control) creates an epistemic community because of shared normative beliefs and knowledge about social and physical phenomena (Adler, 1992). Actors can 'learn new patterns of reasoning and may consequently begin to pursue new state interests'. (Haas, 1992: 2) This is certainly the case in terms of European integration and the development of the EU. Within the EU, nation states, through their interaction with other community members, develop a different set of interests.

Adler (1997b) cites post-war Western Europe as 'the most advanced community region so far'. Like Deutsch, Adler claims that in pluralistic security communities, there is a strong 'core' around which other states gather. Haas notes that:

> Members of transnational epistemic communities can influence state interests either by directly identifying them for decision makers or by illuminating the salient dimensions of an issue from which the decision makers may then deduce their interests. The decision makers in one state may, in turn, influence the interests and behaviour of other states, thereby increasing the likelihood of convergent state behaviour and international policy coordination, informed by causal beliefs

and policy preferences of the epistemic community. Similarly, epistemic communities may contribute to the creation and maintenance of social institutions that guide international behaviour. (Haas, 1992: 4)

But where new loyalties lie, or where the new 'home' is situated, depend on a number of factors, and some which do not immediately comply with the 'social episteme' of that new home. It must be remembered that a state will act within a transnational grouping according to its own intersubjective meanings. These meanings can shift over time and through the experience of cooperation and increasingly common norms, but in certain cases, conflict ensues over this transition. Recalling the example of Britain's relationship with the EC, it is clear that British norms derived from a particular understanding or interpretation of Britain as an 'island nation'/former colonial power/former major world actor, which resulted in a reluctant approach to European integration. Over time, this view has shifted, but remnants of the 'Britain versus Europe' debate (particularly with respect to symbolic issues such as the pound) are still a matter of debate within the British nation-state.

Correspondingly, new developments will alter socially constructed meanings and in turn alter interests. The end of the Cold War meant that the US and the former USSR had to radically reconstitute their identities and interests. At the same time there is a reciprocal process occurring. It is not only the interests and identities of nation-states that produce norms, but also other units outside the state. For instance, when talking about security communities, the process of 'learning norms' and internalising them likewise reproduces this process. In the membership negotiations to the EU, neutral Austria, Finland and Sweden had to 'learn' how to fit into the EU community. Similar values and institutions were not enough (see Chapter 6). These new members had to 'behave' as member states. Adler looks to Eastern European states after the Cold War wanting to join NATO, the EU or the WEU in order to become a part of a 'political community'.[16] Efforts to 'fit in' create a process of adopting and internalising certain norms, which in turn reconstitutes the identity and interests of nation-states or actors. Just as Eastern European states 'learn' how to be 'good' European states via democracy, the market economy and subscribing to many 'Western' values, so too do other states 'learn' the processes and norms that result in a shift in the identity of the nation-state. These triggers of change are largely exogenous, but become endogenised. Identity, interest and action are based on these exchanges and processes, and do not derive solely from the internal or external environment. What happens internally within the state determines how the state perceives itself and acts towards others. But how the state interacts with its external environment also conditions identities. If neutrality is examined from this premise, rather than the narrow view of a small state responding to the external environment, a broader interpretation of neutrality can be achieved.

Conclusion: constructing Swedish neutrality beyond the realist paradigm

By reassessing neutrality as a constitutive part of nation-state identity and interests, a different image of neutrality emerges that departs from the limited interpretation provided by mainstream international relations theory. There are indeed certain 'constants' or norms pertaining to neutrality that cannot be divorced from an alternative reading, but this does not deny certain 'truths' central to neutrality. Rather, is it an attempt to rethink neutrality through a constructivist agenda that opens up different avenues of consideration. The story of neutrality has largely been a neglected one. However, by locating neutrality closely to issues of state identity, a different interpretation may emerge. The crucial point, as will unfold in following chapters, is that regardless of what foreign policy stance a country adopts, it is adopted for reasons strongly linked to the internal make-up of that state. 'States cannot survive without a sense of identity, an image of what marks their government and their citizens from their neighbours, of what special contribution they have to make to civilization and international order. Foreign policy is partly a reflection of that search for identity.' (Wallace, 1991: 78)

In the following chapter, I adopt the constructivist approach to the origins of Swedish neutrality. Rather than focus on external determinants which led to the decision to become a neutral state, I concentrate on the domestic forces within Swedish political society, and issues of identity. By applying a constructivist view to the basis of Swedish neutrality, I explore its historical roots and its more ideational ambitions, and investigate how neutrality forms part of the 'collective meanings' that make up Sweden.

NOTES

1 On this, see Bjereld, 1995b; Cox and MacGinty, 1996; Dahl, 1997; Farrell, 1995; Gustenau, 1999; Laursen, 1997; McSweeney, 1998; Ojanen 2000a; Ojanen et al., 2000; von Altenbockum, 2002.
2 Whilst I argue that the conceptualisation of neutrality has been incomplete, there are a number of claims that can broadly be accepted. Realist assumptions about the neutral state have lent some important defining characteristics to neutrality. Neutrality *is* a state-centric foreign and security policy. Its main concern or end goal is to guard the sovereignty of the state. Therefore, I do not argue against the notion of *the state* or conceptions of *sovereignty*.
3 Bodin also claimed that it is advantageous to play off states against each other: 'And again, what better way is there of maintaining one's state in all its strength than to stand aside when one's neighbours ruin one another?' (Bodin [1576], 1992: 138)
4 Third image constructivism largely accepts the neo-realist notion of systemic theory. This is largely Wendt's domain, where he distinguishes between the state's corporate identity (its internal human material and ideological characteristics) and its social identity (the meaning actors give to themselves whilst taking on the perspective of others). For some, this does not go far enough in explaining changes in nation-state identity and social structures (Reus-Smit, 1996; Zehfuss, 2001; see also 'Forum on

Social Theory of International Politics' in *Review of International Studies*, 26 (1), 2000; Palan, 2000).

5   Touraine is more commonly recognised for his work on social movements, but his insights on institutions ('the mechanism through which cultural orientations are transformed into social practices'), *instituting* and social reproduction are useful for constructivists (Touraine, 1988: 40).

6   The LN's Provisional Constitution (September 1996) begins with a 'separation treaty' that would establish a Provisional Government of Padania (the regions that form part of the LN).

7   The Lombard League, which is part of the LN, campaigned on the federalist platform with the slogan 'Nearer to Brussels than to Rome' (Laffan, 1994) but has shifted from favouring a federal Europe and has taken a distinctively anti-European stance.

8   Even in terms of economic cooperation with the EC, the Swiss rejected the plan to participate in the European Economic Area in 1992, which would have given Switzerland access to the single internal market. The Swiss Germans were against the proposal, whereas the Swiss French supported it (*The European*, 17–20/12/92). In March 2000, 77 per cent of voters rejected a referendum calling for early negotiations to join the EU. Although pro-EU camps in Switzerland are not interpreting the results as a signal against EU membership, the Swiss Federal Committee for a Direct Democratic Neutral and Sovereign Switzerland (an umbrella group of about 20 anti-EU grass-roots groups) calls the vote significant in terms of Swiss reluctance to join (*EU Observer*, 26/04/01).

9   For instance, compared to Finnish and Swedish, or Hungarian and Romanian, there exist negligible distinctions in etymology, syntax and pronunciation between Croatian and Serbian, or Russian and Ukrainian. But Croatian and Ukrainian are markers of national identity. 'Nation-builders' remain uneasy about their closeness. This is seen in attempts to standardise written Croatian and Ukrainian, which implies privileging the variants of vocabulary and syntax whose distance from Serbian and Russian are greater (Neumann, 1999: 7; see also Levinger and Lytle, 2001).

10 Berger and Luckmann (1971) discuss mythology as a 'conceptual machinery' of the symbolic universe and Bell examines the category of myth in collective memory and national identity (2003), but largely myth is dealt with more extensively in sociological works.

11 Austrian neutrality was not referred to in the State Treaty of 1955, but was etched out in the Austrian constitution (Constitutional Law of 26 October 1955 on the Neutrality of Austria), which signified Austria's intention to enter into neutrality of its own free will (Austrian Federal Government, 2000: 199).

12 Nonetheless, the right-wing FPÖ have at times revived the idea that neutrality was an imposed or 'artificial' status placed upon Austria. This idea was supported by the right-wing *Verband der Unabhängigen*, the predecessor of the FPÖ (Missiroli, 1994: 6). The FPÖ has switched its views on Austrian neutrality in the past (once supporting it) but in more recent times has argued for its demise (Schultz, 1992: 175 and 178).

13 Rusi (1987) comments that the term, first coined by the academic Richard Löwenthal in the late 1950s, became part of international foreign policy vocabulary to mean Soviet dominance (see also Quester, 1990: 34). There appears to be some disagreement in the literature on the origins of the term, nonetheless. Lukas (1992: 60) claims that it was coined by German politician Franz-Josef Strauss. Maude, on the other hand, notes that the term grew out of Karl Gruber's references to 'finnische Politik' in his 1953 publication on Austria *Zwischen Befreiung und Freiheit* (1982: 4).

14 Post-war leaders, such as Presidents Mannerheim, Paasikivi and Kekkonen advocated a flexible line with Russia, in the belief that once the USSR had satisfied its strategic

interests with regard to Finland, the relationship would be more secure. In pursuit of this, the Paasikivi-Kekkonen line set the pattern for Finnish relations with its neighbour. It involved two courses of action. The first was to convince the USSR of Finland's 'goodwill', the second to build up its military power to guard against external aggression (Karsh, 1986a: 267).

15 The arguments over whether US neutrality was influenced by power politics rather than republicanism are explored in articles by Sofka (1997) and Bukovansky (1997).
16 Adler (1997b) discusses this in the sense of internalising norms and transforming identities and interests. However, as further chapters will explore, the central issue arises when new norms confront old established ones.

3

Neutrality as a Social Democratic project: tracing the origins of Swedish neutrality, 1814–1945

If NEUTRALITY IS 'what states make of it', then the conceptualisation of neutrality can go beyond mere isolationism and provide a more complex reading of the neutral state. By examining the normative basis of Swedish neutrality, a competing story emerges that is central to questions of identity and how modern Swedish neutrality would be practised. This chapter examines the origins, debates and ideas that have influenced the development of Swedish neutrality from 1814 to 1945. Through a constructivist perspective, this chapter explores how identity and neutrality have been deeply intertwined from the outset, and how Karl Johan's[1] neutrality fuelled an important battle of ideas that was to influence the development of Sweden, both politically and strategically.

Sweden went from being a hegemonic power to a defeated one, and neutrality was intended to signal a new path which aimed for peaceful relations, democratisation and state-building, which the SAP supported and made part of its political platform. This new vision of Sweden had to compete, nonetheless, with the idea of the 'warrior state' or attempts to regain glory. Neutrality came to reflect this period of nation-state formation, and consequently mirrored divisions within Swedish society as to what sort of nation-state Sweden *ought* to be.

The chapter then moves on to explore Swedish neutrality through both world wars, and experiments in international cooperation with the League of Nations. Neutrality endured and over the years became part of the progressive elements of Swedish politics, which took in the view of the 'good society', solidarity and the *folkhem*. This chapter aims to highlight what Stråth (2000a: 371) calls the 'historical continuity' of Swedish neutrality – that in order to understand neutrality's embeddedness in present-day Sweden, one must explore the meanings attributed to Swedish neutrality, which have endured since its inception. Showing how neutrality was cemented in deeper terms

Neutrality as a Social Democratic project

than the context of the anarchic international system prepares the ground for Chapter 4, which explores Sweden's post-war neutrality policy as it became more principled and overtly tied to the SAP's vision of extending solidarity to the external realm.

'Peace, neutrality, and non-intervention': interpreting Karl Johan's 'Rock'[2]

After separating from the Kalmar Union in 1521,[3] Sweden developed into a strong centralised state, built on the merger of interests between the nobility, the free peasantry and the royal house (Rokkan, 1981: 56). Sweden soon emerged as a hegemonic power on the European stage. Swedish expansionism reached its zenith during the sixteenth and seventeenth centuries, and resulted in wars with Russia, Poland, Germany and Denmark. Involvement in the Thirty Years War established Sweden as a Baltic power. Its decline came in 1709 at the Battle of Poltava and the subsequent losses of territories (Jervas, 1986: 7–9; Lundkvist, 1973). From this point onwards, Sweden's position altered from a hegemonic power to a struggling state. Although Sweden was part of the early Leagues of Armed Neutrality, neutrality was invoked to protect trade, not as a principled policy. With Sweden's political and military power reduced, Karl Johan in 1814 issued a state maxim and Swedish neutrality formally came into existence.[4] In 1818, he proclaimed to the Swedish Diet:

> Separated as we are from the rest of Europe, our policy and our interests will always lead us to refrain from involving ourselves in any dispute which does not concern the two Scandinavian peoples [Sweden and Norway]. At the same time, in obedience to the dictates both of our national duty and of our national honour, we shall not permit any other power to intervene in our internal affairs. (Cited in Barton, 1930: 326)

The common explanation for Sweden's choice of neutrality was that it was a *realpolitik* decision, or the calculated choice of a small state with few options. Divorced from power politics and military entanglements, Sweden opted to preserve its independence through neutrality rather than look to an alliance. In his 1834 memo, the King announced that Sweden was an 'insular power' and 'would abandon all illusions which might endanger the calm she enjoyed of her existence as a state'. (Cited in Swartz, 1996) Neutrality was part of a pragmatic 'strategic calculus' – the assumption that the Nordic area was outside the conflicts and interests of the great powers (Huldt, 1995: 139).

A closer reading reveals some implicitly normative features which informed the King's 'system of neutrality'. The emphasis on 'insularity' is somewhat misleading in light of the broader aims of Swedish neutrality at this point in its history. The *realpolitik* reading of Swedish neutrality interprets insularity to mean isolationism; however, the reference to insularity has more to do with state-building (and, as Malmborg points out, a desire to rid Sweden of 'foreign corruption' (Malmborg, 2001: 73)). The loss of empire and the lack of resources forced Sweden to turn inward, concentrating on the internal development of the state, rather than entertain expansionist ambitions.

Karl Johan also held the expectation that neutrality would be an enduring feature of the Swedish state (Huldt, 1995: 139). This in itself was an unusual declaration to make at the time. Neutrality was always considered a wartime policy and to speak of it as a peacetime policy was 'not the practice of the time'. (Wahlbäck, 1986: 11) Sweden did not codify its neutrality, nor was it bound by international treaty. A number of motions were presented to the parliament between 1890 and 1910, to issue a formal declaration of permanent neutrality. These were rejected in favour of maintaining a flexible form of neutrality that would be open to interpretation by the regime (Sztucki, 1991). As few rules existed for neutral states during the early nineteenth century, the parliament recognised that neutrality would technically be worthless unless respected by the great powers.

Neutrality signified a different approach to the external realm. It was an enlightened ideal stemming from the evaluation of 'the costly and in the end futile attempts during earlier centuries to play power politics through wars and alliances'. (Sundelius 1987: 5) Neutrality was intended to symbolise a *new* Sweden, with a desire to mitigate regional tensions and repair damaged inter-state relations. For instance, Karl Johan accepted the loss of Finland, provoking deep division. (The Swedish cabinet had chosen Karl Johan for the throne in the hope that he could lead Sweden into a war with Russia, with the support of Napoleon, and thereby regain Finland). The idea of Sweden as a *nation* became entangled in the debate over Finland. Esaias Tegnér's poem *Svea* (which was awarded the first prize by the Swedish Academy in 1811) captured this idea of reclaiming Finland 'within the frontiers of Sweden'. (Kurunmäki, 2000: 9–10 and 16) Sweden's possession of Norway also caused controversy as Karl Johan treated Norway as an equal partner, not as a security buffer to consolidate Sweden's position against Russian expansionist threats. Norwegians were permitted their own constitution, parliament and government. The peace and prosperity of Sweden and the Nordic region was tied to Sweden's neutrality posture. The first signs of Sweden's active internationalist neutrality can be detected in Karl Johan's mediation efforts between England and Russia after the Napoleonic Wars.[5] The intentions of neutrality were more complex than the *realpolitik* explanation offered. It signified a shift from an expansionist state to 'good neighbour' state.

The intention of Karl Johan's neutrality was 'to be ourselves when we determine our policy, to be ourselves when we assert our independence and to speak our minds clearly'. (Cited in Wahlbäck, 1986: 8–9) However, the problem was that the Swedish 'self' was highly contested. Neutrality signified a new path for Sweden, but it also triggered an intense domestic debate about Swedish identity. Although Sweden was no longer a dominant power in Europe, various groups in society wished to see Sweden return to a level of strength and greatness. Malmborg notes that despite foreign policy being the preserve of royalty even in the nineteenth century, Karl Johan was surrounded by liberal Scandinavianist opinion which had emerged in the 1830s (Malmborg, 2001: 93). In the Scandinavian Movement (1840–1870) and the Gothic Society, there was a promotion of hopes for a Nordic Union under a Swedish dynasty. The Gothic Society (*Götiska Förbundet*) was also part of the Romanticist movement of the time and important in articulating a particular image of nation-building in Sweden. The Gothic Society promoted the idea of an organicist link between the *folk* and the nation. The idealisation of the peasant became part of popular myth. Erik Gustaf Geijer, a leading member of the Gothic Society, believed that the *folk* constituted the past and the present; memories, customs, and traditions are passed between the *folk*, which unite the *folk* as a unit (the nation) (Kurunmäki, 2000, pp. 9–10 and 16). Supported by academics and the upper-middle classes, the movement drew upon the links between the Scandinavian countries' shared language, culture, social and economic conditions. Some of the more radical Scandinavianists wanted a common constitution and parliament for the region (Wendt, 1981: 19). Pan-Scandinavianism was influenced by the push for national unification in Italy and Germany at this time and signified a united front to emerging external phenomena, such as pan-Germanism (Laursen and Olesen, 2000: 61). Successive rulers entertained hopes of returning Sweden to a position of greatness and subsequently neutrality was not practised uniformly. In solidarity with Denmark during its war with Prussia over Schleswig and Holstein in 1848, Sweden was technically 'non-belligerent'.[6]

Efforts to create good relations with Russia provoked even deeper divisions. Russia was the long-standing enemy of Sweden, and still smarting over the loss of Finland to Russia, many Swedes attacked the idea of a friendly posture towards this enemy. Liberal elements in Swedish society wanted to encourage ties with Britain[7] and France, rather than the reactionary regimes of Russia, Prussia and Austria. Hence, Karl Johan's desire to establish good relations with Russia conflicted with the past understandings of Russia, and pan-Scandinavianism is linked to past glories and ideas of an organic link with its Nordic neighbours. This was a period of what Wendt calls 'self-reflection', and Sweden went through a process of 'changing the game'. (1992: 419) In the formative decades of Swedish neutrality, Sweden was struggling between past conceptualisations of self (as the 'warrior' state or dominant power) and the new direction that its neutrality policy *intended to take it* (harmonious relations with other states, including former enemies). Ruth argues that the

Swedish national consciousness was tied to an 'heroic' rather than a 'peace-loving' image of self: 'the mythology of the "great-power" era long outlasted its political foundation'. (1984: 70) The oscillation between Scandinavianism and strict neutrality by Karl Johan's successors is related to the conflicts between different internal political sentiments and self-perception rather than indecisiveness as such over Sweden's neutrality policy. Against such a background, neutrality would come to take on a different significance with the rise of democratisation in Sweden.

Neutrality, democratisation and the rise of political parties

Internal power struggles defined Sweden for much of the twelfth to eighteenth centuries, and the development of democracy was not entirely smooth. Although the *Riksdag* was established in 1435, for centuries a provincial form of democracy existed, and there was intense division between the four estates (nobles, peasants, burghers and clergy), resulting in power struggles up until the end of the eighteenth century. In 1809, a new constitution ended absolutism[8] in Sweden, granting executive power to the king, financial control to the parliament and legislative power to be shared by both (Andrén, 1981: 50). It was intended to balance power between the estates and the monarchy,[9] and encourage greater public interest in political matters and radical debate about the idea of the nation, inspired by the French Revolution. The restoration of the freedom of the press led to the creation of the newspaper *Aftonbladet* in 1830, which was critical of the government (Hallendorff and Schück, 1929: 371). Literary circles also contested certain images of Sweden as the warrior state. Generally, it can be said that Geijer and Tegnér, writing at the start of the 1800s, glorified Karl VII as Sweden's 'war hero' whereas Strindberg (writing later that century) adopted a critical view of Karl VII's reign. Strindberg was also critical of Geijer's dominating idea of Swedish history, being that of 'the history of her kings'. Strindberg was considered anti-establishment by writing about the Swedish people (see Bergström, 1990; Moerk, 1998). The influence of the Enlightenment and liberalism grew in the mid-late nineteenth century, and there was widespread dissatisfaction with the power of the monarchy and ruling elites.

In the 1840s, popular movements (*folkrörelserna*) began to form. These were made up of religious and temperance movements, consumer cooperatives and workers' movements. Religious reforms of the 1860s were compounded by the rising temperance movements (numbering around 470 at the time) (Svanström and Palmstierna, 1934: 402), which were a reaction against societal change within local communities (Rokkan, 1981: 66–8). Sweden was a 'poverty-stricken nation' (Stromberg, 1986: 99) and such conditions led to mass emigration between 1850 and 1930, mainly to America.[10]

The rise of Pietism inspired a different political culture to develop, compared to continental Europe. Scandinavian Lutheranism was cemented during the seventeenth to nineteenth centuries, influenced by the Danish poet and theologian N. F. S. Grundtvig, who advocated a 'folk-church movement' with the aim of educating the peasantry. In 1842, legislation was enacted to provide mandatory primary education (*folkskola*), and the peasantry accessed education through the church (de Vylder, 1996). With the decline of the nobility, the peasantry developed into a strong social and political force, bolstered by the mythologised image attached to it during the Romanticist period. Estate representation for the peasantry (usually the land-owning peasantry) was particular to Swedish political culture. According to Stråth, the peasantry were an important social group, which brought a pragmatic and consensual perspective to Swedish politics, believing in compromise to create the 'good society' (2000a: 364).

This consensualism stems from individuals cooperating against a harsh climate in order to survive and this approach infiltrated its way into the working practices of corporate enterprises. Close but isolated village communities of pre-industrial rural Sweden formed agricultural cooperatives and in the industrialising cities, the labour movement formed similar organisations (Logue, 1999: 166). The idea that the corporation helps sustain the society dates back to the *bruk* (the small town that revolves around a factory in the countryside), which would tend to society's spiritual and educational needs. In these 'factory villages' or working communities, the *bruk* played a central role in social and work life and was well established before industrialism occurred (Enzensberger, 1989: 24; Ruth, 1984: 78–9). According to Ruth, the *bruk* plays a key (but often neglected) part in what eventually came to encompass themes of the *folkhem*.[11]

The *folkrörelserna* 'provided a cultural framework and historical heritage for politics'. (Stråth, 2000a: 364) The popular movements became channels for 'social communication'; establishing both an emerging political culture and a specific set of enduring values, which would permeate Swedish political culture during the following century. The ideal of the 'good society' (or the 'humane society') (Åsard and Bennett, 1997: 90) encompassed themes such as egalitarianism and equality. Sweden's egalitarianism stems from the practices and living conditions of its yeoman farmers. *Jämlikhet* ('equality'), a Social Democratic term, according to Mouritzen (1995: 11) was 'the egalitarian passion that has been almost as important as moral force'. (Ruth, 1984: 56) The effort to promote political and economic rights resulted in a rejection of the 'natural' inequalities that wealth and the economy produced. Compromise envelops both the political and social elements, seen in corporatist and interest mediation, and social engineering through public policy-making (Lane, 1991a: 1). Stromberg claims that the modern Swedish welfare state and the *folkrörelserna* came from the same historical context, that of 'solidarity in the face of a professed ideological liberalism'. (1986: 99) This form of universalism, which would later become a firm tenet of the SAP, began at an early stage. Around these central concepts of solidarity and equality, an emerging political and social culture began to form, which would provide the foundation for the key elements of what would later become the Swedish Model.

In 1865, the *Riksdag* became bicameral and the four estates system was abandoned. Stemming from the four estates system and propelled by industrialisation[12] and urbanisation in the 1880s, party groups began to form in the *Riksdag*. The Rural Party (*Lantmannapartiet*) in the Second Chamber was the first political party formed, dominating the *Riksdag* until the 1880s. From the time the *Riksdag* was reformed, the liberals and the conservatives became the key political groupings. The Liberal Party,[13] which formed in 1895, gained the support of the middle and lower classes with their radical views on voting rights and parliamentary democracy. Commonly associated with the temperance movement (which had the support of the working class and the middle class), the Liberals were also opposed to the build up of Swedish defence and preferred a neutral stance. The Liberals and the Social Democrats were unanimous in their support for neutrality as a method to curb the power of the King, who under the 1809 constitution, was able to declare war (Norman, 1993: 304). Parliamentary democracy was opposed by the Conservative group (later to become the Moderate Party), which formed the General Electoral Association (*Allmänna valmansförbundet*) in 1904. This group was representative of the old aristocracy. What was to become the most important political grouping, the *Socialdemokratiska Arbetarepartiet* (SAP) emerged in the late 1880s. The SAP, however, would not find electoral success until the 1930s.

The SAP: origins and ideology

In 1881, influenced by debates in Germany and Denmark, August Palm introduced Sweden to Social Democratic thought. In 1882, he established the Swedish Social Democratic Workers' Association, and its journal *Folkviljan* ('The Peoples' Will'), which published the first Social Democratic programme. His speech at the Hotel Stockholm in Mälmo set out how socialism would end capitalism's exploitation of workers and contended that workers needed to identify with Social Democracy, build organisations, circulate their own newspapers and push for universal suffrage. Within less than a decade, in 1889, the SAP conducted its first congress. However, the question of how to achieve socialism – by evolutionary or revolutionary means – revealed internal divisions amongst Social Democrats. It was the former which gained ground and came to characterise the stance of Swedish Social Democracy. Amongst the Marxists, humanists, Christian socialists, anarchists, pacifists and prohibitionists that made up the 1889 congress, ten separate programmes were offered. Of these, two main groups predominated. One offered a 'Stockholm' version of the German Social Democratic Gotha Programme (a reformist Social Democratic programme advocating parliamentary reform and rejecting revolutionism) with some local reforms. The second, from the Mälmo delegation, espoused a Marxist revolutionary approach. To compromise, the new party opted for a broad statement of principles, supporting universal suffrage to revolution[14] (if need be). The SAP did not adopt a revolutionist stance. Rather, it aimed to incorporate the interests of society with a vision of socialism which was to be achieved gradually.

In his 1886 Gävle speech ('Why the Worker's Movement Must Become Socialistic'), the SAP's first leader Hjalmar Branting suggested that the working class movement would become socialist through a process of historical development. Capitalism, with its free competition and large-scale production, lowered wages and drove small producers out of business, replacing the guild system with an impersonal one. Branting argued that the goal was to make capital the common property of society; socialism meant recognising the processes of social change and reordering social institutions. In this speech he called on workers to organise into unions and a political party (Tilton, 1991: 15–19). Swedish society was underdeveloped at the time, but rather than seek revolution to enforce change, a more piecemeal approach was adopted, focusing on factory legislation and universal suffrage, sufficiently satisfying the Mälmo delegation.

The SAP tied itself to the rising industrial working class and the emerging trade union movement. In 1898, trade unions formed a central organisation, the Swedish Trade Union Confederation, or LO (*Landsorganisationen Sverige*). The importance of the partnership between the SAP and the LO cannot be overstated. Through this partnership, much of the implementation of the SAP's vision of socialism came to fruition, and the LO was closely involved in SAP policy-making. The LO was more than an interest group, and Heclo and Madsen (1987: 19) go as far as to claim that they were important social actors deeply engaged in the political process. What Olsen labels as Sweden's 'Liberal period' (1820–1932) saw the rise of business associations, which added to the growing strength in employer solidarity. Key associations included the association of engineering industries, *Verkstadsföreningen* (VF) in 1896; the central employers' confederation, *Sveriges Arbetsgivareföreningen* (SAF[15]), in 1902, representing large companies and small business; and the association of industries, *Sveriges Industriförbundet* (SI) in 1910. At this time, the SAF was well organised compared to the LO. The conflict over union rights that culminated in the December Compromise (1906) between the Metal Workers'

Union and the Swedish Engineering Employers' Association ended up favouring capital (Olsen, 1992: 52–3). However, it also set an important precedent for centralised collective bargaining, which was to be a feature of labour-capital relations in the future. It negotiated the pattern of relations between unions and employees, whereby the LO accepted the employers' right to 'hire and fire' in exchange for employers recognising right of association for workers (Delsen and Van Veem, 1992: 85; Lewin, 1988: 19).

This period also marked a change in external relations, and the new political groupings had an impact on events. The issue of Sweden's union with Norway, for example, proved a dividing line between the Conservatives, and the Liberals and Social Democrats, or what Logue (1989: 46) referred to as the chasm between 'military nationalism' and 'the cultural nationalism of the democratic movement'. The Conservatives rejected Norwegian calls for independence and supported a strong defence system for Sweden. The mediating influence of the Conservatives' first leader Arvid Lindman, proved successful in mitigating the factions within the party who also wanted to halt moves towards parliamentary democracy (Hadenius, 1997: 16–19). When Norway in 1905 dissolved its union with Sweden, Germany offered Sweden aid against a possible Norwegian rebellion. Yet strong pressure from the Social Democrats (who threatened strike action) forced the Swedish government to allow Norwegian independence (Logue, 1989: 43). Sweden could have easily dominated Norway in its quest for independence, yet refrained from doing so. Ruth (1984: 70) claims that at this stage, the nostalgic view of Sweden as a great power ended, and Sweden 'politically and morally matured'. Sweden's neutral stance contributed to its response to the loss of Norway. Neutrality had come to mean more than simply staying out of conflict. The concern for good relations with Norway is connected to the original intention of neutrality set out by Karl Johan. Swedish neutrality, however, was about to be tested in the wider context of the First World War.

From neutrality to international community: Swedish neutrality during the First World War and the League of Nations

With the outbreak of the First World War, Sweden's conservative government declared neutrality, as a result of which a 'truce' over neutrality ensued between the political parties.[16] The Conservatives preferred neutrality for trade reasons, whereas the Liberals and the Social Democrats had always supported a neutral policy for Sweden. Yet, at this time, there was little attachment to the notion of neutrality as an 'ideal in itself'. (Stern, 1991: 81) Sweden used its neutrality to remain out of conflict and there was little opportunity to practise internationalism.

Neutrality during this time was about protecting sovereignty and trade,

Neutrality as a Social Democratic project

especially shipping. Britain intended to use its powerful maritime position to halt Germany's supplies by closing the North Sea. In 1912, Churchill and Lloyd George proposed a blockade against Germany to be applied to neutral ports (Antwerp and Rotterdam), 'whatever the political costs', and the rationing of exports from Holland and Belgium so as to leave little surplus stock to export to Germany (Salmon, 1993: 123–7). Sweden was also targeted as a potential supplier to Germany and much of the Swedish economy was, in some senses, controlled by British interests. British and US pressure over exports to Germany almost brought Scandinavia to the brink of starvation (Ogley, 1970: 86). Britain blacklisted Swedish firms that did not follow their instructions regarding exports (Wahlbäck, 1986: 24–5) and the Transito affair[17] revealed the depth of concern that Britain held over Sweden due to the latter's reliance on German imports. Sweden appealed to the US against this and other violations of neutral rights, but Wilson, in 1914, accepted the British blockade and did not defend the Paris Treaty which granted neutral rights (Malmborg, 2001: 112–13).

Despite Sweden twice proclaiming its neutrality (first, on 3rd August 1914, and then again five days later with Norway), Russia suspected that the declaration of neutrality was merely a cover in order to link up with Germany. Russia, at this point in time, had good reason to think such. Pro-German sentiment was powerful amongst the Swedish nobility and King Gustav V (1907–1950). (On this subject, see Malmborg, 2001, particularly Chapter 3.) Russia believed that Sweden would cooperate with Germany in order to reclaim Finland (Logue, 1989: 45). There was also deep historic suspicion of Russia and many Swedish ministers held the view that Russia's defeat was in Sweden's interests. As a result, despite the declarations of neutrality, the Swedish Foreign Minister privately informed Germany that Sweden would be a 'benevolent' neutral whilst assuring Germany's enemies that it would practise 'strict' neutrality.

Prior to the outbreak of WWI, Sweden played a passive role on the international stage. Despite its association with the Palme years, the term 'active neutrality' was actually coined in the 1920s. Branting regarded an active neutrality policy as a core component of a peace doctrine. After WWI, Sweden moved more towards democracy, international arbitration, disarmament and internationalism (Hopper, 1945; Stern, 1991: 82–3). The SAP cooperated with the Liberal Party over universal suffrage, which was achieved in 1918. However, the SAP did not find electoral success. Voters were not attracted to the radical debates within the SAP over the issue of nationalisation. By the 1920s, the issue was dropped and the SAP pursued a path of economic planning as the route to socialism[18] (Olsen, 1992: 95–6). The SAP made up three brief minority governments in the 1920s (1920, 1921–3 and 1924–6).

Escaping WWI relatively unscathed, Sweden cooperated with plans for international peace. The first Liberal–Social Democratic coalition government nominated Sweden's membership in the League of Nations, and Branting was a key figure in facilitating Sweden's entry in 1920. Membership of the League provided an opportunity to practise internationalism guided by the rule of law. Sweden accepted the ruling of the League of Nations regarding the Åland Islands, returning them to Finland.[19] Sweden also gave up its seat on the permanent council in order to facilitate Germany's inclusion into the League (Archer, 1996: 454; Sundelius, 1990: 117). 'These early decisions to give primacy to enduring systemic values over more narrowly defined and immediate national interests set precedents for the future Swedish orientation in other multilateral forums, such as the United Nations.' (Mörth and Sundelius, 1995: 103)

Branting was prepared to abandon Sweden's neutrality, which he regarded as largely determined or guided by the belligerents. During its membership of the League, Sweden did not refer to itself as 'neutral' (Wahlbäck, 1986: 30–1). With the League of Nations, 'new conditions' arose which would give Sweden the chance to play a role in preserving peace. In Branting's view, neutrality allowed 'the world to go its own way outside us' and the League offered a chance for Sweden to contribute to an international order (cited in Norman, 1993: 303).[20] The League was seen as a forum for active neutrality and internationalism, and Sweden's pro-League voices also expected the United States to join, being the largest neutral at the time. The League of Nations was seen as compatible with the Social Democratic ideal of promoting disarmament (Sweden began a process of unilateral disarmament in 1925) and international cooperation, and these 'were the cornerstones of the proper working class foreign policy'. (Logue, cited in Stern, 1991: 83–4) Branting and Östen Undén (Foreign Minister, 1924–26) tried to include 'new principles of international morality' in the Covenant. Sweden had faith in the prospect of an international order guided by the rule of law. Stern writes that the domestic political scene in Sweden in the inter-war period became mirrored on the international front. As domestic politics peacefully graduated from elitist rule to a stable, consensual system based on mass parties and organised interests (Mörth and Sundelius, 1995: 102–3; Norman, 1993: 303; Stern, 1991: 83–4), this approach also guided Sweden's efforts externally. Sweden was interested in international reform and exporting its values and norms onto the international level, 'to change the world to fit Swedish ideals'. (Sundelius, 1990: 117)

However, other elements in Swedish politics were decidedly against membership of the League of Nations. The Conservatives had a strong pro-German sentiment and did not support the League as guarantor of the peace. They preferred neutrality with a strong army (Stråth, 2000a: 361). Left-wing socialists (later the Communists) saw the League of Nations as a capitalist plot, and the agrarians were also opposed. Opposition came from both extremes of the political spectrum and the general approach was to regard the League as a continuation of the *status quo* established under the Versailles Treaty of 1919. But the government stressed that it would be possible to reform the framework of the League (Norman, 1993: 303). Participation in the League of Nations exacerbated the divide between the realist and the moralist view of Swedish neutrality. The shift in Swedish foreign policy from that of an expansionist military state to a neutral one was part of a 'learning process'. The moralist view regarded Swedish neutrality as part of 'the forces of progress' and placed Sweden as 'the harbinger of a new international order'. (Ruth, 1984: 70)

Italy's invasion of Ethiopia in 1935 pushed Sweden towards withdrawal (discussed in Chapter 1). The League was beginning to be recognised as an organisation with different rules for different situations, favouring the interests of the great powers. Collective security was failing and the League did not address other security concerns, such as the Spanish Civil War, and the *Anschluß* (Ogley, 1970: 122; Tingsten, 1959: 477). It also seemed that the concerns aired by the Swedish government in 1923 actually became quite prophetic:

> the obligation arising out of a joint guarantee would increase the danger of her being drawn into war to an extent entirely out of proportion to the increased risk incurred, from the same cause, by certain other countries. There is, no doubt, hope that the day will come when all States will agree to regard any disturber of the peace as a common enemy, against whom they will be prepared to take up arms immediately. But ... we have not yet reached that stage, and there is no reason to suppose that we shall reach it in the near future. In the present disturbed conditions of the world, no Swedish Government could ask the representatives of the nation to undertake international obligations possibly involving Sweden in warlike operations, which might appear to the nation to be in no way connected with the vital interests and independence of the country. (League of Nations Documents 1923 and Records [1930], 1994: 276)

Sweden withdrew from the collective security obligations of the League in 1936. This did not encounter much opposition from the major parties of the time (Conservative, Agrarian, Peoples' Party, who pushed for Swedish rearmament). Expansion of military personnel and the *Riksdag* passing into law of the conscripted Home Guard Units in 1940 indicated a desire to rely on its own defence rather than enter into military alliances. The Home Guard Units were small defensive units which were called up during war to protect towns and public factories in Sweden. Together with the '*Lotta*' (the corps that assisted the Home Guard with tasks such as administration and house-keeping), a sense of community emerged around the Home Guard (Swartz, 1996), strengthening the notion that security should be dealt with within the confines of the state.

External pressures also came to bear. Regional tension arose, with the threat from Germany controlling the Baltic Sea traffic through the Gulf of Bothnia (due to the Anglo-German Naval Agreement, 1935, where England agreed to withdraw from Baltic Sea). It was through the Gulf of Bothnia and the Swedish port Luleå that approximately 50 per cent of Germany's iron ore imports were derived. Hence, Britain's withdrawal from the Baltic Sea facilitated Hitler's stronghold in this region. The Anglo-German Naval Agreement permitted Germany to increased its navy to one third of the size of the British navy. Sweden began to reconsider its policy, particularly in light of Hitler's announcement that 'We are the masters of the Baltic', which caused grave concern. A poll conducted in April 1936 by the newspaper *Nya Daglit Allehanda* revealed that 94–95 per cent of Swedes wanted to withdraw from the League and fortify its own military defences to protect itself (Swartz, 1996).

Thus there was a clear shift away from inter-war idealism and plans for international solidarity and cooperation. A mistrust of alliances, especially with the failings of the League, bolstered public support for armed neutrality. Sweden turned to strict neutrality and concentrated upon building up a strong defence which would be necessary to deter belligerent forces and ensure sovereignty and independence. For those who supported Swedish membership of the League, the return to neutrality was seen as a backward step. According to Andrén (1991: 81), worldwide international solidarity within the framework of organisations such as the League of Nations meant more than neutrality. Sweden's participation in the League, as Eric Bellquist wrote in 1921, revealed a more 'peaceful' example of a nation suppressing national self-interest in favour of international cooperation (Steene, 1989: 168–9). Undén, keen on international cooperation, wrote in his personal papers in August 1935: 'Neutrality may be for a long time the only viable policy after the failure of international solidarity. This fact may be accepted with resignation. But the apostles of neutrality will never be numbered among the liberators of mankind.' (Cited in Norman, 1993: 305) Sweden participated in the League of Nations primarily on the basis of adherence to international law. The sovereignty of nation-states was important, but the anarchic international system required order and justice, and this was largely the Scandinavian approach to international cooperation. The League was to function in a technocratic manner, based on international law, which was to establish particular norms about relations between states and the mediation of conflict. The failure of the League and its internationalist ambitions forced Sweden to abandon its more idealistic approach to the international realm. The League was revealed to be a neat arrangement for the victorious powers to maintain the *status quo* and there was little in the way of equality between members. Sweden's faith in international cooperation was seen as falsely naive.

At this point in time, the literature on Swedish neutrality after Sweden's

Neutrality as a Social Democratic project

departure from the League of Nations takes on a largely realist tone. The retreat away from international cooperation in favour of neutrality was read as isolationism, and combined with Sweden's military build up, appeared to confirm that Sweden as a small state was responding to the anarchic international system. The decision to reinforce Swedish neutrality with a strong defence deterrent injected a degree of pragmatism into foreign policy. As Per Albin Hansson (leader of the SAP and later Prime Minister between 1925 and 1946), explained: 'The strengthening of our defence preparations serves merely to underline our fixed determination to keep our country outside the conflicts among others and, during such conflicts, to safeguard the existence of our people.' (Swartz, 1996) Domestically, Hansson was pushing the idea of the *folkhem* and there was a strong sense that Sweden was turning inward and concentrating on achieving consensus within society.

Sweden returned to neutrality, but the 1930s signified a new period in Swedish domestic politics. When the rise of fascism coincided with a decline in Social Democracy in most parts of Europe in the 1930s, the economic programme offered by the SAP gained ground due to a more pragmatic approach, mixing a modified version of Keynesian economics with the socialist ideal. This formula brought the Swedish SAP to power in 1932 and began the establishment of the hegemonic position of Social Democracy (Padgett and Paterson, 1991: 9; see Chapter 4). The SAP also had the support of the Agrarians, with the 1933 crisis agreement (a compromise package on agricultural tariffs), which began a period of a so-called 'Red-Green Coalition' (Eddie, 1994: 204; Lewin, 1988: 143). The SAP's economic policy was seen as the 'middle way' (the term coined by Marquis Childs in 1936) between capitalism and communism, or trying to marry socialist ideals with the institutions of the liberal capitalist society. According to Childs, the combination of cooperatives, trade unions, and state competence over private monopoly was the formula for Sweden's success.[21] Heclo and Madsen (1987: 3) remark that Swedish politics and policy during this period were characterised by 'enlightened argument, human government programs and moderate compromise – the middle way between authoritarianism of the left and the right'.

Social Democracy encompassed a concern for the welfare of 'the worst off in society' by managing the market economy, lowering unemployment and looking towards economic growth in order to finance welfare and a decent standard of living. 'The state, the consumer, and the producer have intervened to make capitalism "work" in a reasonable way for the greatest good of the whole nation.' (Childs, 1936: 161) As Meidner (1992: 165) contends: 'In Sweden mass unemployment is considered a social evil and a waste of human and economic resources.' Hampden-Turner and Trompenaars note that Sweden's success in bridging capitalism and social values reveals that capitalism need not be a 'ruthless struggle among self-interested adversaries'. The Swedish approach to the market and modes of production embrace 'externalities' that include the environment, humanitarianism and concepts of social rights (1994: 237–8).

Sweden's 'middle way' drew much interest, particularly in the USA. As Logue explains, Childs' 1936 publication impacted upon the US 'with the force of an intellectual hurricane'. Hit heavily by the Great Depression, and increasing strikes and pickets, 'the image of a small, civilized northern country that seemed to have developed a humane and effective response to economic collapse caught the fancy of the nation'. (Logue, 1999: 162) For Americans, the Swedish experience facilitated acceptance of President F. D. Roosevelt's New Deal and allayed fears of state intervention and loss of economic freedom. Visits to the Swedish Cooperative Union by Americans 'in search of the secret of the middle way' genuinely took Swedes by surprise. Gunnar Myrdal, the SAP economist, had to stress to Sweden's American counterparts that the image of utopia was non-existent – Swedes were poor by American standards. In the post-war era, various books portrayed Sweden and Scandinavia as the apex of modernity. The idea of Sweden's social progressivism was largely seen by the outside world as a distinctive trait, something particular to Sweden and the Scandinavian region. This image persisted for a number of decades, and was seen by many as the model to emulate or export. In 1949 Walter Galenson observed that Scandinavia was 'a social laboratory for the Western world'. (Cited in Einhorn and Logue, 1989: 6) Likewise, in 1965, Danish writer Henrik Stangerup wrote: 'Scandinavia of today is the world's avant-garde society. What is taking place among us will happen in other countries tomorrow ... [which] will be of profit [to] the entire world around us.' In Europe, German and Austrian leftists shored up the idea, as Brandt, Wehner, Kreisky and others anticipated the spread of the Swedish Model (Ruth, 1984: 63–6).

Padgett and Paterson (1991: 1) define Social Democracy as a combination of socialism and liberalism: 'It is the product of a division in the socialist tradition between those who seek to realise socialist ideals within the institutions of liberal capitalist society (social democrats) and those who remain outside those institutions with the objective of superseding them through revolutionary force (communists).' However, Padgett and Paterson's description of Social Democracy departs drastically from the Swedish version. Whereas Social Democracy is generally described as a way to circumvent the excesses of capitalism by working within the system, rather than seeking extreme revolutionary methods to bring about change, the Swedish version takes a different approach. Rather than seeking strength in its difference to other ideological models, Swedish Social Democracy sought to incorporate the views of society into its vision of governance. According to Heclo and Madsen (1987:

27), 'Social Democrats have captured the idea of the nation – they have successfully interpreted the national identity as one of an ever-reforming welfare state, a national social community always striving to make itself more of a community.' The Swedish Social Democrats were adept at carving out their own interpretation of socialism and social values. This often translated into concrete legislative goals: the introduction of the law on industrial safety (1912); the first old age pensions (1913); universal suffrage (1918); and the eight-hour working day (1919). The tradition of consensus established in the *Riksdag* in the late nineteenth century became an important part of the way in which the SAP achieved many of its goals. The SAP used that consensus in terms of its own policies, encasing them in a rhetoric which applied to the whole of Swedish society. The SAP adopted neutrality as part of its own platform. It continued the economic, social and political reforms that were a strong feature during the reigns of Oscar I, Charles XV, and Oscar II. In fact, reformism became a key part of the SAP dialogue – it was not enough to introduce legislation and policies to further socialise Swedish society – these initiatives had to be revised continually. Furthermore, the SAP borrowed metaphors, such as the *folkhem*, and made them a key part of its political programmes and platforms.

Social Democratic institutions have been so embedded within the nation-state and approaches to the market that it would be negligent to ignore their impact on society and the individual. Much of the Social Democratic ideology has embedded itself within the belief systems of the major parties that constitute Swedish politics. Per Albin Hansson's government left a vital mark on Swedish politics. The idea of the *folkhem* captured not only what the Social Democrats set out to achieve, but the imagery and imagination of the entire nation. Since Sweden was ethnically homogenous, the notion of the People's Home hit a positive note for Swedes, and captured the preference for consensual politics over adversarial political relations. The *folkhem* was 'the vision of a government as a home that protects the nation's people as much as a family's home protects each of its members'. (Åsard and Bennett, 1997: 86) In his 1928 *Riksdag* debate, Per Albin Hansson described the metaphor as such:

> The basis of the home is togetherness and common feeling. The good home does not consider anyone as privileged or unappreciated; it knows no special favourites and no stepchildren. There no one looks down upon anyone else, there no one tries to gain advantage at another's expense, and the stronger do not suppress and plunder the weaker. In the good home equality, consideration, cooperation, and helpfulness prevail. Applied to the great people's and citizen's home this would mean the breaking down of all the social and economic barriers that now divide citizens into the privileged and the unfortunate, the rulers and subjects, into rich and poor, the glutted and the destitute, the plunderers and the plundered. (Cited in Tilton, 1991: 126–7)

Although this rhetoric has long been regarded as deriving from Social Democratic origins, its history reveals that it was initially a phrase used by non-Social Democrats. Alfred Petersson, a conservative who later switched to the Liberal Party, first coined the term in the early twentieth century. At the time he used the phrase, it loosely referred to 'the good society' and working together for the collective good. But it was an underdeveloped sentiment that was later improved upon by Rudolf Kjellén, a political scientist and conservative member of parliament.[22] Kjellén used the term in a different sense, in a plea for national unity after Sweden's break with Norway in 1905 (Åsard and Bennett, 1997). Kjellén held an 'organicist' concept of the state, viewing it as an individual or living organism, with constituent parts. He is noted for his use of metaphor in his writings, but metaphors for Kjellén were a way to explain radical change. His plea for national unity after the loss of Norway is premised on the notion that the loss of a 'part' of the 'living organism' does not denote weakness. He was inspired by Tegnér's poem *Svea* with reference to the loss of Finland ('torn like a pound of bloody flesh from the heart of the state') but claimed that Sweden's loss was compensated for by internal development.

Under Hansson, this metaphor became a powerful political tool. According to Lawler, Hansson 'took what was originally a vague, organicist conception of society, which emphasised national cohesion above all, and wedded it to a radical programme of social reform such that the metaphor was to become central to the preservation of social democratic hegemony throughout the region'. (1997: 568, see also Åsard and Bennett, 1997: 91–5) Its original meaning was intended to be descriptive, but Hansson used it as a critical label. He employed the phrase to attack inequalities in Swedish society: 'If Swedish society is going to be a good citizen's home, class differences must be eliminated, social services developed, economic equalisation achieved, workers provided a role in economic management, democracy carried through and applied both socially and economically.' (Cited in Tilton, 1991: 127) The central tenets of the *folkhem* were universalism, democracy and solidarity. Hansson rejected the discourse of class struggle when discussing the *folkhem*, and instead he spoke of 'people'. The same notion applied to other political parties. Ideology was not important – unity was essential. According to Hansson, 'A truly strong policy can only be won by uniting conflicting wills and by gathering the many to common work and co-operative effort. That applies to the labour movement and that applies in no lesser degree to the entire society.' (Cited in Tilton, 1991: 142) Despite the broad consensus on the *folkhem*, there were some disagreements over its meaning and implications. Interestingly, Ernst Wigforss (SAP ideologist, discussed below) never used the term as he regarded it as a patriarchal construct. [23]

The metaphor of the *folkhem* clearly carried weight, and some of the vision of the SAP began to be put into practice. In the same year, the *Riksdag* approved the

Collective Bargaining Act and the establishment of the Labour Court (1936) which protected by law the right to association and negotiation. In 1932, the SAP gained office, with cooperation from the Farmers' Party. It was this that marked the beginning of its dominant role in Swedish politics, and the start of the SAP programme of reform and solidarity. In 1938, the most important agreement between industry, government and labour was formulated, known as the 'Basic Agreement' or more commonly, the Saltsjöbaden Agreement, named after the town where the agreement was drawn up. Seen as both an SAP and LO document, it covered collective bargaining and industrial action. A central part of its provisions included limiting industrial action that posed a threat to industry. It also permitted grounds for examination in cases of dismissal in certain circumstances. According to Korpi (1982: 133), the Saltsjöbaden Agreement meant that labour would avoid using government power to interfere in the relationship between parties in the labour market. The relationship between the parties would be regulated amongst themselves. More importantly, the Saltsjöbaden Agreement established a precedent of consensus between labour and employer organisations. This so-called 'Saltsjöbaden spirit' was to persist well beyond the 1950s (Lundberg, 1985: 3).

Nevertheless, the outbreak of the Second World War would test Sweden's neutrality for a second time. Without anticipating the full extent of events to come, plans for a Scandinavian Defence Union (SDU) were abandoned in 1937 when the Danish government withdrew from the proposal, considering it 'utopian'. Nordic unity did not extend to security cooperation (Logue, 1989: 48). Whilst Sweden in the inter-war period was preoccupied with internal politics and plans for international cooperation, the rise of the Nazi Party in Germany would force Sweden to address the tyrannies of the anarchical international system. The markedly idealistic phase was over.

The Second World War and Swedish neutrality

Sweden formally declared its neutrality in September 1939 when Germany invaded Poland and when the UK and France formally entered the Second World War. However, Sweden's neutrality policy during WWII would draw harsh criticism from the outside world. For the Allied powers, Sweden violated the rules governing neutrality and assisted Germany economically, thereby prolonging the war. For the USSR, Sweden's policy was likewise dubious in its non-belligerency towards Finland; and for the neighbouring Nordic countries that endured German occupation, Swedish neutrality was simply a betrayal. The following section outlines key events that marked Swedish neutrality policy as opportunistic; Sweden was seen by the outside world as a 'modern Jezebel' following a 'coolly selfish and even callous policy'. (Joesten, in Steene, 1989: 170)

For many commentators, Swedish neutrality during WWII lacked integrity for the basic fact that Sweden was seen to side with the stronger belligerent. According to Joesten, Swedish neutrality progressed from strict neutrality (at the start of the war), to non-belligerency (in the case of Finland), to unabashed bias towards Germany, culminating in support for the Allies when the path of the war turned against Germany. Only between September and November 1939 did Sweden remain strictly neutral, adhering to The Hague Conventions and the joint declaration of neutrality laid down by the five northern European states at the Stockholm Conference of 1938 (1945: 324). There was no immediate threat to Sweden at this stage. But events would soon turn, and Sweden's intention of remaining out of the conflict proved to complicate the credibility of its neutrality policy.

When Russia attacked Finland, Sweden adopted a posture of non-belligerency with respect to the Russo-Finnish War. For Sweden, the Soviet attack on Finland during the Winter War of 1939–40 was an emotive issue. Domestic opinion urged Sweden to assist the Finns. However only humanitarian aid was provided. Yet approximately 20,000 volunteers went to Finland to fight alongside the Finns. According to Lennmarker, Swedish officers could leave the army, and at times it was openly known that they would leave for the purpose of contributing to the Finnish war effort – 'No questions asked.' (Interview, Lennmarker, 18/08/98) The phrase 'Finland's cause is ours' became a national slogan (Hadenius, 1997: 55; Hedin, 1943: 51; Interview, Lennmarker, 18/08/98). Russia's annexation of Swedish parts of Finland during the Napoleonic Wars, and Finland and Sweden's close cultural heritage and history of union, combined to produce a sense of solidarity with the Finns. Russia had long been the 'traditional enemy' of Sweden and the presence of a Swedish minority in Finland also caused concern. Finland was regarded by Sweden as 'the bulwark of her own security, and as a sister state'. (Joesten, 1945: 325)

Yet Sweden was not in a similar position when it came to the question of Germany. To begin with, Sweden's trade with Germany was massively important. Swartz's study emphasises the significance of trade to Sweden and how it oriented Swedish policy and actions. In 1938, 24 per cent of Sweden's exports went to Great Britain, and 18 per cent to Germany. When WWII broke out, trade agreements were signed with both powers in order to ensure open trade routes. However, the German blockade of the North Sea resulted in trade with the West being cut by 70 per cent. Subsequently, trade with Germany (within the blockade) rose (Swartz, 1996). Sweden's trade with Germany in iron ore was criticised by the Allied powers and seen to contribute to the maintenance of the German military war effort. Sweden supplied 40 per cent of Germany's total supply of iron ore in 1939, exported 10 million tonnes of iron ore to Germany in 1939, and 9.5 million in 1943.[24] Sweden was economically cut off from its usual markets, and in this sense, Sweden acted as it saw fit, in order to survive economically and avoid occupation.

Sweden regarded the dilemma in two ways: it could either make concessions to Germany, thereby breaching its neutrality, or, quite plainly, could be occupied and Germany would make use of its resources anyhow. Sweden opted to grant concessions to Germany, and this became the greatest source of criticism of Swedish policy during WWII from the Allied powers (and Denmark and Norway, which were occupied by Germany in 1940). Sweden's action attracted criticism from the British government who regarded it as a 'serious breach of neutrality' and the exiled Norwegian government was also angered by Sweden's view that hostilities between Norway and Germany had ended (Hedin, 1943: 52–3). Churchill was particularly critical in his 1940 London broadcast about neutral actions during the war: 'We have the greatest sympathy for these forlorn countries, and we understand their dangers and their point of view; but it would not be right, or in the general interest, that their weakness should feed the aggressor's strength and fill to overflowing the cup of human woe.' ([1940] 1974: 6200)

Sweden agreed to allow access of Red Cross personnel and medical supplies to Nazi troops. In July 1940, it was officially announced in Stockholm that an agreement had been reached whereby German officers, on leave, could travel unarmed. This went against The Hague Convention which does not permit a neutral state to allow a belligerent to move troops through its territory. The newspaper *Göteborgs Handels-och-Sjöfartstidning* reported that Germany used the opportunity to move major forces and equipment to Norway, and that these forces were, in fact, carrying arms. In April 1943, the American–Swedish News Exchange (an agency of the Swedish Board of Information) officially denied the extent of the concession. But the transit did not just serve military personnel on leave: after the outbreak of German–Russian war in June 1941, Sweden ceded to Germany a demand for passage of one fully-armed and equipped Nazi division on the way from Norway to Finland. Known as the 'Engelbrecht division', this concession caused great controversy regarding Sweden's neutral status (Åström, 1987: 13; Joesten, 1945: 327). The US State Department estimated that approximately 250,000 separate trips were made by German troops through Sweden (US State Department, 1998: 4). Sweden also allowed Germany to anchor its anti-submarine nets in its territorial waters, and permitted belligerent aircraft to fly overhead and land. Although limited to mail planes, this was exploited for military use.

For Germany, it was not enough that Sweden assist economically. Nazi neutrality experts, such as Dr E. H. Bockhoff, put forward ideas about 'integral neutrality'. A country had to show not only military and political neutrality but also *Volksneutralität* – neutrality of the people, or ideological neutrality.

For Himmler, Sweden held racial appeal and the Nazi regime was keen to link the German *volk* and the Nordic peoples. 'Moral neutrality' was also an interest of the Nazi regime with regard to neutral states and Hitler envisaged a larger *Großdeutchland*, where Sweden would be similar to Bavaria (Leitz, 2000: 52 and 22). Germany was concerned that the partisan attitude of the Swedish press might turn the government from its policy of neutrality and that Sweden would join the war on the side of Germany's enemies (Wahlbäck, 1986: 54). The Swedish press, which had been anti-Nazi since 1933 (Hopper, 1945) soon faced restrictions. In Sweden, the press was under the control of a number of councils and the Government War Information Board regulated military information. The Press Council also issued warnings and 'urged discipline'. Despite state neutrality, the press expressed the opinions of the public, who were not necessarily 'neutral', particularly in relation to emotive issues such as Finland. The German government protested against the Swedish press, and the Press Council and the Information Board issued warnings that reports should not favour 'one side at the expense of the other'. This applied to headlines as well, and there was the added stipulation that editorials and surveys must also be 'strictly objective'. (Swartz, 1996) The government of the time had to restrict any pro-Allied or anti-Nazi sentiment in newspapers, magazines and books. Editors were dismissed or imprisoned and even the arts (theatre, films and exhibitions) were affected by this censorship.

In the context of the time, the threat of German occupation was intense. The pressure Sweden faced during the height of German strength during the war is sometimes under-emphasised. Hedin claims that Sweden was expecting invasion at any given moment and mobilised almost 500,000 men in preparation (1943: 52). After the *Anschluß* of Austria and the Munich agreement, there was firm pressure on the Scandinavian states by Nazi Germany to sign non-aggression pacts. Denmark signed such; Finland and Sweden had prepared their defences, having undertaken rearmament in the 1930s (Logue, 1989: 48).

After the Russian victory at Stalingrad and the Allied victory in Tunisia in early 1943, Swedish neutrality shifted in favour of the Allies. Checks on public opinion relaxed and in April 1943, a mass meeting was held in the Stockholm Concert Hall, demanding that the government end the transportation of German troops across Sweden. The Social Democratic federation of trade unions played a strong role in this, and Sweden suspended this concession in August 1943. Germany's sinking of two Swedish trawlers in Danish waters and the downing of a Swedish courier plane led to Sweden taking into asylum 7,000 Danish Jews (in 1943), 35,000 Estonian refugees and approximately 70,000 Finnish children. Count Folke Bernadotte arranged the transport of 19,000 Danish and Norwegian concentration camp prisoners to Sweden (Logue, 1989: 50). In June 1943, Sweden decreased its supplies to Germany[25]

(US Embassy, Stockholm, 1998). The Swedish Minister in Berlin formally protested against the deportation of Danish Jews to Poland. After further incidents, relations between Sweden and Germany worsened and Sweden sent home German academics. However, the decline in trade with Germany and the increase in trade with the Allies created similar pressures for Sweden. Churchill placed a large amount of pressure on Sweden to join the war effort (Joesten, 1945; Karsh, 1988: 52–4; Norman, 1993).

Criticisms of Sweden's actions and its shifting neutrality policy have largely flavoured how the world remembers certain events of WWII. Joesten describes Sweden's foreign policy as a type of 'homespun isolationism based on egoism and fear'. (Cited in Steene, 1989: 171) Indeed, Sweden's actions did not comply with the principles and rules of neutrality, and for countries such as Denmark and Norway, which endured Nazi occupation, Swedish neutrality appeared selfish and isolationist, certainly not in keeping with Nordic solidarity. The following section examines the domestic debate over Swedish neutrality during the Second World War, and how the Swedish political elite viewed these criticisms.

The domestic debate over wartime neutrality

In Sweden, views of the war and Sweden's involvement with Nazi Germany have produced two distinct readings. It is widely accepted by the Swedish political elite and the public that Sweden's policy of neutrality was the most appropriate option for Sweden during WWII (Interviews, Hall, 11/08/98; Landerholm, 25/08/98; Nordgren, 13/08/98; Rohdin, 12/08/98). However, this was accompanied by deep uneasiness over the nature of the war and Sweden's concessions to Nazi Germany.

The main purpose of Sweden's neutrality policy was to keep Sweden out of war and maintain full national sovereignty. There was fear that internally Sweden could be divided over the war. Although Swedish sentiment was clearly on the side of the Allies ideologically, elite forces were pro-German. After the 1930s, according to Lennmarker, Sweden was culturally and linguistically close to Germany. Berlin was regarded as a 'metropolis' until the 1940s.[26] In 1941, according to the *Völkischer Beobachter* (an anti-Semitic, propagandist German newspaper), concessions to Germany were forced through the Swedish Council of Ministers by the intervention of King Gustav V 'against the trade union leaders'. King Gustav was also threatening abdication 'rather than risk war by saying no'. (Logue, 1989: 49–50) There was also an air of pessimism in the first stages of the war, and politicians and business interests were convinced that Germany would be victorious. The then Swedish Foreign Minister Christian Günther (not aligned to any political party), publicly claimed that Sweden was essentially on 'Germany's side'.

(Karsh, 1988: 45) Regardless of Günther's personal views, it was the general opinion of the government and policy-makers that minor concessions to neutrality were more important than sacrificing sovereignty.

The Social Democrats were largely opposed to granting concessions to Hitler, and feared that such actions would work to support a German new order in Europe. Olof Palme (Prime Minister 1969–86), writing in the 1980s, noted Undén's criticism in 1940 of the Nazi doctrine for a new international order (*Lebensraum*): 'A durable peace can never be built upon such a division of the dwellings of the earth that the smaller peoples are reduced to being mere squatters in the Lebensraum of some great power.' (Cited in Palme, 1982: 245) During the war, Hansson's coalition government (which included all political parties except the Communists) was primarily concerned with maintaining national unity and cohesion. Most accounts from the Swedish side stress that Swedish involvement would have led to German dominance in the region on a larger scale, not to mention the end of Swedish sovereignty. Åström claims that:

> We did accept a certain number of concessions after pressure from [Germany]. Some of them – not all of them, some of them – were contrary to international law. But the reason was simply because here are the German troops standing in large numbers in Denmark and Norway after April 1940. We were surrounded by Germans all around the Baltic, Finland and Norway was under German control at the time. We were surrounded on all sides by an aggressive Nazi regime. And so then to say 'no we refuse this, we refuse this' at the risk of being daily occupied by Germany, that was a difficult decision to take. And we can either say that the decisions that were made to give in to certain German demands was [sic] taken with absolutely democratic manner by the parliament. So it was not something that was done behind the back door. (Interview, Åström, 13/08/98)

Hedin, writing in 1943, claimed that: 'Had Sweden ... been subjugated by the Germans, a German–Soviet conflict might have been precipitated before Germany had finished with the Low Countries and France, to say nothing of Britain.' (1943: 52) Former Prime Minister Rickard Sandler said in 1942: 'What is now happening in Norway can happen, if we do not take care of our own house, to any honest Swedish citizen.' (Cited in Hedin, 1943: 56–7) Gunnar Hägglöf (1960: 153) remembered only too well Stalin's line to the Finnish delegates on October 1939: 'I am sorry, gentlemen, we cannot do anything about geography.'

The experiences of neutral Sweden surrounded by occupied states and open to the possibility of attack left a deep impression upon the nation. According to Beindorf, the transportation of German troops, food rationing, blackouts, and the conscription of men and women for stand-by duty in the Home Guards heightened the daily sense of direct threat. This combined with domestic factors at the time, with the government stressing solidarity to protect the *folkhem* (2001: 9). The uniting features of the *folkhem* were pitted against the outside world, which was seen as destructive and conflictual, full of social and physical risks (Van Ekecrantz, 1997: 405). There was an extremely tense combination of maintaining the solidarity of the nation in the face of aggression, coupled with a sense of guilt about not having been directly involved in the war.

Swedish neutrality has been an underlying theme in film and literature since the 1940s. Ingmar Bergman's 1957 film *The Seventh Seal* is said to reflect the anguish of a neutral nation, numerically and physically disadvantaged, standing aside from conflict and bloodshed (Hampden-Turner and Trompenaars, 1994: 241). Similarly, the 1942 film *Ride this Night!* portrayed the dilemma of protecting home against external threat and malice[27] (Beindorf, 2001). Marika Steirnstedt's drama *The Outrage* (1944) dealt with neutrality and censorship (Martinsson, 2000). Ingmar Bergman's 1968 film *Skammen* ('Shame') critiqued the Vietnam War and Sweden's WWII neutrality (MOMA, 2000). An interesting parallel is drawn in the realm of popular culture with the case of the US. Before the attack on Pearl Harbor, the US film industry was essentially divided on the war and America's isolationist position. However, the attack presented the industry with a 'golden opportunity' to make films that shaped 'popular perception of and support for the war'. According to Loy, the foreign battlefield was reflected in the homefronts of B-Western films, where 'soldiers in Stetsons' underscored themes of identity and encouraged citizens to support the war effort (Loy, 2003: 198–200). The zeal of the film industry at times surpassed or conflicted with the Office of War Information (OWI) (Cole, 2001: 137; Loy, 2003: 198).

As a small state in an anarchic international system, Sweden's main intention was to remain out of the conflict. As Åström contends, 'it is not neutrality alone that saved us, but also – and mainly – strategic and political circumstances largely beyond our control'. (1989: 17) Neutrality was justified in geo-strategic terms, and on this point, most political parties were in agreement that neutrality was the appropriate path for Sweden. For Lennmarker (Moderate Party MP), 'the traditional way of keeping your independence is, of course, to keep predatory powers away ... during the '50s, that was the absolute – you had Stalin and the Soviet Union – there was no ideas about neutrality as an ideology. Hard, hard realities.' (Interview, Lennmarker, 18/08/98) As claimed in Chapter 1, due to the position of these small neutral countries and the demands of belligerents, at times it was impossible to avoid violating neutrality. Sweden exhibited a combination of positive and negative traits during WWII. Neutrality was the tool for this, but the maintenance of Swedish neutrality relied on the belligerent respecting that status. However, this was not the case and despite the codification of rules on neutral rights, belligerents placed pressure on neutral states. Germany's demand for ideological neutrality was also a significant factor in this equation. Neutrality was Sweden's way of maintaining sovereignty, and a belligerent was demanding domestic censorship. The military weakness and economic needs of Sweden at the start of the Second World War placed serious pressures on Sweden's commitment to maintain full neutrality. As Karlsson explains, 'Even if formal neutrality is upheld, neutral countries will seldom be able to interpret this neutrality in the strictest sense. Small states which try to remain neutral are often forced to adapt their interpretation of neutrality to the stronger part in the conflict.' (1995: 37) Additionally, when the Second World War began, The Hague Convention on neutral duties was considered out of date – there were no clear guidelines for economic warfare (Leitz, 2000: 4). For Sweden, the importance was independence, and as such it practised a 'pendulum policy' as it did in relations between Russia and England in the 1800s (Raymond, 1997: 140). I make this point not as an exoneration of Sweden's dealings with Nazi Germany, but rather in relation to how neutral states are criticised in general for not participating in the act of armed conflict.

Nonetheless, the critical views on Swedish neutrality altered somewhat in retrospect. Ruth points to an internalised moral sense of right that Sweden managed to remain out of the conflict: 'the feeling of being the guardian of civilised values remained a vital collective force, in a sense, linking the very project of neutrality with the Allied war effort'. (1984: 88) Many would not agree with Ruth's view, particularly the occupied Scandinavian states. Joesten, who for many years was highly critical of Sweden's policy, actually altered his view in 1945, saying that Sweden was not ultimately pro-German but its policies were derived from economic necessity and security and hence could be interpreted as being 'pro-Swedish' (Steene, 1989: 171). The recent US State Department's report on neutral trade with Germany during the Second World War also claims that although neutral actions did help sustain the German war effort, the neutrals were in a vulnerable position (US State Department, 1998: 3). Additionally, neutrality at the time was a legal concept, and 'standards of morality have evolved since the war that may not have existed then'. (US State Department, 1998: 5)

Although in retrospect, it is a different matter to judge the actions of certain countries without considering the context of the time and the threats faced, a clear point must be made with reference to the nature of WWII. The ideology of Nazism and the nature of WWII brought a different understanding of 'war' to the world. Few would defend Germany's war quest as a 'just' one. As Walzer (1992: 253) claims, Nazism was 'an ultimate threat to everything decent in our lives ... We see it – and I don't use the phrase lightly – as evil objectified in the world, and in a form so potent and apparent that there could never be anything to do but fight against it.' The behaviour of states during WWII has had a massive impact on internal and external identity and policy, even to this day. For instance, Germany's struggles over its war history have resulted in a reluctance to militarise (or be seen to militarise) (Berger, 1996: 334; Zehfuss, 2001: 321). The decision in 2001 to accept the request of the US to provide 3,900 troops to join the military operations in Afghanistan (or the 'fight against terrorism') provoked controversy in the Bundestag.[28] Given the magnitude of the Second World War, it is therefore unsurprising that Swedish neutrality was not viewed through sympathetic lenses. However, Sweden's neutrality policy would change substantially in the post-war period (as Chapter 4 deals with), and some believed that Sweden pursued a more principled form of neutrality because of this experience.

Conclusion: imagining Sweden

The period of Swedish neutrality from 1814–1945 was essentially one of Sweden redefining itself and its place in the international anarchic system. Karl Johan's neutrality formula and his desire to form good relations with the outside world, however, were obscured by a number of factors which resulted in neutrality being widely perceived as a calculated and self-serving policy. Neutrality during this period was part of an attempt to carve out a 'new possible self' (Wendt, 1992: 420). Swedish identity, which was highly contested since its loss of power, became tied up with neutrality. Neutrality represented a new path for Sweden, but there also existed a strong urge to recapture its position of military strength in the region. Subsequently, neutrality was interpreted differently over the decades in relation to Sweden's place in Europe and what type of nation-state it should become. Neutrality during this period was not overtly internationalist nor was it explicitly principled. It was employed to keep Sweden out of conflict and maintain sovereignty and trade. Swedish neutrality was flexible, and therefore open to criticism that Sweden was not in fact neutral. Such criticisms were justified to a large degree in terms of Sweden's neutrality policy during the Second World War.

Although Sweden was regarded as an isolationist neutral state which benefited from war through its neutrality policy, the events and experiences of WWII would contribute to the development of a particular Swedish identity and a new approach to external phenomena in the post-war era. Sweden's neutrality during the Second World War would build on a historically-defined process of self-identification, which would shape its post-war active neutrality policy. The following chapter explores the post-war era of Sweden's active internationalism and doctrinal neutrality. It is during this period that neutrality became deeply anchored to Social Democratic goals such as the welfare state and active internationalism, marking a new phase in Swedish neutrality.

NOTES

1 Jean Baptiste Bernadotte (1763–1844), a French marshal, was appointed by the *Riksdag* in 1810 to succeed the throne upon the death of Charles XIII (who died without heirs). When Bernadotte became King of Sweden in 1818, he adopted the title King Karl XIV Johan (referred to as Karl Johan henceforth) and converted to Protestantism.
2 According to Barton (1930: 360) the 'watchwords' of Karl Johan's foreign policy.
3 The Kalmar Union united Sweden and Norway under Danish rule between 1397 and 1521. In 1520, the Danes invaded Sweden to control revolts, which was met by a peasant uprising against King Christian of Denmark and his Swedish allies, led by Gustav I Vasa. Heclo and Madsen date the formation of the modern Swedish state to this revolt. Under Vasa, a hereditary, independent monarchy was installed in 1527, and the powers of the nobles and the clergy were curtailed in favour of the state (Heclo and Madsen, 1987: 9–10).
4 Widmer dates the origins of Swedish neutrality to 1814 (1989: 22), but this appears to be disputed to a slight degree. Others take its source to be later, in 1834, when Karl Johan's memorandum to the Russian and British governments declared Swedish neutrality regarding the Near East Crisis (Lindström, 1997: 2).
5 Cramér reads this mediation differently, though, claiming that it was reflective of Karl Johan's turn against Napoleon after acceding to the Swedish throne (1989: 68).
6 Under Oscar I (1844–59) Sweden sent several thousand troops to Fyn in northern Denmark, which freed up Danish forces to amass in the south (Wahlbäck, 1986: 11–12). His successor, Karl XV (1859–72) also supported Scandinavianism and wanted Sweden to have a more influential role in European politics (Elgström, 2000: 256). King Karl XV tried to involve Sweden in the Prusso-Danish War of 1864, in the hope of forming a Scandinavian union with Denmark and Norway and reclaiming Finland. Karl XV promised the King of Denmark that Sweden would join in an alliance to defend Schleswig against Germany, although the government was opposed to such a move and the Swedish military at this stage was weak, forcing Karl XV to withdraw his commitment. Logue writes that Karl XV entertained the notion that the King of Denmark might adopt him and hence provide an opportunity to re-establish a single Scandinavian state (Jervas, 1986: 8; Logue, 1989: 43; Stiernlöf, 1989).
7 In the 1820s, Swedish neutrality was balanced more in favour of its trading partner Britain than its rival Russia (Elgström, 2000: 252; see also Raymond, 1997: 140). Indeed, Karl Johan expected Britain to protect Sweden if neutrality failed (Huldt, 1995: 141).
8 Autocracy particularly characterised the regimes of Karl XI (1660–1697) and Karl XII (1697–1718), with periods of oscillation between absolutism and demands for representative rule (lasting until the first decade of the nineteenth century, according to Rokkan, 1981: 58).
9 Nonetheless, national assemblies were aristocratic and the assembly of the four estates which replaced them was not entirely participatory. Elections at this time were not universal. Voters had to satisfy financial requirements and this therefore excluded almost all labourers, clerical workers and small landowners. Women were not permitted to vote. Rokkan (1981: 61–2) attributes this to the establishment of estate representation, which he claims diluted strong pressures for further extensions of political rights. Political democracy in Sweden proceeded at a slow pace, compared to Denmark and Finland, which experienced a sudden extension of political rights in 1849 and 1906 respectively.
10 Swedes that had emigrated as early as the mid-seventeenth century established a

colony on the Delaware River. Swedish migration to America peaked in the late 1860s, reaching a record high in late 1880s. During the Great Depression, many Swedes returned to the homeland (Barton, 1999).

11 The same principle reflects modern industry's approach to 'pulling together'. When BAHCO (B. A. Hjorth and Co., a tool and machinery company established in the late nineteenth century) workers were laid off, there was a concerted effort by management to relocate them, rather than be indifferent to their fate. Anders Lindstrom, one of the business leaders of the company, stated: 'This wasn't charity, it was common sense. We had to have people pull together, trust each other, trust management, and come through the crisis by helping each other.' (Hampden-Turner and Trompenaars, 1994: 239 and 250)

12 Although industrial development was slow, when it took off it did so at a rate that surpassed Britain and Germany's per capita GNP growth. Technological developments in iron and chemical processing, and power generation (electricity) saw the establishment of companies which were to become a major part of Swedish industry to date (such as ASEA, SKF, Atlas Copco, L. M. Ericsson, Alfa Laval). (Hampden-Turner and Trompenaars, 1994: 258)

13 The Liberals were initially called the National Liberal Federation (*Frisinnade Landsföreningen*). The Liberals split in 1923 between the Protectionists and the Liberals, and merged again in 1934.

14 Radical socialism had a difficult time gaining ground in Sweden as industrialisation occurred later in comparison to other European countries. Sweden adopted the Lassallean view of the state as an association of the population that could be used to legislate a socialist order over time, rather than the Marxist revolutionary view (Olsen, 1992: 93–4).

15 In 2001, the SAF was dissolved and merged with the Federation of Swedish Industries (*Industriförbundet*) to form the Confederation of Swedish Enterprise (*Svenskt Näringsliv*). *Svenskt Näringsliv* later formed the SFN (*Stiftelsen Fritt Näringsliv* or the Swedish Free Enterprise Foundation) with *Näringslivet Fond*, its predecessor, in March 2003.

16 However, by 1916, this truce began to collapse, with the Social Democrats and the Liberals attacking the trade policies of the government. As the new cabinet was made up mostly of senior civil servants and industrialists, most of the decisions coming out of government were pro-German (the financier Knut Wallenberg acted as Foreign Minister, but was pro-British). The 1917 Russian Revolution also forced a split in the SAP, with its more radical component breaking away and forming the Left Party (*Socialdemokratiska vänsterpartiet*) which would contest the 1921 election as the Swedish Communist Party (*Sveriges kommunistika parti*) (Hadenius, 1997: 26–8). Sparks and Cockerill note that there was a minute number in the SAP interested in the possibility of Sweden's involvement with Germany in the war, to defend 'Western civilisation against Russian barbarism'. This resulted in three members being expelled from the party (1991: 94).

17 Transito was an organisation established in 1915 to control the transit of goods over Swedish territory to Russia. Disguised as a joint stock company, it was actually controlled by Britain and influenced imports and exports, despite the disapproval of the government (particularly PM Hammarskjöld) and the King of Sweden. Swedish economic interests remained under foreign control until the end of the war (Ørvik, 1953: 50–1).

18 Most of the nationalisation in Sweden has been carried out by non-socialist administrations. The Liberal government set up the Swedish Tobacco Monopoly in 1915, in order to fund its 1913 pension plan. In the early 1900s, the Conservative government

The social construction of Swedish neutrality

established the iron-mining company, LKAB, and the Wine and Spirits Company in 1917 to control alcohol consumption (Olsen, 1992: 101).

19 Swartz (1996) notes, however, that there was no pure consensus on this issue. Foreign Minister Rickard Sandler was opposed to handing over the Åland Islands, and to Sweden's strict neutrality policy of the time.

20 Branting was widely regarded as an advocate of collective security – in the right environment. As a 'constitutional pacifist', he supported security based on principles of justice, arbitration and law, rather than force. He was highly engaged in efforts towards such a platform on the international level, acting as Sweden's representative to the Paris Peace Conference in 1919. He pushed for the adoption of the Covenant of the League of Nations, brought Sweden into the League of Nations and was named to the Council of the League in 1923. He was also chairman of the Assembly's Committee on Disarmament (1920–21), a member of the Council's Committee on Disarmament in 1924 and participated in settling the Greek–Italian conflict of 1923. Branting also acted as a 'rapporteur' in disputes between Britain and Turkey and was involved in drafting the Geneva Protocol (The Nobel Foundation, 2000).

21 Likewise, as Galbraith observed, the role of Swedish cooperatives also played an important part in redressing inequalities in the market place in terms of private power or competition. In his theory of countervailing power, Galbraith claimed that consumer cooperatives in Sweden were instrumental in curbing cartels (1952: 125–8 and 140).

22 Kjellén was elected to the Second Chamber of the Swedish parliament from 1905–8, and to the First Chamber between 1910 and 1918, representing the 'Young Conservatives'. Tunander describes him as a 'socially concerned nationalist', who held anti-liberal and anti-socialist views. He disagreed with the socialists' maximalist view of the state, and likewise distrusted the liberals' minimalist state (2001: 453). Malmborg highlights his affinity for Germany (regarding Sweden as 'the outpost of the Germanic tribe') and fear of Russia (Malmborg, 2001: 108).

23 Wigforss was first elected to parliament in 1919, and was a member of the directorate of the SAP between 1920 and 1952. In 1925–26 he was Minister of Finance and was on the executive committee from 1928–52 (Tilton, 1991: 41). Jenson and Mahon shared his concerns about the use of the term from a feminist perspective: the *folkhem* meant the dilution of more ambitious plans. For instance, Hansson's idea of the role of women did not move beyond the more 'family-oriented' stance, and that plans for rationing out housework and equal wages were omitted from the 1944 programme (1993: 80–1).

24 According to Stuart Eizenstat (US Under-Secretary of State for Economic, Business and Agricultural Affairs (1997–99) and head of the US State Department's investigation into neutral trade with Germany), 'Sweden provided Germany's wartime industry in some years with up to 100 per cent of its requirement in iron ore.' (US State Department, 1998: 3; see also US Embassy, Stockholm, 1998)

25 Sweden in 1944 voted in the *Riksdag* to participate in the Safehaven Programme, which was intended to stop Germany from transferring assets to neutral countries return looted property, and prevent key individuals from the military and security establishment of Germany escaping. In the same year, Sweden supported the Bretton Woods Resolution VI, which directed neutral countries to prevent the transfer of assets belonging to governments, institutions and individuals in occupied countries (US Embassy, Stockholm, 1998).

26 However, after the war it shifted to Anglo-Saxon culture: 'English became the first foreign language to [be taught] in the schools. Some people went to the United States to advance that. Industry, more or less ... financial services became Americanised.' (Interview, Lennmarker, 18/08/98)

Neutrality as a Social Democratic project

27 Interestingly, Olof Palme featured in a controversial film called *I Am Curious (Yellow)* (1967), in which he was interviewed discussing the class system in Sweden. The film was controversial for its sexual references which were considered rather racy when it was made (see Eldridge, 1997).
28 Chancellor Schroeder threatened to resign if the Bundestag would not approve the sending of forces. Plans to send troops to the NATO-led force in Macedonia were opposed by Christian Democrats and Social Democrats, and nearly broke the coalition (BBC News, 19/09/01).

4

Sweden's post-war neutrality doctrine: active internationalism and 'credible neutrality'

> Ideas are not only for active politicians. If they are to have the ability to penetrate, in practical politics, they must be anchored in the population. (Olof Palme, 1968, cited in Stern, 1991: 77)

AFTER THE Second World War, the SAP began its long period in office and neutrality became more principled, activist, and internationalist. Social Democratic ideals of solidarity, equality and reform were played out through Sweden's active neutrality policy. Sweden developed a distinct profile on the international stage through its UN membership, commitment to solidarity with the developing world, pursuit of disarmament, peacekeeping and mediation, and criticism of the superpowers during the Cold War. Sweden did much to provide an alternative view of security. In this sense, Sweden departed from the dominant understandings of neutral states as mere objects in the anarchic international system. Neutrality need not be an isolationist or self-interested policy, as the dominant realist view explained. Neutrality could be 'what states make of it'. Sweden's combination of neutrality and Social Democracy defined Sweden as a specific type of active neutral, one which went beyond the 'good offices' label commonly associated with neutrals, and was interested in translating Social Democratic norms and values to the international arena.

As the constructivist view holds, identities are fluid, and can be transformed by a variety of internal and external phenomena. Foreign policy does not occur in a vacuum and the external posture of a state is essentially conditioned by its internal make-up. Neutrality, under SAP hegemony, became part of a wider Social Democratic project: neutrality was the platform from which a particular form of global socialism could be enacted. During this period, the SAP consolidated key domestic norms and institutions, which were widely accepted by Swedish society. Neutrality, along with the welfare state and the Swedish Model, became such a consensual point of reference for Swedes that it was rarely questioned. Neutrality was developed as a Social Democratic *myth*, one which became an important part of Swedish identity.

Sweden's post-war neutrality doctrine

This chapter is divided into two parts: the first explores the influence of SAP hegemony and how certain SAP values and norms became widely accepted and entrenched, shaping a particular self-identity and picture of 'Sweden'. This builds on the social origins of Swedish neutrality outlined in the previous chapter, and anchors Sweden's post-war active neutrality policy and internationalism in a domestic context. The second part of this chapter investigates how Social Democratic norms were played out through Sweden's neutrality policy and active internationalism: essentially how Sweden 'exported' its norms to the international level.

Hegemonic Social Democracy: the SAP in power

Enzensberger notes that the Social Democratic party 'dominates Swedish society ideologically, morally and politically, whether it is in office or not'. (1989: 6) The political dominance of the SAP and its ideology has been said to be 'hegemonic'[1] for a number of reasons. Many point first to the fact that the SAP has had an almost uninterrupted period in office. After forming minority governments and then governing through a wartime grand coalition, the SAP's 1944 Post-War Programme led them to govern alone until 1951, when they entered into a 'green-red' coalition. This has allowed the SAP to cement its presence politically and instigate its economic and social programmes. Few West European Social Democratic parties can claim such long periods in office, and often share power in coalition governments. The *ideological* influence of the SAP, however, does not wholly derive from its electoral strength. The SAP consistently polled on average 40 per cent of the vote in elections, and often had to rely on support from other parties in order to get proposals passed in the *Riksdag* (Einhorn and Logue, 1989: 307).

What is significant about the SAP's dominance of Swedish politics has been its ability to shape not only the economic and social profile of Sweden, but also to gain widespread support for its particular vision of Swedish society. It achieved this by translating its policies and ideals in universal terms (discussed below with reference to the Swedish Model and consensus). The SAP captured an ideal of Swedish society, and due to its political dominance, was able to socalise this vision so it had widespread appeal, incorporating existing institutions and social bases, such as the trade union movement, as its own. The ability of the SAP to gain consensus for its programmes and encase them in universalist terms established the party as a hegemonic political force in Sweden. Thus, 'Hegemony need not consist of unanimous or even majority support: it consists of the fact that almost everyone, knowingly or unknowingly, dances to the tune of the leading party.' (Heclo and Madsen, 1987: 23)

In the case of Swedish Social Democracy, incremental gains would be achieved through the established order, and by including a variety of opinions and actors. Consensualism is the key. Some regard this as pragmatism, but this does not fully capture the strong ideological element of Swedish Social Democracy. For instance, Tingsten, in the 1950s, claimed that pragmatism and the rejection of Marxism left the SAP ideologically bereft (Tilton, 1991: v). This view generated heated debate, and was opposed by Korpi, Sainsbury, and Lewin in particular (Olsen, 1992: 91–2). Tilton especially takes issue with this, claiming that a strong ideological undercurrent pervades the SAP, its policies and rationale, and to deny such is to negate much of the ideals that guide Sweden internally and externally (1991: 4). For Lane (1991b: 222), a neo-liberal, Sweden's form of 'democratic socialism' is highly ideological. The following section explores some of the key components of the Swedish Model that translated SAP policy and ideology.

The Swedish Model

According to Lane, the Swedish Model was a 'conflict resolution device' which mediated interaction between key social groups in industrial society, replacing class conflict with cooperation, both within parliament and outside of parliament (1991a: 5). The essence of the Swedish Model appears to be stable party government with its leanings towards consensus and its network of neo-corporatist institutions in a mixed economy which embraced pragmatic bargaining between capitalism and social values. Prior to this, the SAP had established a successful consensus between unions, employers and government through the Saltsjöbaden Agreement (see Chapter 3). This consensual form of relations was enveloped in a rhetoric that stressed solidarity and reform.

Having contributed to the establishment of political democracy in Sweden, the SAP began to work towards its next objective, economic democracy. Plans for such were developed in the post-war era by key SAP figures, such as Wigforss, Per Albin Hansson, Alva and Gunnar Myrdal (members of SAP government and key reformers), Gösta Rehn and Rudolph Meidner (SAP economists), Tage Erlander (Prime Minister 1946–69) and Olof Palme. The Swedish Model came to exemplify central ideas and goals that constituted a specific approach to the relationship between labour and capital, state and individual.

Essentially, the Swedish Model is comprised of three parts: economic growth and full employment founded on a modified Keynesian demand-management programme (Wigforss' theoretical model) and an active labour market policy (the Rehn-Meidner model); welfare provisions based on social solidarity, egalitarianism and universal coverage; and the 'solidaristic' wage policy, introduced through collective bargaining that aimed to reduce wage differentials (Wilks, 1996: 94).

It must first be pointed out that the Swedish Model has been an 'elusive' phrase (Weiss, 1998: 86), contested and debated both within Sweden and abroad. Many writers will describe the Swedish Model as composed of the welfare state, corporatism[2] between government, unions and employers, and the ideology of the SAP. Lane describes the Swedish Model as a mixture of what Rustow refers to as the compromise model[3] and Heclo's hegemonic model. For Lindbeck (1997: 12–13), the Swedish Model is a form of economic and social organisation, an institutional arrangement whereby society is dominated by large and centralised institutions. I interpret the Swedish Model to consist of the three parts described previously, but these components could not operate successfully without the dominance of SAP ideology. Furthermore, implicit in the mechanisms of the Swedish Model are consensus and reform. All aspects work together to produce a particular image of 'Sweden' domestically and externally.

The Rehn-Meidner Model

The first component is the core of the Swedish Model, arising from an economic plan to marry full employment with low inflation and economic stability. Developed by Rehn and Meidner in the late 1940s to early 1950s, its basic propositions are a centralised wage, with equal pay for 'comparable work', an active labour market policy and restrictive fiscal and monetary policy to fight inflation and high profits (Meidner, 1992: 160). By tightening the differentials between wages of low-productivity sectors and high-productivity sectors, growth and structural change could be accelerated. As the latter sectors expanded, the former became obsolete. The role of the unions with active labour market policies then placed redundant workers in the expanding sectors of the economy, with the government providing mobility grants and subsidies towards this. The ulterior motive was to facilitate social control over capital and alter the structure of industry and capital. Meidner was firmly committed to full employment, not merely for the longevity of the economic programme of Social Democracy, but for more resilient reasons such as providing a good standard of living for the unemployed and avoiding demoralisation (Meidner, 1992: 169).

The Swedish brand of Keynesian economics differed from the norm. In the 1930s, Swedish Keynesianism disagreed with the assumption that economic power had shifted from the capital to the managerial class. There was still a strong belief that it was possible to control capital. State ownership was never an important part of the SAP's functionalist form of socialism. Party theorists in the 1960s instead looked to reduce the ownership functions of capitalists via an active labour market policy and state investment funds. This was linked to the idea of democratic control over the economy, stressing other factors such as cultural and educational opportunities for fulfilling the individual. A strong line of humanist socialism featured in the Swedish approach (Padgett and Paterson, 1991: 25–6). These determinants were worked out between industry and labour with the aim of channelling resources into certain areas of the economy which would be more productive. This tripartite association carved a 'distributive' form of capitalism.

The SAP also encouraged the strong and active participation of the labour movement in its economic model. Under the Labour Market Board (LMB), an active labour market policy was implemented whereby labour and business were equally represented. Made up of the main organisations, the LMB was a forum for the regulation of corporatism. Hence, political bargaining was firmly entrenched into the institutional fabric of the socio-economic order and became institutionalised (Jenson and Mahon, 1993: 81; Padgett and Paterson, 1991: 195). There is 'institutionalised' support for the party in collective affiliation through the unions. These labour institutions produce a working class culture that incorporates housing, youth movements, tenants' unions, and pensioner organisations, amongst others. As Linton observed, the influence of the labour movement affected the everyday lives of Swedes during the SAP's decades in power: Swedes socialised, shopped, and were educated 'in the warm bosom of the labour movement'. (Tilton, 1991: 3) A sense of working class identity was engendered by practice, as union interests were linked to national interests. The consensus that marked Swedish politics was encouraged by the methods of the SAP. For instance, after the 1948 election, Erlander established the 'Thursday Club', which included representatives of economic interest groups (namely from agriculture and blue- and white-collar unions) to discuss political and economic issues. This was overtaken in the mid 1950s with the so-called 'Hapsund democracy' where a series of conferences resulted in wide-ranging discussion.[4] Non-socialist groups adhered to the SAP vision of society and their interests were included in decision-making. Hence, the Rehn-Meidner model and its strong labour union involvement created an inclusive political and social culture.

The welfare state

The welfare state plays a distinctive role in the Swedish Model, extending welfare provision beyond the basics and linking welfare to societal goals and aspirations in line with the idea of the 'good state' and the *folkhem*. The SAP programmes of the 1940s and 1950s aimed to adhere to principles of universalism, unconditional entitlement and the institutionalisation of the welfare state as a vital part of society. The establishment of the Swedish welfare state involved harmonising the interests of wage-earners and beneficiaries, creating solidarity, and linking the welfare state to principles it had hoped to achieve for society as a whole. The welfare state was also connected to the desire to use political devices to inhibit market forces and their divisive effects (Padgett and Paterson, 1991: 137–8).

For Esping-Andersen, the Swedish welfare state differs from other models in its extension of social rights – the 'essence of social policy' – and attention to decommodification and social stratification. Decommodification refers to the idea that a service is rendered as a matter of right and an individual can maintain a livelihood without relying on the market. Social insurance mechanisms cannot free the individual from commodification unless the individual is free from market dependence. By social stratification, he refers to how the individual is treated in the acquisition of social rights, for instance, the stigmatisation of means-tested social welfare (Esping-Andersen, 1991: 21–4). Liberal welfare regimes, such as those of the US, Canada and Australia, involve means-tested assistance, modest universal transfers and basic social insurance. Benefits are claimed mostly by those with low income, the working class and those dependent on the state. A traditional liberal work ethic is the norm, which halts social reform, and entitlements are stringent and stigmatised. Corporatist welfare models, such as those of Austria, France, Germany and Italy maintain status differences, and the state will only interfere as a last resort (Esping-Andersen, 1990: 9–11 and 26–8).

For the Swedish welfare state, welfare is universal, built into the fabric of society and intended to assist individuals throughout life. It is not simply about the relationship between workers and capitalism, but is far more inclusionary in that it takes into account how these structures impact on the individual and society. Erlander held a firm belief in a 'strong government'; that government should be founded on the wishes of the majority and that this majority is united by common values. Connected to the idea of the 'strong government' is the 'strong society' and this was to be achieved by the long-term goal of extending the social security system (Ruin, 1991: 61). Ryner's understanding of the distinctions between the more liberal models and those of the Scandianvian variety stem from the fact that demands for social protection held more saliency in Sweden, than say, in the US. For Ryner (2002: 62), 'the social democratic labour movement managed to maintain an alliance with agrarian forces, and pre-empt what emerged in the United States: an alliance between financiers, industrialists, and agrarian interests, that watered down the interventionist density in the mode of regulation in favour of market reforms'. The Swedish welfare model is a universalist one, and ties in with the rhetoric of the *folkhem*, that it is the responsibility of the state to look after society.

Solidaristic wages policy

In the mid 1950s, the solidaristic wages policy came into action and introduced a firm link between organised labour and capital. According to Rehn and Meidner, the solidaristic wage policy was a way to circumvent the usual system of wage freezes to control inflation. Through the solidaristic wage policy, employers were required to pay equal wages for equal work, regardless of the profitability of the firm (Olsen, 1992: 10). Wage levels were settled by the level of profitability of the most productive companies and industrial sectors on a national level. This meant that weaker firms could not be protected by artificially depressing wages and that competition from more productive firms would halt price rises. Subsequently, this implied that some industries would be forced to close, but this would have been redressed by Sweden's active labour market policy. The gap would therefore be resolved by retraining and labour mobility schemes to relocate labour to more profitable sectors (Padgett and Paterson, 1991: 144–5). A centralised labour movement board (*Arbetsmarknadsstyrelsen*) absorbed these workers, and the SAP's introduction of a superannuation scheme would shift investment towards greater control of the economy, as employers and employees contributed to a state-administered fund. More importantly, the solidaristic wage-earner policy would create wage equality and class solidarity amongst workers. The policy would give unions an active rather than a passive role (Olsen, 1992: 10).

However, the solidaristic wages policy was not successful. Firms that made a high profit managed to escape paying higher wages due to the wages policy. In order to resolve this problem, in the 1970s, collective wage-earner funds were proposed to allow workers to invest in the firm. This was to alter the private sector's dominance over the capital market (discussed further in Chapter 5). These were derived from the 1944 Post-War Programme. Wigforss' *The Working Class Movement's Postwar Programme* of 1944[5] also aimed to transform capitalism by economic planning and social welfare, but not through the nationalisation of industry. Economic planning for full employment would extend social control over the organisation of production and increased production would maintain social welfare measures (Tilton, 1990: 48). The post-war 'harvest' period saw the Social Democrats achieve full employment, a basic retirement system, child benefits, a universal health insurance system, more progressive taxation, an active labour market policy and housing subsidies, to name a few of the major successes (Tilton, 1990: 4). The welfare state was to be the way to fulfil the SAP's previous project – economic democracy and social democracy, as well as political democracy, which had already been achieved.

Sweden's post-war neutrality doctrine

Consensus and reform

The vital point about the Swedish Model was that it inspired a positive set of relations not simply between labour and capital, but also proved a point of consensus between political groups. Initiated under Hansson's grand coalition of the SAP, the conservatives, the liberals and the agrarians, it signified a turn in Swedish politics that revealed a wide form of consensus between all social classes rather than an adversarial style of politics. Coming out of the war years, employees refrained from demanding higher wages, consumers adhered to rationing, manufacturers froze prices and a general sense of optimism prevailed. The acceptance by the conservatives and the liberals of the SAP model which required state involvement in economic affairs was a massive turning point, as these two political parties traditionally disagreed with such a stance.[6] Thus, the Swedish Model not only created a specific set of policies to redress the inequalities of the capitalist system, but it also produced a particular pattern of relations within Swedish politics and society.

For Sainsbury, the success of the SAP has been its emphasis on 'programmatic renewal' of Social Democracy in Sweden (1991: 39–40). Rather than ideas, it has been the creative revision of policies and their content which accounts for SAP political dominance. However, this view does not fully explain the values that have underpinned and constructed social and political life in Sweden. In many countries, dissatisfaction with government programmes can often result in the loss of office and triumph of the opposition. In many respects, Social Democracy has proven itself to exist more as a *folkrörelse* (or 'popular movement', see Chapter 3) that has as its core a reforming aim. There exists more to Swedish Social Democracy than simply 'changing the programme'. The SAP has remained a dominant force in Swedish politics and society because it has been able to make its view of society and politics the dominant view amongst the population. There is a sense of society as a 'social laboratory'. With its tendency for reformism, Sweden creates and recreates itself 'using the political process and public policy to create a more or less coherent and explicitly social democratic vision of itself'. (Heclo and Madsen, 1987: 6) The ability to instil a particular model of how a society should work and what values it holds central, had the effect of creating specific norms about issues and policy. The combination of universal policies, consensus and reform established norms between state and market, which filtered down to society and the individual. The following section explores the impact of such ideas and rhetoric, and how they became embedded in the Swedish mindset.

Imagining Swedish society: SAP rhetoric and metaphors

The SAP vision of Swedish society was further disseminated through its use of specific rhetorical tools and metaphors, which encapsulated the 'Swedish way' as something quite unique and exceptional. Chapter 3 discussed Hansson's use of the *folkhem* in political discourse, and in the post-war era, the *folkhem* gained increased significance since the SAP was in a position to pursue its objectives of economic and social democracy. The notion of the *folkhem* came to epitomise the Swedish welfare state and became a consensual point of reference between political leaders and competing political ideologies. According to Nordstedt's Dictionary, the term has become synonymous for the 'Swedish Welfare State' (1993: 225).

The effects and intricacies of the Swedish Model established a particular set of relations and expectations between state and market, but this also impacted upon society and the individual. Under the Swedish Model, universalism and decommodification were distinguishing features of the Swedish welfare state and encapsulated under the rubric of the *folkhem*. Under the rhetoric of the *folkhem*, the combination of policies and ideologies merged to engender a strong sense of collective identity and community. Linked to the idea of the *folkhem* was the strong value of *solidarity* in political discourse, which, according to Lawler (1997: 568), became socially embedded due to domestic legislation and the regional and foreign policies of Sweden (and Scandinavia).

Social Democratic rhetoric also found its way into popular culture and made up journalism's 'discursive events' of the time. The post-war period represented a time of dynamism in Sweden, symbolising unity. Van Ekecrantz writes that at its height in the mid 1950s, the rhetoric of the *folkhem* coincided with booms in industry and construction, culture and ideology, which

> came to serve as effective *metaphors* in the general utopian rhetoric of the People's Home ... These metaphors represented the positive, constructive and democratic forces in society. They stood for the common and shared values, interests and ways of life, for the bridging of distances between people, groups and social classes, for consensus and social integration. (Van Ekecrantz, 1997: 404–5)

Similarly, as Sweden progressed industrially in the late nineteenth century, such symbolism was prevalent in events such as the Stockholm Exhibition of 1897. During the late 1890s, the average real income of the Stockholm middle and working class increased, and the Exhibition came to stand as a metaphor for an optimistic future where class differences might be diffused (Pred, 1995: 32–4). Likewise, with the Stockholm Exhibition of 1930, themes of solidarity, social responsibility and individualism were captured. Architecture, construction, and consumer goods reflected a new type of modernity and functionalism in Sweden. Social Democratic ideologues, such as the Myrdals, equated radical architecture with socialist reform (Pred, 1995: 162), and were closely associated with the group of radical architects who were prominent in the new functionalism in the 1930 Stockholm

Exhibition. Their manifesto *Acceptera* argued for using modern technology to form a just and functional society and strongly influenced Swedish urban planning, housing and industrial design, which the Myrdals took up in their housing policy (Tilton, 1991: 146–7). Alva Myrdal advocated modern socialist housing and public daycare. For her, the people's home meant men and women participated in both the workforce and responsibility at home (Jenson and Mahon, 1993: 80–1). The Myrdals and the SAP put much faith in modernity, scientific rationalism, and social engineering, particularly in relation to the role of the state in housing, childcare and other social programmes (Eliæson, 2000). The Swedish attachment to the metaphor of the *folkhem* persisted well into the 1980s, influencing discourse and practice (Lawler, 1997: 568). The idea of the People's Home is a sedimented one, and part of the 'collective stocks of knowledge' that Berger and Luckmann refer to (see Chapter 2).

This had a profound effect upon Swedish society. In SAP ideology, the sense of individualism relates to social well being. Swedes in general are not comfortable about the idea of individual rights over that of the social group or community. As Palme put it:

> Democratic socialism starts with the social situation of the individual. The liberty of the individual will benefit most if he is able to find paths to a sense of community with others, to cooperation and solidarity. The individual must be able together with others to control his own situation and to influence his own surroundings. (Palme, 1972: 18)

Pred (1995: 136) claims that this notion of the individual had the effect of evening out (or obliterating) class differences. As such, a 'narrative of progress' became the discourse of the time, whereby popular movements were elevated 'so as to cement the interests of individual and society, so as to suggest that what is economically good for the nation as a whole is good for everyone'. Furthermore, this sense of freedom of the individual is not merely left to the dynamics of a capitalist market economy. The SAP's understanding of equality meant that the state must not only regulate the inequalities of the market, but must also ensure that this equality is universal and not simply rhetorical. The state had to ensure that equality is concretely promoted by government policies, such as education, health, childcare, care of the elderly and housing. Alva Myrdal explained that equality in Sweden carried different connotations. It rejected 'the traditional liberal idea of equality of opportunity, which is based on the assumption that we are all equal at the outset'. For Myrdal, the liberal conception of equality bred further inequality, and it was the onus of society to alter social circumstances 'throughout life, not just at the beginning'.[7]

For Hampden-Turner and Trompenaars, Swedes in general approach work from a reciprocal perspective. The individual is important, but 'the fulfilment and destiny of the individual lies in developing and sustaining others' through their work. In this sense, the dilemma between individualism and wealth creation is balanced and resolved by social obligations. The search for meaning between society and the individual was captured at the time by the term *lagom*, derived from Old Norse, meaning 'the right to satisfy yourself as well as others'. (1994: 244 and 258) *Lagom* is a multifaceted term that encompasses such ideas as 'just right', 'in moderation', 'sufficient', 'appropriate' and 'suitable'. (Mörth and Sundelius, 1995: 125; Ruth, 1984) It is a moral and quantitative judgement. This notion has played a part in the style of politics that Sweden adopts, in its consensual nature that is open to compromise, and essentially close to the values of equality, or having access to the 'common cake'. The expression derived from the drinking habits of ancient Swedes, where a jug of beer would be passed amongst men, making the rounds (*gå laget om*; *lag-om* being short for *laget om*). 'To drink more than one's share from a community jug is of course unforgivable, but drinking too little is equally unsociable; it means opting out of the common spirit.' (Ruth, 1984: 60–1) This also relates to Swedish views and consensus on the welfare state. Even though the more conservative elements in Swedish politics want to change the welfare state, there is still a strong obligation to protect the less well off in society. Thus, a shared understanding of the obligations of the state towards society underscores the Swedish self-identity.

As Delanty puts it, 'reality can only be known through our cognitive structures'. (1997: 112) The SAP provided the cognitive structures for Swedish reality and identity. The Swedish Model 'interlocked' (Logue, 1999: 165) a humanist approach to economic phenomena. The Social Democratic norms and values that underpinned the Swedish Model provided a particular identity for Sweden. By its specific institutions, such as the Swedish Model, and the processes of consensus and reform that it produced, the SAP was crucial in shaping Sweden's internal identity. Neutrality is part of the collective meanings that construct domestic politics in Sweden. Foreign policy is as much a product of internal as well as external phenomena: therefore, the separation between foreign and domestic politics leaves serious omissions in explaining or understanding what drives state action.

Understanding the significance of Social Democratic ideology is crucial to understanding *how neutrality is particularly embedded* in the Swedish popular opinion. This is not to suggest that neutrality is not embedded in other neutral states. Finnish neutrality and Austrian neutrality, for instance, can claim to be as deeply sedimented in public opinion, but its sources differed, and as a result, the neutral policies of these countries are tied to different meanings and associations. But Sweden differs from other neutrals in that its Social Democratic programme was inherently connected to how it presented itself to the external realm and how internal norms guided Sweden's international behaviour. This is where the significance of domestic policy informs external policy. Domestic politics does matter – Swedish neutrality was as much a point of reference in terms of identity as the Swedish Model was, and became linked to key themes implicit in the SAP ideology, such as conflict resolution and solidarity.

It should be noted, however, that some (particularly non-socialists) take a different approach to Sweden's active neutrality policy. According to Sverker Åström, one of the key shapers of Sweden's post-1945 neutrality policy, Swedish neutrality was simply a response to the international environment, based on 'pragmatic strategic considerations' (Interview, Åström, 13/08/98). It has little to do with ideology or altruism. Such an explanation remains unsatisfying. Despite Åström's view of Swedish neutrality, many Social Democratic leaders, such as Palme, did not define neutrality in such narrow terms. Such a stance also denies any impact of history, political processes and vital underlying social and cultural influences. Åström's explanation remains unconvincing because he concedes that the public maintains a strong attachment to neutrality,[8] that it is 'deeply rooted in the minds for all Swedish citizens'. (Åström, 1989: 17) If neutrality were merely a policy of 'pragmatic strategic considerations', how did it come to be so important to the public? In order to answer this question, the following section examines Sweden's post-war neutrality policy, drawing on the social, historical and political background of Sweden in order to argue that neutrality is not simply the posture adopted by weak and small states, but is part and parcel of what constitutes the internal aspects of the nation-state and nation-state identity.

The beginning of active internationalism: Sweden and the UN

Soon after WWII, the development of the UN re-ignited Sweden's interest in internationalism. In 1946 the Swedish government sought the approval of the *Riksdag* to apply for UN membership. Nonetheless, there existed some wariness toward international cooperation, given Sweden's disappointing experience in the League of Nations. This tension was reflected in Undén's and Hägglöf's stance on the subject of international cooperation and the question of neutrality. Undén, as Foreign Minister in 1945, was prepared to 'abstain from neutrality' in the interests of internationalism, but was wary of great power dominance in the UN, and Sweden being drawn into any bloc (Schlesinger, 1991: 85). Hägglöf, on the other hand, was a realist in the sense that he held little hope for any form of international cooperation in terms of security. Peace could only be achieved if the superpowers were 'held in check' under the UN (and the use of the veto in the Security Council was regarded as a means of doing so). For Hägglöf, neutrality belonged to the 'balance of power' and had no place in international organisations. With the Cold War in its embryonic stage, there was much discussion on whether collective security and cooperation could be successful. Sweden would participate in the UN, but in a government statement in 1948, it was disclaimed that should 'the new security organization [be] undermined by the political formation of blocs or even paralysed in its capacity to take action, our country must be free to choose the path of neutrality'. (Cited in Norman, 1993: 306) The value of the UN was recognised but so too were its limitations (Andrén, 1989: 178; Tingsten, 1959: 477).

By this stage, the tensions between East and West had begun to take tangible form. Any utopian hopes in the post-war era were already beginning to look premature as the Truman Doctrine and the Marshall Plan (and the rejection of it by the East) set the lines of division. Although Undén wanted Sweden to have the option of remaining outside of conflict, this was looking increasingly unlikely. Alliances such as the Brussels Pact (1948), NATO (1949) and the Warsaw Pact (1955) were forming and Soviet pressure on Czechoslovakia and Finland caused uncertainty. The advent of nuclear technology also convinced Undén that Sweden, and indeed the Nordic region, should remain out of the 'line of fire'. This reasoning was combined with the consideration of Sweden's place in the international system as a small state. Although the literature would suggest that Sweden readily accepted its position as a 'peripheral player' on the international scene, this idea is rather off the mark. Sweden accepted Marshall Aid, but recognised that there were both economic *and* political ties to this (Karlsson, 1995: 40).

In response to mounting tensions, Undén, in May 1948 (although talks had commenced in 1947), proposed a Scandinavian defence alliance. For Undén, independent security was a possible alternative should the UN come under bloc division. The plan for a Scandinavian Defence Union signalled on the part of Sweden concern over what shape internationalism would take in the post-war period, and a desire to secure the North of Europe against the possibility of external threats. According to Stern, Undén was wary of the superpowers and was not certain that strict neutrality would be enough to ensure Sweden's security (1991: 87). Sweden's plan for a Scandinavian Defence Union was intended to have neutrality as its core component, to create a 'league of neutrals' (Huldt, 1998: 39). His concern about Denmark and Norway joining NATO was combined with a desire to protect the security of small states but was seen by others (particularly the superpowers) as an attempt to extend neutrality to the Nordic region (Stern, 1991: 87).

Under the context of the emerging global divisions, the superpowers were suspicious of plans for a Scandinavian Defence Union. The Soviet Union was convinced that it would result in a Western alliance, or have some link to it. The concept of neutrality was frowned upon by Marxist–Leninist thought, as the view was that there could be no neutrality in the struggle against capitalism (Geier, 1999: 25). Overall, however, the Soviet Union preferred a neutral Sweden with an active form of neutrality (that would, of course, serve the interests of the Soviet bloc).

The position of the USA, however, was more hostile. According to Karlsson, the US government was against the notion of a neutral defence union forming in Scandinavia. Neutrality, particularly in a time when countries were clearly in one camp or another, signalled an ideological void that could be exploited by either side. The stance of neutrality caused insecurity amongst the superpowers. As such, neutral states came under pressure to clarify their position and assert their allegiances (see Chapter 1). Between 1947 and 1950, the USA also tried to persuade Sweden, Denmark and Norway to join NATO. The American ambassador in Sweden during this time, H. Freeman Matthews, began a strong campaign against Swedish neutrality, claiming that Sweden would find it difficult to remain outside of another world war and that it risked Soviet occupation if it did not join a Western military alliance. Swedish neutrality, according to Matthews, was an attempt to fight 'isolationism [with] isolation' (Karlsson, 1995: 41) and he urged Denmark and Norway not to follow this path. The US National Security Council (NSC) policy 28/1 (1948) stated the US position towards Swedish neutrality:

> To make perfectly clear to Sweden our dissatisfaction with its apparent failure to discriminate in its own mind and its future planning between the West and the Soviet Union; to influence Sweden to abandon this attitude of subjective neutrality and look toward eventual alignment with other Western Powers in such form as may be found collectively acceptable; and at the same time to refrain from forcing Sweden into an attitude which would be unnecessarily provocative toward the Soviet Union. (NSC [1948], 1994: 106)

The same policy sought to place economic pressure on Sweden and hamper plans for a Scandinavian defence union, giving priority to states which cooperated with the US in security (Karlsson, 1995: 40–1; NSC [1948], 1994: 107; SOU, 1994: 101). The US also expressed concern about Sweden's pursuit of trade with the East[9] and instigated a firm policy towards Sweden which included the threat of blocking supplies of essential commodities, to denying Sweden entry into the UN, the World Bank and the International Monetary Fund (IMF). Such a stance affected Sweden because Western Europe and the USA became the main markets for Swedish goods. After the war, Sweden took a multilateral approach with attempts to regain Western European markets and bridge trade with Eastern Europe for Swedish commodities. The US was determined to ensure that Sweden would neither be drawn into the Soviet sphere nor be a victim of Soviet aggression.

The plan for a Scandinavian Defence Union failed, echoing the aborted plans that emerged in the 1930s for a Scandinavian alliance (see Chapter 3).

Norway, the lynchpin in the plan, remained unconvinced that the proposed defence union would receive the much-needed military material from the West (mainly the US) so long as neutrality was part of the SDU's constitution (Sundelius, 1989: 108–12). Norway was not confident in Sweden's ability to provide such material and wanted cooperation with the West; Sweden felt that such cooperation would put Finland in a difficult position with the USSR.[10] In 1948, Iceland, Norway and Denmark joined NATO.

Therefore, from the end of the Second World War until the late 1940s, Swedish neutrality struggled to gain acceptance externally and was subject to pressures from exogenous sources. The beginning of Cold War tensions saw Sweden investigate a number of options for its security, such as membership of the UN, and the possibility of Scandinavian coordination. With the failure of a Scandinavian Defence Union, Sweden returned to an independent neutral posture. Underlying this phase, however, was a deep suspicion by the superpowers (particularly the US) of Sweden's intentions and ability to maintain a firm policy of neutrality that would not show bias nor invite aggression and thereby destabilise the North of Europe. Despite these complications in the post-war era, it was also during this time that a clear doctrinal definition was developed, and this became the platform from which the Social Democratic project of extending solidarity to the external realm was based.

Credible neutrality: Sweden's security doctrine

After the failure of the Scandinavian defence alliance, the *Riksdag*, in 1949, agreed on a distinct formula for Sweden's neutral policy. Swedish neutrality was defined as 'non-participation in military alliances in peacetime aiming at neutrality in war'. The 'Swedish Model' of security involved three key concepts: non-participation in military alliances; an independent and strong defence; and strong public support for neutrality. These three elements amounted to a 'credible' neutrality policy – neutrality would be respected both internally and externally (Goldmann, 1991: 123).

The first element, that of non-alliance, is underscored by what Carlsnaes calls the 'logic of precommitment'. (1993: 12) Swedish neutrality is primarily intended to ensure the maintenance of sovereignty. In this sense, it was interpreted to mean no entanglements in alliances or organisations that can be linked to an alliance in peacetime. This was also a legacy from Sweden's experience of neutrality, particularly during WWII. After the war, Sweden was heavily criticised, especially by the USA, for its 'pendulum policy' (see Chapter 3). Swedish neutrality was seen as biased and not credible by the outside world. Now, Sweden's insistence on developing a credible neutrality policy was paramount. For this reason, Sweden did not join certain organisations, such as the European Coal and Steel Community (ECSC).[11]

The second element, that of independent and strong defence, was intended to support this commitment, and also emerged from Sweden's experiences during wartime. Memories of the violations of Belgian and Norwegian neutrality forced a pragmatic assessment that in order to remain neutral, Sweden must dissuade belligerents from violating its neutrality. Based on an awareness of its geographical position, size, and limited resources, Sweden would have to ensure that it would be able to repel attack. The consequence otherwise would be that neutrality would become meaningless. The core of the security doctrine of Sweden was a desire to remain in peace coupled with a 'total defence' which was not purely military, but civil, economic and psychological (Andrén, 1989: 182; Logue, 1989: 36). The logic behind this was that Sweden wished to create the impression that any aggression towards it would be unprofitable and futile. By developing a strong defence and not permitting the use of Swedish territory by an external power, Sweden would create or contribute towards conditions for peace in Europe. Also, Sweden must be *seen* to be a credible neutral if it wanted to avoid having its neutrality violated in a conflict situation. Therefore, a credible neutrality policy needed to be founded on resources and intention or resolve (Jervas, 1986: 37).

Another aspect to this formulation was the post-war consensus on neutrality policy, which lent it meaning and credibility. Public support for neutrality was regarded as vital, and as such grew to be a part of collective identity in Sweden. As Bukovansky claims, collective identity requires both external recognition (respect by other powers) and internal recognition (public support) (1997: 210). Undén's formulation of foreign policy was to pave a 'third way' between East and West without links to either that could harm or influence Sweden's policy option of neutrality (Norman, 1993: 307). Here Swedish neutrality was overtly defined as a Social Democratic project, linked to SAP ideals about the internal and external realm. It was Undén's intention to combine neutrality with the SAP tradition of reformism, international cooperation based on international law, and the extension of neutrality to the wider international context: an *active* form of neutrality that sought to reach collective solutions within the framework of the UN. Armed neutrality would also ensure the security of the region. Sweden could very easily have located its neutrality in an isolationist category, but by attaching it to Social Democratic goals and policies, neutrality became part of the SAP project. This came to be labelled the 'Undén line' (Noreen, 1989: 254), which was to be followed by future SAP leaders.

The preference for neutrality and participation in international institutions was a way to mark Sweden's independence from European integration and (superpower) global dominance. Undén's 'third way' echoed Sweden's cultural and geographic distance from continental Europe and the establishment of the Swedish Model reinforced Sweden's unique stance. In the post-war years, Sweden did not feel the need or desire to participate in establishing a pan-European organisation. Sweden's neutrality had spared it the experience of two world wars which devastated continental Europe. The purpose of the establishment of the EC was to overcome the nation-state, which was regarded as the primary cause of war and aggression. The main political parties at the time, the SAP, the Liberals and the Farmer's Party, regarded the nation-state as the main forum for political and societal issues, and were not sympathetic to a collective European unit (Malmborg, 1994: 1). The metaphor of the *folkhem* cemented this and encouraged a positive view of what society could achieve within the boundaries of the nation-state.

Thus Spinelli's vision of a federal Europe, and his call for 'the abolition of the division of Europe into national, sovereign states' (Spinelli and Rossi, 1985: 472) hardly sent pulses racing in Sweden. Åström summed up the feeling in Sweden about the European project, claiming that Sweden's non-participation in WWII and geographical and historical separation produced a 'mental barrier'. 'That idea for us at that time, it had no real reality, because we had not been at war. We did not feel in our *guts*, so to speak, the absolute necessity.' (Interview, Åström, 13/08/98) Quite simply, the EC was not a project that suited Swedish interests. Sweden's tension with the EC can be interpreted as the case of two different understandings of international cooperation. As Huldt explains, 'Europe' to most Swedes meant the CSCE (the 'UN' of Europe) rather than the EC (1995: 149). Although Sweden adopted a low profile in the first decade of its UN membership, participation in the UN did not call into question Swedish sovereignty. UN membership was an opportunity to extend Social Democratic understanding of solidarity to the external realm, as well as a chance to reform the international system.

Bolstering this stance was Sweden's deep involvement within its own region. Nordic ideas of progressivism have resulted in a high level of interconnection within the Nordic region. The Nordic Council (of which Sweden has been a member since 1952) created a common labour market and passport union (1954), industrial development fund (1972) and an investment bank (1975) (Logue, 1989: 59). The style of cooperation was interparliamentary and non-binding (Saeter, 1993), and furthermore, participation in the Norden project did not call into question the principle of state sovereignty, as the EC project implicitly did (Malmborg, 1994). Swedish membership of the European Free Trade Association (EFTA) in 1960 was regarded as a way to circumvent membership whilst obtaining some market benefits.

Much more than open borders and free movement amongst Nordic peoples, Nordic cooperation was also strong on the international level. The Nordic countries held similar norms and policies on development cooperation and aid, gender, the environment, and disarmament, for example. This has developed since the 1960s and across a different range of levels (government offices, development cooperation agencies, multilateral cooperation with developing countries).[12] There existed a strong reliance on international law amongst the Nordic states, which was highly valued in terms of mediating conflicts between nations. The Nordic states, according to Joenniemi, did not 'equate security with brute force but understood it more broadly as a reciprocal relationship'. (1990: 205)

It is this basis of common norms and identity that also integrated the Nordic region in the area of security. The Nordic system did not internalise the 'bloc logic' as deeply as other European states. However, regardless of how the Nordic states came to view security in their region, realists preferred to look upon the Nordic states as part of the balance of power (Joenniemi, 1990: 206). In the Cold War environment, the Nordic states created an effective buffer zone, with two neutral states, Sweden (as armed neutral) and Finland (its connection to the USSR), and Denmark, Norway and Iceland in NATO, striking a stable security balance (Huldt, 1988: 318). Denmark and Norway had a specific arrangement with NATO that meant that during peace, nuclear weapons or allied troops were not permitted to use their territory. The Nordic balance preserved the security in the region for both the superpowers and the Scandinavian states. Despite the failure of the Scandinavian defence alliance, the resulting security formula that came to be called the 'Nordic balance' produced an arena of 'low tension' and minimal superpower presence (Wahlbäck, 1992: 3). Domestic stability amongst the Nordic states prevented a sudden change in alliances or balance (Logue, 1989: 54–5). For Deutsch, the Nordic region was a 'pluralistic security community' (1957: 6), or a 'zone of peace'.[13] A shared sense of culture, history and economic links has ultimately strengthened consensus and cooperation in the region. It was a form of cooperation that had its roots in the pan-Scandinavianism of the last century (see Chapter 3) and differed to the project of European integration that was emerging on the continent. Therefore, Sweden's approach to security and the external realm was grounded in a specific doctrine of neutrality, strengthening links in the Nordic region and on the wider scale, active internationalism, which the following section will explore in more detail.

Sweden and the UN: extending solidarity to the international community

Given Sweden's antipathy towards European integration and its reliance on neutrality and Nordic cooperation for security, membership of the UN provided the most appropriate platform to extend Social Democratic solidarity and practise internationalism. Initially, Sweden adopted a 'low profile' in its first period of membership of the Security Council (1957–58). Sweden abstained from voting in the General Assembly in 1951 on China's aggressive actions towards Korea. Concern for Swedish neutrality and wariness towards the ability of the General Assembly (rather than the Security Council) to decide on such matters explains Sweden's early reluctance to speak out. Hammarskjöld practised 'discrete diplomacy' in the case of Pakistan and India over Kashmir, perhaps cautiously because of the strong Cold War overtones of the conflict. Despite adopting a cautious approach during its first term in the UN Security Council, Sweden provided a field hospital during the Korean War in the 1950s and did not support the American-led majority in the General Assembly (Mörth and Sundelius, 1995: 103). Sweden also was part of the UN supervisory team in a mediation capacity after the conflict, notably in the Neutral Nations Supervisory Commission (1953) which was based on the Korean Armistice Agreement. Sweden was beginning to find its feet as a mediator, but also as an actor in the international environment.

It was in its second term on the Security Council (1975–76) that Sweden began to take a more pronounced approach. External circumstances permitted a more active role in this decade – the Security Council had expanded and different dynamics were at work. New issues were entering the agenda – mediation between the North and South, human rights, international development, disarmament and economic issues widened the scope for Sweden to offer its 'good offices'. Sweden developed a working relationship with Third World countries, helping them to formulate their proposals to the UN in terms that would make them easier to adopt.

Sweden's participation in the UN, nonetheless, allowed a different side of its neutrality policy to develop. Rather than merely acting on the sidelines, Sweden saw the UN as a platform to project its particular brand of internationalism which was to give it the label of an 'active neutral'. Although doubts were raised about the stipulations of the UN Charter (Chapter VII, which gives the Security Council the power to prevent, by military means, the violation of international law), Sweden took the opportunity to turn neutrality into a policy which did not denote an isolationist stance when world politics were concerned (Lindström, 1997). The concern was emphasis on solidarity and bringing a Social Democratic element into the operations of the UN. Swedish participation in the UN has tended to revolve around a number of issues, such as mediation and peacekeeping, disarmament, and development. Sweden was also a key critic of superpower behaviour in the UN. The following section explores these issues in broader detail, discussing how Sweden adopted an active neutrality policy that went beyond the general 'good offices' role of neutral states and sought to extend Social Democratic solidarity and norms to the international level.

Mediation and peacekeeping

Mediation, bridge-building and peacekeeping have long been a part of Sweden's international profile, and can be traced back to the initial years of Swedish neutrality under Karl Johan, and Count Folke Bernadotte, who mediated in the Palestinian–Israeli conflict in 1948. Dag Hammarskjöld acted as Secretary-General of the UN between 1956 and 1961 and introduced the concept of preventive diplomacy in the 1950s relating to the Suez crisis and conflict in Lebanon. Palme served as a special representative of the Secretary-General whilst mediating between Iran and Iraq between 1980 and 1984. More recent examples include former Prime Minister Carl Bildt, who served as High Representative in the Bosnia-Herzegovina crisis, Ambassador Rolf Ekéus, who since 1991 has led the UN Special Commission on Iraq, and Ambassador Jan Eliasson, elected as President of the UN General Assembly in 2005.[14]

Within the remit of the UN, Sweden has also been a strong contributor towards peacekeeping in the international arena since the late 1940s. Countries that have seen Swedish peacekeeping contributions include Croatia, Guatemala, Sierra Leone, Congo, Eritrea/Ethiopia, Kuwait and other Middle East countries, East Timor, Cambodia, Kashmir, Korea and Afghanistan. Recently, Sweden has been involved in an even wider range of UN peacekeeping missions (including NATO, KFOR and SFOR operations), and has contributed over 70,000 personnel to UN peacekeeping operations.[15] This involvement in UN activities signals a willingness to participate in active internationalism, and Sweden, along with the Nordic states, places much importance on legitimising the authority of the UN to act in such matters. Participation in peacekeeping missions, for instance, has strong domestic support across the Nordic states (Eknes and Eide, 1994: 4), and is the preferred avenue of the public with regard to international involvement in crises. Sweden and the Nordic countries are also noted for their commitment to peace research. Institutes such as the Stockholm International Peace Research Institute (SIPRI, established in 1964 as Erlander's initiative for a peace research institute to celebrate Sweden's 150 years of peace), the Central Defence and Society Federation, the Peace and Development Research Institute (PADRIGU) at the University of Gothenburg, and the Transnational Foundation for Peace and Future Research (TFF), in Lund have played a prominent part in academia and public interest in Swedish debates. Institutes for studies in international affairs are, in general, established for the purpose of public debate and are widely seen as 'public service institutions'. Sweden's *Utrikespolitiska Institutet* (the Swedish Institute of International Affairs) was established in 1938 as such.[16]

Mediation constitutes a key part of Swedish active neutrality. As a neutral state, Sweden is seen to be impartial and is trusted by both parties to the conflict/dispute. Palme regarded the role of the neutral state as extremely important in the Cold War scenario: 'Our policy of neutrality has given us the possibility and therefore the responsibility for contributing actively to building bridges between East and West.' (1982: 237) For Eliasson, neutrality has given Sweden 'a specific image' within the UN (1989: 8). Here the ideal of Undén, that of a 'third way' in international politics, comes into practice. The wider application relates not merely to Sweden playing the role of 'good offices' as a neutral. Mediation signifies an active concern for stable relations between conflicting states, thereby contributing to the possibility of achieving a sustainable peace. Attached to Sweden's mediation efforts is its adherence to rules and principles of international law, which has long guided its approach to international conflict. Whilst most countries participate in some forms of mediation or peacekeeping, the distinction in the case of Sweden is that there is a strong emphasis on a broader framework to resolve not only the conflict at hand, but the causes of that conflict. Mediation and peacekeeping are part of a wider internationalist framework and neutrality plays a strong foundational role. More importantly, the meanings attached to mediation are a strong part of the domestic political set-up. As discussed in the previous chapter, consensus plays an important role in domestic conflict resolution. On the international stage, Swedish domestic norms inform how it acts within a wider international context. Mediation is by no means an exclusive practice to Sweden – other states also give mediation importance in international affairs and conflict resolution. Yet from the perspective of a neutral state, Sweden's emphasis on mediation as an important tool derives from broader questions of the causes of conflict and peaceful ways of resolving them. Mediation and peacekeeping are components of Sweden's broad approach to the external realm, based on domestic norms.

Disarmament

Nuclear disarmament initiatives have also raised Sweden's profile as an activist state. The advent of nuclear weapons called into question Sweden's neutrality formula, which relied on a credible defence. Swedish defence was based on conventional weapons, and in the event of a nuclear attack, such arsenal would prove useless. The military and conservative circles argued for a Swedish nuclear defence, eschewed by Undén, who preferred to limit nuclear weapons and testing. Possessing a nuclear capability could have also troubled the consensus that neutrality enjoyed (Agrell, 1986: 199). Undén instead pushed for disarmament initiatives in the UN, such as the proposal in 1961 for a 'nuclear-free club' whereby members would cease obtaining nuclear weapons and support the end of nuclear testing.[17] The subsequent Partial Test Ban Treaty (PTBT) mirrored his initial proposals. In 1962, Sweden and seven other alliance-free states (including ten states from the Eastern and Western blocs) formed the UN Eighteen Nation Disarmament Commission (ENDC), working towards a complete ban on testing (although this did not convince other nuclear states to do likewise) (Stern, 1991: 62).

Sweden proposed a comprehensive test ban in 1965 and adopted the Non-Proliferation Treaty (NPT)[18] in 1968. Sweden has also acted as a technical and diplomatic expert in other multilateral negotiations, such as the Disarmament Conference in Geneva, and has been active in the CSCE process since 1972, and as part of the Neutral and Non-Aligned (N+N) Group.

Disarmament was regarded by Sweden as a universal goal for all states, not simply an effort from the superpowers, and encouraged horizontal non-proliferation. For instance, Sweden preferred wider initiatives for a nuclear-free zone that included all states, rather than Kekkonen's 1963 nuclear weapon-free zone proposal which aimed to protect the Nordic countries from the effects of nuclear weapons (Prawitz, 1994). The decision in the 1960s not to develop indigenous nuclear weapons fed back into the international response to the proliferation of nuclear weapons and the subsequent arms race that characterised much of the Cold War tensions. Disarmament for Sweden was tied to wider global issues, such as the position of small states within a bipolar international system.

This was particularly pertinent as events began to turn in the 1970s, when the strategic situation in Northern Europe altered. The Nordic region had been considered a buffer zone, but NATO's dual track decision and the heightening of tensions made Northern Europe an area of interest and competition to the superpowers (Sundelius, 1987: 21). Since the 1940s, the USSR had been building up the Kola Peninsula and the Murmansk area. NATO began referring to Northern Europe as 'NATO's most exposed flank' or a 'new strategic front'. Ballistic missile nuclear submarines (SSBNs) grew in importance in the race to maintain a credible second-strike capacity. The advent of the cruise missile had serious implications for neutral states in particular, who feared that their airspace would be violated. The development of technology was now becoming a major concern. This growing threat was noted in the 1979 and 1985 Swedish Defence Committee Reports which focussed on the increased build-up in the region[19] and the consequences for Nordic security (Huldt, 1988: 319).

The 'new Cold War' raised concerns about the arms race and the position of small states in the face of increasing superpower tensions. Palme in 1974 also linked the importance of small states making clear their position in relation to the superpowers: 'Vi lever i en tid av allt stakare hegemoni för supermakterna. Deras makt är oerhörd... Den utrecklingen kan innebara en fara för de små nationernas självständighet.'[20] For Palme, the processes of détente and peace were linked to Sweden's national security: 'That policy is being formed by the interplay between foreign policy, defence policy, policy for international disarmament, trade policy and aid policy.' (1982: 240) Within Palme's rhetoric is the simple idea of exporting norms – the ideals of solidarity and universalism take on stronger notes in this instance. His stance on nuclear issues also garnered public support. Discussions between Nordic ministers from 1981 on a Nordic nuclear weapons-free zone filtered down to public debate which 'served to strengthen the nuclear weapon-free status of the region'. The promotion of Nordic security in relation to the international community worked to strengthen the non-proliferation regime, heighten confidence in the region and limit and reduce arms (MFA (Finland), 1986: 3). In 1982, the Palme Commission produced a report called *Common Security – a Program for Disarmament*, which looked to deeper international cooperation and examined the concept of a common security for all. It also proposed a 300km-wide nuclear-free corridor in central Europe. The following year, Palme and Carlsson participated in the 'Six-Nation Initiative', which aimed to pressure nuclear states to cease testing and resume negotiations towards disarmament (Stern, 1991: 52). The first joint Nordic meeting to discuss a Nuclear Weapon-Free Zone (NWFZ) met in Copenhagen in 1984, bringing together the Nordic political parties and labour unions to discuss initiatives. Sweden's efforts towards disarmament were based not only upon a neutral's 'good offices', but were linked to global concerns for stable security and were also connected to the position and input of small states in the bipolar era. Sweden's disarmament initiatives were supported domestically and regionally. Disarmament has been pursued with equal vigour in the 1990s, and Sweden has been vocally critical of the former USSR and the USA in terms of their commitment to treaties and conventions.[21]

Overseas development assistance

Sweden has been a frontrunner in its commitment to overseas development assistance (ODA). A consistently generous contributor to the UN budget, Sweden has met (and exceeded) the UN goal of 0.7 per cent of GNP for development assistance since 1974.[22] In the 1980s, Sweden surpassed the 0.7 per cent target and in the 1990s, maintained this level despite its economic recession.[23] In 2003, Sweden allocated 0.81 per cent of GNI (SIDA, 2003). According to the budget bill of 2005 (presented to the *Riksdag* in September 2004), development assistance is set to increase further (0.882 per cent of GNI). In 2006, it is expected to increase to 1 per cent of GNI (MFA, 2005). Sweden has also spearheaded the Millennium Development Goals in pursuit of a 'holistic perspective on global development'. (MFA, 2004: 3)

Nonetheless, aid is not simply about generosity, but the ideals behind humanitarian internationalism. The aid policies of the larger, industrialised countries are generally conditional, and in the realist view, are driven by self-interest. Adopting a universalist approach to ODA, Sweden's humanitarian internationalism is deeply linked to domestic norms and neutrality. For Noël and Thérien (1995: 552), Social Democratic governments tend to give more generously in aid, guided by socialism and universalism: 'welfare principles institutionalized at the domestic level shape the participation of developed countries in the international aid regime'. Pratt's study of humanitarian internationalism identifies three different varieties: liberal internationalism, reform internationalism, and radical internationalism. Liberal internationalism holds that states have an ethical obligation to the poor, but this is mixed with a strong commitment to an open multilateral trading system, with the view that stable economies create a stable international economic order. In the mid-1970s, reform internationalism gained ground, adopting a more critical view of the international economic system. Reform internationalists argued that the international economic system disadvantaged Least Developed Countries (LDCs) and that a fairer distribution of power within international financial, monetary, trade and development institutions was to overcome the inequalities of capitalism – or as Pratt called it, 'Social democracy applied internationally.' Radical internationalism emerged in the late 1970s, marked by hostility to consumerism and the ethics of capitalism. Radical internationalists were also hostile to bilateral aid agencies, and trade institutions such as GATT and the World Bank (Pratt, 1989a: 17–20; see also Stokke, 1989: 12–14).

For Gunnar Myrdal, the 'moral ambivalence' that could be produced by the welfare state bred a style of democracy that fostered nationalism and protectionism. This could only be countered through developing a 'welfare world'. 'By extending this domestic logic into the international sphere, international society could be transformed through peaceful means to benefit its many weaker members.' (Mörth and Sundelius, 1995: 118–22) Sweden sought to make this a part of its domestic and external approach to tackling poverty, inequality, economic and environmental deprivation and gender issues on the global level. Aid has become institutionalised in Sweden, with specialist government agencies such as *Nämnden för internationellt bistånd* (NIB, created in 1961) or the Committee for International Assistance, which established the guidelines for Sweden's aid policy. Aid would be used to further 'social equality' in countries with different political and social systems. The Swedish overseas aid programme signified that welfare and peace were the concern of the nation, but that this was mutually reinforcing and universal (Lawler, 1997: 569; Södersten, 1989: 159). Erlander regarded foreign aid as a 'moral obligation', linked to the idea that 'assistance was an expression of a feeling of moral duty and international solidarity'. (Södersten, 1989: 157) This view is still prevalent in Sweden. In its 1997 report on poverty, the Swedish Ministry of Foreign Affairs maintained that fighting poverty was a global and 'moral' responsibility (MFA, 1997b: 7). This position is also linked to Sweden's aid and development efforts in multilateral organisations, such as the UN. Furthermore, development and aid constitute an extension of the *folkhem* ideal. Instability abroad is understood to affect stability at home, and Sweden's actions internationally feed back into domestic society, as Svante Sandberg, Secretary-General of *Forum Syd* (the Swedish NGO Development Centre) explains: 'We in Sweden can also learn a great deal from their experiences. Their ideas and thoughts can revitalize our society.'[24] The donor–recipient relationship is marked by 'partnerships' rather than vested interests and the root causes of insecurity and poverty are viewed through the broad spectrum of education, standard of living, access to information technology, gender imbalances, and economic barriers (MFA, 1997b: 8).

Sweden's 'reform internationalism' has sought to alter the conditions of international trade which produce poverty and unfair trading practices, and links in with the principles of the universal welfare state domestically. In the 1970s, Sweden was part of the Like-Minded Group,[25] an informal group of western industrialised middle powers which supported the South's demands for a New International Economic Order (NIEO) (Løvbræk, 1990: 32; Pratt, 1989b: 205). From 1974–81, the NIEO dominated North–South relations, and wide-ranging, intensive negotiations were established under the aegis of the United Nations Conference on Trade and Development (UNCTAD). Its key proposals were to create a new international economic institution, the Common Fund, and international agreements on commodity access for Third World producers. The NIEO also pursued the goal of gaining a more substantial role for Third World states in the management of major international development, financial and trade institutions (Pratt, 1989c: 26–7). Another key goal of the Like-Minded Group was to convince states such as the US, the UK, and Germany (at a time when neo-liberal ideology dominated) to grant concessions and become involved in international economic reform. By the early 1980s, it became clear that these states would not accept such reforms, and the NIEO lost its momentum (Pratt, 1989b: 206).

Despite the perceived failures of the NIEO, the principles behind it and Sweden's involvement reveal much about the normative aspects of Sweden's international outlook. The Like-Minded Group was largely associated with reform internationalism, the view that 'the global distribution of income and resources is unjust and morally indefensible' (Södersten, 1989: 155). Reform internationalism contained a strong Social Democratic link, 'an extension to these issues of attitudes and values that had first developed in regard to class tensions in domestic politics'. (Løvbræk, 1990: 33) The idea of the state in modern social democratic theory places importance on state interventionism in economic matters 'because there can be no equivalent to state ownership at the international level'. (Løvbræk, 1990: 35) For Stokke (1989: 9), aid policy is 'part of a cluster of domestic policies', and like foreign policy, reflects domestic traditions and norms. Reform internationalism linked with the Swedish domestic welfare model. Just as the SAP programme concentrated on reforming the injustices inherent within capitalist society, this is also viewed on a global scale as an imperative, not only to peace and stability, but also to wider notions of solidarity. The picture of Sweden's active internationalist profile so far reveals that Social Democratic norms and values have been pursued on the international level. Neutrality was the platform from which to perform these 'good offices', but Sweden was actively internationalist on the basis of its domestic norms. In the next section I examine Sweden's more critical approach to international phenomena.

Criticism in the UN

Reform internationalism as enacted by Sweden also had a directly political accent. Stemming from the Hammarskjöld era of the 1960s, Sweden firmly understood its place in the UN as a small state confronting larger powers in solidarity with weaker states (for instance, Sweden voted with developing countries on key issues in the UN General Assembly). Sweden used its neutrality and its UN membership to act as the 'moral conscience' on international political issues. Solidarity with the underprivileged 'is regarded as a moral responsibility' for Swedes (Kärre and Svensson, 1989: 231). Åström cements this ideal when he states: 'The right to express solidarity with this cultural community, to criticize phenomena that are contrary to our democratic principles and to basic human rights, to demand respect for international law and for the interests of the small nations, is one right we refuse to relinquish.' (1987: 11–12)

Solidarity with small and weak states became vociferous during the 1970s, particularly under Palme.[26] His main objectives under the UN were promotion of international law, human rights, conflict resolution and disarmament. Palme carried on the Undén line of criticising South Africa's apartheid system and was also critical of human rights abuses in Eastern Europe. Perhaps the most noted example is Sweden's criticism of America during the Vietnam War (what Palme called 'an abnegation of human dignity') (1972: 8). Stockholm made clear its difficulties with the USA's South East Asia policy and the US view of Sweden was that of a 'troublemaker', aligned to the peace movement.[27] For America, connection with the peace movement at this time denoted difficulties with US policy. The US ambassador was returned to the US for talks on the declining relations between the two countries over the Vietnam issue. Sweden heightened diplomatic ranking to Cuba, and named an ambassador to communist China, giving him credit as an envoy to North Vietnam. When Palme became Prime Minister, the US threatened to stop Swedish exports to the US if Sweden gave aid to North Vietnam, and to close the Gothenburg consulate (the oldest, established in 1797 by Washington). Nixon refused to see Palme ('that Swedish asshole', as he so eloquently put it) on his visit to Washington (Tunander, 1999: 193). Relations worsened in 1972 when Palme drew similarities between the US bombing of Vietnam and Nazi crimes (Zakheim, 1998: 122). In 1973, diplomatic links were severed. The relationship between the US and Sweden was downgraded, but not totally destroyed.

Here Sweden again overturned the accepted notion of the remit of the neutral state. Expected to provide 'good offices' and adopt an isolationist international stance, Sweden rejected this characterisation of neutrality by using neutrality to pursue its norms and values internationally. The combination of mediation, peacekeeping, development assistance, and disarmament plus criticism of great powers set Sweden out as a state that punched above its weight.

Conclusion: a Swedish interpretation of neutrality

Sweden's post-war credible neutrality doctrine was an important example of an active neutral state breaking out of the assumed role of neutrals. Sweden's extensive good offices, however, was not merely part of a different interpretation of neutrality. It was also inspired by the desire to extend solidarity and Social Democratic principles and values to the international realm. Palme, in particular, 'shattered the monopoly enjoyed by the traditional view of neutrality as isolationist, objective, and remote, instilling a dauntless "moral duty" for partiality into Swedish neutrality'. (Stern, 1991: 89)

The crucial point of the development of Swedish politics and society up until this time has been the resilience of a number of key themes: consensus, universalism, equality and solidarity. In the post-war era, neutrality became more doctrinal and consistent compared to the swings and uncertainties that characterised Swedish neutrality in its formative years. This provided a legacy that marked Sweden out as a different sort of political actor on the global stage. These actions that go beyond the mere confines of isolationism show that neutrality can be 'what states make of it'. In the following chapter, I examine how the basis of Swedish neutrality, Social Democratic ideology, came to be challenged in the 1970s, which laid the foundations for a serious questioning of neutrality in the 1990s.

NOTES

1 Heclo and Madsen's use of the term 'hegemony' differs to the Gramscian use of the term, which implies *coercion* and consent. On this, see Cox, 1993.
2 Padgett and Paterson describe corporatism as the 'interlocking network of relations between the apparatus of government and the state... and organized interests'. (1991: 190) Esping-Andersen considers Swedish corporatism to be based on ideals such as fraternity, where status and identity in the modern capitalist age formed around occupational groupings that attempted to maintain traditional status distinctions (Esping-Andersen, 1991: 60–1 and especially Chapter 3).

Sweden's post-war neutrality doctrine

3   Rustow, in his 1955 publication *Politics of Compromise*, claims that the combination of political stability and sustained economic growth was the result of the social confrontation between SAP (and its affiliates) and the non-socialist parties (Lane, 1991b: 222).
4   Named after the estate where the meetings took place. Tilton writes that these forums did not include scope for groups to participate in decision-making. This forum continued until 1964. By this stage it was increasingly criticised by the left and the right, namely for bypassing parliament and ignoring the opposition (1991: 184; Heclo and Madsen, 1987: 24).
5   Olsen writes that Wigforss originally proposed a 'public investment fund' as early as 1928, but this plan was not put into practice as the SAP endured electoral setbacks in the 1920s (1992: 33).
6   Lewin notes that the Liberals only accepted the SAP's expansionist economic policy during times of economic depression, and still held to the view that the state should not intervene in business during normal economic periods (1988: 159–62; see also Chapter 3).
7   From *The Alva Myrdal Report – Towards Equality*, cited in Dickson, 1972: 24.
8   Åström separates official policy from public perception. During the course of my interview with Åström, he agreed that neutrality was connected with Social Democratic hegemony, but there is a difference between labelling neutrality idealistic (with which he strongly disagrees) and the public regarding it in sentimental or psychological terms.
9   Further measures, such as the US Export Control Act of 1949 and the establishment in 1950 of CoCom (the Coordinating Committee for Multilateral Export Controls) likewise hindered trade with the East for Sweden. CoCom was a multilateral organisation designed to coordinate export measures and stop the export of commodities to the Soviet bloc that could be used as weaponry (Dörfer, 1987: 191–2; Karlsson, 1995: 38–49; NSC [1952], 1994: 114–5). In 1962, the Export Control Act was widened to include not only military but economic items. During the détente era, the Act was amended (Export Administration Act, 1969), lifting many previous restrictions. George Kennan, in his memoirs, remarked on how the Department of State wanted to 'jam' the NATO alliance closer to the Soviet borders (Andrén, 1987: 144; Schlesinger, 1991: 86).
10 Under the TFCMA (Noreen, 1989: 253; Wendt, 1981: 27–9). This sentiment was also noted amongst my interviewees: Interviews, Bohlin, 13/08/98; Hall, 11/08/98; Hugemark, 26/08/98; Nilsson, 13/08/98; and Tobisson, 18/08/98.
11 The ECSC's treaty stipulations would not permit Sweden to be a 'free agent' under Article III of the Treaty of Rome, which established the Common Commercial Policy (CCP). This article gave the EC the power to conclude commercial agreements with non-member states (Title IX (Ex-Title VII), European Union, 1997a). Sweden also threatened to pull out of the Council of Europe when it proposed to link the European Defence Community (see Chapter 5) to NATO (Schlesinger, 1991: 87; Wahlbäck, 1992: 3).
12 The Nordic Council of Ministers was established in 1971 (its predecessor was the Committee of Nordic Ministers which was established in 1959). Since 1994, cooperation has been more informal at all levels, but cooperation between regional divisions is still regular, mainly in the area of bilateral and multilateral development cooperation (Østergaard, 1997: 2).
13 On this, see Archer, 1990, 1996; Brundtland, 1971; Möttölä, 1988; Mouritzen, 1995; Wahlbäck, 1994; Wendt, 1981.

14 On bilateral mediation, Herbert Ribbing (1966–8) mediated over the dispute between Thailand and Cambodia; Olof Rydbeck mediated in the Western Sahara; Emil Sandström, Supreme Court Justice, headed the UN Special Committee on Palestine. His partition plan was later adopted by the General Assembly in 1947. Gunnar Jarring acted as a mediator between Pakistan and India over Kashmir in 1957 and the Middle East in 1967–91. Hammarskjöld also played a vital role in establishing the UN Emergency Force, the UN Forces in the Gaza Strip and at Sharm el Sheikh in the 1950s (Eliasson, 1989: 8–10).

15 Sweden has been involved in the UN Truce Supervision Organisation in Palestine (supervising the armistice of 1948); the UN Emergency Force I in Gaza and the Sinai (1956–67); UNEF II in the Sinai (1973–1979/80); and UNIFIL, the UN Interim Force in Lebanon (1978). Swedish participation has also included election monitoring for EU missions in the Balkans and for the OSCE in Georgia.

16 Across Scandinavia, peace research and peace institutions have been active for many years. In 1959, the Norwegian Parliament established the Norwegian Institute of International Affairs (NUPI); Oslo's Peace Research Institute Oslo (PRIO) was established in the same year. Finland's Tampere Peace Research Institute (TAPRI) was founded by the Finnish parliament in 1969, and Finland also boasts the Finnish Institute of International Affairs (UPI). Copenhagen's Peace Research Institute (COPRI) was established in 1985 and the Danish Institute of International Affairs (DUPI) was formed in 1995. Nordic universities also house a number of peace-oriented departments and research offshoots, such as the Department of Peace and Conflict Research at the University of Uppsala (Sweden), the Chair in Empirical Conflict Research, at the University of Lund, the Department of Political Science, University of Helsinki, and the Department of Political Science, University of Århus. Others include the Life and Peace Institute (LPI) (Sweden), the Centre for Conflict Management (Norway), the Institute for Alternative Development Research (IADR), Oslo, the Norwegian Nobel Institute, the International People's College (established in 1921 in Denmark), the Peace 2000 Institute (Iceland), and the World Futures Federation (Finland).

17 Denmark and Norway, although without nuclear capability, were reluctant to adhere to a treaty which might have infringed upon their NATO commitments (i.e., should Denmark or Norway need to receive nuclear weapons in an emergency) (Herman, 1998: 518–9).

18 The NPT was a disappointing result for those states working towards disarmament. It relied on superpower initiative, and France, China, India, Israel and South Africa did not sign it. Alva Myrdal (Sweden's first minister for disarmament and Sweden's chief negotiator at the ENDC between 1962 and 1974) suggested that major powers should renounce a first strike, negotiate a comprehensive test ban treaty, and pledge to never attack a non-nuclear state (Herman, 1998: 514–9).

19 In the early 1980s, Sweden experienced a number of Russian submarine incursions in Swedish territorial waters. Recent reports also reveal that in the 1960s, US nuclear submarines violated Swedish territorial waters (*Radio Sweden*, 27/12/02).

20 'We exist in a time of increasingly marked hegemony for the superpowers. Their power is unprecedented ... this development can only mean a danger for the independence of the small nations.' (Cited in Kleberg, 1977: 61, my translation)

21 In the 1990s, Sweden supported the CTBT, START II, and used international law (citing the International Court of Justice Advisory Opinion regarding the legality of the threat or use of nuclear weapons) to pursue non-proliferation. Sweden was also critical of the US and Russia for not ratifying the Chemical Weapons Convention of 1996, sup-

ported the Biological and Toxic Weapons Convention, and pursued an active policy on anti-personnel landmines (Sweden destroyed its stockpile of anti-personnel landmines in 2001, two years ahead of the deadline of the 1999 Mine Ban Treaty). Sweden also ratified the Amended Protocol II of the Convention on Certain Conventional Weapons.

22 Kärre and Svensson note that Sweden's ODA between 1964 and 1973 ranged between 0.21 per cent to 0.56 per cent of GNP (1989: 232), but had large contributions to multilateral institutions, normally channelled through UN agencies.

23 The Netherlands reached over 0.9 per cent during this time. In 1980, Sweden allocated 0.78 per cent of GNP; in 1983, 0.84 per cent; in 1985, 0.86 per cent; and in 1986, 0.85 per cent to ODA (Pratt, 1989a: 8). In 1995/6, Sweden gave 0.83 per cent, and in 1997, 0.7 per cent (MFA/SIDA, 1997: 5). The estimated budget framework for international development cooperation in 1999 was 0.705 per cent of GNP. This was a reduction on the 1998 allocations due to changes in GNP forecasting (MFA, 1999). This figure increased to 0.73 per cent in 2000, 0.73 per cent in 2001, and 0.74 per cent in 2002 (MFA, 2000: 19). To date, Sweden has contributed US$750m to UN programmes, funds and specialised agencies and in 2000, Sweden's share of the UN budget amounted to 1.084 per cent (Permanent Mission of Sweden to the UN, http://www.un.int/sweden/).

24 See MFA/SIDA (1997: 5) and in particular, the MFA's 1997 report *Preventing Violent Conflict* which adopts a post-modern approach to conflict and insecurity, seeking a long-term vision of UN, regional and sub-regional proposals for conflict resolution.

25 By the end of 1984, the Like-Minded Group had twelve members: Australia, Austria, Belgium, Canada, Denmark, Finland, France, Ireland, Italy, the Netherlands, Sweden and Norway. It linked together liberals, conservatives, Christians, and socialists (see Løvbræk, 1990).

26 To the criticism of the Moderate Party, the SAP in the 1970s supported colonial liberation movements such as the Movement for the Popular Liberation of Angola (MPLA) in Angola; the African Party for the Independence of Guinea and Cape Verde (PAIGC) in Guinea-Bissau; the African National Congress (ANC); the South West Africa People's Organisation (SWAPO) in Namibia, and Frelimo in Mozambique (Bjereld, 1995a: 23).

27 Palme, not yet Prime Minister, participated in a demonstration against the Vietnam War in 1968, alongside the North Vietnamese ambassador to Moscow. Palme's actions were defended by Erlander. British philosopher Bertrand Russell wanted to set up a mock 'war crimes trial' in Stockholm to examine America's role in the war in 1968 (Tunander, 1999). Sweden also accepted US deserters from the armed forces.

5

The crisis in Swedish Social Democracy: paving the path for a new identity

As the previous chapters have shown, the link between domestic and foreign policy is a deeply intricate one. Swedish neutrality has been part of the development of the modern Swedish state, and in the postwar period, neutrality was an explicitly Social Democratic project, tied to the ideals of the Swedish Model and the metaphorical imagery of the *folkhem* and solidarity, creating a specific set of collective meanings which were then exported to the external realm. Not all neutral states practise their neutrality in the same manner, and Sweden's active internationalism and comprehension of the more normative aspects to such an international stance give weight to the reasoning that not all neutral states are isolationist or seek to preserve a limited set of self-interests.

During the 1970s, Sweden reached the apex of its active internationalism with Palme's distinctive stance on global issues, but domestically the Swedish Model and SAP hegemony faced a series of challenges. The 'golden era' that defined Sweden domestically in the 1950s and 1960s came under attack. This chapter explores the so-called decline of the Swedish Model and SAP hegemony in order to establish that as domestic phenomena changed, this would prepare the ground for a gradual reconsideration of Sweden's neutrality policy in the 1990s, which is the focus of the following chapter. During this period of decline, neutrality remained unchanged and unquestioned. This was still the era of the Cold War and neutrality was still widely seen to be the appropriate stance for Sweden. Yet the questioning of embedded Social Democratic norms and institutions would lead to the eventual questioning of neutrality, which is a strong part of the SAP ideology and value system. This rupture or 'crisis' of Social Democracy contained strong implications for the reconsideration of neutrality policy. Although its sources and causes are disputed amongst academics, as discussed below, the essential point is that the challenge to Social Democratic hegemony opened up a number of new ways of thinking about the state and the international for Sweden. Here the constructivist idea about shifting identities is captured, as the change in domestic values and identities in turn reshaped Sweden's external profile and opened the path for a different turn in Swedish neutrality. Whilst contemporary observers identify a decisive shift in Swedish domestic politics with the Bildt government of the early 1990s, in this chapter, I argue that the domestic shift has its roots in developments from the early 1970s. This chapter, covering the period of the 1970s to the late 1980s, explores another stage of development in Swedish identity and ideology. It begins by examining the decline of the Swedish Model debate, and then moves on to discuss attempts to steer Sweden in an alternative ideological direction with regard to the welfare state and the market. It then analyses the impact of ideological challenges of the 1970s – ranging from the offensive of Swedish business interests and the rise of Swedish think-tanks, which tried to bring a different debate about the market into public discourse, to the SAP's 'Third Way' programme of the 1980s and the debate about EC membership.

The end of the golden era? Domestic and external challenges to the Swedish Model

To summarise developments, the Swedish Model experienced its 'golden age' in the 1950s and 1960s. The Rehn-Meidner model planned to achieve high employment, wage equality and a wide-ranging welfare state. The ideology of Social Democracy inspired consensual political and industrial relations, a universal welfare state system and a programme of policy renewal and reform. The strong connection between the SAP and the LO was vital for constructing economic developments and policy. The metaphor of the *folkhem* held together a particular mental image of the Swedish nation as a family, where the state took care of its members. Solidarity was a key theme in Social Democratic discourse and policy, both domestically and externally. This created a particular set of expectations with regard to the state and the market, and the relationship between society and the individual. By the end of the 1950s, and arguably until recently, a basic welfare state was accepted even by conservative elements in society[1] (Einhorn and Logue, 1989: 14–15). The institutions established by the SAP became sedimented in Swedish politics and society.

However, a combination of exogenous and endogenous factors combined to test the resilience of the institutions of the Swedish Model. The first domestic challenge can be located with the rise of the new left in the late 1960s. Objections to economic and technological change in industry (particularly with regard to Fordist production relations) prompted concern over the impact on the welfare state and increasing inequality, which, despite plans to address this, revealed the 'limits of the distributive model' (Weiss, 1998). Ruth

(1984: 61) claims that during this period, 'the limits-to-growth message mingled with a newborn nostalgia, especially among urban youth, for the simpler rural values of Swedish life a generation earlier'. In 1966, the LO Congress examined the consequences of technological change in the workplace; the stress and pace of work, instability in employment and loss of influence. Palme (1972: 17) (Minister for Transport and Communication at the time) recognised that 'technical developments are moving progressively faster, but human conditions change slowly'. Reports of the 1960s, such as the 1965 *Commission on Low Income* and the 1968 *Level of Living* survey, revealed that despite the growth of the welfare state, inequality was rising (Olsen, 1992: 16; Ruth, 1984: 89–90). The discontent of the 'red wave' reflected labour unrest and a critical view of capitalism and the capitalist state. This group was also joined by the 'green wave' which employed the *lagom* idea in its concern over nuclear power, and was critical of Western affluence and the business community (Zetterberg, 1984).

The Lindbeck[2] Commission claimed that these new groups challenged the established power groups in Swedish society, and represented a legitimacy crisis in the Swedish Model (Lindbeck et al., 1994: 17). For Ruth, labour unrest could be regarded as a reaction to the elite and paternalistic nature of the notion of the 'common good' (Ruth, 1984). Yet there were other aspects to this turn. After the SAP split from the Agrarians in the 1950s, the former spent much energy in the following decade trying to capture the white-collar vote (and gaining 40 per cent of it). Subsequently, this meant a shift in SAP policy as it sought to accommodate its new electorate. The *folkhem* was developed and expanded to include white-collar workers and working women,[3] adopting 'more family members as well as their re-identification'. (Jenson and Mahon, 1993: 85) Although at the time blue-collar workers accepted the changed circumstances as part of a wider form of equality between the two sectors (in keeping with the SAP's aim of universalising society), the blue-collar membership of SAP was gradually being displaced. Cooperation became 'issue oriented' and it became more difficult to obtain working parliamentary majorities in the *Riksdag* to handle social issues. The SAP's courting of the white-collar vote also affected labour–union relations. White-collar unions gained strength,[4] triggering a confrontation between unions in the coming decade (discussed below).

The discontent resulted in a spate of strikes in the late 1960s to early 1970s. The Kiruna miners' strike (1969–70) started a broader wave of wildcat strikes involving some 25,000 workers, such as at the Volvo plant in Gothenburg, and then a second major wave in 1974 (Ryner, 2002: 127). The Kiruna strike was important in the sense of challenging Social Democracy to continue to improve the conditions of working life. When the workers in the state-owned iron mines in northern Lapland stopped work for three months in protest against working conditions, the Social Democrats shifted their emphasis from the material aspects of progress to the quality of work. Workers rebelled against their limited power in the work environment and felt that the spirit of the 1938 Saltsjöbaden Accord was being defeated, particularly as wage and benefit levels lagged behind those of white-collar workers (Ryner, 2002: 128).

The response to these challenges saw the SAP work towards *economic democracy* in the workplace, highlighted in the party's *Programme for an Active Industrial Policy* in 1968 which adopted a statist approach and planning. The LO weighed in with its proposals, such as *Industrial Democracy* (1971) which focussed on co-determination in management and worker representation on company boards. A series of legislative measures came into force in the 1970s[5] but the three most important initiatives were greater state intervention in industrial restructuring; the restriction of managerial power and greater input by workers in decision-making (co-determination law); and collective share ownership of industry through the wage earner funds (Wilks, 1996: 96).

The most important piece of legislation was the 1976 *Act on Co-Determination at Work* (*Act on Employee Participation in Decision-Making*) which allowed unions to be consulted at various levels within the company before major changes were enforced that would affect employees. Management had to negotiate with labour for joint rights in all matters regarding hiring and firing, organisation of work, and key decisions which affected the workplace, which matters were previously at the discretion of business.[6] The intended aim echoed Wigforss's slogan from the 1920s ('democracy cannot stop at the factory gates') but this conflicted with the established pattern of allowing business to have the right to manage: 'Once the LO and SAF began to take Wigforss's slogan seriously, business began to question the value of a set of institutions whose distributions were becoming more and more asymmetric, from business's point of view.' (Blyth, 2002: 204) However, the wage earner funds proposal entailed a 20 per cent profits tax on corporations, and was regarded as 'a frontal assault on the sanctity of private ownership'. While the Co-Determination proposals had the support of the bourgeois parties, and were eventually accepted by the employers' confederations, the wage earner funds sought to 'socialize the economy'. The revenue raised from the funds would be used by the unions to buy out business interests, part of the SAP's vision to democratise ownership of Swedish industry, and the LO vision of 'capitalism without capitalists' (Blyth, 2001: 9; Henrekson and Jakobsson, 2003). Legislation such as the Co-Determination Act and the wage earner funds initiative were perceived by business interests to be a step too far, a break with the corporatism that had underpinned Swedish labour relations since Saltsjöbaden.

The evidence of disquiet over the Swedish Model and domestic changes came in 1976, when Thorbjorn Fälldin's bourgeois coalition broke the SAP's long rule that had been in place since 1932.[7] The coalition came to power largely on the issue of nuclear energy. Although disavowing the wage earner funds, the Fälldin government actually nationalised some major industries and allowed government debt to grow (Blyth, 2002: 208). Nonetheless, the Fälldin government attempted to introduce modest measures to control spending. It planned to reduce part-time pension benefits from 65 to 50 per cent of income; increased use of fees for some types of medical care and housing; and transferred to local authorities responsibility for social services, similar to the social-liberal Danish model, that had less state management of the economy (Andersson and Mjøset, 1987: 232–4). There were also plans for reducing sick pay from 90 to 80 per cent of income. These proposals were due to come into force in 1983 but were never implemented because the Social Democratic Party returned to government in 1982 (discussed later in this chapter) (Swank, 1999: 106).

The shift to a bourgeois government in Sweden coincided with domestic developments and the broader international turn towards neoliberalism. The global recession of the late 1970s–early 1980s is largely cited as the source of the Swedish Model's decline. The Organisation of Petroleum Exporting Countries' (OPEC) pricing strategy and the oil crises of 1973 and 1979 combined with a decrease in growth and productivity in the world economy. The price of raw materials skyrocketed and interest rates increased (Sperling and Kirchner, 1998: 221–2). There was increased competition from Japan and the newly industrialised countries in traditional Swedish export industries (steel, textiles, shipping), and the breakdown of the Bretton-Woods international monetary system affected Sweden's economy. The figures for Sweden during this period reveal the extent of the economic downturn. In the 1960s, Sweden's average annual growth was 4.5 per cent. In the 1970s, this dropped to 1.7 per cent (Olsen, 1992: 8). Average annual productivity growth fell (1961–73: 3.2 per cent; 1973–79: 0.6 per cent), industrial production declined by 6.2 per cent between 1974 and 1982, and the balance of payments due to terms of trade decreased. In 1982, foreign debt was 21.7 per cent of GDP (compared with net credit in 1974 of 5.3 per cent GDP) (Ryner, 1994: 386–7). It appeared that the Swedish Model, which was intended to secure Sweden economically, could not be immune to external economic influences.

Domestically, Sweden experienced a 'blue wave', a reaction against the legislative measures of the 1970s that was regarded by private industry as an attempt to socialise the economy. In neighbouring Norway and Denmark, the rise of conservativism was evident as 'Progressive' political parties began to take ground. From the post-war period until the 1970s, most economists advocated Keynesianism, but neo-classical theory then came to the fore

(Nordlund, 2000: 32). In the United States, a 'back-to-market' ideology guided economic policy in the 1980s, with Reagan reducing the influence of the state in the economy and restricting eligibility criteria for welfare. Developments in the labour market and the strong neoliberal flavour of economic policies diluted the welfare state in the USA and benefits were provided by the employer, not the government. Similarly, in the UK, Thatcher's efforts to restore market discipline were coupled with a strong anti-welfare state proclivity. Furthermore, under Thatcherism, the market was the *only* solution – summed up neatly in the catchphrase *'there is no alternative'*. France pursued a state-led response to the economic crisis until the mid-1980s, when austerity programmes replaced the expansionist and redistributive policies of the socialist government. In West Germany, the Christian Democratic Government looked to deregulation and the curbing of labour union power. This, combined with developments in the international economy and the growing currency of neoliberal views, encouraged business interests to take on a more active and more offensive stance in Swedish politics and political debate.

Since Swedish capitalism has been highly export-oriented, it is perhaps unsurprising analysts have been drawn to the globalisation explanation. Wilks (1996: 89–90) claims that globalisation and capitalist restructuring has contributed to this breakdown and it is important to understand the Swedish Model as 'a system related to a period of history bound by two major crises of global capitalism'. By this he means that the first crisis of the 1930s helped establish the class compromise as a national response to the threat of global economic uncertainty. The second crisis, from 1973 onwards, is an undoing of the class compromise as a result of globalisation processes and a shift of power to capital. The breakdown of the corporatist model did not only affect Sweden. As Stråth claims, on the European front, there were attempts to save the tripartite bargaining model by projecting it onto the European level. The European Trade Union Confederation (ETUC) formed in 1973 (stemming from the Confederation of the European National Federations of Industry in the 1950s) in an attempt to foster a new type of 'Euro-corporatism'.[8] In 1977, the MacDougall Report to the European Commission recommended a European Keynesian strategy to cope with the economic crisis, but this plan was rejected in favour of the OECD McCracken Report of the same year. This report pursued a more liberal approach based on the market. For Stråth, this signalled a 'new language' which rejected the assumption that national governments could successfully manage the economy (2000c: 402–4; see also Weiss, 1998: 91). The fact that Swedish firms increasingly relocated overseas meant that they escaped domestic labour unions, claims Pestoff, and contributed to the breakdown of centralised collective bargaining (2001: 2). In order to understand the domestic shift in the broader context of the neoliberal age, the following section explores how business interests mobilised not only to promote their interests, but to challenge the prevailing Social Democratic discourse and institutions that had structured Swedish politics and society. Most explanations about the decline of the Swedish Model look to the international context and the rise of neoliberalism; indeed, this is an important feature of the debate about change in the Swedish Model, but how this change materialised domestically is the crucial question.

Mobilisation of business interests in the 1970s: SAF gains teeth

Domestically in Sweden, the 1970s signalled change not simply in economic realities but also in ideas. Challenges from the left and the right combined in different ways to restructure the Swedish Model, but the serious battle of ideas came from the business community, who sought not only to protect their interests as corporatism fractured, but to explicitly revise accepted norms and ideas that the Swedish Model were built on in the first place. In order to effect change, capitalist interests needed to convince the wider public that the Swedish Model was no longer feasible.

In the wake of the wage earner funds proposal, business interests adopted a more aggressive stance in light of the perceived attacks on business' right to manage and the threat to private ownership that the funds implied. The rise of the 'blue wave' in Sweden was a reaction against profits squeeze, higher employer contributions to finance social consumption, and the juridification of the labour process. Smaller entrepreneurs, who increasingly made up the ranks of the SAF, had been disinclined towards tripartite accommodation (Ryner, 2002: 143). For Swedish business interests, the signing of the Co-Determination Act signalled the end of tripartite corporatism, and that the SAP had allowed the LO so much leverage meant the terms of the Saltsjöbaden agreement were effectively over. The SAF planned to stage a lockout of over 200,000 workers, which was avoided at the last moment (Blyth, 2001: 11) but this was an early signal of employer activism which was to reach new levels in the 1980s.

In the early twentieth century, business interests were not an effective power bloc in Sweden. Organisations such as the SI and the Director's Club[9] regarded socialist planning as contrary to economic rationalism, but fell into accommodation with the SAP after it won the 1936 elections. However, the core view that planning was synonymous with 'totalitarianism' or had echoes from the Soviet bloc remained. During the 1940s, the SAF and the Director's Club drew on Cold War discourse to discourage support for such a strategy (Ryner, 2002: 72 and 98) and set up organisations such as NÄSO (Joint Committee for Private Commerce and Industry) and enlivened the Swedish Free Enterprise Foundation (NÄFO) to ward off the 'stagnationist' threat of the

SAP's economic policies (Blyth, 2002: 214). In the post-war era, Swedish capitalists exercised power through labour and influenced policy through organisations such as the SI and the SAF, and the Association of Bankers (*Bankföreningen*). The strategy of the SAF was limited to providing 'technical advice' to public commissions, tripartite boards and research institutions (creating and funding institutions such as the SNS and IUI), rather than through mobilising national leadership. However, these groups took on a more activist profile when the prerogatives of production and ownership were challenged in the 1970s. The powerful Wallenberg sphere, which previously took a subdued role in the SAF, began to adopt a leadership role. The appointment of Curt Nicolin in 1976 as SAF chairman saw the organisation adopt a non-compliant stance, and Ryner claims that from this point onwards, SAF ideology and policy became 'hyperliberal', advocating market relations principles in all aspects of social life. At this juncture, the SAF sought to intervene in public debate (Ryner, 2002: 69–71) and actively worked to shift public opinion. The effect of this was to 'normalise' the debate on the market within the setting of the Swedish Model, and business foundations offered large amounts of funding to university departments 'to investigate questions of particular interest to business, such as profitability and inflation'. (Ryner, 2002: 176)

These two issues, profitability and inflation, were the key intellectual tools that business and capital employed in order to counter the arguments against the wage earner funds and other initiatives that were considered to deprive these groups of their control over industry. But, as Blyth (2002: 222) contends, 'brute' economic facts were not enough to dislodge decades of embedded institutions and practices. Ideas were needed to 'play the crucial role in determining both how to break such an order and how to shape the institutions that replace it'. Towards this end, the SAF sought to influence the public and, according to Sture Eskilsson (former director of the Swedish Employers' Confederation), ensured that in debates, an 'ideology of business could emerge'. (Ryner, 2002: 144) In the 1978 campaign against the wage earner funds, 'Free Enterprise Days' were organised in municipalities, and students and journalists were targeted by the SAF to get the pro-market message across. This was achieved by providing material for distribution to schools, supporting student and youth organisations, using evening papers to espouse their views and setting up regional SAF offices. Campaigning returned to the approach adopted in the 1940s, reviving the discourse of totalitarianism and central planning, and campaign material portrayed the SAP in black and white compared to the use of colour imagery to show the merits of free enterprise. The message was 'free markets and free choice' (*Marknad och Mångfald*) (Ryner, 2002: 146).

Seeking to contribute to the intellectual debate, business put money into creating and managing an ideological apparatus, including publishing houses, advertising agencies, and conducting seminars and workshops. The *Studieförbundet Näringsliv och Samhälle* (Centre for Business and Policy Studies, or SNS), founded in 1948, published material and organised conferences and seminars, with its central concerns being economic policy and growth, labour market issues and the welfare state. Timbro, established in 1978, published 22 books between 1978 and 1982 (half of these on free market and the wage earner funds issue[10]). Ratio, the publishing house, dealt with theoretical and philosophical debates (Ryner, 2002: 170–1). The SAF had the resources to pursue this strategy – from the late 1970s until 1987, SAF dues doubled, providing over 1.5 billion dollars (in 1987 prices). The SAF used these resources primarily to fund conflict resolution and for propaganda, and employed much of its funds against the wage earner initiative. To gauge its financial strength, Blyth points out that during the 1982 election, the five main political parties spent a combined total of 69 million kronor on campaigning. The SAF spent between 55 and 60 million kronor on the wage earner funds issue *alone* (Blyth, 2002: 210). After 1979, the SAF also sponsored many young politicians, such as Carl Bildt, and the sponsorship of these politicians in turn radicalised the Moderate Party further towards a neoliberal stance (Ryner, 2002: 125).

As Ryner and Blyth rightly claim, the influence and rise of business interests has altered the balance of power in Swedish politics and society. Their aim was to set Sweden on a new path economically, which would challenge mainstream SAP thinking about the nature of the economy and government intervention. This effort to redirect thinking away from the welfare state and the Swedish Model cohered with international developments, lending strength to the arguments for a rational approach to the economy that favoured market forces rather than government intervention. More than an alternative economic view, these moves to influence policy and opinion had deeper implications which were to impact upon Swedish society. For instance, the discourse of Swedish public debate moved significantly towards neoliberalism, as Boréus's study of language and rhetoric in the major newspapers *Dagens Nyheter* and *Svenska Dagbladet* explains.[11] The SAF's campaigns used language that shifted from collective forms of identification to individual referents, for instance its slogan *satsa på dig själv* (count on yourself) (Jenson and Mahon, 1993: 95). Van Ekecratz (1997: 408) also notes in his study of the Swedish media that in the late 1980s, there was less mention of 'we' (which had traditionally been the case) and more mention of 'I' in journalistic discourse, reflecting 'the general ideological changes that have taken place since the 1950s, from a collectivist to an individualistic political culture'. Zetterberg's metaphor of the 'Old Sven and Ugly Swede' (1982) captures this shift as well. The 'Old Sven' is the class-oriented voter who trusts in the collective purpose of the labour movement. The 'ugly Swede' is the self-interested individual who is less likely to vote along class lines, is suspicious of authority and bureaucracy, and is associated with material security and affluence (Heclo and Madsen, 1987: 39–40). The image of the *folkhem* was changing under new pressures, becoming less salient in line with social and political change. For Ringmar (1996: 84), metaphors have 'life cycles' and new metaphors emerge that 'point to new connections between things, events and phenomena, and identify new possibilities that need to be explored'. Whilst the Fälldin government survived only briefly,[12] the ideas of Swedish business interests were to have a lasting impact, not only in terms of providing an alternative debate, but influencing the SAP upon their return to power in 1982.

The SAP and the Third Way in the 1980s

When the SAP returned to power in 1982, the Swedish Model was entering a crucial stage. The developments from the 1970s pointed to a dramatic shift in the economic and ideological landscape in Sweden and internationally. Between 1973 and 1982, Sweden's economic performance was below the OECD average. Unemployment was low, and mass unemployment did not hit the Scandinavian states until the early 1980s compared with Western Europe (Notermans, 2000: 23). The active labour market policy shifted those made unemployed to more profitable firms. However, in the mid-1960s, manufacturing jobs declined dramatically (from 35 per cent to 20 per cent of the workforce). The solution was the public sector, which absorbed these workers. The growth of the public sector in Sweden during this period was massive. Between 1973 and 1980, public sector employment rose by 38.7 per cent, double the EC rate of 16 per cent. Between 1960 and 1992, employment fell by around 300,000 in the private sector, but rose by over 900,000 in the public sector (Henrekson et al., 1996: 266; Weiss, 1998: 88–95). The expansion of the public sector was regarded by business interests as producing a cumbersome welfare state and placing pressure on public spending.

Underlying the economic problems were the increasing tensions and breakdown of corporatism. Opposition to the wage earner funds issue had been pursued with almost religious zeal by business interests (Blyth, 1998: 9; Ruth, 1984: 57). In 1983, the SAF organised a rally against the wage earner funds in Stockholm, bussing in around 100,000 supporters. The mobilisation of business against the funds manifested itself in union relations, when *Metall* defected from central bargaining in the same year. The SAF added to this by doing the same prior to the annual SAF/LO negotiations. As centralised bargaining was a key feature of Social Democratic success, its breakdown had deep political ramifications (Notermans, 2000: 34). There was an increased attempt by some unions (such as the Association of Engineering Industries

(*Verkstadsföreningen*, VF)) to bargain independently. Despite pleas for solidarity by Kjell-Olof Feldt (Minister of Finance, 1982–90), the motto of the SAP of 'sharing the burden collectively' was not generally accepted. Individualism overtook the traditional response of solidarity and inter-union rivalry began to mark union relations (Agell and Lommerud, 1993: 577).

Economic growth and industrial production declined as wage costs and domestic inflation rose, and to finance the deficit, Sweden borrowed from abroad. The first oil shock meant a rise in energy prices and the international recession of 1974–5 put further pressures on Sweden's finances, as exports fell and recovery was slow internationally. In 1977, the Krona was devalued twice and the second OPEC crisis in the late 1970s produced further economic problems (Henrekson et al., 1996: 254–5).

The solution of the Social Democrats was to embark on a programme of deregulation and wage restraint. This was to have long-term consequences for its support base and the nature of the Swedish Model. The SAP's Third Way[13] programme (*tredje vägens politik*) involved a 16 per cent devaluation of the Krona to assist Swedish exports (Meidner, 1992: 164). The aim of the government was to increase net exports, fixed investment and profitability. Savings were encouraged over consumption. The devaluation plus restrictive domestic fiscal and monetary policies were aimed at halting the protection of stagnant parts of the economy and raising productivity. The budget would be balanced by lower spending and increased revenue (Ryner, 1994: 392–3).

The 'third road' adopted by the Social Democrats in 1982 was a large step away from the traditional approach of the Rehn-Meidner model of macroeconomic policy. Stemming from the 1981 'crisis report' of Feldt and Ingvar Carlsson, it edged away from the wage earner funds[14] to promote public investment in favour of greater austerity measures and budget cuts to stabilise the economy and stimulate private investment (Blyth, 2002: 220). The LO rejected the SAP's policy of devaluation, adhering to classic Keynesianism, claiming that domestic demand must be stimulated through increased public investment in infrastructure and transport. The Social Democrats' plans for devaluation and wage restraint were decided without consulting the LO. Although its congress approved the economic plan in 1981 and acknowledged the need for wage restraint, the LO held the firm view that wage restraint needed to be linked to collective profit sharing (wage earner funds) (Pontusson, 1992: 310 and 314). The SAP regarded the Third Way programme as an alternative to the neoliberal doctrines of Reagan and Thatcher. Feldt linked this new economic approach to the continued Social Democratic plan for ideological and economic development:

> If we, with our large public sector, high level of taxation, and strong union movement, can succeed in restoring economic stability as well as creating a dynamic and growing economy, then the demands for systemic change [in a neoliberal

direction] will have been dealt a severe blow. If we succeed, then we have shown that solidaristic, collectivist solutions not only are superior to individualist solutions with regards to social justice – they also create better conditions for economic growth ... For the future of Social Democracy, the success of this strategy can prove itself to be as important as the political breakthrough in the 1930s. (Cited in Ryner, 1994: 389)

Nonetheless, the prescriptions of the Third Way were not Keynesian in nature, with its emphasis on cutbacks in public expenditure and reducing the budget deficit by stimulating the private sector (Notermans, 2000: 27). The strategy of the Third Way was considered successful between 1983 and 1985. During this period, export demand rose and industrial production expanded. Unemployment remained low and the budget deficit was reduced. But signs of 'malfunction' soon set in (Henrekson et al., 1996: 255).

In 1985, the government deregulated the capital and foreign exchange markets, and would no longer borrow from abroad. Swedish interest rates rose and a 'norms based' monetary policy was employed to contain inflation by exerting market discipline on the wage bargaining process (Ryner, 2002: 149). The 'November Revolution' of 1985 saw ceilings abolished on bank lending (which would later lead to the government bailing out banks that could not reclaim loans) and cuts to the welfare state (in pensions, health, and parental insurance) (Svensson, 2002: 211). Strikes became an increasing feature of industrial relations in Sweden: in 1986, unions representing 60 per cent of the workforce were on strike footing (Ryner, 1994: 404). The relationship between the SAP and its support base had been damaged.

Rydén and Bergström note that there has been a decline in class-related voting since the 1970s, where they cite 10 per cent of the electorate switching their loyalties based on single-issue politics[15] (1982: 4). Blue-collar support for the SAP declined, as reflected in the number of unions affiliated with the LO, which decreased from 46 in 1945 to 24 in 1980[16] (Heclo and Madsen, 1987: 19). In 1956, blue-collar workers made up 53 per cent and salaried workers 26 per cent of the electorate. By 1988, the former had fallen to 41 per cent and the latter had risen to 47 per cent. The growth of white-collar unions – public sector employees in union federations rose from 26 per cent to 44 per cent between 1960 and 1988 (Weiss, 1998: 99) – meant the SAP sought their support and it weakened the LO's authority in wage-bargaining and wage solidarity. SAP policies in 1989–91 alienated the blue-collar vote and did not attract enough white-collar support. The changing landscape of trade unionism in Sweden was partially a reflection of events in other Western industrialised countries at the time. In the UK, trade union power decreased along with a drop in the number of full-time jobs (Coates, 2000: 92). Thus the changes in SAP policy were more significant in terms of the breakdown of the relationship with the labour movement which according to Andrew Martin, 'provided the language' for the Swedish Model (Tilton, 1991: 189). The shift in collective bargaining undermined the cohesion of the labour movement.

The changes in the international economy go some way to explaining Sweden's economic crisis during this period, but closer examination of the overall ideological climate lends a different twist to the tale. With the rise of business interests and their efforts to change public thinking about the state and the market in the 1970s, it is important to view the crisis of the Swedish Model in terms of domestic efforts to rethink the Swedish Model and the welfare state. Neo-classical economic arguments against the welfare state and government intervention in the economy became the norm, entering into the discourse and ideology of Swedish political and social life. One of the more interesting arguments about the decline of the Swedish Model offered by Ryner and Blyth is that the SAP itself became convinced by the arguments of the business community and was persuaded that the welfare state could not be maintained in a climate of global economic change. Ryner claims that by the mid-1980s, neoliberal norms permeated state-management circles, particularly in the Ministry of Finance and the central banks, which explains the change in policy in 1985 (2002: 116). Sweden was not alone in this revision, as a new wave of bureaucrats and policy makers became prominent in other states such as Denmark, Australia and New Zealand (Schwartz, 1994). The SAP had bought into the 'sclerosis thesis', that Sweden must adjust to the demands of the global market and respond to technological change (a position championed by Calmfors and Lindbeck, and more recently, Ryner argues, by Esping-Andersen (Ryner, 2004: 102)). Blyth is in agreement with this viewpoint, and argues that Lindbeck's defection from the SAP and his shift towards monetarism inspired a new generation of economists to follow suit: 'Once Lindbeck shifted, the discipline as a whole shifted, and what was once unthinkable was fast on its way to becoming a new orthodoxy.' Pro-market ideas began to gain ground in official government reports and Swedish economic journals, such as *Ekonomisk Debatt*. Similarly, Timbro sough to influence the press, particularly *Dagens Nyheter* and *Dagens Industrie* (Blyth, 2002: 215–18), and neoliberal think-tanks formed links with similar organisations in other countries (Schwartz, 1994: 539), shoring up the pro-market message. Korpi also examined this trend in relation to the arguments pushed by Swedish economists close to decision-making that the welfare state and Sweden's economic growth placed Sweden behind other European countries – or the 'eurosclerosis diagnosis' (Korpi, 1996). Economists wedded to the view that Sweden's growth was in decline had an important influence on policy and spreading this particular message, despite the argument being open to serious debate.[17] Timbro itself coined the phrase 'suedo sclerosis' for the Swedish case, to denote the idea that the Swedish welfare state was too large to manage over time and will become a burden (Blyth, 2002: 218).

Despite the ideological battle that was being waged, other commentators note that these challenges had a somewhat limited effect on notions about the welfare state and its sustainability in the neoliberal climate (Svensson and Öberg, 2002). Swank points to the extension of social rights by the Social Democrats between 1982 and 1991, citing an increase in child allowance and unemployment benefits (but acknowledging cuts to public health care spending in 1983) (1999: 107). Nordlund's study of welfare state dismantling in the Nordic countries during the 1980s claims that on the whole, cuts to social protection were minimal (2000). Where other countries experienced drastic austerity measures and cuts to welfare programmes during the 1970s and 1980s, Sweden in comparison had a strong welfare state. The difference with Sweden, as Pfaller et al. (1994: 275–9) note, is that the 'institutional tracks' were laid that allowed the country to cope with economic crisis: 'To get the same results as Sweden, other countries would have had to come up with major institutional innovations at a time when it was not at all propitious to them. The Swedish welfare state responded under stress in a different way because some time in its history it had acquired an institutional disposition to do so.' (Pfaller et al., 1994: 286–7)

By 1988, the Social Democrats had managed to turn the economy around. Between 1983 and 1988, the economy grew at the rate of 2.7 per cent per annum and the balance-of-trade deficit was transformed into a surplus. The improved business climate in the private sector compensated for the closure of uncompetitive businesses. Yet the economic recovery was short-lived. There was still a struggle with inflation (which was at 8.8 per cent in 1989 (de Vylder, 1996)). Since 1985 Sweden's GNP average growth was 2 per cent per annum, below the OECD average of 3.5 per cent (Stein, 1991). Sweden's national debt for the fiscal year 1984/5 reached 64.6 per cent of GDP.[18] Despite this, it was clear that Social Democratic ideology had undergone some kind of revision. The Swedish Model had gone from being 'exceptional' to 'problematic'.

In 1987, Feldt pushed for a series of tax cuts, and foreign exchange controls were removed. In 1990, the SAP's main concern was containing inflation, and due to a series of developments such as the rise in oil prices as a result of Iraq's invasion of Kuwait, the effect on the Swedish economy was a rise in interest rates, with a deficit that was expanding. Tax cuts meant less revenue as government expenditure rose (Blyth, 2002: 225–6). Furthermore, efforts to revive collective bargaining in 1990 fell to pieces. When Feldt invited the SAF, the LO and TCO to Haga Castle for discussions, there were expectations that this would result in a second Saltsjöbaden (*Saltshöbadsavtal*). The SAF rejected the talks, with its chairman Ulf Laurin declaring that 'after a long illness, the Swedish Model is dead'. (Blyth, 2002: 227; Pestoff, 2001: 3 and 8)

The SAF's withdrawal from collective bargaining gave it the confidence to push more aggressively its vision of privatisation and Laurin announced that 'the centre of gravity in SAF's work has shifted to idea and opinion formation. It is ideas that change the world ... SAF is the driving force in changing the system.' (Cited in Blyth, 2002: 228) Convinced by arguments that the Swedish Model and the welfare state could no longer be sustained in their original form, arguments developed towards a consideration of deeper integration into the global economy. This clearly meant membership of the EC.

European integration reconsidered

For Sweden, the dominant lesson of the 1970s was that the Swedish Model and the welfare state were no longer immune to external economic phenomena. Alternative strategies and ideologies entered the discourse of Swedish society, pushed largely by business interests who no longer felt that corporatism was a workable solution. Efforts to turn around public opinion were not limited to a questioning of the welfare state and the Swedish Model alone. Business interests began to push for Swedish membership of the EC, and this signalled another major shift ideologically. Sweden had previously discounted the idea of EC membership. Under Social Democratic hegemony, the EC was regarded as incompatible both economically and politically. Economically, the golden age of the Swedish Model excluded consideration of joining the European economic recovery project that emerged in the early 1950s. The commitment to a credible neutrality policy also excluded membership on a political level.

Neutrality had kept Sweden out of both world wars, and there was little identification with plans to reconcile French and German animosities through a union of states, federal or otherwise. Sweden was active internationally and maintained a successful welfare state without the need for supranational cooperation. The debate about EC membership was framed in terms of how such a project would reduce or dissolve the distinctive features of 'self', or 'Swedishness'. In the 1960s, the left in Sweden was strongly opposed to EC membership, or 'the dangers of the *four C's*: capitalism, conservativism, colonialism, and catholicism'. (Åström, 1989: 33, original emphasis) European integration was cased in the rhetoric of reconstruction and harmonisation with the expectation that economic ties would prevent war. Nationalism was targeted as the source of aggression between nations. As Neumann points out, Sweden already had a similar arrangement with its Nordic neighbours that was not premised on the basis of a 'war threat' but on common values and culture (1999). The arrangement was also informal, which was seen to preserve the individual identities of the total. Nordic cooperation did not touch on questions of security and defence policy. The EC, on the other hand, had entertained plans since the 1950s to form a common foreign and defence policy. Under the Pleven Plan, a European army was proposed, with an institutional structure that would have transformed the common market into a political body. Despite the failure of the European Defence Community (EDC) in 1954, attempts were made throughout the following decades to revive the idea of political union that contained a common security element (European Parliament, 1983: 15).

On the economic front, however, in the 1980s the EC began to work towards realising its goal of a single internal market. The acceleration of the EC's economic ambitions presented a potential solution to Sweden's economic problems. Sweden sought a looser set of economic arrangements with the EC. In 1961, Sweden applied for associate membership of the EC in order to strengthen economic ties. The main concern of Sweden was to separate economic cooperation from political cooperation. In the same year, Tage Erlander, at the congress of the Swedish Metal Workers' Union, rejected the proposal for full Swedish membership in the EEC on the grounds that it was incompatible with neutrality. For Erlander, the EC was construed as the 'economic arm' of NATO, since the original six member states were tied to the Atlantic Alliance (Erlander [1961], 1997: 78). In 1967, after Britain's second attempt to join the Community, Sweden reconsidered engaging in a 'flexible' relationship with the EC, so long as its neutrality policy remained intact. Sweden began to regard cooperation with the EC in a more positive light. This was the time when supranationalism and federalism were on the decline in the EC. De Gaulle had successfully increased the importance of the nation-state within the EC, most notably by rejecting the British application (twice) for EC membership and staging the French walkout of the Council of Ministers in 1966 in the so-called Luxembourg Crisis, which resulted in the use of the veto in the Council of Ministers in areas of 'vital national interest'. Within this political climate, Sweden regarded closer economic cooperation to be in its interest and felt that its sovereignty could be protected. In 1972, Sweden signed a Free Trade Agreement with the EC for a reduction of tariffs on industrial commodities. Sweden's engineering, steels and electronic industries were becoming more integrated into EC markets (Miles, 1994: 7–8). Cooperation extended in the same decade to cover joint technical and research ventures.

Ross notes that the SAP pursued economic relations with the EC quite vigorously in the 1980s. The non-socialist government of 1976 did little to prioritise EC relations (Fälldin was actually critical of the EC and against Sweden forming deeper ties with the organisation). Palme was the first Swedish Prime Minister to visit the EC Commission in 1983, and he actively sought relations with the EC based on 'solidarity' (Ross, 1991: 120). Full membership was not a possibility; the monetary policy of the EC's Werner Report and the political implications of the Davignon Report of the 1970s (which aimed to strengthen political cooperation) would have compromised Sweden's credible neutrality policy. In 1987, a policy paper was submitted to the *Riksdag* that recommended Sweden prepare to join the EC, and that border controls between Sweden and the EC be removed in order to protect firms and consumers from isolation in the Single European Market (Miles, 1994: 10). Negotiations resulted in rejection of membership, but there was agreement that Sweden should seek further economic relations with the EC.

In 1984, the EC Luxembourg conference extended the provisions of EFTA to include increased cooperation, joint ministerial meetings annually, and a goal to create a European Economic Space/European Economic Area (EES/EEA). This would allow EFTA states to access the 1992 single internal market of the EC without EC membership. The enlargement of the EC in the 1980s to include the southern European states of Spain, Portugal and Greece meant that economically, it would be harder to compete with the EC and have access to the wider EC market. The EC Commission's White Paper of 1985 on the single European market was set to invigorate the Community economically, after its period of stagnation in the 1970s. The impact of the global economic crisis of this period made the EC realise that it would have to be increasingly competitive against markets such as the USA and Japan (Hakovirta, 1987a: 266). The Single European Act (SEA) (1986) also solidified the position of the EC as it concerned institutional reform and placed the development of the single internal market at the centrepiece of its rationale. The Delors Presidency's proposal for a broader European Economic Area (EEA) proved an insufficient solution.[19]

By the time it became apparent that the possibility of actual EC membership might be the only solution around the question of increased economic cooperation with the expanding Community, the situation in the EC had changed. After the Delors Presidency, neoliberalism came to characterise the policies of the EC. The influence of Thatcher, multinationals, industrial associations, financial interests, pressure groups (such as the Bruges Group), think-tanks and pro-business strands in Germany's Christian Democratic Union–Christian Social Union (CDU–CSU) and Free Democratic Party (FDP) and other liberal/conservative continental European parties became key forces within the European Commission (Hooghe and Marks, 1997: 9). At the same time, in Sweden, business interests began placing pressure on the government to apply for membership and open up the Swedish market. The effects of the global market came to play an important role in the lead up to the general election of 1991. Investment abroad increased from 10 per cent in 1985 to 28 per cent in 1989. As foreign investment grew in the 1980s, the balance-of-payments deteriorated and in the late 1980s profits were reinvested abroad rather than domestically. With the Single European Market, direct investment in the EC rose as well (between 1986 and 1990, the increase was from 24 per cent to 73 per cent). Legislation controlling foreign exchange and currency were abolished in 1989, resulting in a rapid outflow of Krona. A shift of power to capital was clearly occurring (Wilks, 1996: 103–8). Now it was a matter of not if but when Sweden would join the EC as a member state.

Debating the decline

The debate about the decline of the Swedish Model has been academically divisive, open to different accounts about the beginning and nature of its 'end'. Critics of the Swedish Model have been anticipating its demise for some time, and the global recession of the 1970s provided the proof that Sweden's economy was out of step with the rest of Europe, if not the global economic community. The debate is broadly divided between those who support the 'dismantling hypothesis' and the 'durability hypothesis' (Nordlund, 2000). Supporters of the 'dismantling hypothesis' such as Lindbeck and Pontusson argue that the dynamics of international competition and industrial change are incompatible with the idea of full employment and the universal welfare state. Korpi, Rydén and Bergström, Tilton, and until recently, Esping-Andersen make the case that although transformation has occurred, the welfare state remained strong and in the case of the Swedish Model, dismantling the welfare state was not such an easy task because Social Democratic norms and apparatus had 'remained intact'. (Tilton, 1991: v) Furthermore, others question the potency of the globalisation/international economy argument. According to Weiss, the new 'logic of capitalism', which meant that economic globalisation limited what national governments could do, is an incomplete explanation. The capital mobility argument contains no causal logic – Swedish corporations already had overseas subsidiaries (1998: 85; see also Lindbom, 2001, for the case of Sweden in the 1990s). Companies such as Aga, SKF, Electrolux, Ericsson, Nobel, and Swedish Match were all founded between 1860 and 1914 but were 'internationalised' within a decade (Hampden-Turner and Trompenaars, 1994: 258). The shift of Swedish capital to overseas markets and bases was already well under way at the time of the global recession – the Swedish economy was always primarily export-oriented. Between 1970 and 1976, approximately 3,700 mergers occurred (Thompson and Sederblad, 1994: 240).

The debate about the decline of the Swedish Model is important in terms of ideas and the formation of new ideas and understandings about established institutions and issues of identity. Swedish politics and society are symptomatic of the underlying tensions in the political discourses that constitute Swedish political culture. For a long time, societal consensus has been the 'glue' that has held the political and social fabric of society together. The challenges to this are not merely an expression of a change in discourse, but imply something deeper. Jenson and Mahon succinctly point out that in the past, debates have occurred within Swedish politics, but within the 'hegemonic language' of Social Democracy that has become the norm: 'Representative organizations – parties, unions, social movements, for example – which once successfully promoted a particular set of identities, become vulnerable as the "naturalness" of their capacity to represent comes into question.' (Jenson and Mahon, 1993: 76–9) In the 1985 election, the conservatives challenged the Social Democratic hegemony, calling for a 'change of system' to allow more private initiative and less reliance on the state. Despite the Social Democrats' warnings that the neoliberals wanted to dismantle the welfare state, the opposition received an electoral boost, whereas the level of support for the Social Democrats remained the same (Heclo and Madsen, 1987: 30).

What is important to the debate about the Swedish Model is that the phenomena of globalisation, in combination with the rise of neoliberal ideology, produced a different set of expectations and discourse. For the critics of the Swedish Model, Sweden was out of step with the rest of Europe, if not the world. This neoliberal discourse was captured by the right (particularly in the 1990s by Bildt's claim that neoliberal solutions were the 'only' viable option for Sweden) and employed to re-direct Sweden's interests and ideology towards greater liberalisation and the erosion of years of Social Democratic policies. Policy change, particularly in a country such as Sweden where the SAP ideology was so entrenched, does not occur overnight. In order to change the policies, there had to be a decisive shift in the ideology that guided these SAP policies.

Conclusion: reconstructing SAP ideology?

The decline of the Swedish Model in the 1970s and 1980s came to signify something deeper than an economic crisis. For Pred (2000: 12), 'Whatever the word *crisis* may be taken to mean, from the early 1990s onwards, it became a commonplace part of everyday Swedish, a term as much used in popular face-to-face discourse as in the discourses of the political arena to the mass media.' The perceived unravelling of the Model coincided with a questioning of many long-held Social Democratic 'truths': there was widespread dissatisfaction with the SAP and the relationship between the SAP and the LO altered during this period. Business interests began to mobilise and attempted to change not only policy, but public opinion towards a more rationalist, neo-classical economic position. In the late 1970s, the rise of neoliberal economic theories and their application in Europe and the USA brought a particular resonance to conservative or liberal arguments that the welfare state was no longer sustainable. This all worked to dislodge embedded Social Democratic institutions such as the universal welfare state and the accepted role of government intervention in the economy. As Rosamond (1999: 666) contends, the phenomenon of globalisation and the neoliberal ideology that claimed to accompany it was presented as a structural fact, a necessary set of policy preferences for economic openness and budgetary constraint.

Why should this matter to those interested in Swedish neutrality? The shift in the Swedish Model is vital because it indicated that on the domestic front, a change in ideology was in process. The ideological premise of the SAP had changed, and with it its institutions that formed the basis of not only the Swedish Model but neutrality. When these were confronted and questioned in the mid-1970s, a new set of values and a new rationalism appeared as an alternative. The language of neoliberalism gained dominance in the series of challenges to the SAP model of society, over and above the rise of new leftist groups, and a different image or idea of the *folkhem* was being manufactured during the 1980s by conservative elements (Tilton, 1991: 127). Yet this shift in ideology which underlined both the Swedish Model and Swedish neutrality was still difficult to shake. Forty years of SAP norms and practices create a specific idea of Sweden's place domestically and internationally. Such constructions of self are highly ingrained, yet identity is not a static phenomenon. The process of developing an affinity with a new set of (European) identities has been another chapter in Sweden's process of self-identity. The rhetoric of globalisation and neoliberalism opened up a particular path towards this identity, yet Sweden's relationship with the EC would be contested on grounds that had been established by Social Democratic hegemony. In the following chapter, I assess how the question of Europe became a pivotal debate in Sweden and how it led to a process of questioning Sweden's neutrality.

NOTES

1   Tilton, however, concedes that the conservatives back social measures only because it is electorally unpopular for them not to do so (1991: 7–8).
2   Led by former SAP economist Assar Lindbeck, who resigned from the SAP over the wage earner funds issue.
3   It was not until 1971 that the radical socialist-feminist Group 8 was able to influence the discourse of the SAP and highlight remaining problems regarding gender which were overshadowed by the effort to achieve consensus and class solidarity. Issues such as sex discrimination, child care and parental insurance had been sidelined in the past within the discourse of the *folkhem* (Jenson and Mahon, 1993: 89–91).
4   The Central Organisation of Salaried Employees (*Tjänstemmännens Central Organisation*, or TCO), was established in the 1920s to represent white-collar workers. The TCO contains three main groups: the TCO-K (local government employees), the TCO-S (state employees) and the PTK (*Privattjänstmänna-kartellen*) representing salaried employees in private industry. SACO (*Sveriges Akademikers Centralorganisation*) caters for high-level white-collar workers with university education. In 1974 SACO merged with the National Federation of Civil Servants (SR) to form SACO-SR, consisting of professional and high-level civil servants and Swedish military officers (Heclo and Madsen, 1987: 19–20).

5   See Tilton, 1991: 223–4. The *Act on Employee Representation on Boards* (1973, 1976) allowed workers to elect two representatives to the boards of private corporations and public agencies. Unions were given more say in the work environment with additional legislative measures, such as the *Job Security Act* (1974), which regulated hiring and firing of employees. In the same year, the *Promotion of Employment Act*, required employers to inform unions before dismissals or layoffs occurred. The right to free time and paid time for union activities was recognised in the *Shop Stewards Act* (1974), and the *Work Environment Act* (1974, 1978), addressed the physical and psychological impact of the work environment on employees, giving workers the power to enforce safety measures in the workplace.

6   Despite the Co-Determination law, it soon became apparent that workers would have little input into decision-making, as management generally did not follow their suggestions. Workers became frustrated by their lack of input, as Olsen pointed out: 'According to some cynical Swedish workers, this only means that employers now have to honk the horn before they run over the workers.' (1992: 28)

7   Centre Party leader Fälldin formed a coalition government with the Conservatives and the Liberals. He was seen as the opposite of the intellectual and sophisticated Palme, with views on decentralisation and individual values.

8   Sweden was not included in this initiative, but according to Stråth, the Swedish metal workers' trade union was interested in these discussions. Personal correspondence, with Stråth, 20/11/01.

9   Otherwise known as the 'manager's club', this group of five CEOs of the largest export companies formed in 1933 with the goal of returning bourgeois parties to power (see Ryner, 2002; and Anderson and Snow, 2003: 97).

10 Publications by Timbro have on the whole been critical of the Swedish Model and the welfare state. An autonomous centre, The Centre for Welfare Reform, was created within Timbro in 1999. Timbro is part of the Swedish Free Enterprise Foundation (SFN). In March 2003, the Confederation of Swedish Enterprise and *Näringslivet Fond* founded SFN.

11 In the late 1970s there has been a shift to the right in public debate on a range of issues. Between 1969 and 1977, there existed positive attitudes towards the public sector, but after 1980, other ideas entered the debate, such as privatisation, and views that the welfare state was too costly. Debate on development assistance and the third world became increasingly problematised in line with neoliberal arguments about aid policy. See Boréus, 1997.

12 The Fälldin government collapsed over disagreements about nuclear energy with its coalition partners. Fälldin called a national referendum on the issue of nuclear power, which his coalition partners did not support, and resigned in 1978. The government was briefly lead by Liberal Ola Ullsten until 1982 (Heclo and Madsen, 1987: 41–2).

13 Jenson and Mahon define the 'Third Way' as a rejection of Thatcherite concern with inflation and also the reflationary programmes of the Mitterrand Government in its first two years in power (1993: 92–3). Meidner used the term 'third way' with reference to the wage earner funds, to signal a different economic system from both capitalism and state-controlled communism. 'The middle way' more aptly described the extension of the welfare state, although Feldt used the term 'third' way in a different sense, that of the distinction between 'excessive expansion and the excessive reduction in demand'. (1992: 17–18)

14 By 1983, a 'symbolic and watered-down' version of the wage earner funds was permitted to survive (to be eventually abandoned under Bildt in 1991) (Ryner, 2002: 143).

15 Lane, however, notes this phenomenon occurring in other Nordic countries as well, where the new middle class were less attached to traditional political parties and ideals. Norway in the last twenty years has experienced electoral disruption, with less party identification and increasing voter volatility. Denmark experienced electoral upheaval in 1973, combined with a welfare state backlash. In Finland, disinterest has come to characterise the electoral system (1993: 316–17).

16 Weiss contends that between 1960 and 1988, the LO's constituency fell from 75 per cent to 58 per cent of organised labour (1998: 99).

17 On this, see Korpi (1996) who outlines the astonishing misuse of data and figures by such interests to make the case that Sweden was comparably worse off than its European neighbours in terms of economic growth. Korpi also suggests in this article that the lack of objectivity extends to a form of censorship as alternative views (such as his own) were excluded from debate. Comparatively, see Hay and Watson (2003) on the British case and how the 'crude business school globalisation' thesis has dominated political discourse within New Labour.

18 Sweden experienced high national debt figures during most of the 1980s. National debt at the end of the fiscal year (as a per cent of GDP) was as follows: 1981/2: 50.3 per cent; 1982/3: 57.2 per cent; 1983/4: 60.5 per cent; 1984/5, 64.6 per cent; 1985/6: 62.9 per cent; 1986/7: 59.5 per cent, and 1987/8: 53.6 per cent (SAF, 2000: 60).

19 The EEA was to create common decision-making institutions, requiring EFTA states to adopt a large amount of the EC's *acquis communautaire* (the body of rules, legislation and regulations that constitute the EC) without actually having much impact in decision-making.

6

A new Swedish identity? Bildt, Europe and neutrality in the post-Cold War era

THE DEVELOPMENTS of the 1970s and 1980s set in train a series of challenges to the Social Democratic institutions and norms established since the post-war period. During these two decades, core assumptions about the Swedish Model were questioned, and the ability of the SAP to realise the utopian society it envisaged ideologically was not only hampered but in some respects abandoned in the light of new logic and new ideas. Despite these challenges to the Swedish Model, Swedish neutrality was not questioned during these times. But the direction of debate and discourse indicated that neutrality would no longer enjoy its privileged position as part of SAP hegemony and power. In 1991, the SAP lost office to Carl Bildt's Moderate coalition. Bildt did much to cement the changing views about the economy and the state which were espoused by business interests during the 1970s and 1980s. Courting ideas of European integration and the dramatic shift in the international system which was to occur with the end of the Cold War, meant neutrality was also open to review. Whereas in the 1980s, neutrality was on safe ground, despite the ideological affront to Social Democracy, in the 1990s under Bildt, neutrality came to be seen as part of the previous order and not apt for the new international setting.

This chapter begins by examining the post-Cold War security environment and the debate surrounding the question of the role of the neutral state. Bipolarity had given way to a new discourse that focused on the inadequacies of the nation-state and cooperation between countries in order to resolve common security risks. Indeed, the whole definition of security underwent revision, and for many realists, neutrality's *raison d'être* had disappeared. At the same time, the EC was transforming into the EU, and its long-term goal of political union began to take shape in its plans to develop its CFSP. The impact of the demise of bipolarity and the acceleration of plans for European integration prompted debate in neutral and non-neutral countries as to the purpose and relevance of neutrality. The chapter then moves on to discuss the Bildt coalition government of 1991–94. Under Bildt, Sweden's shift towards Europeanism accelerated and his vision of locating Sweden away from exceptionalism towards 'normality' and a European identity underscored the important shifts emerging in Swedish politics, society and identity. The end of the Cold War introduced a new phase of identity reconstruction as Bildt offered an alternative vision of security for Sweden which involved essentially abandoning the legacy of neutrality in favour of greater European security cooperation. Bildt's approach to internationalism and the Swedish Model is discussed as part of the changes that Sweden endured during the early 1990s.

Post-Cold War security and European security

The collapse of the Soviet Union, the unification of Germany and the end of bipolarity ushered in a new era in international relations and ideas about states, security and cooperation. With the withdrawal of the USSR from Eastern Europe, the European security environment underwent a massive shake up and redefinition. Military power declined as the primary tool of statecraft, while a broader security agenda emerged. Rather than the *amount* of security, the focus had turned to the *nature* of security (McInnes, 1993: 71). For Hansen, instability *between* and *within* states became a key feature of the new era (1995: 119). The demise of East–West tensions certainly did not produce peace – in fact, uncertainty can be said to have characterised the immediate aftermath of bipolarity's demise. During the Cold War years, the enemy was clearly defined. Subsequently, security was broadened to include economic, immigration, and environmental threats. Terrorism, civil conflict, human rights and individual security rose to the top of the security agenda. Interdependence and cooperation became the key to tackling the diffuse and varied security problems that emerged in the post-Cold War era. It was increasingly argued that new threats could not simply be dealt with via a military response or the nation-state alone and required cooperation between states, international organisations and a multitude of non-state actors.[1]

In IR theory, the breakdown of bipolarity engaged academics in a reassessment of the new world order. Realist and neo-realist orthodoxy was subject to a barrage of criticism and the discipline of IR opened up to explore new interpretations. Waltz (1993: 76) expressed concern about the prospect of an unbalanced hegemon in the international system and predicted that without the threat of the Soviet Union, NATO would lose its rationale and cease to exist. Instead, NATO refashioned for itself a different role with new institutions, moving from a doctrine of 'flexible response' to its 'New Strategic Concept'. Nuclear weapons were re-cast as 'weapons of last resort' and there was a shift away from the forward defence principle in conventional forces.

Security was no longer concerned with military factors but with political ones, emphasising democracy in former Warsaw Pact countries, non-military cooperation in science and environmental policies, and additional measures for arms control. NATO would focus more on 'soft' security and broader cooperation with the view to bringing in more member states. NATO discourse also shifted accordingly, with an emphasis on inclusive language that stressed unity. Despite predictions that some of the former Warsaw Pact nations would adopt neutrality in the new setting, most instead sought NATO and EU membership. Membership of such organisations signalled more than securing economic and security interests. At Hungary's NATO accession ceremony in the US in 1999, the Hungarian foreign minister stated: 'The decision was not only about security. NATO accession is also about returning Hungary to her natural habitat. It has been our manifest destiny to rejoin those with whom we share the same values, interests and goals.' (*Radio Free Europe/Radio Liberty*, 20/12/99)

Shared values, interests and goals also characterised the European response to the changed security and political environment. The EU anticipated playing a more prominent role in European security and expectations were raised for a more coherent European security policy after decades of slow movement in this area. By the 1990s, the US signalled its reluctance to maintain a presence in Europe and the disharmony of the EC during the Gulf War[2] pushed the issue of political and security cooperation high on the agenda of the 1991 Maastricht Summit. The Maastricht Treaty on European Union opened up a new chapter for foreign and security policy coordination, improving the largely ineffective European Political Cooperation (EPC). Although the CFSP remained an 'intergovernmental pillar' of the Union, its creation was extremely important because of its intentions: 'The common foreign and security policy shall include all questions related to the security of the Union, including the eventual framing of a common defence policy, *which might in time* lead to a common defence' (my emphasis). The WEU was to form 'an integral part of the development of the Union, to elaborate and implement decisions and actions of the Union which have defence implications'.[3]

The CFSP's objectives were to 'to safeguard the common values, fundamental interests and independence of the Union'; strengthen the security of the EU member states; strengthen international security and 'develop and consolidate democracy and the rule of law, and respect for human rights and fundamental freedoms'. There was also a concerted effort to avoid the disharmony of the EPC days, with the establishment of 'systemic cooperation' between member states and joint actions in 'areas in which the Member States have important interests in common'. (Council of the European Communities, Commission of the European Communities, 1992) Thus, the EU's security profile began to gather substance, and closer cooperation between member states on security harmonisation was a key rationale of the CFSP. The CFSP and the post-Cold War security setting signalled a new approach to international phenomena based on ideas of community, cooperation and interdependence. This was to have a decisive impact on neutral states such as Sweden, which were now considering EU membership.

Confronting the new: neutrality and the Swedish Model

Whereas in the 1980s, economic integration with the EC gained saliency, in the 1990s, membership of the EC was becoming an economic, a political, *and* an ideological issue. The perceived failings of the Swedish Model undermined the established hegemony of SAP norms and values, and set the path for a new discourse and debate about Europe. Neutrality and the Swedish Model had always been the reason for Sweden's refusal to contemplate full EC membership. Now the Cold War was over, and by the early 1990s, Sweden was in the throes of a major economic crisis, a late result of the global recession. Sweden's membership in EFTA guaranteed access to markets, but little input into decision-making.

Under the SAP government, membership of the EC was pursued, but not overtly. Within the party, opinion was divided on the issue of EC membership. The 'modernisers' supported membership, believing it would assist Sweden's export-driven economy, which in turn would fund the welfare state. On the other side, the 'traditionalists' felt that the goals of Social Democracy could be better achieved outside the EC. For the latter, the EC was not democratic enough. It lacked advanced policies on working conditions and full employment. National sovereignty was linked to democracy and the pursuit of peace on the international level, and the prevailing view was that this could not be maintained through EC membership. The rank and file of the SAP was also wary of ceding neutrality, despite the end of the Cold War. The leadership of the LO largely supported membership, taking into account the EC's plans to develop a social dimension, and was lured by the promise of increased export-led growth which would protect employment.[4]

The question of EU membership could no longer be avoided, but the issue was articulated in very different terms between the Social Democrats and the non-socialists. For the Social Democrats, it was vital to gain grassroots support and to be pro-EU in a 'social democratic' way. The EC was an opportunity to expand Social Democratic norms to a wider level; Sweden could maintain neutrality and hopefully promote key Social Democratic values and institutions to the European level. Membership of the EU had to be compatible with the ideological underpinnings of the SAP. For the non-socialist parties, particularly the Moderates, support for the EU was pitched at the level of distancing Sweden from its Social Democratic heritage, and was a way to become 'part of Europe'. For the Moderate Party, the EC was the solution to ridding Sweden of some long-held 'myths' such as neutrality and the welfare state.

In the October 1990 austerity package, the government announced (in a footnote) its intention to submit an application for membership of the EC.[5] Despite succumbing to the 'politics of inclusion', Carlsson did not soften his stance on neutrality and argued that neutrality was necessary in the new unpredictable security climate. He also set the parameters for involvement with the EC in 1990 by stating that if the Maastricht summit adopted a common foreign and defence policy, then membership would be 'impossible' for Sweden (Sundelius, 1994: 179–80). At a time of widespread uncertainty over the European security situation, this line of thinking was not restricted to neutral countries alone, as Dunne et al. (1998: v) have noted; despite the end of the Cold War, there was 'no consensus on what has replaced it'.

When the *Riksdag* approved the application for membership in December 1990, it was with the intention of maintaining neutrality and non-participation in military alliances. The Parliamentary Standing Committee on Foreign Affairs in 1990 concretely stated that neutrality permitted Sweden to pursue an active internationalist role and its credibility should not be jeopardised. The Committee did not exclude Swedish participation in a wider European security context but noted that neutrality has always been regarded as an obstacle to such participation by the great powers, who had viewed the neutral and non-aligned with 'suspicion' in the past. By late 1990, Carlsson officially supported EU membership (as opposed to comments earlier that year that Sweden's credible neutrality might be compromised). With the end of the Cold War, he explained, neutrality had lost some of its 'moral' force. If a pan-European security and peace could be a reality, then Sweden should strive to be a part of it (Carlsson, 1991). Carlsson regarded EC membership as compatible with the maintenance of Swedish neutrality. Sweden submitted its application for EC membership in 1991.

Where the Social Democrats were reluctantly dealing with the possibility of EC membership, the non-socialists would come to play a greater role in this debate. The austerity package adopted in 1990 banned strike action and froze wages for two years. Parliament refused to give its approval. In 1990, a vote of no confidence in the *Riksdag* forced the government to resign amid labour unrest. Support for the SAP had been declining since 1989, when their popularity rating had only reached approximately 30 per cent. Capturing the youth vote also seemed to be a struggle (support stayed between 20 and 25 per cent compared to 44 per cent in 1988). During the election campaign, the SAP campaigned on safe traditional issues, focusing on high standards in public service with the slogan 'Sweden is unique'. The Liberals and the Moderates used the slogan 'A New Start for Sweden'. The left in Swedish politics in general faced electoral problems. The Green Party faced a political climate where economic issues ranked high compared to environmental ones, and failed to make the four per cent threshold. Parties that traditionally supported ideas about the *folkhem* (Centre Party and Liberals) also experienced electoral fallout, despite forming part of the new coalition. But the underlying explanation of the shift must be located in developments of the previous decade. Bildt's vision of setting Sweden on a new path held a particular resonance at a time when the Swedish Model faced crisis and Europe's transformation seemed to offer a resolution to not only economic problems, but the possibility of new avenues of cooperation.

A 'New Start': the Bildt government and the Swedish Model

When Carl Bildt won office from the Social Democrats in September 1991, he became Sweden's first conservative Prime Minister for 60 years. The SAP had their worst performance at the polls since 1928.[6] Bildt's coalition government, made up of the Moderates, the Liberal Party, the Centre Party and the Christian Democrats, did not gain the absolute majority that the polls predicted, with 46.6 per cent of the vote. The coalition government did not have control of the *Riksdag* and had to seek the support of newcomers *Ny Demokrati* (New Democracy) which campaigned on an anti-tax and anti-immigrant platform.

Bildt's coalition put forward their 'New Start' package (Bildt and Liberal leader Bengt Westerberg's joint manifesto of 1991) which aimed at a re-evaluation of the 'middle way'. Taking his cue from the 'New Right' of American and British politics, Bildt aimed to restore economic growth and remedy economic stagnation via cuts in taxation. 1991 was labelled the 'tax reform of the century' as it went further in reducing marginal taxes than reform in other countries.[7] The issue of tax reform had been growing since the previous decade, mirroring the increasing discontent over high rates that had in the past been accepted as a necessary function of funding the welfare state. High taxes were cited as the reason why Swedish firms relocated overseas and for Sweden's apparent lack of international competitiveness. According to Anders Hall, political advisor in the Moderate Party in 1998, Sweden's 'unique' position had changed (Interview, Hall, 11/08/98). There was no longer a blanket assumption that high taxes to support the welfare state should be accepted, especially in comparison to other European countries which have lower tax rates. Furthermore, many in the non-socialist camp do not regard the welfare state as 'value for money' anymore, according to Jesper Haglund of the Christian Democrats.[8]

The public sector was targeted as the source of Sweden's economic ills, as it employed over one third of the workforce and consumed roughly 60 per cent of GDP. Deregulation and privatisation (including the sale of public-owned housing and the privatisation of Swedish State Railways, Swedish Telecom and Swedish Post) were part of the reform. Housing subsidies were reduced, child allowances frozen and taxes on capital and property were reduced. Outward investment was encouraged, and the traditional limitations on foreign ownership of Swedish companies, shares and properties were lifted. The emphasis shifted so that individuals, families, cooperatives and private companies began to take more responsibility for welfare services. Bildt's plans to cut back the public sector had strong support from employers' organisations and business groups. In 1991, the SAF unilaterally withdrew 6,000 representatives from the governing bodies of public administration at local, regional and national level. This, according to Pestoff (2001: 5–6) 'dramatically changed the situation overnight'. A year later, Bildt terminated the formal corporate representation on public administration boards, and the SAF's influence was part of this move.

Bildt's 'revolution by choice' in education, social and health services was an important part of reshaping the welfare state in line with European levels. And 'choice' was presented as freedom and options, rather than Social Democratic formulas and limitations (Eddie, 1993: 9; Svensson, 2002: 212-3). In the 1980s under a Social Democratic government, privatisation was a dirty word, largely regarded as an attack on the welfare state. This view altered in 1989 when the Carlsson Government began to reconsider its stance on what services should be managed publicly or privately (in preparation for EU membership and with the realisation that the welfare state had to be cut back in order to maintain it). Citizens began to be regarded as 'users' and 'consumers', causing a demarcation between 'consumer solutions' and 'collectivist solutions'. Privatisation had become a practical rather than an ideological issue (Montin and Elander, 1995). In this sense, Social Democrats made room for Bildt's justification in introducing such concepts, since the former were becoming more interested in contracting out and introducing competition within the public sector rather than their traditional position of solidarity and equality.

Bildt's solutions raised a number of debates in economic and political circles. Although a shift in thinking had already taken place academically and amongst economists, Bildt set up the Lindbeck Commission to provide suggestions on economic change. The Commission itself was intended to be 'objective and expert' in nature, but there were also criticisms that it was created to legitimise the government's policies.[9] By this stage, Lindbeck himself was convinced of the need to cut welfare and reform institutions in order to respond to global competitiveness. The Commission's report declared that there were three basic problems in the Swedish economy – stability, efficiency and growth. Also, the economic crisis in Sweden was a crisis of politics and institutions. Sweden did not adjust to external economic crises, and the economic problems could be traced back to the expansion of the welfare state in the 1970s. Sweden fell from third place in 1970 in the OECD's ranking of the world's richest countries to fourteenth place in 1991 (SAF, 2000: 8). Additionally, labour market legislation and wage bargaining, two key Social Democratic initiatives, were considered responsible for macro-economic instability and harming the dynamism of the economy (Lindbeck et al., 1994: 10–13). The report recommended the liberalisation of the labour market, reduction of unemployment benefits, and the decentralisation of wage negotiations in the public sector (Lindbeck et al., 1994: 50). It also suggested cuts in public spending and revenue increases, more working hours to raise productivity and to reduce capital costs, open competition in commerce and industry, the curbing of some trade union rights, reform of the social security system and public sector cuts (Lindbeck et al., 1994: 73–94).

For Bildt, the problems of the Swedish Model could be resolved by EU membership, which would tie Sweden firmly to market discipline and shift Sweden away from its provincial attitude towards the welfare state and government intervention. The push to join the EU, according to Blyth, can 'perhaps best be understood as an attempt by business and the conservatives to let the economic ideas and institutions of the EU achieve by international convergence what they had failed to do through domestic reform'. (2002: 231) Business interests and organisations supported EU membership, regarding it as a way out of the trade union maze and a chance to weaken the Swedish Model. In 1990, the then Volvo executive Pehr G. Gyllenhammar said: 'We need to liberate ourselves from our national myth [of the Swedish Model] ... The only way of saving our jobs and our standard of living is for us, Swedish citizens, to become real Europeans, exposing ourselves to real competition.' (Nyberg, 1996) Edging away from the welfare state and Swedish Model through European integration was considered to be the only solution in an era of liberalisation and global competitiveness – or as Bildt coined it, 'den vägens politik' ('the only way policy'), echoing Thatcher's mantra of 'no alternatives'. (Blyth, 2002: 229; Gould, 1995: 3) This view was now the official line of the government, and from a position of power, Bildt's coalition had the perfect opportunity 'to render it organic in civil society'. (Ryner, 2002: 154)

This opened up what Marcussen and Roscher (2000: 351) refer to as a 'critical juncture' – 'a window of opportunity for party elites to deconstruct, reconstruct and manipulate given nation-state identities'. The task of convincing a broader audience of the problems of the Swedish Model had long been in the making, but on the question of neutrality, the Bildt government was on relatively new ground. Since the post-war era, neutrality had been the 'taboo' subject in Swedish politics and had long enjoyed a wide consensus. In the next section, I explore how Bildt aimed to rid Sweden of yet another myth – that of neutrality.

Bildt's 'non-neutrality' and the accession negotiations for EU membership

Neutrality had always been a point of consensus in Swedish politics, but for the non-socialists, the ideological overtones the SAP had given to Sweden's neutrality policy since the 1960s had always been problematic. For non-socialists, the option of neutrality was simply a *realpolitik* decision, a rational choice for a small state such as Sweden, which had 'nothing to do with altruism or anything but pure national interest'. (Interview, Rohdin, 12/08/98) Now in office, Bildt was in a position to articulate not only the 'realist' view of Swedish neutrality, but argue for a rethinking of neutrality in the light of EU membership and European security cooperation.

In his first ministerial speech to the *Riksdag* in October 1991, Bildt introduced a revised 'foreign and security policy with a European identity'. (Miles, 1994: 13) Bildt's speech to the *Riksdag* in January 1992 confirmed the 'hard core' of neutrality, reiterating that 'the core of our security policy is still military non-alignment' and that 'Swedish defence is for Sweden only'. (Wahlbäck, 1992: 1–2) With the Centre Party (which supported neutrality) as part of the coalition, Bildt could not wholly abandon neutrality. But recognition of a new security reality in Europe saw Bildt align Swedish security interests with those of the EU. The effect of the new security formulation engendered a sense of uncertainty regarding Sweden's security policy, prompting discussion of labels and meanings. 'Neutrality', according to Bildt, was not an apt term to describe Swedish foreign and security interests (*Svenska Dagbladet*, 25/11/91). Although Bildt adhered to the 1949 definition (substituting 'aiming for neutrality in war' for 'with a view to neutrality during war'), he clearly interpreted the meaning of neutrality differently. By rejecting the term 'neutrality', Bildt aimed for a less weighted description of Swedish foreign policy. Using the term 'non-alignment' removes the concept of 'ideological neutrality' (Dahl, 1997: 19). Since the 1950s, Swedish neutrality was dogmatic, deeply embedded in the national culture and rarely questioned publicly – do to so 'would be political suicide for any aspiring leader'. (Sundelius, 1990: 124) However, Ekengren and Sundelius claim, this shift in terminology occurred long before Bildt's overt redefinition:

> The traditionally important neutrality term was erased from official speech even before Sweden officially became a party to the Maastricht Treaty and to its second pillar through its membership ... The transition from an image of Sweden as the committed neutral to a committed European seemed to have been fully completed well ahead of the beginning of the membership negotiations, at least at the top of the government. (Ekengren and Sundelius, 1998: 135)

Bildt's statement was controversial because it appeared as a sudden, arbitrary decision to distance Sweden from the label of neutrality. The Social Democrats claimed that during his period in office, Bildt 'krossat neutralitetspolitikens stentavlor' ('smashed the stone tablets of neutrality policy') (*Svenska Dagbladet*, 15/02/96). The language that he employed also came to be included in a new discourse about neutrality, but this time neutrality was not a uniting abstract that held certain notions of Swedishness together – rather it became a cause for concern. This 'sterile isolation' (Bildt, cited in Ingebritsen, 1997: 33) began to take on negative overtones.

The important difference between Bildt's redefinition and the gradual phasing out of the phrase 'neutrality' from official discourse is that the SAP were conscious of the way the Swedish public view neutrality and how deeply ingrained it has become. MP Viola Furubjelke thinks 'it is much more political when you're talking about neutrality' although she conceded that the connotations of such a political term created 'the impression of a passive country and a government which doesn't understand that the Cold War is over'. (Interview, Furubjelke, 18/08/98) Fellow Social Democrat Britt Bohlin preferred the term 'non-alignment', 'but if you ask someone in the street – everybody called it the "neutrality policy"'. (Interview, Bohlin, 13/08/98) Undén preferred to use the term 'neutrality' rather than 'non-alignment' (which had a different meaning), to preserve Sweden's status should a war erupt. The Swedish Commission on Neutrality Policy in 1994 stated that non-participation in alliances with the view to remaining neutral in war was 'often referred to as the "Swedish policy of neutrality"'. (SOU 1994:11: 8) The phrase *alliansfrihet* is used more often in discourse with and about Europe because of the ideological baggage of the phrase 'neutrality': 'In contrast, they misunderstand neutrality and neutrality policy. They perceive this as our not wanting to participate, but instead preferring to be outsiders. There is no prestige attached to this issue. A new use of language merely makes it pedagogically easier for us.'[10] Within the SAP, the revised terminology is accepted, but the importance of neutrality to Swedes is still beyond dispute. It is still a 'key word' for Swedes today but according to Åström, Bildt's re-labelling is 'of very, very small importance'. (Interview, Åström, 13/08/98)

These domestic reinterpretations of Swedish neutrality were not only based upon a conservative rejection of the SAP-defined neutrality policy, but must also be viewed in the context of the accession negotiations, which commenced at the time of the Bildt coalition winning office. Sweden's accession negotiations were held concurrently with those of Austria and Finland. Austria had applied to join the Community in 1989, and Finland followed Sweden by submitting its application in 1992. The reasons for their membership bids differed to that of Sweden. Primarily, the end of the Cold War had opened up an opportunity for Finland to regain a sense of independence after decades of close ties with the former USSR. Additionally, the security vacuum left in the wake of the dissolution of the Soviet Union caused a heightened sense of insecurity in Finland.[11] Its relationship with the former USSR altered with the end of the TFCMA (the 'No' campaign stressed tensions with Russia over EC membership). Similar to Bildt's redefinition of Swedish neutrality, Finland also relabelled its policy soon after submitting its application to join the EU to 'military non-alignment and a credible national defence'. (Arter, 1996: 615) EC membership was also important in terms of economics.[12]

For Austria, EC membership was a way to resolve the country's economic problems which struck in the mid-1980s. In 1985, Austria's state-owned industries neared bankruptcy and economic growth was slow. Among the EFTA neutrals, Austria had the highest amount of exports to the EC (Luif, 1990: 189). With the end of the Cold War, membership was also seen as a 'return to Europe'. Some groups were keen to shed neutrality, which was regarded as a condition imposed on Austria in exchange for its autonomy.[13] Debate on membership began in the mid-1980s, prompted first by large business interests and small- and medium-sized companies. The Austrian People's Party (ÖVP) supported EC membership, in opposition to the Austrian Socialist Party (SPÖ). In 1987, the new coalition of the SPÖ and the ÖVP placed EC membership at the centre of its foreign policy objectives (Luif, 1998: 117–8).

All three applicants, nonetheless, intended to maintain their neutrality upon joining the EC. Foreign Minister Pertti Paasio (1990: 58) in 1989 claimed that Finland would 'hold fast' to neutrality and PM Holkeri (1990: 59) stated that neutrality would not limit Finland, but in an integrated Europe, 'neutrality is more, rather than less, important'. The implications of EU membership for neutrality were downplayed to the public, declaring the CFSP to be a mere 'political declaration'. Chancellor Vranitzsky likened the CFSP to an idea or concept without flesh and bones (*The European*, 08–10/02/91). At this point in time, the neutral states were confident that the CFSP might not go as far as full security integration, with a common defence. The years of intergovernmental cooperation under EPC verified the view that the interests of the nation-state had the upper hand over supranational ambitions. Ireland, after all, was a neutral member state and had managed to keep its neutrality intact. The stipulations of the CFSP were not widely regarded as a threat to neutrality by the pro-EC supporters – it was expected that national interests would take precedence, given its intergovernmental nature. In the realm of defence, the wording of the treaty was vague and member states could employ the veto in terms of vital national interests. Ireland, during the CFSP negotiations, insisted on the EU allowing some independence via Article J.4, which promised not to 'prejudice the specific character of the security and defence policy of certain Member States'. (Council of the European Communities, Commission of the European Communities, 1992: 126)

However, the demands of the CFSP were more ambitious than those of EPC. Under the Maastricht Treaty, the EC had become a 'Union', and in pursuit of this deeper identity as a Union, there would be less inclination to permit opt-outs on foreign and security policy. The purpose of upgrading the Community's foreign and security policy was to make it more effective and binding under the CFSP – and regardless of however vague the wording of the CFSP remained, it was unlikely that the development of a common security policy would be halted.

The intention to retain neutrality became a problematic point in the accession negotiations. There was minimum controversy over adherence to the economic regime and regulations of the EU, as the majority of legislation had already been adopted through EFTA membership, but neutrality was problematic for the European Commission.[14] Austria learnt an early lesson when it included neutrality in its application for membership, along with the firm commitment to keep it unchanged. The then Foreign Minister, Alois Mock (1990: 37), tried to make amends by offering neutrality as 'an asset in a new, favourable situation of broad cooperation between East and West'. Despite this, the EU was still dissatisfied. Austria's intention to retain neutrality caused concern and the Commission recommended Austria 'redefine' its neutral status. The EC was particularly concerned that Austria would not adhere to the *acquis communautaire* on the issue of neutrality.[15] There was concern that a neutral bloc would form in the EU and that the CFSP would not be implemented. Neutrality was still regarded as a state-centric policy, out of date and incapable of adapting to the new security circumstances. According to Cox and MacGinty (1996: 124), neutrality was unable to confront 'the logic of interdependence and integration'. It offered no value as a security policy because it was 'a selfish policy of national interest'. It was expected that member states participate in the CFSP and its implementation fully, and not act as an obstacle to its development. The neutral states had to be seen to support the EU in action as well as in rhetoric. Subsequently, the position of the three neutral applicants shifted accordingly during the course of the accession negotiations.

Because inclusion into Europe was considered more desirable than remaining outside of its economic benefits, the applicant states tried to bend their foreign policies towards the preferred EU position. In 1992, the Austrian parliament gave its support for Austria's involvement in the development of a collective European security network. Austria announced that it would act as an observer in the WEU. Austria's then President, Thomas Klestil, questioned the viability of neutrality in the EU and claimed that Austria was no longer strictly neutral since allowing Allied aircraft to use Austrian airspace during the Gulf War (Lahodynsky, 1992: 24). Austria wanted to send out a clear signal to the EU that its neutrality would not pose an obstacle to its application for membership, and the objectives of the CFSP were accepted in principle (Neuhold, 1994a: 29).

Sweden and Finland downplayed neutrality as a major issue in their applications for membership. Finland, despite being more open to a broader interpretation for neutrality since the end of the Cold War, still preferred to maintain it due to uncertainties with the former USSR. There was recognition, nevertheless, that neutrality was a condition of its relationship with Russia and 'never an end in itself but only a means of safeguarding ... national existence and security'. The idea of the EU deciding matters of security still remained slightly problematic for the Finns, yet in 1993, Finland accepted the provisions of the CFSP and 'closed the chapter' on this issue (Suominen, 1994: 12–13).

Under Bildt, there was more enthusiasm to involve Sweden in Europe's anticipated security network. In 1993, Sweden accepted the Combined Joint Task Forces (CJTF) to strengthen the European Security and Defence Identity (ESDI[16]) in NATO, and the WEU's role in peacekeeping. Bildt was heavily criticised in the same year over his statement that if the security of the Baltic states were threatened, then Sweden could not remain neutral. Aware of public concerns about neutrality, Bildt tried to present the CFSP as an opportunity for Sweden to ensure a 'clear northern European dimension' to the CFSP whilst continuing its traditional path of involvement in the CSCE, the Council of Europe and the UN. The EU and the WEU should be regarded as 'new opportunities to build peace in different parts of Europe'. (Bildt, 1993) Yet the language Bildt employed signalled that Sweden could no longer be stubborn on neutrality policy, and that broader European security should be placed above narrow national interests:

> Logically speaking, anyone who considers that Sweden should not participate in peace-keeping and peace-enforcement should not expect any other country to do so either. What is wrong for us cannot be right for others. (Bildt, 1993)

For the Moderates, neutrality has long been a rhetorical tool of the Social Democrats to control public and parliamentary debate or 'arouse certain feelings'. (Interview, Hall, 11/08/98) For Huldt, the new thinking on neutrality was a welcome relief: 'Today, is it embarrassing to consider the amount of energy that went into woolly thinking about "neutrality" as ideology when the logic of the strategic realities (and history) was quite satisfactory as explanation of the Swedish position.' (1996: 1) Less importance is given to public perception, as a member of the Moderate Party explains neutrality as 'a rather esoteric thing and foreign policy is rarely discussed in our election campaigns'. (Interview, Lars Tobisson, 18/08/98) Comments such as these, however, remain wide of the mark. Had neutrality simply been adopted to face the strategic realities he speaks of, then its reinvention (or abandonment) would be an uncontested transition.

The questioning of neutrality, nonetheless, was intended to not only steer public opinion towards the conclusion that Swedish security now lay with European cooperation, but came to signify everything that was dubious about 'paternalistic' Social Democracy. Not only did the Swedish Model rule out *choice*, but neutrality was turned from a moral principle, as it was broadly understood, to an immoral position. In 1991, a controversial book *Heder och Samvete. Sverige och andra världskriget (Honour and Conscience: Sweden and World War II)* by Maria-Pia Boëthius was published, which was critical of Sweden's neutrality policy and its accommodation of Nazi Germany. Boëthius claimed that Sweden has never confronted its past and that it profited from its wartime actions as a neutral state. But more importantly, Boëthius raised some questions about the nature of Swedish society and the taboo subject of neutrality. In an interview with *Dagens Nyheter*, Boëthius claimed that Sweden's 'consensus society' and the 'common good' were defined by politicians and scientists without the involvement of the people. This social engineering precluded other views (*Dagens Nyheter*, 21/10/97). Although this view of neutrality was criticised,[17] the book was timely in that questioning Social Democratic wisdom was in full swing. Furthermore, in 1992, Bildt commissioned an investigation into allegations that Sweden was not strictly neutral during the Second World War, and that Sweden had secretly made security arrangements with NATO.[18] Those who were not enamoured by the more idealistic slant given to neutrality grasped this debate as an opportunity to approach the question of NATO membership and redefining Sweden's position in the new European security architecture.

Such criticisms, however, play on points of definition. For Sweden, the key feature of its neutrality policy was not merely an adherence to a specific legal description of its status. Neutrality was the platform from which to pursue a global role of the active internationalist state, and it mediated political relations on the domestic front. As the SOU report (1994: 50) also points out, conventions such as those of The Hague cater for neutrality in war – neutrality during times of peace 'does not have a corresponding basis in international law'. Neutrality was always seen as the 'sacred cow' of Swedish politics (Andrén, 1991: 67). Under Bildt, debate about Swedish neutrality was seen to be permissible, but this was also an opportunity to rethink neutrality outside of the parameters of the *folkhem*.

Regardless of whether Sweden actually had links with NATO or if Sweden acted morally during WWII, the vital point about these domestic debates is that the established understandings of and attachments to neutrality came under question. Such debates, or challenges to traditional understandings of self with regard to neutrality must be viewed in the context of Europeanisation and shifting identities. In 1993, as Sweden edged closer to its referendum on EU membership, a series of museum exhibitions (*The Swedish History*) opened in Stockholm and other provincial areas with, according to Pred (2000: 28), 'the express intent ... of remythologizing the past so as to reinvent the national ideals which all were to identify'. For Pred, the combination of the exhibition's images plus the new revelations about neutrality 'were in keeping with a larger set of widely recurrent messages: We have always been a part of Europe'. This is what Wendt would call 'altercasting' (Zehfuss, 2001: 323). The EU presents Sweden with a new role or source of identity. The yearning to Europeanise is also related to Sweden's past distancing of itself from the continent. There was an underlying current that neutrality, although useful for protecting Sweden from war, also prevented Sweden from certain 'rites of passage' that a nation-state builds its identity upon, such as war and survival, acting as a filter on Swedish experiences (Sandomirskaja, 1999). This sense of 'missing out' has opened up debate on issues such as NATO membership, which would have never been seriously considered in the past. However, Bildt was not content with raising questions about neutrality and its ideological uses. In the following section, I outline how the cornerstone of Swedish neutrality in practice (active internationalism) also underwent revision.

Bildt and Swedish internationalism

Despite the expectation that EU membership might not necessarily harm Sweden's foreign and security policy, some changes were already occurring. Bjereld notes that during Bildt's term in office, Sweden's traditional posture of voting in solidarity with the Third World in the UN General Assembly declined and voting in favour with the EU increased.[19] Sweden's policy of recognition of states has also altered. In the past, Sweden strictly adhered to the legal interpretation and did not grant recognition of certain states if they did not fulfil specific criteria.[20] However, in 1992, Sweden recognised Croatia and Bosnia-Herzegovina, marking a clear distancing from the principles of international law that it had followed in the past.[21] Although this signalled a break with the Palme tradition, Bildt's recognition (like Germany's decision to recognise Croatia) was an effort to internationalise the Croatian issue. Nonetheless, this also should be viewed in the context of efforts to Europeanise Swedish foreign policy – it is doubtful that a Social Democratic government would have recognised Croatia on such criteria. Other breaks with SAP tradition included Bildt's shift from Sweden's traditional policy in disarmament and arms control[22] and Bildt's decision that Sweden would no longer align itself with the Group of 21 neutral and alliance free states in the UN.

Despite the Bildt Government's alterations to Swedish internationalism, this was not a signal of 'anti-internationalism'. Whilst there largely was consensus over Sweden's international role, there existed different viewpoints as to the motives behind it. For Social Democrats, Swedish internationalism is vital to what defines Sweden and what constitutes the Swedish social and political identity. It engenders a sense of community within, to be exported to the community without. But for non-Social Democratic parties, particularly the Moderates, Swedish internationalism was a way to avoid questions about neutrality in the domestic arena. Sweden's activism on the international front served to divert attention from issues at home, or to present some moral code or voice. The Moderate Party had long been critical of the moral overtones the SAP injected into its active internationalist stance.

For others, Swedish internationalism gave Sweden 'some kind of goodwill among a number of countries in the Third World' but it also signalled an unwillingness to discuss Europe: 'It was a way to channel the foreign policy awareness or attention in Sweden away from European issues ... It was easier to focus the attention to places far off in the Third World.' (Interview, Hall, 11/08/98) A non-attributable source from within the Ministry of Foreign Affairs concurred with this view: 'It was much easier to develop [a position] on Nicaragua or Tanzania or ... Guatemala ... I don't really think that they were consciously thinking in these terms like that, planning a kind of deception of the Swedish public.' Some comment that it was perhaps a feeling of 'guilt', that Sweden emerged from WWII relatively unscathed, and that Sweden had to 'compensate by playing this role'.[23] Södersten claims that Sweden's emphasis on internationalism has been guided by 'a sense of guilt and an attitude of self-confidence' and like neutrality, 'soon became something of a holy cow', not open for discussion (1989: 157 and 174). Wahlbäck explains that Sweden's actions in the international arena and mediation in the UN created an independence that separated Sweden from the bloc alignments. However, Wahlbäck (1992) comments, 'These altruistic and peace-promoting functions of neutrality appealed to many Swedes who were not comfortable with the more hard-nosed security calculations underlying our policy of neutrality.' Rohdin supports this claim:

> Security policy is not about ideals or whatever. It's about pure egois[m] ... It can benefit others as well, to play that role, but you don't *play* it because of the others, you play it because of your own interest ... we used this position consciously ... But one should not forget about cause and effect. It is not in order to be able to play this role that we were neutral. It was that we could play this because we happened to be neutral for other reasons. There is a world of difference. (Interview, Rohdin, 12/08/98)

The changes to Swedish internationalism, in its focus away from issues such as the Third World towards European issues are, for some, a cause for regret. Helena Nilsson, former MP for the Centre Party, claims Sweden is now 'occupied with European affairs' at the expense of developing countries (Interview, Nilsson, 13/08/98). For Annika Nordgren, former MP of the Green Party, the shift is viewed in more critical terms. Within a globalised economic environment, there is more need to support the Third World, and now there is 'just silence'. (Interview, Nordgren, 13/08/98) Some Social Democrats do express an underlying concern about the alignment to Europe in the UN. There is some hope that Sweden may influence the EU, as Furubjelke states: 'I think that it's a bit worrying and I'm a bit concerned, because at the same time, we know that if we can move the European Union a little bit in the direction that we want, then we have maybe gained more... as a small country [than] in the United Nations. But it [does not give us] a very clear profile.' (Interview, Furubjelke, 18/08/98) Åström is more positive about the ability of Sweden to push the EU to higher standards in the UN, and Sweden as such can increase its profile (Interview, Åström, 13/08/98).

Therefore, within the space of a few years, there has been a reconsideration of the traditional way of conceptualising Swedish neutrality and active internationalism. The shifts in both areas have been subtle, nonetheless. There has been no wholesale rejection of neutrality, but the underlying ideological slant given to Swedish neutrality and Sweden's role as the moral voice on the international has stage has been reconsidered. In the following section, I examine the return of the SAP to government and assess the impact of Bildt's brief time in power.

The return of the SAP and debating the Bildt legacy

Regardless of its short time in office, the Bildt coalition government had a decisive impact and dislodged some very sedimented Social Democratic principles and values. Although this largely stems from the domestic changes of the 1980s (outlined in Chapter 5), Bildt brought these alternative ideas into the wider public domain and gave them a considerable degree of legitimacy. The Bildt Government was different to the bourgeois government of 1976–82. Fälldin's Government at least attempted to maintain welfare entitlements and full employment, despite economic recession. The bourgeois government also nationalised more industry in this time than the Social Democrats had done in their years of power. Bildt's pursuit of an EU identity and the neo-liberal approach to the market offered a different idea of Sweden's place in Europe, and ultimately, the international system.

Despite the new ideas, the Swedish economy was running into serious trouble. Between 1990 and 1993, Sweden's GDP fell by almost 5 per cent in terms of volume (SAF, 2000: 7). The recession that the coalition had to govern through had been the worst since the 1930s. In the early 1990s, over 500,000 jobs were lost, and open unemployment went from 1.6 per cent in 1990 to 8.2 per cent in 1993.[24] By 1994, Sweden had a currency crisis, high unemployment, a serious budget deficit and financial markets were volatile. Bildt had succeeded in getting cross-party support for two earlier crisis agreements, but the third failed to garner support. In the run up to the September election, Bildt was behind the SAP in the polls. The business interests that had finally thought they had seen the back of Social Democratic formulas became vocal at the prospect of an SAP victory. In 1994, Skandia, Sweden's largest insurance company, sold SEK 1.8 billion of its government bonds in protest against the government's economic policy[25] and threatened not to buy government bonds unless the budget deficit was cut (Widfelt, 1995: 207–9). One week before the election, Ericsson, Stora, Asea and Volvo published a joint article in *Dagens Nyheter* endorsing deregulation and threatening to relocate overseas. Rehn and Meidner regarded such demands by large companies as 'blackmail' (Widfeldt, 1995: 209; Wilks, 1996: 103–8). Such moves, however, seemed to work in the SAP's favour, according to Blyth, increasing its support amongst the public (2002: 236).

The 1994 election was a general victory for the left in Swedish politics, against a backdrop of recession and high unemployment. The SAP was returned to government with their best result since the 1970s (45.3 per cent).[26] The Greens received 5 per cent of the vote, and the Left Party gained 6.2 per cent (their best result since 1948). The Christian Democrats retained a low profile with 4.1 per cent (due to internal division over the EU) (Wörlund, 1995: 286–8). New Democracy, which was never a serious political option, failed to reach the 4 per cent threshold, gaining only 1.23 per cent of the vote (Eddie, 1994: 204).

Bildt tried to present a different story about Sweden. His policies and rhetoric were a clear shift away from established Social Democratic norms, which had become entrenched. But could they become embedded? Sweden has been influenced by SAP hegemony for over four decades, and as such, Social Democracy defined the nation as well as the nation-state. For instance, on the issue of taxation, it became the norm under the Bildt government to argue for tax cuts, but for the Swedish public, taxation was a key part of the functioning of the welfare state. The position of the SAP had been that the public accepted high taxes: 'The Swedish population, if we ask them ... "could you give a bit more tax, for better health care?" – sixty per cent say yes.' (Interview, Bohlin, 13/08/98) Although Bohlin cites a broad figure, studies appear to support her claim. Despite assertions that the Swedish public is growing critical of high levels of tax, according to Edlund (2000) and Steinmo (2002) there is little empirical evidence to support such claims.[27] Concern over welfare, women's rights, open democracy and neutrality was still a part of the public memory of self, despite Bildt's efforts to turn European integration into a positive thing for Swedes. It is useful at this point to recall Finnemore and Sikkink's notion of 'cognitive frames'; norms are built, become sedimented, and as new ideas enter the established framework, norms become 'competitive'. As constructivists contend, identity is not a fixed phenomenon. The Bildt Government did much to view Europe through a different set of lenses, but Bildt's new vision was set against decades of Social Democratic hegemony and socialisation. Subsequently, the debate about Europe had been 'normalised' (Lawler, 1997: 574 and 583) under the Bildt years, but the majority of Swedes wanted to enter the EU through the Social Democrats. What Bildt proposed had to fit in with the Social Democratic understanding of self and especially of 'other' (in this case, the 'other' being Europe), but as Marcussen and Roscher note:

> Elite groups promoting a specific nation-state identity or a concept of political order need to make these new ideas fit with pre-existing identity constructions embedded in political institutions and culture. New ideas about just political order have to resonate with these classical notions of political order and, if this fit is not commonly perceived to be evident, then national elites will attempt to construct a compatibility between old and new ideas. (2000: 348–9)

Under the Bildt Government, there was little in the way of bridging this connection between established Social Democratic norms and the new direction the non-socialists wanted Sweden to adopt. The Bildt Government was doubtless cautious about too much disengagement from Social Democratic norms (evidenced in the rewording of neutrality but maintaining the commitment to independent defence) but Bildt's image of Sweden envisaged a new set of ideological notions. Despite the revisions under the Bildt Government, neutrality (or 'military non-alignment') had not been discarded. In fact, there is little evidence that even a conservative government would so readily abandon it (evidenced in the Moderate Party's present approach to NATO membership, which is 'no rush' to join). Bildt's vision presented an alternative avenue through which to conceive of Sweden's place in global politics and what can be achieved within the confines of the nation-state. Ruth's point, made in the decade before, suggests that although certain myths have become destabilised, there has been confusion on what has replaced them, or what gives Sweden its particular distinctiveness: 'Myths are socially useful only as long as they are not consciously perceived as myths.'[28]

'Yet,' as Lawler states, 'myths matter.' (1997: 571) Myths are part of the collective idea of self and inform and corroborate the experiences of the nation. Although neutrality was mythologised, the existence of myths, as Berger and Luckmann contend, 'does not prevent their entering as elements into the reality of everyday life, sometimes in a very decisive way'. (1971: 48) Swedish neutrality is as much a part of the collective awareness as, for instance, Finnish war experiences with the Soviet Union. Despite the questioning of such myths, they are still resilient and are a reference point by which to gauge the change of direction. Identity formation can be subject to change, but that change occurs against the established ideas of self.

Conclusion: from the *folkhem* to the European home?

In the early 1990s, it was not only the Swedish Model and neutrality that was challenged, but the norms and institutions that had long been a part of what constituted 'Sweden' also came under review. The competing views over 'Sweden' – the Old Sven versus the Ugly Swede – changed the nature of how the public viewed government, the economy and the welfare state, neutrality and Europe. However, identities are never fixed and these remain highly contested stories. The Social Democratic account of the Swedish Model and neutrality may have shifted but a number of cornerstones remained, and contained a high degree of resonance for the Swedish population. The deep divisions over the welfare state were indicative of an underlying sense of threat or loss of the Swedish Model or Swedish way. This mixed with the new rhetoric of Bildt that argued that Sweden was no longer the prosperous, exceptional state, and its economic and welfare system was out of step with other nations and international economic change.

As Marcussen and Roscher posit, political leaders 'must be able to convince a wider audience that a particular moment in history indeed constitutes a crisis situation whereby nation-state identities are up for negotiation'. (2000: 352) Despite its short period in office, the Bildt Government articulated a different image of Sweden and of Europe. There was a clear attempt to move away from neutrality and the underlying ideological basis of society that was established by the SAP. Thus, a particular crisis of identity emerged, which involved a destabilising of traditional structures. Nonetheless, the embeddedness of SAP norms and values (when pitted against an alternative European identity and a neo-liberal direction) meant that Swedes were not entirely convinced of this new direction. The SAP returned to government in 1994 and took Sweden into the EU. But the Bildt years had a decisive impact on the debate about Europe and about *Sweden* itself. As Blyth contends, even though Bildt had taken Sweden as far as possible from its established institutions, the effect was that any forthcoming SAP government would find it difficult to change course (Blyth, 2002: 231). The following chapter examines Sweden as a member state of the EU and the path the SAP adopted in the process of Europeanisation.

NOTES

1 Others claim that the 'new thinking' in security has not matched practice. On this see George on the first Gulf War, where he argues that Machiavellian power politics still characterised new conflicts (1994: 2–3).
2 The disharmony of the EC member states drew sharp criticism from the US. Despite the initial united front, the member states pursued their own national interests when military action began. France refused to place its forces under US command and attempted to secure its own peace deal with Iraq via secret diplomacy. Britain cooperated closely with the US, rather than with its European counterparts. Constitutional restraints

limited Germany's involvement and Belgium refused to sell ammunition to Britain. In the words of then Belgian Foreign Minister, Mark Eyskens, the EC was 'an economic giant, a political pygmy and a military larva'. (See Salmon, 1992)

3 The designation of the WEU (a separate body from the EU) as the 'defence arm' of the CFSP also created a number of disagreements amongst member states. France and Germany wanted to make the WEU more operational, whereas Italy wanted to go further and merge it with the EU. However, Denmark and Britain preferred to keep the WEU out of the picture as much as possible, preferring to strengthen transatlantic links.

4 The rank and file of the LO were opposed (Miles, 2000: 221–25). Only one out of two SAP rank and file supported membership, and the negative voters were predominantly part of the LO (63 per cent of LO members were against membership) (Svensson, 1994: 2). The unions largely saw membership as a threat to the Swedish Model and the welfare state. Most political parties from the left were opposed, but trade interests and the non-socialists largely supported membership.

5 Carlsson did not inform the governments of Finland or Norway of Sweden's intention to join the EC, breaking the tradition of cooperation and interdependence between the Nordic countries on matters of international politics and economics (Aunesluoma, 2001: 2).

6 The SAP gained only 37.6 per cent of the vote, with the share of the vote dropping by 5 per cent (Eddie, 1994: 203–5).

7 In 1991 the top rate of income tax was cut from over 80 per cent to 50 per cent. Corporate and capital tax was also reformed, and the marginal tax rate was reduced from 57 per cent to 30 per cent (Steinmo, 2002: 840 and 850).

8 Interview, 13/08/98. Other interviewees also echoed this opinion but more so in the sense of frustration over how the welfare state was managed.

9 Korpi challenged the arguments of Bildt and the Lindbeck Commission by saying that Sweden was still very affluent compared to other countries with a fast growth rate. Bildt's Liberal Minister for Health and Social Affairs also claimed that there was no need for drastic welfare cuts, and, more importantly, that Sweden should not follow the path of the USA or Japan (Gould, 1995: 11–13).

10 Schori, cited in Lindmarker, 1991: 9. It should be noted that the term 'neutrality' has often been used more outside of Sweden than inside (Interview, Lennmarker, 18/08/98). The term *alliansfrihet* denoted non-aligned countries so neutrality was the key reference term for Sweden (Stråth, 2000a: 372). Malmborg claims that the term *neutralitetspolitik* (neutrality policy) only entered the Swedish language in 1891, and *alliansfrihet* came into use more in the 1950s as military alliances formed, in order to indicate Sweden's neutrality in wartime (2001: 3).

11 In the Russian parliamentary election of 1993, Zhirinovsky's statements that Finland should be annexed as part of the Russian Federation prompted alarm in Finland (Fitzmaurice, 1995: 228).

12 Between 1991 and 1994, Finland suffered a serious economic recession, with unemployment reaching 18 per cent and economic production falling by around 7 per cent (*The European*, 18–24/01/96).

13 The debate over the legitimacy of the Austrian State Treaty has drawn various opinions within the political parties. Generally, the FPÖ question neutrality (but switched in the past if it was politically convenient) and want the State Treaty abolished. The SPÖ and the Greens defend both, and the ÖVP holds the middle ground.

14 Some issues, such as welfare provisions, environmental standards, and agricultural policy, required some revision. See Commission of the European Communities, 1992; 1993a; 1993b; 1993c; and House of Lords, 1993.

A new Swedish identity?

15 See Commission of the European Communities, 1991: 6; Neuhold, 1994b: 24. Belgium was also critical of Austria's neutrality and claimed that a neutral state 'could not be satisfactorily integrated into the Union'. (Phinnemore, 1995: 364) Austria held the view that neutrality was compatible with the EEC Treaty (Articles 223 and 224) which concerned the maintenance of peace and international security. However, it was up to the European Court of Justice to decide if this article was in agreement with Austria's constitutional neutrality. It was widely agreed by experts that no opt-outs could be obtained for neutrals so long as the ECJ was the final arbiter (Luif, 1990: 188–99).

16 It was not until 1994 that the US began to accept the notion of an ESDI, and the establishment of a European pillar under NATO with the WEU. The US in particular was concerned about the EU duplicating NATO's role in security when the EU began to push for a separate military capacity to handle crises in Europe (Van Staden, 1994: 150).

17 Within Sweden, the impact of Swedish guilt from WWII is debatable. Despite investigations of the extent of Sweden's complicity with Germany, 'it would be false to say Sweden's past is a burning issue'. (*Reuters Press*, 05/01/98) I would concur with this point. In the course of my interviews and fieldwork, many MPs and foreign policy experts did not agree with Boëthius's claims. According to Landerholm, 'she is quite isolated in her views'. (Interview, Landerholm, 25/08/98) Arvidsson is not certain that Boëthius is taking into account the context of the time (as most interviewees acknowledge) but concedes that the debate is 'perhaps important'. (Interview, Arvidsson, 11/08/98) One unattributable source responded by saying that her views are rather cynical and could possibly be seen to devalue neutrality's moral position.

18 In the 1990s, various reports claimed that Sweden was an 'informal member' of NATO, and sought military assistance from the West in the event of an attack by the USSR. The Commission on Neutrality Policy investigated the claims, but found little evidence to back them up (see SOU, 1994: 31–5). The issue was revived again in August 1998 by the conservative broadsheet *Svenska Dagbladet* and within academia Tunander's 1999 article prompted much criticism. Based on a series of interviews with many 'unattributable sources', Tunander claims that Sweden was 'plugged into NATO' on a high level. Kronvall et al., (2000) found his piece to be 'weak', full of 'conjecture' and lacking in empirical evidence. The view that Sweden was NATO's 'secret 17th member' garnered little reaction in public opinion (Dahl, 2002: 143).

19 In 1990, Sweden's UN General Assembly votes with the Third World tallied 46 per cent, compared to 54 per cent with the EU. In 1991, the figures were 25 per cent and 75 per cent respectively, and in 1992, 13 per cent and 87 per cent respectively again (Bjereld, 1994: 9). Austria experienced a similar shift with the end of the coalition government and the election of a new ÖVP majority government (1966–70). Interests developed more towards Western Europe and attention towards the Third World declined, with the position reversed when the SPÖ was politically strong, most notably during the Kreisky era, which pursued a more active model of neutrality (see Benke and Wodak, 2001: 37; Luif, 1986: 26–7).

20 When examining Sweden's track record of recognition afforded to new states, Sweden employed a strict policy of abiding by UN rules and legal formulations. A new state, in order to receive recognition, must adhere to the criteria established in international law (i.e. it must contain a people, a defined territory, which is organised under a state authority which has full control over the territory). On this basis, Sweden did not recognise the provisional revolutionary government (PRR) in South Vietnam in the 1970s, nor did it recognise Western Sahara, East Timor and the Palestinian state of the PLO on the West Bank and Gaza. The same policy was adopted for the DDR until the

Hallstein Doctrine was abandoned in 1972; nor did it recognise North Korea until 1973 (Bjereld, 1994: 6–7).

21 Only two principles were fulfilled in these cases – the existence of a 'people' (Croats and Bosnians) and territories (Croatia and Bosnia-Herzegovina) but the governments were not in control of their territories. Sweden took into account political considerations, that Croatia had undertaken to respect human rights and democracy and issue guarantees for national minorities (Bjereld, 1995b: 188).

22 Sweden abstained from voting on freezing nuclear weapons, explaining that the wording of the 1991 Resolution 45/59 was no longer relevant (even though it voted in favour the previous year), and again abstained from voting on Resolution 47/64D on the annexation of the Golan Heights by Israel, citing similar reasons. In some cases between 1990 and 1993, Sweden altered its vote with no explanation whatsoever (Bjereld, 1995a: 189–90).

23 Interview, Rohdin, 12/08/98. In her discussion of neutral states in the UN, Baker Fox claimed that neutral states compensated for their inactivity on security and political questions by focussing on social and economic issues (Baker Fox, 1965: 781)

24 These figures are based on percentage of the Swedish labour force, and include those engaged in government-subsidised job training programmes (SAF, 2000: 10; also *The European*, 19–25/08/94).

25 Shadow finance minister Göran Persson (who would become Prime Minister in the 1998 election) announced a new economic plan which involved increased taxes and spending cuts of SEK 61 billion. The non-socialist parties criticised his plans for a 5 per cent 'solidarity tax' on incomes over SEK 200,000. Persson also aimed to reintroduce the 'double taxation' of share dividends that the Bildt Government had ended. This would have meant both a corporate tax and a personal income tax (Aylott, 1995a: 423–4).

26 The election campaign of 1994 was markedly different to previous ones. Concern arose over the perceived 'Americanisation' of Swedish politics. The 1994 SAP election campaign made use of consultants and pollsters. The SAP had hired advisers from Bill Clinton's election team for the 1994 campaign (Aylott, 1995: 423). Åsard claims that the involvement of such campaigning techniques and the reliance on the media played an insignificant role in the election; the influence of American style politics and methods is minimal, yet this may be a future trend (1999).

27 Edlund's (2000) study shows that there is little empirical evidence of a long-term trend of increased discontent over taxation between 1981 and 1997. Particularly between 1981 and 1991/2, discontent had decreased. There are some indications that there has been a gradual increase during the 1990s (especially between 1996 and 1997). Edlund contends that cuts to the welfare state and the less universal flavour of welfare reform are a key cause for concern amongst Swedish citizens.

28 See Ruth on the backlash against Social Democratic norms and ideas (1984: 56–60).

7

Into Europe with the SAP: Sweden as an EU member state

> Our country has lost its way these last few years. We have all the problems everyone else has. Our famous middle way has disappeared with inflation and unemployment and doubts about the future. We are no longer special. (Björn Linnell)[1]

THE BILDT LEGACY did much to redefine Swedish identity and neutrality and in light of Sweden's bid to join the EU, can be regarded as an attempt to 'normalise' Sweden through the discourse of neoliberalism. Nonetheless, as Blyth noted previously, the post-Bildt era would not necessarily mean an easy return to traditional Social Democratic principles and ideology. When the SAP returned to power in 1994, it managed to secure a positive referendum for EU membership, and Sweden became a member state in 1995. During the referendum campaign, division still remained over joining the EU, both among the public and within the SAP itself. An EFTA Barometer poll of 1992 revealed that Swedes were wary of the EC deciding health and social welfare policy, education, industrial and cultural policy, and security and defence (EFTA Barometer, 1992). At the SAP congress in Gothenburg in September 1993, the issue of EU membership was adjourned and the party adopted a 'wait and see' approach. Carlsson kept a low profile, allowing his ministers to choose which campaign to support. In August 1994, the Swedish government submitted its Bill to Parliament, which proposed that the Parliament should accept Sweden's accession to the EU.

Although Carlsson agreed with Bildt that Sweden should join the EU, the difference lay in what aspects of membership would be prioritised (Miles, 2000: 226). Swedes were more comfortable with the Social Democratic reasons for joining the EU – the idea that Sweden would be able to export its norms and values onto the EU level and through this hopefully repair the welfare state and the Swedish Model. Some positive signs that this might be possible existed at the time – the leftward turn in European politics and the limitations of Maastricht's voting structure favoured small states, so it appeared that there would be some room to achieve these goals.

The result of the November referendum was 52.3 per cent yes, with 46.8 per cent against. Voter turnout reached 83.3 per cent (Svensson, 1994: 1).

Voters in the south of Sweden scored high on choosing to go with the EU, but figures were lower in the north, particularly those constituencies close to the Norwegian border (Jahn and Storsved, 1995: 25) (Norway rejected EU membership for the second time). Women, who made up a large number of public sector employees, were especially against EU membership, fearing loss of welfare provisions for childcare. Fitzmaurice (1995: 231) claims that without a Social Democratic government, obtaining a 'yes' vote for EU membership 'would have been very difficult if not impossible'. Social Democratic voters were reluctant to vote yes to help Bildt in 'achieving his goal of bringing Sweden into the EU in order to pursue the dismantling of the Swedish Model by market reforms'.

Sweden has had to make the shift from *nation-state* to *member state*. Subsequently, membership of the EU has reshaped Swedish politics, policy and identity in a number of ways. This chapter examines Sweden's integration into the EU from 1995 to 2000, focusing on the impact on Swedish neutrality, cooperation in European security circles, and whether Sweden is adopting a 'European identity' as a result of these changes. From a constructivist perspective, I argue that during this period, Swedish identity and neutrality were 'up for grabs'. Sweden's economic, social and security policies would now be devised with greater reference to its involvement in European integration. Beginning with an analysis of Sweden's early input into the CFSP, I outline how pressure began to increase on issues of security cooperation and integration. Against this background, I then consider how ideas of European identity and integration have affected Sweden as it adapts to the European model. The domestic debates over Europe and neutrality are then given attention, as well as a focus on how EU membership impacted upon other European neutrals and the tensions that appeared in Nordic cooperation and solidarity during this time. Sweden thus faced another period of self-reflection and a reassessment of its own identity.

The initial years of Swedish EU membership and security cooperation

When Sweden became a member state of the EU, it was keen to appear unproblematic in terms of European security cooperation. The SAP did not alter Bildt's redefinition of Swedish neutrality when it returned to power. Sweden was aware that neutrality carried a certain stigma in a Union which aimed to achieve its long-term vision of political and security integration. As such, upon joining the EU, Sweden signalled its acceptance of the CFSP and the *aquis communautaire*. Sweden became an observer state of the WEU, joined NATO's PFP and its Planning and Review Process (PARP), and the EAPC. Sweden also enthusiastically supported Baltic security cooperation, EU membership for Latvia, Lithuania and Estonia, and their bid for NATO membership.

Sweden was still wary of giving security guarantees to other states, which was part of the WEU Treaty (Article V). There were also concerns over the EU solely making security and defence decisions without the involvement of the UN, the OSCE, or the Council of Europe. Sweden wanted to pursue a broader type of security that included peacekeeping, mediation, and dialogue between states, rather than immediately opt for a militarist path. At this early stage of membership, Sweden did not want to appear problematic with regard to security cooperation, but was also reluctant to stray too far from its established methods of securitisation.

Despite concern about the EU's approach to security, there was little expectation that the CFSP would tightly commit Sweden to a pan-European defence initiative. The necessity for unanimous voting on decisions related to defence and the vague wording of the Maastricht Treaty meant that Sweden did not regard the more complex issues of defence as binding. Despite committing to the CFSP, Sweden (along with Finland) reiterated the right to decide its own security policy and for neutrality to be respected (Halonen and Hjelm-Wallén, 1997b; Hjelm-Wallén, 1996). Even Bildt (1997: 10) recognised the importance of national interests in the EU, claiming that member states should not 'submerge their national foreign policies into a common European one'. Nonetheless, it was not the intention of the EU to keep the CFSP static.

Post-Maastricht: the neutrals' impact on the CFSP and increasing pressure for integration

In order to make the CFSP both workable and credible, its decision-making structure and instruments would require further clarification. The provisions of the Maastricht Treaty were due for revision at the Amsterdam Summit in 1996, and the crisis in the Balkans heightened the urgency for the EU to develop its external capacity beyond rhetoric. The neutral states were particularly keen to develop a broader interpretation of security in the EU, by emphasising the importance of the inclusion of the UN, the OSCE and the Council of Europe. Sweden and Finland were concerned about a military emphasis gaining precedence in the development of the CFSP. The Finnish-Swedish memorandum of April 1996 (to the forthcoming Intergovernmental Conference (IGC)) submitted the proposal that the WEU take on board the 'Petersberg tasks' of humanitarian assistance, peacekeeping and crisis management. Furthermore, Sweden and Finland stressed that all states should be involved in decision-making on an equal basis, regardless of their membership of military alliances (Memorandum from Finland and Sweden, 1996). The Swedish-Finnish Memorandum faced criticism from other member states. Those preferring a more ambitious CFSP regarded the memorandum as too intergovernmental. It also allowed neutrals to have a voice in operations involving the WEU, in which they were not full members.[2] During the Amsterdam Summit, Sweden and Finland pushed for the Petersberg tasks to be included in the CFSP, and this was adopted in the Amsterdam Treaty of 1997.

Sweden emphasised expanding the 'soft' security profile of the EU in order to bring its own security traditions and norms to the European level. The success in importing the Petersberg tasks into the remit of the CFSP inspired a confidence in the EU as a progressive organisation which prioritised the broader aspects of security cooperation that had characterised the neutral outlook on security matters. The Petersberg tasks steered EU security cooperation away from questions of militarisation and promoted discussion of the EU as an alternative security organisation in the post-Cold War era, reviving ideas such as Duchêne's notion of a 'civilian power Europe'.[3] Sweden and Finland support this conceptualisation of security in the European context, stressing solidarity between member states in foreign policy, and a strong reliance on joint declarations and sanctions, which 'is the EU's strongest weapon in the event of a crisis'. (MFA, 1998: 15)

Although Sweden and Finland were successful in contributing their ideas about European security and made an early substantial impact upon the CFSP, the Amsterdam provisions signalled a tighter commitment to fulfilling the aims of security integration. Stressing loyalty and solidarity, the Treaty asked member states to 'refrain from any action which is contrary to the interests of the Union or likely to impair its effectiveness as a cohesive force in international relations'. (European Union, 1997b) In terms of decision-making, the Amsterdam provisions decreased the use of unanimous voting on certain aspects of the CFSP.[4] Furthermore, some member states pushed to give the EU 'a genuine capacity to act' (Blair, 1999). After criticisms of weakness after the Kosovo crisis, integration stepped up pace. The Cologne Summit of 1999 examined cooperation beyond crisis management and increasing the range of military and non-military 'response tools' available to the EU, with the suggestion of transferring the functions of the WEU to the EU (later adopted) (Keohane, 2001: 7). For Sweden, there was still concern about mutual guarantees for security and defence, and the distinction between crisis management and defence (Lindh, 1999). The Helsinki European Council of December 1999 went beyond crisis management, exploring the possibility of member states committing military forces, and the development of a 'Common European Security and Defence Policy' (CESDP[5]). The Helsinki Summit adopted the aim of creating a European Rapid Reaction Force (ERRF) of 50–60,000 troops by 2003, which could be readily deployed within 60 days and operational for one year. This force would concentrate on humanitarian and rescue missions, peacekeeping, and peacemaking in crisis management (European Union, 2001); and peace*making* is a different business to peace*keeping*. The Nice Council (December 2000) later approved new permanent political and military bodies, such as the standing Political and Security Committee, a Civilian Crisis Management Committee, the Military Committee, and the Military Staff.[6]

European security integration was touching on sensitive areas for Swedish neutrality. The Helsinki Summit left many in Sweden feeling that the CFSP was moving too fast (Vaahtoranta and Forsberg, 2000: 14–15). Simultaneously, neutrality still raised concerns within the EU. Neutral states' objection to the WEU's integration into the EU proper was criticised by other member states. It was widely claimed that neutrals wanted the benefits of security yet did not want to participate in the 'nuts and bolts' of obligations (Ojanen, 2000a). The EU was developing the apparatus and the vision to go somewhere beyond soft security tasks. For Missiroli (1999: 46–7), the softer options of the Petersberg tasks had the possibility of escalating into defensive measures. Should this happen, military non-alignment would undermine 'the political credibility of the defense "dimension" of the CFSP'.

The wider context: European security cooperation and European identity

As the EU moved towards deeper political and security cooperation, it simultaneously tried to cultivate a European identity which would bind member states together by something more than shared economic interests. Under a CFSP, the EU could present a united front in international affairs, and its position in international relations would be based around a number of common values and interests (see Chapter 6). This had been lacking in the past. The change from an economic club to a political one required more than a united policy; it had to be based on unifying principles and values that were applicable to all member states. Benedict Anderson (1991: 53) rightly comments that 'in themselves, market-zones, "natural" geographic or politico-administrative, do not create attachments. Who will willingly die for Comecon or the EEC?' If such units are to develop or create such attachments, we must look to how they create meanings.

In addition to shared norms and values, the EU placed much weight on common heritage, history and culture to form the basis of a European identity, forming what Adler calls a 'cognitive region' (1997b). Indeed, the EU has a range of symbolic and discursive tools that in a sense 'manufacture' an identity; it has its own flag, anthem and vocabulary ('directives'; 'regulations'; '*acquis communautaire*'; 'co-decision'; 'subsidiarity'; 'the democratic deficit') that are *sui generis* in nature.[7] Integration has developed via treaties, policies, institutions and processes. Diez (1999: 601) contends that the politics of integration discourse has produced 'Europe' or the idea of 'Europe'. The 'language' of the EU does not merely *describe* itself as a polity, but *constructs* that polity (and thereby the norms and values it encases).[8] The signing of the ECSC Treaty created the first European institutions and a system of governance establishing a 'remarkable collection of speech acts' in the form of declarations, treaties, decisions by the ECJ, and so forth. This led to various actions and modes of integration, which in turn reinforced the idea of 'Europe'.

The idea of Europe nonetheless remains a contested one. The European sense of identity springs from various factors, such as the Greek-Judeo-Christian heritage, Humanism and the Renaissance, the Reformation, the Enlightenment and the French and Industrial Revolutions. Rather than the 'melting pot' of the American variety, European identity has been more about 'unity in diversity'. (Neuhold, 1996: 29) This is largely due to the fact that countries join the EC/EU for different reasons: economic need (the UK, Sweden), political rehabilitation (Germany, Portugal, Spain, Greece), security (Finland, Belgium) or internal cohesion and international substance (Italy, Luxembourg). Thus, the members of the EU subscribe to certain aspects of European integration which fit their national profile, but will not readily subscribe to all.

For Stråth (2000b: 19), *the idea of Europe* is not the same as the idea of European identity. Ideas about Europe date back centuries, in the hopes for a pacific union of the type espoused by Kant and others. The European resistance movement against fascism in the 1930s shaped a particular vision of 'Europe' which eventually came to fruition through the ECSC. Therefore, in considering the *sui generis* nature of the EU, we are perhaps witnessing the modelling of a new pan-European identity that is united in broad conceptions about democracy, human rights, conflict resolution and rule of law. Yet there exists some doubt over the 'commonality' of the new model. Sperling and Kirchner (1998) claim that the changes in the European state system in 1989 did not unify Europe. There were still different levels or spheres of involvement amongst European states. The economies of European countries are not the same, and not all European states are members of the same international organisations. The EU is a complex decision-making unit, with differing procedures and rules depending on the policy area. Although the EU is trying to foster the 'we-feeling' that Deutsch (1957: 36) counts as important for pluralistic security communities, as a whole, its identity is disjointed. It suffers a 'democratic deficit'; it is seen as highly bureaucratic and lacking in legitimacy.

European identity is thus interpreted in different ways. As Delanty (1995: 1) points out, every age invented the idea of Europe according to the context of the times. For certain countries, the ideal of Europe is engaged at different points and in differing contexts. Europe is a social construct, 'an idea as much as a reality'. For the Czech Republic, the notion of belonging to Europe is tied to its desire to separate from Slovakia. For the UK, and especially Scandinavia, there is talk of 'going into Europe' as opposed to Central and Eastern Europe states who talk of a 'return to Europe'. (Delanty, 1995: 137) Stråth (2000b) and Burgess (2000) claim that European cultural identity emerges at a point of crisis in order to create a sense of shared interests and heritage. In terms of a common foreign and security policy stance, a common identity was emphasised when the EC was heavily criticised over its disarray during the Gulf War and its perceived failure in the Balkan crisis in the early 1990s. During the period of 'Euro-sclerosis' in the 1970s, the Copenhagen Summit of 1973 pursued a common European identity, invoked to produce solidarity and unity. A great part of the discussion about a European identity is based upon what it can potentially be. It contains different interpretations and means different things to different people. As Burgess put it: 'Europe has an identity thanks to the reality that it cannot decide what that identity is. Europe's experience of itself ... is the experience of a *question*, the question of Europe.' (2000: 432, original emphasis)

Thus, the creation of such a construct can be regarded as a challenge to the nation-state and sovereignty. The identities of the nation-state can be confronted by the larger project of European integration, as ideas of self compete against emerging norms, values and policies. Although Sweden has been able to influence the CFSP, this does not imply a one-way exchange. As a member state, Sweden's actions and policies have shifted accordingly. In 1997 Sweden established diplomatic missions to NATO, and has officers and civil servants working as partnership staff in NATO staff structures (Vaahtoranta and Forsberg, 2000: 16). In 1998, Sweden and Finland announced their willingness to place their military forces at the disposal of the WEU (with UN or OSCE mandate for action) (Lindh and Halonen, 1998). In November 2000, the then Foreign Minister Anna Lindh also announced that Sweden would contribute army, naval and air units plus approximately 1,900 men for EU peace support missions (which were to be dealt with on a case-to-case basis and would require a UN mandate).[9]

By way of the integration process, the idea that European and Swedish security values were inconsistent began to break down. The EU came to be regarded as a 'security project' and a 'peace project' rather than a 'capitalist' one (SOU, 1997: 11). This view of the EU has been the prevalent one, particularly under the Persson Government, and government rhetoric places much value on shared norms between Sweden and the EU. Political elites are redefining Sweden in light of its EU membership and identify with the Union's values and principles. This marks a distinctive change from the traditional SAP stance on European integration, which was once considered to be a project that had little in common with Swedish interests. The Persson government, which took over from Carlsson in the 1998 election, has been far more pro-European and open to shifting public perception about neutrality than its predecessor, which came into Europe with a party divided on membership.[10] This new conceptualisation of the EU has permitted a more involved form of security cooperation by Sweden. For Persson (2000), Sweden's membership of the EU opens up opportunities to 'steer the agenda ... in a Europe that is increasingly progressive, a Europe that is increasingly marked by common values'.

Disengaging neutrality and bringing in NATO: the official and public debate

The debate about Sweden's wider circles of involvement in European security prompted more public commentary by key government and military figures of the possibility of Sweden joining NATO. The pursuit of NATO membership occupied newspaper, television and parliamentary debate, and had the effect of bringing such topics into everyday discourse. The Commander-in-Chief of the Swedish army, Johan Hederstedt, explained: 'We take part in the military handling of crises within the European Union, which is an alliance. This is contrary to our security doctrines, which ought to be updated.' (*EU Observer*, 22/11/00; *Dagens Nyheter*, 22/11/00) The former Defence Minister Anders Björck claimed 'I will not be surprised if Sweden would join NATO within the foreseeable future.' (1998) The Moderate Party was keen to dissolve what Bo Lundgren called 'this spineless security policy'.[11] During the Bildt years, the possibility of NATO membership began to be articulated publicly, but in the context of the time, Sweden was not yet an EU member state – it was aspiring to be one. As an EU member state, such debates about European security integration and NATO membership began to be linked to the discourse of being an EU member. For the Moderate Party and the Liberal Party, NATO membership was regarded 'as a natural conclusion ... to European cooperation in all things. That doesn't necessarily lead us to the conclusion that Sweden should apply for NATO membership tomorrow, but we see it as the *natural end point* of more and more close cooperation with NATO and with our Western powers.' (Interview, Hall, 11/08/98, my emphasis) In a sense, these could be seen as 'natural' topics for discussion, as Sweden seemed to progress from being a neutral state to an active participant in European security.

Bildt's position won the support of *Dagens Nyheter*, which declared in January 1997 that he was one of the few who dared 'to think aloud' on the issue. According to Bildt, 'only backwards-looking fundamentalists' would cut off Sweden's options on NATO (*Wired from Sweden*, 17/01/97). Neutrality came to be viewed as part of the old Social Democratic order – the order that did not fit with the realities of the globalising world economy and political integration with Europe. For the Moderates, EU membership meant that Swedish neutrality 'is no more' (Interview, Landerholm, 25/08/98). Yet it was not enough simply to dismiss neutrality – something else had to take its place. During Bildt's time in office, NATO and European security cooperation provided this potential replacement. However, with the return of the SAP to power, there was some expectation that a return to a neutral position would come about. Conscious of public sensitivity about NATO, the SAP attempted to downplay the issue, but Bildt's discourse and new ideas had opened up a debate about Sweden's relationship with NATO, and from this point on, there was little room to reverse.

The SAP tried to discourage debate about NATO membership. In a public debate with Bildt in 1998, Lena Hjelm-Wallén (Foreign Minister, 1994–98) claimed it was 'dangerous' to talk of NATO membership: 'Either Sweden is militarily non-aligned or we aren't. As long as we are, we must together make sure that non-alignment is respected and the rest of the world has confidence in it.' (*Wired from Sweden*, 09/02/98) For the Moderates, Sweden's interests could be better served as part of NATO, particularly if Sweden continued to send troops on NATO-led peacekeeping missions. But for Hjelm-Wallén, offering security guarantees and being part of a military alliance was 'not the central feature of today's work for a pan-European security order'. (1997b) The SAP was interested in furthering cooperation with NATO on a range of issues (peacekeeping and regional security, for instance) but this had yet to filter down to the public. Opinion polls consistently revealed that around 40 per cent of the public were against NATO membership.[12] There remained strong nostalgia on the issue of neutrality – it formed part of the collective memory of Sweden's experiences during two world wars and has defined Sweden's distinctive stance internationally. During the Kosovo crisis, NATO's bombing campaign in early 1999 and the EU's role in this provoked criticism across the political spectrum in Sweden. Persson and Carlsson called the action 'illegal', and were angered at the lack of UN mandate for the action.[13] Bildt openly criticised both the EU and NATO (Møller, 1999: 14–15). According to Persson, neutrality still 'colours our attitude and Sweden's role in Europe and the world'. (Persson, 1999)

Despite the public's 'coloured attitude', there was awareness amongst the SAP leadership that neutrality still mattered to the Swedish public. This could be detected in the duality of Anna Lindh's (Hjelm-Wallén's successor) speeches on Swedish non-alignment, which recognised the importance of a 'credible' policy – but in the past, credibility in foreign policy meant *not* being part of Europe. Lindh had clearly stated that a policy of military non-alignment 'best serves security, both for us and the world around us' despite claiming that Sweden's membership of the EU means that Sweden is now part of a political alliance: 'The changes have meant that the concept of neutrality policy and the self-imposed restrictions this implied in order to lend credibility to our policy, have lost significance.' (Lindh, 1998) Lindh's dual message reflected both the sensitivity of neutrality to the Swedish public, mixed with the reality of Sweden's new commitments in Europe.

Swedish Euroscepticism and competing norms and values

Whilst debate may have opened up about neutrality, the public were also sceptical of European integration and its implications. European identity was always perceived to have been the opposite of Swedish experience. Swedes largely remain suspicious of federalism in the EU and according to polls, Sweden is the most anti-EU member state, surpassing the UK and Denmark. Eurobarometer polls between 1995 and 2004 show that Sweden has ranked the highest negative response in every year for the question of support for EU membership and perceived benefits of EU membership (Commission of the European Communities, *Standard Eurobarometer Reports*, 1995–2004).

Swedes in general are also negative about the economic implications of EU membership, witnessed in Sweden's slow movement towards EMU and its later rejection of EMU entry in the 2003 referendum. According to Åsbrink (1998), Sweden's non-participation in the Euro is political. The public remained uneasy over its impact on the welfare state and the transparency of EU institutions such as the European Central Bank. Key organisations and union groups were not convinced that EMU would address unemployment, poverty and social inequality.[14] For Persson, Sweden will eventually have little option but to join: 'It's impossible for us to say no. We only have two options. *Yes* we want to enter now or *Yes* we want to enter later.' (*Radio Sweden*, 15/11/99) Persson anticipates the construction of a modernised European social model and active welfare states in the EU (Swedish Parliament, 2000a).

But the EU is in many ways the antithesis to the traditional Social Democratic model that shaped many of the institutions and norms that constructed Swedish politics and identity. The more progressive elements of traditional Social Democratic ideology will find little ground in a market-based organisation. With the Swedish Model widely considered to be inappropriate to European economic goals, there has subsequently been a shift in perception and ideas under the Persson government. Key figures in Swedish business welcome further integration with the EU, considering the Swedish Model over and blaming the poor state of the economy on Sweden's 'voluntary isolation' from external markets; and the publications of pro-market think-tanks pursue the question of Sweden's lack of competitiveness as a result of the welfare state.[15] Persson's close link with Tony Blair is presented as the more progressive arm of EU economic discussion, but there remain substantial differences between SAP socialism and the so-called 'third way' of New Labour. New Labour embraces social justice, but the discourse is located primarily in terms of the 'individual' and by default, the market place. Social justice should be pursued on the basis of 'the equal worth of each individual'. (Blair, 1998: 3) Despite Blair's nods to concepts that remain an intrinsic part of the Social Democratic agenda (equality, social solidarity, community, so he draws very much on the 'communitarian' tradition here), he pays more attention to economic forces and pragmatic methods of achieving such goals.[16] Emphasis on individualism differs from the Swedish idea about the individual; Blair still talks of stable families and stresses partnership between business and government but is rather reticent on workers' input into such decisions. The SAP, along with the LO, SACO and TCO, on the other hand, are pushing for workers' rights on a European scale.[17]

Regardless of the public view of European integration, it is questionable whether the SAP will be able to influence European integration to the degree it expects. The SAP has indeed been active in terms of importing certain norms and values to the EU, especially in the area of environmental protection, transparency (public access to official EU documents, now a principle of the Amsterdam Treaty) and to some degree, gender equality. But the reality is that Sweden has to deal with 24 other member states whose ideological and political norms differ. This has already arisen in the area of gender, where Swedish views have already being challenged[18] and the more radical ideas of gender equality are becoming more mainstream in Sweden.[19]

In another area, Sweden's long-standing rules on alcohol are also facing upheaval. Upon joining the EU, the state monopoly on alcohol was challenged by the ECJ, which claimed it broke competition laws (this was later overruled). This has remained an important debate in the Swedish press and parliament.[20] Sweden has the highest alcohol taxes in Europe. After Finland and Denmark reduced alcohol taxes, and neighbouring Estonia and Latvia joined the EU, *Systembolaget*[21] has experienced losses from cheaper alcohol coming into Sweden after its exemption from the EU over personal imports ended in 2003. The issue of alcohol taxes reflects two sides to the story. Compared to most of Europe, where drinking is considered a private activity, in Sweden it is more so a public issue, perceived to have negative consequences for society as a whole. In Sweden, the control of alcohol is related to 'the two core principles of universalism and decommodification that emerged out of decades of social democratic hegemony'. Thus, the state has a 'moral obligation' to restrict sales and distribution (Kurzer, 2001: 147–8). On the other side, the argument for tax cuts and an end to *Systembolaget* is largely in the vein of free market principles and making Sweden 'normal' compared to its European neighbours.

In many senses, the Swedish debate about EU membership has gone beyond past differences between European and Swedish norms to a question of whether to adapt or adopt EU norms. The SAP under Persson clearly aligns Sweden's interests with those of the broader European community as part of its discourse of solidarity, but the changes in security policy, domestic policy and accepted social norms reveal a gap between the public and the leadership. The following section investigates how Europeanisation is affecting other neutral states and altering Nordic cooperation, both of which influence Swedish neutrality and internationalism.

European neutrals and Europeanisation

For many of the European neutrals, membership of the EU has largely been understood as a 'return to Europe' (Ireland, having been a member of the EC since 1973, is a rather different case). Finland, although it cooperates with Sweden on security initiatives, is more pro-EU than Sweden. For the Finns, European security was a release from the 'straitjacket of our Cold War neutrality' (Valtasaari, 1999) and seen as a natural shift back to a true (West) European identity (Browning, 1999). Neutrality has been openly criticised in official circles, with Max Jakobson (former diplomat and once an ardent supporter of Finnish neutrality) dominating the debate. Jakobson claimed that important security decisions will in future be made in NATO (not the EU/WEU) and that Finland ought to avoid being left out of the decision-making process.[22] Polls, however, consistently show high levels of hostility to the idea and a preference for non-alignment (usually in the range of over 70 per cent supporting non-alignment) (*EU Observer*, 11/12/01). The debate in Finland has been more open because technically the TFCMA is obsolete and EU membership also represents a chance for Finland to have an international voice, which it could not have during its close relationship with the USSR. Finland has been active on the Nordic Dimension and other EU-related initiatives and, like Sweden, hopes to bring into the EU its 'own traditions and values, which bring new nuances to the policies and working methods of the EU'. (Halonen, 1998)

In Austria, the debate about the future of neutrality is tied to the desire to etch out a European identity and wider participation in European security. Benke and Wodak, in their analysis of a televised debate on neutrality and NATO membership in 1998, note that NATO dominates the discussion 'while neutrality never becomes the predominant focus of the interaction'. (2001: 42) In its Coalition Agreement (2000), the Federal Government decided to pursue within the EU 'a guarantee of mutual assistance between the EU countries' in security matters. The federal constitutional law on neutrality would also be redrafted so Austria could fully participate in the CFSP towards this end.[23] There has been much discussion about plans to reassess 'without taboos ... a reorientation of the Austrian security and defence policy'.

(Ferrero-Waldner, 2001) Furthermore, the option to join NATO remained 'open'. (Austrian Government, 2000: 115) The Austrian leadership has been positive about the issue of NATO for some time, with Vice-Chancellor and Minister for Foreign Affairs, Wolfgang Schüssel stating that NATO enlargement was of 'civilizational importance' (1997) and Klestil arguing that neutrality is incompatible with NATO. NATO enlargement to include Austria's neighbours has also encouraged a positive view of military alliances.[24] Neutrality is no longer a contentious issue for the centre-right government as it was for the Social Democratic government that presided over Austria's accession to the EU (*The Guardian*, 05/11/01). Such verbal acrobatics, nonetheless, signify that although the Austrian leadership is ready to move on NATO membership, and move on from neutrality, it is still constrained by public opinion and legal barriers. Neutrality remains a fixture of Austrian identity, despite officials pushing to locate Austrian identity in a European context.

For Ireland, neutrality has also undergone reinterpretation. Ireland was the only neutral member state of the EC, but managed to combine membership and a neutral stance because foreign policy cooperation within the Community was so weak under EPC. Ireland joined the EC as part of its efforts towards industrialisation and modernisation which started in the 1950s. Ireland wanted to decrease its dependence on Great Britain economically, and the economic reasons for membership outweighed the political (Laffan and Tannam, 1998: 70). However, in the 1990s, there has been public debate about the nature and relevance of Irish neutrality, with a growing number of political commentators arguing for its abandonment. Irish neutrality, according to McSweeney, 'has no other significance in Ireland than symbolically to placate the ghost of Frank Aiken and postpone the day when Irish policy-makers will face the political and moral challenge of our EU membership'. (1998) Former Taoiseach Garret FitzGerald has been outspoken about Ireland's assistance to Britain during the Second World War, but still maintains that there exists 'a general sentiment favouring certain enduring values in foreign affairs'. (*Irish Times*, 19/10/96) In 1996, support for neutrality was still firm, with almost seven out of ten wishing to maintain neutrality. The government's decision to apply for membership of PFP caused consternation amongst political parties, particularly Fianna Fáil and the Greens, and the government's 1996 White Paper on Foreign Policy did similar by advocating closer links with the WEU.[25] Taoiseach Bertie Ahern has insisted that neutrality is consistent with the security dimension of the EU. Ireland joined PFP in January 1999, yet this was expected to go no further and the government announced that it has 'no intention' of joining NATO or the WEU (*Financial Times*, 29/01/99).

Within Switzerland, there has been debate over the place of neutrality in the context of possible EU membership and the post-Cold War era. The Swiss government has recognised 'the increasing gulf between the realities of security policy and the status of neutrality' (Swiss Government, 2000: 21). Although Switzerland adhered to the basic legal principles underlining its neutrality policy, changes have been instigated that permit involvement in collective security in the context of the UN. In June 1993, parliament passed a federal law permitting Swiss troops to serve in peacekeeping operations under the UN and OSCE. Swiss neutrality is being reinterpreted in wider terms, although it is still recognised that neutrality remains a taboo subject (Rösch, 1993). In May 2000, Switzerland held a referendum on opening up the country to the EU: 67 per cent of the population approved, and as a result, Switzerland now has a series of bilateral agreements with the EU, which cover technical barriers to trade, agriculture, transport, research, and the movement of people (DFA/DEA Integration Office, 2000). The Swiss are moving away from an isolationist stance: in March 2002, 55 per cent of the population voted to join the UN.[26]

Malta's prior reluctance to join the EC has been due to its neutral stance, but is also related to ideas about Maltese identity and battles between the two main political parties. The Maltese Labour Party, which under Dom Mintoff aligned the country with its Arabic past and favoured neutrality, is in opposition to the conservative Nationalist government, which sees Malta as European and Christian (Gerber, 2000). The former has criticised the ruling Nationalist Party over its zeal in its pursuit of EU membership, preferring an industrial free trade zone with the EU (a 'Switzerland in the Mediterranean' policy) and a continuation of Maltese neutrality, which saw the tiny state 'punch above its weight' on the international stage as part of the Non-Aligned Movement. For the Nationalists, however, neutrality represents the brand of socialism that Mintoff championed, and his antipathy towards Britain and the US. The debate in Malta about Europe and neutrality has been constructed around ideas of identity and Malta's future role in Europe.

Europeanising has involved a questioning of neutrality. Whilst official debate shows a preference for Europeanisation, neutrality, or military non-alignment, remains deeply attached to public sentiment and ideas about the nation. On some levels, the debates in neutral countries contain some similarities in terms of identity and recasting the role of the state, but the discourse and discussion is specific to each country's historical, social, economic and political circumstances. This period of self-reflection and rethinking of neutrality and identity also signals the possibility of less solidarity amongst neutrals as EU member states. As the following section outlines, shifting patterns of solidarity also affect Sweden in terms of Nordic cooperation in the context of the EU.

Fractures in Nordic solidarity

In the early 1970s, Palme expected that 'whatever their relationship to the common market, the Scandinavian countries must stick together'. (1972: 7) When Sweden joined the EU, it was assumed that Nordic solidarity, if anything, would strengthen. This has not materialised. Despite Nordic cooperation on initiatives such as the Northern Dimension, and a desire to export their norms and values to the European level, EU membership has highlighted some divisions amongst the Nordic states.

Finland, for instance, is more positive about European integration than Denmark or Sweden, who adopt a more sceptical, anti-federalist attitude. Finland supports a strong Commission, and is prepared to give up its veto power in the Council of Ministers for greater cooperation. Denmark and Sweden support intergovernmentalism and a stronger Council of Ministers. In the EP, Nordic MEPs infrequently join forces, and stick to their political groups (*Helsingin Sanomat*, 31/10/00). This has resulted in the Nordic states forging alliances with other European states.[27] Sweden and the UK have similar views on monetary union, and the Persson Government also finds common ground with Blair's New Labour on issues such as globalisation. Sweden and the UK also have 'shared values' with regard to improving the effectiveness of the UN in conflict and crisis management, as a joint article in *The Scotsman* by Lindh and Robin Cook demonstrates (1999).

Within the EU, the Nordic states cooperate on regional issues with a specifically European focus: assistance to the Baltic states, relations with Russia, and the Northern Dimension Project. Since independence in 1991, the Baltic states have had close cooperation with Sweden, Denmark and Finland, including bilateral and multilateral assistance in trade, political, social and security cooperation.[28] The Northern Dimension project attempts to assert the North as a distinctive region, different to 'Westerness' and based on 'Nordicity'. As Joenniemi puts it, this adds to the 'plurality of the EU' and works towards dispelling the image of the EU as 'a closed and unattainable "club" with very fixed external borders'. (1999: 3) This may appear to contribute a unique Nordic presence within the Union; however, tensions have reportedly arisen due to perceived competition between the Nordic states. Sweden has been blamed for trying to act as 'leader' in the European North and its tactics are alienating its Nordic neighbours (Hansen, 1996). Competition has overtaken solidarity (Mouritzen, 1998: 56; Vaahtoranta and Forsberg, 2000: 5). Furthermore, Finland's National Coalition Party has recently expressed criticism of the Northern Dimension programme, claiming it is not working (*Helsingin Sanomat*, 09/03/05). Denmark's policy of environmental protection is opposed by the Finns, who have a large stake of their economy in the export of pulp. Denmark has lost its role as bridge between the EC and the Nordic countries with new Nordic member states (Pedersen, 1995:

1199–1200). Nordic cooperation in the UN has also declined (Møller, 1999: 4).

Ideologically, there seems to be less in common amongst the Nordic states than in the past. Social Democratic solidarity, which once defined the Nordic region, is also in decline. The Danish Social Democrats were ousted in November 2001 by a centre-right coalition of the Liberal (*Venstre*) Party and the Conservative party. The new Liberal Prime Minister Anders Fogh Rasmussen set out to reform the Danish welfare system, with more emphasis on individualism (Rasmussen, 2002). The Danish general election had a strong voter turnout (87 per cent) and the extreme right-wing party *Dansk Folkeparti* gained nine new seats (it now has 22 seats in the *Folketing*) (BBC News, 21/11/01). A month earlier, the Norwegian Labour Party also faced electoral defeat to a centre-right coalition, which relied on support from the far-right Progress Party. For Maigaard (1996: 17), 'Nordic cooperation is more an expression of a community of attitudes than a community of interests.' At present, it is difficult to predict whether a 'community of attitudes' may still be the case, given the current shift from the left to the centre-right. Cooperation now has a distinctly European character and focus: Sweden may hark back nostalgically to Nordicity, but official speeches confirm that the connection between Nordic states is primarily in terms of trade and anchored more broadly in a European context, despite new cooperation on security policy.[29] The language used is also different in the European setting, as demonstrated by Hjelm-Wallén's idea of Baltic security cooperation: 'The Baltic Sea Region is not just a consumer of peace and security in Europe. It is increasingly becoming a producer. I would like to look upon cooperation in the Baltic Sea Region as a peace project.' (1997b) Security has become a commodity.

Now Nordic interests are pursued in an EU framework, and are not based on any firm notion of Scandinavian exceptionalism. For many, Nordic cooperation has become a 'worn-out expression'. (*Helsingin Sanomat*, 31/10/00) According to Joenniemi (1990: 214), the Nordic states failed to promote their specific approach to security as an alternative in the post-Cold War era: 'The Nordic countries do not seem prepared to generalise from their experiences from the postwar period. They do not trust their model to carry weight if applied in a broader European context.' Mouritzen (1995: 16) makes an interesting point with reference to the realignment with Europe, linking the decline of the Nordic model (of which Sweden was considered the leader) with EU membership (and the change in Swedish neutrality), claiming that the leader has 'now joined the EU class as a student'.

Ruth noted this change in the 1980s, claiming that political culture in Sweden was 'more fragile, less rooted in a firm conviction of its own values'. The logic of globalisation and European integration has taken over traditional views that Sweden was a model for the rest of the world. Uncertainty about the value of Sweden's traditional approach in the post-bipolar, globalised world has translated into the turn towards Europe as the solution to economic and political questions (1984: 54). This was especially the case during the Bildt years and the turn away from Nordic cooperation in favour of European cooperation. Nordic solidarity was a strong part of the SAP platform, and since the changes to the Swedish Model in the 1980s, the breakdown in close Nordic relations is also important from the point of view of Sweden's breakdown in consensus and SAP hegemony. Therefore, patterns of cooperation are changing, and are likely to influence the direction of Swedish neutrality. Sweden, being a member state of the EU, cannot be immune to the pressures of European integration, security changes in other neutral states, and the breakdown in traditional Nordic solidarity.

As constructivists posit, the values and behaviour of an actor will alter in the process of 'learning' new norms and values through interaction. According to Lipschutz (1995: 217) 'Defining security involves establishing a definition of the collective self via-à-vis other collective selves.' At the elite level in Sweden, this is evident in the SAP's approach to European integration and it appears 'most likely that the political practices of Brussels will shape Nordic political practices'. (Stenbäck, 1995: 26) From the integrative process, Sweden re-examined its traditional views and ideas about pan-European security, and this fostered linkages with the EU in terms of common goals and a sense of community bound by mutual understandings (Deutsch, 1957: 22 and 36). Because of EU membership, Sweden regards its security position as positive (less likelihood of being attacked as an EU member state) (Ministry of Defence, 1998: 22). The idea that the EU was a threat to Swedish neutrality decreased and after the Cold War, was turned into a different debate by political elites. Lindh (1999) claims that 'Sweden has a European identity' and with this comes 'European responsibil[ities]'. Sweden began to identify with the European project and saw a role for itself in the construction of a European security community, or as Britt Bohlin claims, this means: 'We can take part. We can belong.' (Interview, Bohlin, 13/08/98)

As a result of Sweden's increasing involvement in European security issues, neutrality has gradually been sidelined. The government's Defence Committee in early 1999 considered dropping the reference to 'neutrality in war'. Åström supported this change, favouring the non-allied status but saying references to neutrality should be removed (Ojanen et al., 2000: 181–8). In November 2000, Persson claimed that neutrality was no longer relevant after the Cold War and that: 'Neutrality does not cover all aspects of our security policy, for example disarmament, non-proliferation of nuclear arms and stability in Europe.' (*Financial Times*, 28/11/00; *Dagens Nyheter*, 22/11/00) Whereas in the past, neutrality was deeply linked to such issues, in the post-Cold War, European security context, it is not. A month later, the

SAP dropped any specific reference to neutrality ('free from military alliances with the view of being neutral in case of war in our near area') without broad debate in the party organisation or the public. In the same month, Lindh told the *Riksdag* that Sweden was no longer neutral: 'It seems that the only scope for the freedom from alliances is that we should be neutral. We want a better definition.' (*EU Observer*, 14/12/00) This was carried through in the government's statement of policy in the *Riksdag* in February 2001, which announced its intention to review the 1992 formula 'to arrive at a better description of the orientation of our security policy'. (MFA, 2001: 7) At this stage, the government still reaffirmed the value of non-participation in military alliances and recognised the strong public support that this policy commands.

Conclusion: Europeanising Sweden?

> There may be more than one discourse in operation within particular states. The interesting question is which of these frameworks of meaning exert influence on foreign policy. It is possible that the foreign policy of a state is split between several frameworks of meaning or that different discourses dominate particular policy areas. (Larsen, 2000: 40)

This statement is perhaps the most accurate way to locate the question of Swedish security policy in the late 1990s. The phenomena of Europeanisation, altered domestic norms and institutions, and new security realities have called into question traditional Swedish frameworks for defining its security stance. Official discourse is trying to pull Sweden in a more European direction, but the attachment to neutrality remains one of the most potent 'myths' from decades of Social Democratic hegemony, and as such, is difficult to dislodge.

Swedish neutrality, despite deeper European integration, had not disappeared because it was part of the basic beliefs in Swedish society. 'The ideal of a policy of neutrality is ... so solidly rooted in the Swedish tradition that it is likely to remain in form longer than in substance.' (Andrén, 1991: 81) Even though 'Europeanization of domestic life was accepted as a necessity', when it comes to neutrality, 'it cuts deeply into the configuration of political forces in society'. Swedish neutrality was domestically viewed as having a *sui generis* character; it differed from the forms of neutrality practised elsewhere in Europe. Subsequently, neutrality was an expression of or a 'codeword for independence'. (Stålvant, 1990: 151 and 158–9) As Berger (1996: 326) notes, it is those beliefs that are more abstract or emotionally-connected that constitute the core of a culture, and these beliefs are difficult to alter.

The nature of neutrality was likewise changing from the roles and definitions that characterised it during the Cold War years. In Gärtner's (1996: 609) opinion, neutrality will change because the context has altered, and will therefore 'have to take on a new meaning'. The neutral countries are participating in the EAPC, WEAG, and PFP. Finland, in 1997, opened a permanent mission to NATO and nominated an ambassador to NATO (Norrback, 1998: 7). Therefore, it appears that neutral states are interpreting their role in Europe through a revision of neutrality. Mediation is no longer the special role of the neutral state and 'good offices' now holds less significance to the neutral profile. Such functions are now being overtaken by other states who are part of military alliances, such as Norway and Canada. As a result, there is wider cooperation on the European level, and the willingness to participate in European security is indicative of a desire to downplay the neutral card, whereas in the past, this was not the case.

Identities, as constructivists argue, are malleable, subject to change. However, change does not come about suddenly. For Sweden, a number of variables have combined to create a change in the traditional security policy established under decades of Social Democratic guidance. The end of the Cold War has widely signalled the obsolescence of neutrality. Bildt's efforts to put Sweden on a European path established the domestic context. The nature of neutrality became subject to popular debate, and subsequently lost some of its taboo status. European integration has become the strongest challenge to the relevance of neutrality as the EU forges a common security identity. However, the public remained moored to a particular image of neutrality and the meanings it conveyed. Neutrality was an important symbol of self in Sweden. Its embeddedness in the fabric of what constitutes 'Sweden' remains a potent factor despite the new direction the government wishes to forge. The language and discourse of inclusion and unity is already influencing how neutral states are altering their security policies in order to 'fit in' with a European vision. Nordic cooperation under European integration is less based on solidarity, more so on European issues. But processes of identification are historical, developing by overlapping and modifying each other. At present, Sweden is at the point where past understandings of Europe are juxtaposed against newer interpretations and realities.

Swedish neutrality is now being placed in the European context, and as such, its continuance will rely on the extent to which it can be proven to be compatible with European security norms and practices. Sweden has been able to contribute its understanding and experience of security to EU policies so far. Yet this understanding will face confrontation as other neutral states increasingly move away from a neutral stance in favour of wider European cooperation. Likewise, European integration will not pause at certain points. Security integration will go beyond the Petersberg Tasks, and there is evidence of this already occurring as non-neutral member states accelerate security cooperation.

Wider participation in European security matters is mediated through a

The social construction of Swedish neutrality

Social Democratic discourse, emphasising traditional ideas of solidarity. As actors integrate, they 'learn' from each other, adopting norms, languages, and symbolic gestures to produce shared meanings and understandings. Sweden is in the process of a form of social, economic, and political integration, and its established norms and practices are confronted with new meanings. But new meanings do not immediately replace old ones, nor do they wither away quietly. So far, Sweden has managed to successfully merge its own understandings with those of Europe. The extent to which Sweden becomes 'European' rests on a number of factors, and here neutrality's embeddeness serves as an important marker between the known past and the hazardous future, where established norms and patterns that shaped the Swedish identity may be discarded or embellished. In 2002, the Persson government rewrote the Swedish security doctrine in a move that many have interpreted as the end of neutrality. This, coupled with the 'war on terrorism', globalisation and Europeanisation, make up the last chapter in the story of Swedish neutrality which is to follow.

NOTES

1 Former editor of *Moderna Tider* (cited in *Specter*, 1998).
2 At the WEU meeting in Birmingham in 1996, it was agreed that WEU observers did have the right to participate in peacekeeping and crisis management tasks and decision-making (Archer, 1997: 1–6), although this debate highlighted the different ideas of securitisation amongst the member states, between those who focussed on alliance-based forms of security cooperation and others such as Finland and Sweden who read security in broader terms.
3 Duchêne's idea referred to the emphasis on diplomatic and economic measures on the international stage rather than military force. Civilian power Europe came to be associated with efforts towards conciliation and arbitration, which Duchêne had hoped would 'consolidate the shift in international relations in Europe from a military to a political emphasis'. (1973: 19–21). This view later became sidelined as Hedley Bull (1983) declared that the EC's lack of military power rendered Europe ineffective on the world stage.
4 In an effort to foster a more 'communitarian' CFSP, the use of qualified majority voting (QMV) was introduced for decisions and implementation of joint actions, common positions or other decisions based on common strategies. This marked a change from the Maastricht provisions which allowed for QMV on a case-by-case basis and wider use of unanimous voting. Member states can still object to the use of QMV if their national interests are affected, but Amsterdam also brought in 'constructive abstention'. This means that if a member state does not agree with a decision, the action cannot be stopped from going ahead (European Union, 1997b).
5 Whilst the ESDI concept stressed burden-sharing between NATO and the EU, the CESDP implies a more ambitious profile for the EU, going beyond sharing resources to political influence and diplomatic leadership (Croft et al., 2000: 504).
6 During the Santa Maria Da Feira European Council in 2000, it was also agreed to establish police officers to be available for international civilian crisis management missions (EU, 2000). The Treaty of Nice (2001) kept to the use of QMV on military and defence decisions, without prejudice to the security and defence policy of member states (European Union, 2001).

7   Delanty rather scathingly dismisses such symbolic gestures, claiming that 'the cultural apparatus of the new institutions was not the stuff out of which new symbolic structures could be built ... Ironically in attempting to move beyond nationalism, the European Community attempted to fashion a European identity using the very tools of nationalism: the flag, anthem, passport, group name and sense of common history.' (1995: 128)
8   Diez looks at the concept of European citizenship with regard to this claim. The establishment of EU citizenship was not merely based on defining citizens in a particular space or area relating to geography, or an economic market, but was in a sense a 'reformulation of the concept of citizenship' in itself (1999: 601).
9   In the *Riksdag*, the Green Party expressed concern about potential EU militarisation and the EU's remit to perform such actions (Swedish Parliament, 2000b).
10 The 1998 election saw the SAP record their worst vote since 1921 (36.4 per cent, a drop of 8.9 per cent since the 1994 election). Voter turnout for the 1998 election (81.4 per cent) was the lowest since 1958, indicating a further crisis in representation and a protest vote against the SAP. Of the political parties, the Left and the Christian Democrats made gains (12 per cent and 11.8 per cent respectively). The election campaign centred on issues such as unemployment, the economy and social welfare. The Moderate Party tried to woo disgruntled SAP voters by targeting tax increases, and the Left criticised cutbacks to the public sector (which was the SAP's formula for 're-establishing politics and safeguarding democracy'). The number of LO members voting for the SAP declined (66 per cent in 1994 to 52 per cent in 1998); many LO votes went to the Left Party (Möller, 1999: 261–3).
11 BBC Monitoring International Reports, 'Swedish parliament discusses new security policy doctrine'. 13/02/02. Text of report by Swedish SVT Europa.
12 There have been some reports that resistance to NATO membership was decreasing (*Svenska Dagbladet*, 05/02/97), but in general, opposition remains the norm, even in today's figures (see Chapter 8).
13 Keohane claims that this is a somewhat disputed point; NATO claimed it had a UN mandate under Resolution 1699 (2001: 4). What troubled the EU neutrals was whether NATO's action was compatible with international law. Austria took the same view as Sweden, denouncing the bombings and denying the use of Austrian airspace to NATO.
14 Some pro-EU Social Democrats argue that EMU would stabilise Sweden's economy and growth, thereby helping the welfare state and increasing social spending. The centre-right parties also believe EMU would bring market discipline to public spending. See Gould, 1999, for further discussion of Sweden's position.
15 See comments by Perh Gyllenhammar (1996) and Peter Wallenberg (*Europe*, 1995) in the mid-1990s, and on think-tank publications, see those of the IUI, Timbro, SNS, and the Stockholm Network.
16 Walker (1998) comments that there is no fundamental questioning of capitalism in Blair's approach. The Swedish 'third way' as a discourse and a practice still informs Swedish industry on some level. When Ford took over the automotive sector of Volvo in 1999, there was overwhelming concern that American business practices or 'corporate culture' would introduce levels of hierarchy in the workplace. Workers want to keep Volvo independent, not expand into areas that it does not specialise in (excessive competition) and ensure that workers' standards are maintained (*Detroit Free Press*, 06/03/99).
17 The emphasis of the Swedish presidency of the EU in 2001 was the 'three Es': enlargement, employment and environment. In 2000, the LO, SACO, and TCO issued a joint

declaration recommending the Swedish presidency to concentrate on the following areas: developing a social dimension; extension of the EU's common employment policy; a more open and enlarged EU; and gender equality.

18 In 1997, a Swedish MEP proposed that the EU act against pornography and prostitution. Sweden's Commission of Inquiry into the sex trade recommended criminalising the purchasing of prostitutes' services, which was enacted in Sweden in 1998. Yet the Dutch chair of the EP Committee on Women rejected Sweden's proposal as being 'too moralistic' and not related to violence against women (Gould, 1999: 168–9). Interestingly, the Dutch are also facing a shift in traditional policies which stem from core values and historical development. The permissive Dutch drugs policy has, since the late 1990s, been tightened and attitudes have become less tolerant towards drug use (Kurzer, 2001: 148).

19 Kulick (2003) observes that new laws on prostitution in Sweden were a response to EU membership, an example of 'moral panic' over opening borders to a wider Europe. In the run up to the referendum on EU membership, the problem of prostitution (identified by *Dagens Nyheter* and *Expressen* as largely from Eastern Europe and linked to organised crime, drugs, and the spread of HIV) was depicted as a threat to Sweden, particularly at a time when prostitution was largely being decriminalised in many European states.

20 *Radio Sweden* has covered the issue on an almost weekly basis, and in the *Riksdag*, the matter has lead to heated debates. The SAP has resisted moves to lower taxes on alcohol purchases, and the KD want to reintroduce limits to the amount of alcohol that can enter the country. The Moderate Party wants *Systembolaget* abolished, and the Liberals have reversed their previous stance (a legacy of the temperance movement) and have called for lower duties.

21 Sweden's *Systembolaget* is the state-run alcohol monopoly, controlling the production, wholesale, distribution and retail of alcohol. Currently, revenues from alcohol sales and taxes go to substance abuse treatment clinics, which are locally run. Of the five state-run alcohol monopolies, only *Systembolaget* remains since EU membership (Gould, 1999: 169–70; Kurzer, 2001: 147–55).

22 This viewpoint was criticised by the then Centre Party leader Aho, and President Ahtisasari, as Finland still adhered to military non-alignment (Arter, 1996: 621–6; see also Joenniemi, 1993: 291).

23 The Foreign Minister claimed that the Petersberg Tasks (now included in the EU Treaty) meant Austria had to amend Article 23 of the Federal Constitution Act, with the addition of Article 23(f), which would permit Austria to partake in combat operations in crisis management, including peacemaking. The new article allows Austria to participate in sanctions decided under the CFSP (Luif, 1998: 125; also Schüssel, 2000: 5).

24 Putin has made clear Russia's discomfort with the prospect of Austria joining NATO. Putin regards Austrian neutrality as 'a valuable achievement which we rate highly'. Prior to this statement, the Russian ambassador in Vienna stated that Austria's joining NATO would amount to a breach of international law (BBC News, 08/02/01).

25 *The Irish Times*/MRBI poll also found that respondents were largely in favour of PFP, anticipating the proposals of the White Paper. The poll revealed that 57 per cent of respondents agreed that member states should defend each other in the event of an attack (*The Irish Times*, 05/10/96).

26 This was, nonetheless, an extremely contested issue, and 45 per cent voted against. The German-speaking Swiss were sceptical of UN membership, due to its cost, the effect on neutrality and sovereignty and general suspicion of the UN Security Council. Christoph Blocher, the right-wing populist, also played on neutrality during his 'no' campaign, employing a poster with an axe superimposed over the word 'neutrality'

(*The Guardian*, 04/03/02).
27 Finnish academics have also downplayed the Nordic connection as it rediscovers its European identity. Historian Matti Klinge has advocated that Finland orient itself towards Germany and Europe, since Nordic cooperation and solidarity were established in a Cold War context, which now no longer exists (Stenius, 1996).
28 There is also an emphasis on bringing Nordic models of conflict resolution and policy-making to the EU, and this is linked with the Baltic states and Russia. A strong emphasis of the project is to support democracy, political stability, economic development, regional cooperation and security in the Baltic states (Knudsen, 1998: 29).
29 Security issues were not discussed in the Nordic Council until 1997 and ministers of defence for the first time participated in a session of the Nordic Council. In October 2000, a plan to coordinate and plan a Nordic crisis management cooperation (NORD-CAPS) was introduced (Nordic Council of Ministers, 2000: 46).

8

The 'war on terror' and globalisation: implications for neutrality and sovereignty

> Neutrality is a concept of the past. (Javier Solana, Secretary-General of EU and High Representative for the CFSP, *EU Observer*, 17/01/01)

ALTHOUGH MEMBERSHIP of the EU and wider participation in European security will essentially determine the fate of Swedish neutrality, the developments in international politics that came after the terrorist attacks of September 11, 2001 have reshaped international relations and with it, added further fuel to the argument that neutrality is now obsolete. Since September 11, there have been additional alterations to the security doctrines of neutral or non-aligned states, and in the case of Sweden, a significant shift occurred in 2002 when then Persson government radically altered the text of Sweden's security doctrine (discussed in detail below). The EU's external dimension has also gathered pace in light of the 'war on terror', with the introduction of new measures to combat international terrorism. The 'war on terror', combined with the EU's economic strength and role in the process of globalisation has a dual consequence for neutral states: European integration essentially implies the downgrading of sovereignty in the field of security, and both globalisation and the fight against international terrorism will impact not only upon the principle of sovereignty but the ability of neutrality as a concept to muster any sustenance in the post-September 11 world. This final chapter analyses these new developments in relation to their implications for Swedish military non-alignment and the future of neutrality in general. It begins by examining the shift in international relations and security in the post-September 11 international order and the amendments to Sweden's security formula which followed in February 2002 (which had been proposed in 2001). The chapter moves on to then examine the increasing pressures on Swedish security policy and sovereignty stemming from European cooperation and the challenges of globalisation. Despite the changes that open up Sweden to options to participate in mutual security, remnants of neutrality remain. The chapter then concludes with a discussion of the possibilities of converting the values of neutrality towards a more progressive European profile in international relations through norm change.

Reshaping the global order: international relations post-September 11

The post-Cold War period was characterised by a sense of uncertainty about the shape and direction of international security. In the 1990s, a number of themes emerged to take the place of Cold War tensions – humanitarian and human rights issues, the impact of globalisation, civil wars and ethnic tensions. For neutral states, this was fertile ground in which to continue with neutrality, and more significantly, the shaping and consolidating of international law and norms. Where the post-Cold War 1990s security agenda was preoccupied with 'new wars', (Kaldor, 1999) ethnic violence and humanitarian intervention (as evidenced in Kosovo and conflict in Rwanda and Somalia), the following decade ushered in a new kind of enemy that was stateless and exploited global networks to secure its goals. After post-Cold War uncertainty, the fight against international terrorism has refocused the objectives and policies of nation-states and international organisations. International terrorism, particularly extremist Islamic fundamentalism, poses, some argue, a threat to 'civilisation' (as interpreted by the Bush Administration, and in an obvious manner giving credence to the predictions of Huntington), but more broadly, it is seen to represent a fundamental challenge to (Western) 'ways of life'.[1] The post-modern 'ways of life' simultaneously became the basis of the terrorist threat to international security, as terrorist networks and organisations operated through the global economy and channels of communication, and within and outside of the state. This, we are told, is the 'dark side' of globalisation (Rasmussen, 2004: 333). In a post-modern world, sovereignty is opaque and threats do not emanate from the traditional sources of the state. As Romano Prodi, Commission President, claimed in a speech one month after the attacks, 'The threat is global, and the terrorists' instruments are global.' (Prodi, 2001) No more than 24 hours after the September 11 attacks, NATO, for the first time in its history, invoked Article 5 of the Washington Treaty, deeming the attack on the US to be an attack on all NATO members (NATO, 2004). Democracy, freedom, and the rule of law are deemed to be at risk against a new enemy which can strike at any time, using a range of devastating methods. The nature of the new threat has instigated a 'state of emergency' within states (Armitage, 2002), creating a 'world risk society' (Beck, 2002) impacting upon security, immigration, banking and finance, policing, intelligence, legislative systems and processes, travel, trade, media and the arts, popular culture, and education. So broad is the scope of the 'war on terror' that it has already been used as a justification for securitisation domestically. The 'war on terror' has been used to legitimise Putin's actions with regard to Chechnya, and Israel justifies its security actions in the West Bank and Gaza under the guise of the 'war on terror' (Roth, 2004). Furthermore, it has been presented as an *ongoing* war and in current estimations, looks set to outstrip the costs of the Cold War (Jackson, 2005: 3 and 16). For Dunne, in the 'war on terror', the US has a 'mission'. (2003: 309)

This 'mission' has been presented in terms which exclude any opportunity for neutralism: 'In the struggle between terrorist killers and peaceful nations, there is no neutral ground. All nations must join in confronting this threat where it arises – before terrorists can inflict even greater harm and suffering.' (Bush, 2003) The 'war on terror' has been linked to a significant turning point in American history – the break with isolationism. Parallels have been drawn between September 11 and Pearl Harbor, presenting a picture that suggests America has been twice caught off guard under isolationism (Weber, 2002). This association of isolationism and vulnerability echoes throughout history (note the Belgian and Norwegian cases discussed in Chapter 1) and is reinforced in the terminology employed by Bush's 'with us or against us' depiction of the 'war on terror'. The events of 1941 'eliminated "isolationism" as a political, intellectual and even a morally defensible force in American life'. (Parmar, 2005: 14) Likewise, September 11 is a call to other nations to abandon a neutral stance. The 'war on terror' is presented as a *just war* and a *good war* (Lawler, 2002; Skidelsky, 2004) from which no nation can withdraw or opt out.

Redefining security: Sweden, neutrality and the 'war on terror'

Prior to the September 11 attacks, the Swedish government announced in its annual statement to the *Riksdag* that it intended to review the 1992 formula of neutrality 'to arrive at a better description of the orientation of our security policy'. (MFA, 2001: 7) In February 2001, the Persson Government secured the changes through an agreement with the Moderate Party, the Christian Democrats, and the Centre Party, and the new security formula was presented:

> The aims of Sweden's security policy are to preserve our country's peace and independence, contribute to stability and security in our vicinity and strengthen international peace and security. Sweden pursues a policy of non-participation in military alliances. This security policy, making it possible for our country to remain neutral in the event of conflicts in our vicinity, has served us well. Looking to the future, it is more apparent than ever that security is more than the absence of military conflict. Threats to peace and our security can best be averted by acting concertedly and in cooperation with other countries. The primary expression of this conviction at global level is our support for the United Nations. As a member

of the European Union, we are part of a community based on solidarity, whose primary purpose is to prevent war on the European continent. (MFA, 2002)

Although the commitment to military non-alignment remains in the text, the new formula also states that Sweden is no longer neutral in the case of war in its immediate surroundings, should an EU member state be attacked (*Dagens Nyheter*, 12/02/02; SAP, 2001). Neutrality is now an *option*, rather than the cornerstone of Swedish security policy. Swedish security is now based on three pillars: cooperation with other countries (with a large emphasis on the EU and the UN); a modern defence; and a modern, free and active non-alignment policy (Persson, 2001b). Persson and Lindh wanted to drop the word 'neutral' from the SAP party programme, yet delegates voted to keep neutrality as an option (*Financial Times*, 09/11/01). The shift in security doctrine was intended to clarify Sweden's foreign policy stance and smooth the path to greater involvement in European security cooperation, and given the timing, cannot be seen to have been a direct consequence of September 11. But Persson's strong condemnation of the September 11 attacks and his promise to stand firm with the US (including support for its actions in Afghanistan) raised concerns that Sweden was about to blindly follow the lead of the Bush Administration. Less than one month after the attacks, Persson stated: 'America does not stand alone ... All democracies stand side by side in the fight against terrorism ... and America has a right to use military force in response to the September 11 terrorist attack – not just a right; it is also a responsibility to the rest of the free world.' Lindh also stated that neutrality does not apply in the fight against international terrorism (Nordic Reach, 2001; Persson, 2001a).

The new position has caused much debate. The Left Party's Lars Ohly described the new security doctrine as 'alarming', and a 'real shift to the right in which the Social Democrats accommodated the nonsocialists on all points'. (*Dagens Nyheter*, 11/02/02) In the parliamentary debate in October 2001, the Left and Green Party expressed criticism towards the Bush campaign, and former Prime Minister Carlsson and Carl Tham (former Education Minister) denounced the US, saying terrorism was understandable in an unjust world order they believe is maintained by the US. Sverker Åström advised that Sweden and the EU should not follow the lead of the US in the fight against terrorism and was critical of Persson's support of the US's 'right' to self defence (Forsberg, 2002: 158).[2] Former Foreign Minister Sten Andersson, who was involved in the Stockholm Process that aimed to resolve the Middle East conflict, accused the SAP of siding with Israel and betraying the Palestinians.[3] Critics within the SAP are becoming more vocal because of Persson's distancing from the Palme tradition, and some SAP members have been sidelined, such as MEP Maj-Britt Théorin (formerly Palme's Ambassador for Disarmament) over her opposition – along with Carlsson and Tham – to

The social construction of Swedish neutrality

NATO bombings in Kosovo which were unauthorised by the UN (Burke, 2001b). She was demoted on the SAP party list of candidates in the 1999 EP election, and replaced by cabinet member Pierre Schori, who supported the bombing campaign, was given first place. More recently, Sweden has come under criticism from Amnesty International and other bodies for its deportation of two Egyptian detainees. The shifts in Swedish foreign policy, to some, indicate a more 'commonplace' or 'acquiescent' style, where Sweden is no longer seen as the radical critic on the international stage but the 'unthinking ally of Washington' (Oberg, 2001; Ramachandaran, 2001). For Oberg, 'Sweden has lost its creative grasp on global concerns and its solidarity with the disadvantaged and finds security in following the herd.' (2000)

The change in doctrine also brought the issue of NATO membership into public debate. In November 2002, the *Riksdag* raised Sweden's status in the NATO Parliamentary Assembly from guest observer to associated member.[4] For Huldt, the revised security formula 'dismantles some of the obstacles that we have put in the way of approaching NATO'. (*USA Today*, 13/02/02) Where Lindh acknowledged that public opinion was strongly against joining NATO (at the time, 49 per cent were opposed) (*Radio Sweden*, 05/03/02), Persson presented the choice in more black and white terms: 'The heart of NATO's security policy is mutual defence guarantees, and we do not want to be a part of that so we should not be a part of the decision-making process.' (*Times of India*, 13/02/02) By counting Sweden out of 'the decision-making process', Persson emphasises that Sweden will be increasingly marginalised if it does *not* join NATO. The NATO question, plus the 2002 revision, imply European security cooperation and maintaining a neutral stance are two contentious and irreconcilable points. Neutrality and Sweden's involvement in European integration are being presented as incompatible themes, rather than as a unique Swedish contribution to European integration.

The 'war on terror' has affected the non-alignment policies of a number of EU member states, and resulted in some heated debates over efforts to shift policy away from neutrality. Since September 11, Austria's neutrality policy has been influenced by the 'war on terror' and broader developments in European security. Days before the attacks, Schüssel indicated that he was willing to renounce neutrality and consider NATO membership after a discussion with George W. Bush. Following the attacks, which he labelled a threat to the 'civilised world', he declared that neutrality does not apply (*EU Business*, 10/12/03). In the same month, both Schüssel and Albert Rohan, the secretary-general of the Austrian foreign ministry publicly supported NATO membership, with the latter declaring that neutrality 'is no longer an issue' and an 'artificial obstacle to a natural development' towards a CFSP (NATO, 04/11/01; NATO, 14/11/01). In December 2001, the Austrian Parliament published its White Paper on the Austrian Security and Defence

Doctrine, which stated: 'The security situation of a European state today can no longer be considered in isolation ... The new challenges and risks to security policy cannot be dealt with by individual states alone, but only through international cooperation in the spirit of solidarity.' (Austrian Parliament, 2001: 1) The Security and Defence Doctrine seems to argue that Austria's neutral status has gradually become more irrelevant. The common line of the Austrian administration has been that since EU membership in 1995, Austrian neutrality has become obsolete in the context of European security cooperation. However, the Security and Defence Doctrine seems to 're-write' this shift to say that the tenets of Austrian neutrality altered *after 1990* with the first Gulf War where 'the legal view came to prevail in Austria that obligations under the Statute of the United Nations take precedence over obligations under neutrality'. The document then adds that the Swiss model of neutrality (that had formed the initial basis of Austria's 1955 neutrality) was thus irrelevant. Accession to the EU, the acceptance of the *acquis*, and plans for a common defence essentially 'restricted' the Neutrality Act. The Amsterdam Treaty and participation in the Petersberg tasks have added to the further distancing of neutrality, making Austria a 'non-aligned state' (Austrian Parliament, 2001: 7). This legalistic approach to Austrian neutrality is presented as a 'continuous "adaptation"', despite the divisions within Austria over NATO's intervention in Kosovo, but in some ways revived neutrality when the issue of using force in Iraq came up. Austria rejected overflight requests for the 'coalition of the willing' and transportation of troops (Federal Chancellery, Austria, 18/03/03; Neuhold, 2003: 16–17). Since the September 11 attacks, Austria has only allowed the US to use its airspace in action in Afghanistan in its fight against terrorism.

Domestically, there are confusing signals in Austria over whether or not neutrality will be finally written out in legal and political terms. Further to the refusal for overflight access, the Austrian government incurred the criticism of the Bush Administration for delaying the transit of US troops from Germany to Italy via Austria, citing the lack of a UN mandate for action in the Gulf (*EU Observer*, 14/02/03). Over a year later in the presidential elections, the pro-neutrality candidate Heinz Fischer beat Ferrero-Waldner, who favoured stepping away from neutrality. Perhaps the most confusing shift has been with the Green Party, one of the traditional advocates of Austrian neutrality, which adopted the 'Safe in Europe' paper which proposes to redefine security policy (some argue in exchange for some influence in government). Although there are expectations from the Green Party that the EP should control a common European security policy, the shift is a clear indication that Austria intends to locate its security profile with that of Europe (particularly in relation to the EU battle groups), even if this implies ending neutrality (*EU Observer*, 09/11/04). Furthermore, the proposed EU constitution and its mutual defence clause has prompted debate over dropping neutrality, and this debate has been tied into a discourse of 'progression' and changing definitions over time, with key figures in the ÖVP claiming that amendments to the Austrian constitution in 1998 to allow participation in peacekeeping operations mean that neutrality is flexible in interpretation and would permit mutual guarantees. A survey conducted by the Austrian Society for European Politics found in February 2004 that 75 per cent favoured an EU army (*EU Observer*, 20/02/04).

In Finland, the issue of neutrality in the post-September 11 era has been a constant feature in news reportage and public debate. Compared to Sweden, Finland has been more reserved with regard to Bush's 'war on terror', and the post-September 11 environment has not encouraged a positive view towards NATO membership. According to Forsberg, only 11 per cent of Finns supported NATO membership and support for sending troops to Afghanistan was low. In a poll before US military action, only 23 per cent of Finns gave their support to strikes (Forsberg, 2002: 160). In 2004, 70 per cent of Finns were opposed to a common EU defence force (*EU Observer*, 16/02/04), although other polls tend to post greater support for European defence initiatives compared to NATO membership. The domestic debate about the 'war on terror' has at times been inflammatory. Foreign minister Erkki Tuomioja linked US unilateralism and its refusal to sign the Kyoto accord to the September 11 attacks. In Forsberg's estimation, Sweden has shown itself to be far more willing to join the US-led coalition against terrorism than Finland. Where Finland has taken a more muted tone, Sweden has engaged in strong rhetorical support. Finnish former chief of defence, Gustav Hägglund (now head of the EU military committee) had suggested it would be logical that Finland and Sweden join NATO by 2010 (*Helsingin Sanomat*, 20/01/04). Sweden and Finland have also signed up to the EU battle groups initiative, forming their own Nordic Battle Group with Estonia and Norway in May 2005 to enhance the EU's RRF capacity in crisis management operations (Ministry of Defence, 2005).

Ireland's handling of the 'war on terror' and its cooperation with the US has placed the debate about neutrality and NATO membership back on centre stage. Prior to September 11, neutrality was seen to be part of the reason for Ireland rejecting the Nice Treaty in the 2001 referendum. During the referendum campaign, the Peace and Neutrality Alliance (PANA) focused on EU militarisation, and Sein Féin highlighted neutrality in its posters.[5] In Sweden, the Nice Treaty debate was far more centred on the issue of enlargement, and Irish Prime Minister Bertie Ahern explained the negative vote in terms of a 'widespread sense of disconnection' between the EU and the Irish people and downplayed neutrality's role in the debate.[6] In 2003, the Irish government allowed the US to use Shannon airport in its military actions against Iraq, prompting renewed calls to drop neutrality and criticism that economic interests took primacy over concern for neutrality. Newspaper reportage has focussed on Ahern's relationship with Blair, and criticism that Ireland is choosing to be a 'US colony' which has abandoned international law.[7] Mass protests and High Court action to challenge the legality of allowing access to Shannon airport shows that the issue of neutrality is not exactly subdued, despite pronouncements of its demise.[8]

For new member state Malta, the debate about neutrality has been entangled in the question of EU accession and the divisions between the main political parties. The Labour Party has been the traditional supporter of neutrality, stemming from the Mintoff era when Malta was seen to punch above its weight internationally. The ruling Nationalist Party has, since gaining office in 1998, given strong signals that neutrality is out of place in the context of EU membership and that neutrality should be removed from the constitution.[9] Since the 'war on terrorism', the issue of neutrality has increasingly become part of Malta's quest to integrate itself into the global economy and be seen to support the US. According to the former Maltese president, Guido de Marco, 'there can be no neutrality between terrorism and its victims'. (2001) Under the Nationalist government Malta has opened its dry docks to service US warships, and by permitting access to Maltese ports has forced a controversial debate about the nature and purpose of Maltese neutrality. Such policy, many argue, has been guided by economic considerations.[10] The need to integrate the Maltese economy in the global market has become a crucial mission under the present government (Calleya, 2002; Fenech-Adami, 2000).

Within the EU the call to drop neutrality increases. Prior to the September 11 attacks, Solana told Austria not to expect solidarity from other countries and the French defence minister has dismissed non-alignment in the EU, claiming it has 'no meaning' (*EU Observer*, 19/01/01). Finland's *Helsingin Sanomat* ran an editorial the following day highlighting the comment in an effort to push Finland towards full integration with NATO and the EU militarily. Further commentaries have attempted to link Finland's reluctance to formally abandon neutrality as a sign of insularity (Archer, 2002).[11] In terms of Nordic cooperation, the 'war on terror' has unveiled further divisions. As of March 2003, Denmark is part of the 'coalition of the willing', has provided contributions to the military effort in Iraq, and has signed the Solidarity Statement with the US. Sweden and Denmark have had strained relations since the Rasmussen Government, with tensions over Denmark's immigration policies. The 'war on terror' has been linked to immigration in Denmark, with claims that the liberal immigration policies of the Scandinavian states provide an inviting base for their activities. Denmark's commitment to internationalism has come under question, with some claiming Rasmussen is aligning Danish interests with those of the US rather than focusing on international cooperation (*Radio Sweden*, 30/01/03; 09/05/03). Norway has backed NATO's invocation of Article V in response to the terrorist attacks on the US, and has faced pressure by the Bush Administration to sign an immunity agreement to protect US troops from the International Criminal Court. Both countries have been referred to by Osama Bin Laden in his taped recordings, whereas his reference to Sweden appears to imply that it has been excluded as a target by Al Qaeda.[12]

In March 2003, the US decision to attack Iraq on the basis that the regime of Saddam Hussein was harbouring weapons of mass destruction was presented to the international community as an essential part of the 'war on terror'. On this issue, the Persson Government has shown signs of returning to a more critical stance in international politics. Already concerned with what is widely regarded as the unilateralist position of the Bush Administration, Sweden has been critical of the US on issues such as the death penalty, withdrawal from major conventions such as the Anti-Ballistic Missile Treaty, the Kyoto accord, the International Criminal Court, human rights, UN aid, and its treatment of the UN. Much of the conduct of the 'war on terror' challenges established Swedish norms with regard to internationalism and international law and human rights. Persson has publicly stated that the US is setting a worrying precedent in its military actions in Iraq with respect to international law and that the US was 'out of step with the rest of the world' (*Radio Sweden*, 26/03/03). Both Lindh and her successor, Laila Freivalds, have criticised the Bush administration for its policies in Iraq and in relation to peace efforts in the Middle East, and Freivalds rejected a demand by the US to confiscate alleged Iraqi assets in Sweden. Hans Blix and Schori have also been critical of the US. Blix has received a high level of support in Sweden for his claims that the US was not wholly concerned with finding weapons of mass destruction in Iraq. Both Blix and Schori have been sidelined by the US in various ways, with Blix claiming to have been the subject of a smear campaign, and Schori arguing that his criticism of US foreign policy has resulted in his nomination for UN administrator in Kosovo being blackballed by the US (*The New Yorker*, 21/07/03). Concern for civil rights and privacy has been a central stance for the Swedish government, despite US demands for sky marshals, and requests for passenger information, on flights to the US (domestically, there have been proposals for monitoring telephone calls and introducing ID checks). In April 2003, the *Riksdag* passed into legislation a new law on terrorism that brings Sweden in line with EU legislative efforts.

European measures to combat international terrorism show strong signs of fulfilling or at least pursuing the norms and values that are still deeply embedded in Sweden. The EU's response to the 'war on terror' has largely been in the area of judicial measures and cooperation. In the days immediately after the attacks, a series of emergency meetings took place in all key EU institutions, resulting in air safety and security measures, and agreement on proposals for a European arrest warrant (Blair, 2004: 205). The Commission published its proposal for a Council Framework Decision on combating terrorism and the European Arrest Warrant[13] (established in December 2001) (OJEC, 2001a; 2001b). Stemming from the decisions taken at the Tampere European Council in 1999, the Justice and Home Affairs Council in 2001 issued measures to combat terrorism which included judicial cooperation, cooperation between policy and intelligence services, actions on the funding of terrorism, border measures, and measures to cooperate with the US.[14] The Plan of Action produced by the Extraordinary European Council meeting (21st September) solidified these earlier initiatives by summarising the EU position, which focused on solidarity and cooperation with the US, enhanced judicial and police cooperation, developing legal instruments through the UN and the OECD, and coordinating the fight against terrorism through a more integrated CFSP and ESDP and global trade activities. The more controversial products of the European initiatives included a common definition on terrorism and terrorists. The EU early on also agreed to give the US access to Europol and the Eurojust system of legal coordination under the Strategic Cooperation Agreement and later agreements with the US, which had been a sensitive issue in the past (Hill, 2004: 150). Europol was to have an anti-terrorism unit, and the Schengen Information System (SIS) would share some data with intelligence services. The European Security Strategy of 2003 also noted that the EU must respond to new 'dynamic' threats and 'be ready to act before a crisis occurs. Conflict prevention and threat prevention cannot start too early.' (European Council, 2003: 7) Despite the references to the need for Europe to develop a 'strategic culture' (echoed in comments by Solana and efforts to establish a European defence agency) the document places solidarity and the primacy of international law and multilateral processes and cooperation as essential to fighting international terrorism.

The EU's emphasis on judicial and international cooperation to combat terrorism has struck a chord with the Swedish government, indicating that the approach of the EU on this matter coincides with the established norms and values that still constitute Swedish identity and its world view. Freivalds has already expressed her concern about US military action in Iraq, and the fact that the 'war on terror' should not be a licence to abuse human rights: 'War on terrorism is a political metaphor, not a justification for extra-judicial acts ... Acts of terrorism are criminal acts, and criminal acts must be dealt with through law enforcement mechanisms.' For Freivalds, the combination of law enforcement responses to terrorism and military acts 'confuses the debate'. (Freivalds, 2004) Persson and Lindh publicly stated that if Sweden were on the Security Council, it would support France, Germany and Russia's veto of a second UN resolution authorising attack, and accused Blair and Bush of undermining the UN. Freivalds and Persson have strongly indicated that they consider the military action against Iraq to be 'inconsistent with the UN Charter' (Freivalds, 2004). Regardless of the show of solidarity, Persson also expressed concern at the prospect of a second Bush term in the run up to the US election. The *Daily Mirror* has reported Persson as saying that Sweden and the EU will 'continue to criticise Bush the same way as earlier. But I do not believe that he will be more willing to listen to it during the second period than during the first.' (*The Daily Mirror*, 04/11/04) The 'war on terror' has returned Sweden to a more internationalism position, with Sweden critical of US unilateralism, and pushing for stronger international instruments to deal with the terrorist threat.

Nonetheless, the 'war on terror' and the progression of European security cooperation have translated into deeper security cooperation between Sweden and its EU partners. In 2003, Sweden and Finland announced their cooperation with NATO member Norway in allowing their military forces to assist civilian authorities in dealing with accidents and catastrophes in the Arctic region (*Agence France Presse*, 29/01/03). The EU battle group initiative is also a part of this cooperation, although Sweden and the other neutrals have expressed concern over the mutual defence clause attached to the EU Constitution (which was later amended to avoid this commitment). Whether neutrality can still be upheld in the EU is questionable, especially since the 2004 enlargement that brings new powers into European decision-making. A number of the central and eastern European newcomers have enthusiastically signed up to the 'war on terror', for instance. With 'old Europe' (namely France) still commenting on the redundancy of neutrality, it appears that 'new Europe' may also be unsympathetic to a neutral stance.

Globalisation, sovereignty and the state

The domestic and international impact of Sweden's membership of the EU goes beyond the issue of neutrality. EU membership has also had a decisive impact upon Sweden's approach to the welfare state and the role of government intervention in the economy. As a member state of the EU, Sweden is implicitly involved in the process of globalisation, not simply from the perspective of a nation with a high export profile and globalisation ranking (Sweden, along with Finland, Ireland, Switzerland and Austria, rank in the top ten) (A. T. Kearney/Foreign Policy, 2005) but by being part of the largest trading bloc in the world. Sweden entered the EU determined to export its own norms and values, and was hopeful that it would have the cooperation of likeminded member states to pursue issues such as poverty, development, and fair trade. In 1997, the then Foreign Minister entertained hopes of a social democratic Europe: 'What is striking is the strong social democratic character of the agenda and the policies on which the EU is now united. We are involved in an important ideological shift. Neo-liberalism has had its day. Hopes for the future now rest with European social democracy.' (Hjelm-Wallén, 1997a) The phenomenon of globalisation could be combined with the welfare state (Pagrotsky, 1997; 2001). Furthermore, trade unions should regard globalisation not as an immutable process, but one which they can influence and change. Workers and unions can shape globalisation rather than be shaped by it and its potential inequalities (Pagrotsky, 2000). Solidarity constituted the key to the Swedish approach to globalisation and fair trade, as Schori explained: 'Globalization must be given a human face, it must be guided by solidarity and inclusion, not by egotism and exclusion.' (1997: 9)

Fast forward five years, and social democracy is on the decline, with centre-right parties gaining ascendancy in the Netherlands, Portugal, Spain and France. Touraine has declared that 'Social Democracy is dead' – free market ideology has successfully edged Social Democracy out.[15] The debate about EU membership and the changes it brings domestically has been integrated into public debates about globalisation and what this means for Sweden. Think-tanks and others have argued that globalisation is good – not simply good but necessary to make Sweden competitive and to instigate a fairer world trading system (Norberg, 2001). The welfare state is presented as an institution past its time:

> The welfare state was never an ideal form of organisation. Its claim to politically define the content of the good life and to monopolise the tools leading to it inevitably violated the principle of the equal dignity of all human beings. This pretension called for restrictions on the independence and freedom of choice of the individual and civil society which is hardly compatible with a social order whose main purpose is the safeguarding of individual freedom.' (Rojas, 2001: 107)

However, opposition to globalisation in Sweden is deeply linked to the issue of the welfare state. Swedish Attac, the Swedish wing of the global Attac anti-globalisation movement, locates their concern about the effects of globalisation on the ability of the Swedish state to protect its citizens. The violent riots in Gothenburg during the EU summit in June 2001 have also been discussed domestically in terms of dissatisfaction with changes to the welfare state and the decline of sovereignty.

Globalisation and sovereignty are broadly considered to be incompatible themes. Pressure to compete in the global economy binds nations in the 'golden straightjacket', according to Thomas Friedman, where growth is encouraged over equality (Brook, 2004: 25). Although Sweden is applauded for its redistributive policies, in recent times taxation, the 'excesses' of the welfare state, sick leave and competitiveness have been key areas of debate domestically. Some research on youth has identified an increase in individualism, perhaps indicating that the ideas of Bildt have had a sedimenting effect.[16] The main point of contention in Swedish society is the balance between welfare (provided by the state) and freedom of choice (which the global market offers). Claims that welfare reduces competitiveness and limits freedom of choice mingle with the SAP rhetoric that both can work in tandem.

The referendum to join EMU in 2003 demonstrated the Persson government's commitment to bringing Sweden in line with Europe. In the midst of the referendum campaign for EMU membership, the Persson government was accused of sidelining key members of the SAP who did not support EMU entry. The public remained sceptical over business interests working with the government (*Radio Sweden*, 26/08/03) and there was concern over the amount of spending by the 'yes' camp on the EMU referendum. According to reports, the Swedish government spent twice as much per person trying to convince the public to vote 'yes' than Bush spent in his 2000 Presidential election campaign, and *Svenskt Näringsliv* spent 500 million krona (€55 million) on the campaign (*EU Observer*, 09/09/03; 21/10/03).

The death of Anna Lindh in September, 2003 was expected to lead to a 'yes' vote in the referendum, given her central role in the referendum campaign, despite the 'no' side leading in the polls. However, Swedes returned a verdict of no to EMU, signalling that Persson's keen support over this European initiative misjudged the mood of the public. In the forthcoming efforts to establish the EU Constitution, Persson has another battle on his hands. The constitution's economic dimension, with its commitment to a 'free and undistorted market' is seen in some quarters as a recipe for neoliberal economics lacking in social protection (BBC News, 11/05/05). Despite the state of the Swedish Model, welfare continues to be a major issue in Swedish politics, regardless of Persson's view that welfare spending must decrease.[17] By comparison, Sweden's welfare provisions remain generous compared to other European states, but the Swedish government faces pressure to 'normalise' economically as a member state of the EU. Evidence of this is most prominent in the imminent changes to the state-run alcohol monopoly (and more recently pharmacies) and changes to welfare programmes. Although many have argued that Sweden has succumbed to a more neoliberal bent, there is still a commitment to exporting specific norms and values, as seen in efforts to promote 'globalisation with a human face' and push for changes in the EU to make trade more balanced with developing countries. In late February 2005, European Social Democratic leaders met in Stockholm under the Party of European Socialists, to discuss the Lisbon strategy revisions with the idea of extending the welfare state across Europe and to tackle issues of unemployment in an effort to promote economic growth with what Persson calls 'the building of a humane society' (*Radio Sweden*, 25/02/05). There may be signs that social democracy is returning to the EU, notably in the change in government in Spain after the Madrid bombings, and the French rejection of the EU Constitution (largely driven by concerns that it was a 'neoliberal' document that would threaten France's social security).

Towards a cosmopolitan reworking of neutrality in the EU?

In contemporary discourses, the subject of Swedish neutrality remains sensitive, despite the obvious efforts to acclimatise the public to the possibility of neutrality eventually being abandoned. Sweden no longer strictly adheres to neutrality in the sense of how it was applied in the post-war era under its 'credible neutrality doctrine'. Under EU membership, the meaning of neutrality has been stretched and expanded to permit actions that would have once been considered contradictory to how neutrality was understood. There is concern that the changes to Sweden's security doctrine signify more than a willingness to support European security efforts – the shift is also indicative of an effort to conform rather than stand out in international affairs. Oberg argues:

> It does not seem important to the defence intellectuals and the decision-makers to explore whether there could be new and different ways to be neutral and whether you could be neutral not between two but among many ... Neutrality has become a bad word, even when it means staying out of war. Instead, side-taking, bravery, moral commitment, conflict management and humanitarian intervention are the words of the day. (Oberg, 2000)

It is unfortunate, according to Dahlsson, that Sweden is downplaying its neutrality because 'constructive international debate demands the presence of as many independent voices as possible'. (1996) Indeed, this seemed to be the assessment about Swedish neutrality for those (this author included) who had hoped that Sweden's unique stance in international affairs would continue, despite the pressures to abandon neutrality. However, in the 'war on terror' and deeper connection to the EU through globalisation, Sweden may have an opportunity to *convert the values and norms of neutrality* towards a more normative appreciation of global politics and action. Neutrality is changing shape in all neutral/non-aligned states. The crucial question is whether Sweden can bring its more critical edge and unique world vision to the European table, so to speak, and work to transform the EU into a normative or cosmopolitan world power.

The post-September 11 world is one which has revealed a serious chasm in transatlantic relations. Much has been made of the differences between the Bush Administration and the EU, with many urging the transformation of the EU into a global actor that can either counter US hegemony or at least balance it or influence it in a positive manner. US unilateralism has serious implications for the development of a coherent and cohesive international community based on the principles of international law and cooperation. For Venn, the current state of international relations can be regarded as 'neo-feudal' (Venn, 2002: 123) and Dunne sees a new problem in terms of international hierarchy (Dunne, 2003). Nye has urged the US to employ 'soft' power over 'hard' and the former French Foreign Minister Hubert Védrine captured the sentiment of European and other citizens when he referred to the US as a *hyperpower* some time before September 11. Védrine's label taps into an underlying mistrust of US power: 'US supremacy today extends to the economy, currency, military areas, lifestyle, language and the products of mass culture that inundate the world, forming thought and fascinating even the enemies of the United States.' (Védrine, cited in Nye, 2002–3: 545) The French defence minister Michèle Alliot-Marie claims that Europe has a stronger desire for peace and solidarity due to its past wars, whereas the US 'have a desire to spread their vision through the whole world'. (*Helsingin Sanomat*, 27/09/04) Mass demonstrations protesting against the war in Iraq surfaced across Europe in February 2003, with protestors numbering from the thousands to slightly over a million.[18] A Flash Eurobarometer survey published in November 2003 showed that 58 per cent of EU citizens preferred the UN and 44 per cent the provisional government of Iraq to deal with Iraq's post-war reconstruction, with the least support for the US (18 per cent). On the question of whether the military intervention in Iraq was justified, a strong majority of citizens claimed it was 'not justified' (41 per cent) or 'largely not justified' (27 per cent).[19]

The war in Iraq, for many Europeans, had little to do with the 'war on terrorism'. The EU and the US have different conceptions of the post-Cold War international order. For the US, the 'war on terrorism' is the licence to reassert US preponderance in a number of areas. The liberal internationalist bent of the Clinton Administration, with its excursions into the Balkans crisis and humanitarian intervention, sat uncomfortably with the new Bush Administration. A year before Bush won office, Condoleeza Rice made clear the direction of the forthcoming administration, amounting to a view that 'power matters': those uncomfortable with power politics, Rice claimed, resort to appeals to international laws and norms. Under a Bush administration, there would be a decisive shift away from Wilsonian internationalism: 'To be sure, there is nothing wrong with doing something that benefits all humanity, but that is, in a sense, a second-order effect.' (Rice, 2000: 47) The combination of this re-interpretation of internationalism (equated with the pursuit of US national interests) and the Bush doctrine of pre-emptive action is a cause of concern for Europeans and highlights the distance between the US and Europe. The EU's strength lies in the 'soft options' of securitisation – international justice, diplomacy, economics and international law – and the current US administration has clearly demonstrated that power matters. Hirsh makes a salient point about Bush's rhetoric and actions, claiming that he is 'defending civilisation' yet his administration dismisses 'the civilities and practices that other nations would identify with a common civilization', such as cooperation, diplomacy and consensualism, 'the social glue' of international society (2002: 20).

Such a stance, where 'the logic of interdependence has been replaced by the logic of getting on-side' (Dunne, 2003) has deep implications for international society. It is here that the norms of neutrality can contribute to a more measured and cosmopolitan profile for the EU. Where the EU presents challenges to the neutral state and its sovereignty, we must recognise that there remain problems for internationalism in US unilateralism and its vision of the world. Swedish neutrality was built on the cornerstones of active internationalism, solidarity and an expansion of international cooperation and conflict resolution. The real test of neutrality's sustainability in the new world order is whether its norms, values and ideas can strengthen international solidarity and cooperation.

NOTES

1 I borrow this term from Johnson, who uses the phrase 'ways of life' in a cultural studies sense to explain the necessary sustaining practices of daily life (systems of meaning, forms of identity) which produce and reproduce meanings. The notion of the threat against 'ways of life' is employed in the rhetoric of Bush and Blair to represent global uncertainties and chaotic events which disrupt the order of ordinary living (Johnson, 2002: 212).
2 Maj-Britt Théorin, Carlsson and Tham are also critical of the USA's claim to this 'legal right', and say that the US is abusing the terms of Article 51 of the UN Charter (Burke, 2001b). In August 2002, Sweden joined the Open Skies Agreement, allowing members to carry out observation flights at short notice, which Sweden argues is important for broader security. The EU had been opposed to the agreement, arguing it breaches competition.
3 Lindh denied this accusation in an interview with *The Times of India* (16/10/01), but Oberg (2001) insists that active political support to the Palestinian cause has been toned down over the years, and Sweden abstained from voting in a UN General Assembly motion which mentioned Israel's 'excessive use of force' (see also Ramachandaran, 2001).
4 The Swedish parliament appointed a permanent delegation to NATO's Parliamentary Assembly in 2004 (Swedish Parliament, 2004).
5 The Green Party also mentioned neutrality, but the No to Nice campaign did not stress neutrality, and paid more attention to the issue of sovereignty (*The Irish Times*, 11/06/01). The former Maltese Labour Party Prime Minister Bonnici supported Ireland's rejection of the Nice Treaty, regarding it as prejudiced against applicant countries and a threat to small state sovereignty (*The Irish Times*, 31/05/01).
6 See *The Guardian*, 16/06/01. Voter turnout for the Nice referendum (35 per cent) was the lowest ever for Ireland. The final results of the referendum were 46.13 per cent in favour, 53.87 per cent against (*The Irish Times*, 11/06/01).

7 See Scott Ritter's address to the Galway Alliance Against War (*The Irish Times*, 07/07/03). It appears that access to Shannon airport has been a lucrative venture. According to the *Sunday Mirror* (12/10/03) Aer Rianta bosses gained €11 million from military flights into Shannon airport. Since 2002, over 300,000 US personnel have passed through the airport, with Shannon airport itself gaining €39 million in landing and refuelling fees (see also Newby and Titley, 2003).

8 See *Agence France Presse*, 28/04/03 and *The Irish Times*, 07/07/03. For commentaries by both politicians and journalists advocating the end of neutrality, see *The Irish Times* 16/01/04, 30/07/04, 29/01/05; *Irish Independent*, 30/05/03, 19/04/04; *Financial Times* 20/04/03.

9 The argument here has primarily centred on a clause in the constitution which refers to 'superpowers' – which the Nationalists consider outdated.

10 Much of the controversy centred on the maintenance contract with the US navy. Dry dock workers under the General Workers' Union, with support from the Labour Party, refused to carry out the work, prompting the government to threaten halting subsidies to the industry. The contract is estimated to be worth millions to the Maltese government. See *The Malta Business Weekly*, 28/06–04/07/2001; *Malta Star*, 08/03/02.

11 Archer equates the inability of Finns to let go of neutrality as almost bordering on a form of racism, despite acknowledging that the norms and values of Finnish neutrality are an engrained feature of Finnish identity, and that in the 'war on terror', Finland's neutralist position has perhaps kept it a non-target for terrorists (Archer, 2004). His views have been criticised by Newby and Titley (2003).

12 See CNN, 29/10/04. The Swedish government has maintained that the risk of a terrorist attack is unlikely on Swedish soil, despite defence and emergency agencies arguing that Sweden is unprepared for such an attack. Analysts have interpreted Bin Laden's mention of Sweden to indicate Al Qaeda's message that it is not 'anti-Western' (*Radio Sweden*, 01/11/04). *Radio Sweden* (22/05/03) has reported that the reference to Norway was perhaps a mistake by Bin Laden (confusing Norway with Denmark).

13 The Moderate Party refused to support two Framework decisions on this issue, claiming it excluded the consultation of national parliament. The EU framework would involve a change in Sweden's justice laws, sparking concern over the EU's broad definition of terrorism, which could be interpreted to mean that protesters could be classified as 'terrorists'. The Greens and the Left were also against the EU framework decision, although it has been argued that the Moderate Party played to the anti-EU mood by initiating a public consultation procedure. The *Riksdag* accepted the proposal in May 2002 (*Statewatch*, 2002).

14 The Tampere European Council of October 1999 established an area of freedom, security and justice in the EU, and proposed the following measures: a common EU asylum and immigration policy; a common European asylum system; fair treatment of third country nationals; and the management of migration flows. A large concern of the Tampere European Council was the issue of convergence of member states in areas of civil law and the fight against crime with a view to deepening the EU's external profile. See European Council, 1999; 2001.

15 Touraine claims that Blair's ideology is centre-right, and German Chancellor Schröder no longer represents the 'new middle' (*EU Observer*, 17/05/02).

16 There have been efforts to rethink the established institutions and symbols of social democracy to reveal their more 'capitalist' leanings. For instance, Hagstrom argues that the *bruk* (see Chapter 3) can be regarded as the 'first capitalist undertaking in Sweden'. (Hagstrom, 2001: 42) Even the idea of equality embodied in Jante's law, the

moral code in Swedish (and Scandinavian) societies that places no one above another, is given the revised treatment, reinterpreted as crushing the creativity and development of individuals (Hagstrom, 2001: 13). On the rise of individualism amongst Swedish youth, see Glans, 2003.

17 Persson had stated that sick leave, unemployment benefits and parental leave should be reduced and suggested changing the social insurance programmes so they are funded by individuals and companies rather than taxes (*Radio Sweden*, 14/11/03).

18 The BBC estimated that in London and Rome, figures were at one million, and 1.3 million in Barcelona. It was not simply Europe that held mass protests – in Australia, the US and the Middle East, large numbers also turned out against plans to attack Iraq (BBC News, 17/02/03).

19 82 per cent of European citizens were also in favour of humanitarian aid from their countries towards Iraq (responding to 'rather' and 'totally' in favour). On the subject of sending troops to Iraq, the majority of EU citizens (54 per cent) were unfavourable. UK citizens, despite the Blair government's support for US action, had the strongest support for the UN in this regard with 72 per cent. Amongst the 15 member states polled, support for the US only reached a high of 24 per cent (Belgium and Denmark) (European Commission, 2003).

Conclusion: The failure of neutrality?

NEUTRALITY HAS ENDURED during major wars and changes in world systems, and still survives despite European integration and a 'war on terror' where no one can be neutral, according to George W. Bush (2001). Despite the efforts to present neutrality as an outdated stance and policy option, we still find that the task of writing neutrality out of policy is difficult. If we are to invest in the notion that the end of the Cold War, the call to stronger international forms of securitisation and a 'war on terrorism' render neutrality a thing of the past, then why is a neutralist stance still the definitive aspect of the foreign policies of Sweden, Austria, Finland, Ireland and Malta? These 'militarily non-aligned' states seem unable to make a decisive break from neutrality (whatever form it takes), which suggests that the issue runs deeper than most would like to present.

We began the examination of the role and place of neutrality in international relations by returning to its origins in Chapter 1. Neutrality has been a concept and practice which has become associated with traits of isolationism, self-interest and folly. The discourse and conceptualisation of neutrality has been one of the most neglected aspects of international relations, in both theoretical and empirical work. Subsequently, it has been misunderstood and in the post-Cold War era, actively dismissed as a lie and an anachronism. Neutrality was never seriously considered to have a normative foundation, and it was commonly deemed to rely on the balance of power, surviving only by fortune's sake. Despite the end of the Cold War, neutrality was still present.

With explanations lacking and predictions that it would only be a matter of time before neutrality was abandoned, this was insufficient. Chapter 2 considered the discourse on the demise of neutrality, but this still did not explain why neutrality remained part of security policy. The task was therefore to look beyond the realist explanations about neutral states, and re-examine neutrality from a different perspective that brought in intersubjectivity, identity and norms. Social constructivism was employed to rethink neutrality as a concept and a practice, uncovering how norms and values become embedded over time, producing their own realities, frames of reference and myths. Viewing neutrality from this prism opened up new understandings of why it was difficult to abandon.

Examining Swedish neutrality from the constructivist perspective drew in the importance of domestic norms and values which became attached to the idea of neutrality, whilst simultaneously reinforcing Swedish identity. Social Democratic ideology presented the image of the *folkhem*, uniting broad societal values which were consensual, and exporting those ideas and visions to the international stage. Sweden distinguished itself from claims of self-interested isolationism by using neutrality as a platform to realise its own vision of an international order guided by justice, equality, and peaceful resolution of conflict. Chapters 3 and 4 examined the domestic and external sides to Swedish neutrality, and explained how the relationship between neutrality and identity became embedded.

Identity, however, is not immutable. In the late 1960s, the heyday of the Swedish Model, its famous 'Middle Way' was confronted by a series of setbacks. Chapter 5 focused upon the influence of new ideas and thinking in the public domain, namely the rise of business interests and a neoliberal discourse. This new voice articulated a different image of Swedish society and identity, arguing that the foundations of the Swedish Model and the ideology of the SAP could not respond to external realities and challenges. Think-tanks and non-socialist parties worked to reset the Swedish mindset with their arguments to curb the welfare state, and business began to get political. The rupture in Swedish politics culminated in the Bildt government, and the timing coincided with the end of the Cold War, which refocused Bildt's efforts to rid the nation of a few myths – including neutrality. Chapter 6 analysed the Bildt government, and its attempts to not simply edge away from neutrality but question many of the norms and values established under Social Democratic hegemony. Pursuing EU membership, Bildt aimed to reorient Swedish identity towards Europe, to *normalise* Sweden. New ideas can be seductive, but identity can be an entrenched thing. Sweden entered the EU under the Social Democrats, largely in the belief that Swedish membership of the EU would be an opportunity to export its norms to the European level. As a member state of the EU, Sweden also influenced the development of the CFSP by introducing its soft security options (in the Petersberg tasks) to the Amsterdam Treaty. However, as Chapter 7 discussed, European integration was not intended to be static. As security and defence cooperation increased throughout the 1990s, neutrality was starting to be regarded as an obstacle to European integration. Under the Persson government, there has been a greater emphasis on European solidarity which has seen neutrality downgraded, and in February 2001, significantly altered. The 'war on terror' and deeper economic cooperation have added further fuel to the argument that neutrality is now obsolete, and Chapter 8 discussed how Sweden and other neutral states have reworked their security doctrines to adapt to the new international system. This final chapter also explored how the norms and values of neutrality could possibly be reproduced on the European platform, charging neutral states with the task of upholding a cosmopolitan or alternative vision of European integration against the banality of a 'war on terror'.

The question of the purpose and role of neutrality in today's international setting is important for a number of reasons. First, the widespread dismissal of the possible contribution of an active form of neutrality to international relations theory limits our understanding of what is viable in political theorising. It is intellectually insufficient to limit our understanding of neutrality to mere isolationism. Neutrality has too easily been written out as an option without exploring what can be salvaged and what can be assigned to the past. Alternative voices and options are needed in an increasingly complex world. Second, to dismiss neutrality is to dismiss a key part of identity and to separate it from what constitutes the state, or as Hopf observes: 'State actions in the foreign policy realm are constrained and empowered by prevailing social practices at home and abroad.' (1998: 179) To neglect to understand the relationship between domestic and external phenomena is to view international relations in a myopic manner. In an era of globalisation, many have bought into the idea that the state has become obsolete. Clearly it has not,[1] and the claims that neutrality holds back further integration and interdependence is a misguided view that neglects an important variable in the processes of globalisation. Sovereignty may be taking on a new form, but it is still the state that creates the conditions for a globalised world. If this were not the case, then we can assume that the world would operate according to very different principles and practices than those we currently experience.

We now live in a more complex and integrated world, where new meanings and new realities emerge and confront each other. Ideas that were once definitive in the past are under reconsideration, moulded to fit current scenarios, creating new values and understandings. The key question is how to negotiate new meanings against the background of past understandings of phenomena. In the case of Swedish neutrality, it would appear that its normative dimension is steadily being eroded in favour of the perceived benefits of European cooperation and integration. Despite widespread support for neutrality, the government bows to pressure to adapt.

But recent events, specifically the 'war on terror' are reinvigorating the debate about *difference*, which permits some space to consider how neutrality could be reworked in a meaningful way in European security cooperation. Rather than become preoccupied over what constitutes a 'neutral action' (for

The failure of neutrality?

instance, participation in European security initiatives which may or may not 'violate' neutrality) what we must concern ourselves with is whether the norms and values that underpinned neutrality continue on in critical form. Neutrality was once the distinguishing signature of those nation-states which embraced a different vision of security and peaceful relations in the international system. The demise of neutrality is not simply about the demise of one particular approach to security – it is about the demise of ideas, norms and values that captured a different view of the world.

NOTE

1 In 2004, Fukuyama argued that post-September 11, states are needed more than ever: '11 September also underscored a key feature of the post-Cold War world. While the great problems of world order in the 20th century were caused by too-powerful nation states such as Germany, Japan and the former Soviet Union, many of the problems of our current age, from poverty to refugees to human rights to HIV and Aids to terrorism, are caused by states in the developing world that are too weak.'

Bibliography

Books and articles

Adler, E. (1992) 'The emergence of cooperation: National epistemic communities and the international idea of nuclear arms control', *International Organization* 46 (1):101–45.

Adler, E. (1997a) 'Seizing the middle ground: Constructivism in world politics', *European Journal of International Relations* 3 (3):319–59.

Adler, E. (1997b) 'Imagined (security) communities: Cognitive regions in international relations', *Millennium Journal of International Studies* 26 (2):249–77.

Agell, J. and Lommerud, K. E. (1993) 'Egalitarianism and growth', *Scandinavian Journal of Economics* 95 (4):559–79.

Agrell, W. (1986) 'Behind the submarine crisis: Evolution of the Swedish defence doctrine and Soviet war planning', *Cooperation and Conflict* 21 (4):197–217.

Albrecht, U., Auffermann, B. and Joenniemi, P. (1988) (The Marstrand Study Group), *Neutrality: The need for conceptual revision*. Tampere: Tampere Peace Research Institute (TAPRI) Occasional Papers No. 35, pp. 1–41.

Aligheri, Dante [1949] (1996) *Inferno. Canto III*. Translated by D. L. Sayers. London: Penguin.

Anderson, B. (1991) *Imagined communities: Reflections on the origin and spread of nationalism*. London: Verso Books.

Anderson, K. M. and Snow, S. G. (2003) 'Forestalling the business veto: Investment confidence and the rise of Swedish Social Democracy, 1932–1936', *Social Science Quarterly* 84 (1):91–110.

Andersson, J. O. and Mjøset, L. (1987) 'The transformation of the Nordic Models', *Cooperation and Conflict* 22 (4):227–43.

Andrén, N. (1981) 'Five roads to parliamentary democracy', in Allardt, E. et al., *Nordic democracy. Ideas, issues and institutions in politics, economy, education, social and cultural affairs of Denmark, Finland, Iceland, Norway and Sweden*. Copenhagen: Det Danske Selskab, pp. 44–52.

Andrén, N. (1987) 'The case of Sweden', in Lodgaard, S. and Birnbaum, K. (eds.)

Overcoming threats to Europe: A new deal for confidence and security. Stockholm International Peace Research Institute (SIPRI). Oxford: Oxford University Press, pp. 134–54.

Andrén, N. (1989) 'Swedish defence: Traditions, perceptions, and policies', in Kruzel, J. and Haltzel, M. H. (eds.) *Between the blocs. Problems and prospects for Europe's neutral and nonaligned states.* Woodrow Wilson International Centre for Scholars and Cambridge: Cambridge University Press, pp. 175–99.

Andrén, N. (1991) 'On the meaning and uses of neutrality', *Cooperation and Conflict* 26 (2):67–83.

Archer, C. (1990) 'The North as a multidimensional strategic arena', in Heisler, M. O. (ed.) 'The Nordic region: Changing perspectives in international relations', *The Annals of the American Academy of Political and Social Science* Vol. 512, November. Newbury Park, California: Sage Publications, pp. 22–32.

Archer, C. (1996) 'The Nordic area as a "zone of peace"', *Journal of Peace Research* 33 (4):451–67.

Archer, C. (1997) '*Finland, Sweden, the IGC and defence*', International Security Information Service (ISIS) Briefing Paper No. 8, pp. 1–12.

Archer, T. (2002) 'Keeping out of it: The hangover of Finnish neutralism and the limits of normative commitments'. Paper presented to The Finnish Institute in London – Young Academics Seminar 8th–9th March.

Archer, T. (2004) *International terrorism and Finland.* FIIA Report. Helsinki: FIIA.

Armitage, J. (2002) 'State of emergency: An introduction', *Theory, Culture and Society* 19 (4):27–38.

Arnold, H. (1989) 'Austria and the European Community', *Aussen Politik* 40 (4):385–96.

Arter, D. (1996) 'Finland: From neutrality to NATO?', *European Security* 5 (4):614–32.

Åsard, E. and Bennett, L. (1997) *Democracy and the marketplace of ideas. Communication and government in Sweden and the United States.* Cambridge: Cambridge University Press.

Åsard, E. (1999) 'The limits of "Americanization" in Swedish politics', *Swedish-American Historical Quarterly* 50 (3):173–81.

Åsbrink. E. (1998) 'Sweden and EMU', Speech to conference at Nordiska Investeringsbanken och European Economics and Financial Centre, Helsingfors, 10th–11th June.

Åström, S. (1987) *Sweden's policy of neutrality.* Stockholm: The Swedish Institute, pp. 5–20.

Åström, S. (1989) 'Swedish neutrality: Credibility through commitment and consistency' in Sundelius, B. (ed.) *The committed neutral. Sweden's foreign policy.* Boulder, Colorado: Westview Press, pp. 15–33.

A. T. Kearney/Foreign Policy (2005) *Globalization index. Measuring globalization.* May/June.

Auneslouma, J. (2001) 'Negotiating economic and political interdependence: Finnish–Swedish relations 1944–73', Paper given to the conference 'Small states in world markets – fifteen years later', Gothenburg, 27th–29th September, pp. 1–17.

Austrian Federal Government (2000) Austrian Federal Constitutional Law of 26 October 1955 on the neutrality of Austria. The Austrian Constitution. Vienna: Herausgegeben vom Bundespressedienst.

Austrian Parliament. (2001) Security and defence doctrine. <http://merln.ndu.edu/whitepapers/Austria-2001.pdf>

Aylott, N. (1995) 'Back to the future: The 1994 Swedish election', *Party Politics* 1 (3):419–29.

Baker Fox, A. (1965) 'The small states of Western Europe in the United Nations', *International Organization* 19 (3):774–86.

Baldwin, D. A. (1995) 'Security studies and the end of the Cold War', *World Politics* 48 (1):117–41.

Barkin J. S. and Cronin, B. (1994) 'The State and the nation: Changing norms and the rules of sovereignty in international relations', *International Organization* 48 (1):107–30.

Bartelson, J. (1995) *A Genealogy of sovereignty*. Cambridge: Cambridge University Press.

Bartelson, J. (1998) 'Second natures: Is the state identical with itself?', *European Journal of International Relations* 4 (3):295–326.

Barton, D. P. (1930) *The amazing career of Bernadotte, 1976–1844*. Second Edition. London: John Murray.

Barton, H. A. (1999) 'Crossings and recrossings: America and Sweden in the twentieth century', *Swedish-American Historical Quarterly* 50 (3):133–46.

Bauer, R. A. (1984) 'The United States and the European neutrals', in Neuhold, H. and Thalberg, H. (eds.) *The European neutrals in international affairs*. The Laxenburg Papers, No. 7. Vienna: Austrian Institute of International Affairs, Wilhelm Braumüller, pp. 81–91.

Bauslaugh, R. A. (1991) *The concept of neutrality in classical Greece*. Berkeley: University of California Press.

Bebler, A. (1992) 'The neutral and non-aligned states in the new European security architecture', *The International Spectator* 27 (1):69–79.

Beck, U. (2002) 'The terrorist threat: World risk society revisited', *Theory, Culture and Society* 19 (4):39–55.

Beindorf, C. (2001) 'Film as propaganda: Linking the past to politics. *Ride this night!* (1942) and the Swedish politics of neutrality', in Vonderau, P. (ed.) *Film as history/history as film*. Working Papers, 'Gemenskaper/Gemeinschaften', Vol. 21. Funded by the National Bank of Sweden's Tercentenary Foundation, pp. 9–15. <www2.hu-berlin.de/gemenskap/inhalt/publikationen/arbeitspapiere/ahe_21.html#cb>

Bell, D. S. A. (2003) 'Mythscapes: Memory, mythology, and national identity', *British Journal of Sociology* 54 (1):63–81.

Benke, G. and Wodak, R. (2001) 'Neutrality versus NATO: The analysis of a TV-discussion on the contemporary function of Austria's neutrality', in Bischof, G., Pelinka, A. and Wodak, R. (eds.) *Neutrality in Austria*. Contemporary Austrian Studies, Volume 9. New Brunswick, New Jersey: Transaction Publishers, pp. 37–68.

Berger, P. L. and Luckmann, T. (1971) *The social construction of reality. A treatise in the sociology of knowledge*. London: Penguin Press.

Berger, T. U. (1996) 'Norms, identity and national security in Germany and Japan', in Katzenstein, P. J. (ed.) *The culture of national security. Norms and identity in world*

politics. New York: Columbia University Press, pp. 317–56.
Bergström, S. O. (1990) 'The debate surrounding August Strindberg's *Svenska Folket*', *Scandinavian Studies* 62 (4):431–48.
Best, G. (1983) *Humanity in warfare. The modern history of the international law of armed conflicts*. London: Methuen.
Bildt, C. (1993) *Swedish security policy in a changing Europe*. Royal Academy of Military Sciences, Stockholm, 7th December. Unofficial translation.
Bildt, C. (1997) 'Europe and Bosnia: Lessons of the past and paths for the future', Address by the High Representative Mr Carl Bildt to the Netherlands Association of International Affairs, The Hague, 27th May, pp. 1–11.
Binter, B. (1989) 'Neutrality, European Community and world peace: The case of Austria', *Journal of Peace Research* 26 (4):413–18.
Binter, B. (1992) 'Neutrality in a changing world: End or renaissance of a concept?', *Bulletin of Peace Proposals* 23 (2):213–18.
Bitzinger, R. A. (1991) 'Neutrality for Eastern Europe: Problems and prospects', *Bulletin of Peace Proposals* 22 (3):281–9.
Bjereld, U. (1994) 'Swedish foreign policy in the light of EU membership – Imposed adaptation or self-determined change of course?', Paper presented to the European Consortium for Political Research (ECPR), Madrid, 17th–22nd April.
Bjereld, U. (1995a) 'Critic or mediator? Sweden in world politics, 1945–90', *Journal of Peace Research* 32 (1):23–35.
Bjereld, U. (1995b) 'Sweden's foreign policy after the end of the Cold War – From neutrality to freedom of action', in Lindahl, R. and Sjöstedt, G. (eds.) *New thinking in international relations: Swedish perspectives*. The Yearbook of the Swedish Institute of International Affairs, 1994–1995. Stockholm: The Swedish Institute of International Affairs, pp. 183–94.
Björck, A. (1998) 'The European security and defence identity', speech to colloquy, Madrid, 6th May. <www.nato.int/docu/colloq/c980504/d980506d.htm>
Blair, A. (2004) 'Diplomacy: The impact of the EU on its member states', in Carlsnaes, W., Sjursen, H. and White, B. *Contemporary European foreign policy*. London: Sage, pp. 189–210.
Blair, T. (1998) *The Third Way: New politics for the new century*. Fabian Pamphlet 588. London: The Fabian Society.
Blair, T. (1999) 'NATO, Europe, and our future security', speech to NATO 50th anniversary conference, Royal United Services Institute, London, 8th March. <www.britainusa.com/sections/articles_show.asp?SarticleType=1&Article_ID=713&i=117>
Blair, T. (2000) *Speech by the Prime Minister at Warwick University*, 14th December.
Blyth, M. (1998) 'The neoliberal moment in Sweden: Economic change, policy failure or power of ideas', Paper presented at the Ideas, Culture and Political Analysis Workshop, Princeton University, May 15–16, pp. 1–22.
Blyth, M. (2001) 'The transformation of the Swedish Model. Economic ideas, distributional conflict, and institutional change', *World Politics* 54 (October):1–26.
Blyth, M. (2002) *Great transformations. Economic ideas and institutional change in the twentieth century*. Cambridge: Cambridge University Press.
Bodin, Jean [1576] (1992) 'The state's need of armed force to protect its interests'

[extract from Six Books of the Republic], in Luard, E. (1992) *Basic texts in international relations*. Basingstoke: Palgrave Macmillan.
Booth, K. (1991) *New thinking about strategy and international security*. London: Harper Collins Academic.
Borchard, E. M. (1933) 'The enforcement of "peace" by "sanctions"', *American Journal of International Law* 27 (3):518–25.
Boréus, K. (1997) 'The shift to the right: Neoliberalism in argumentation and language in the Swedish public debate since 1969', *European Journal of Political Research* 31, pp. 257–86.
Brook, D. (2004) 'How Sweden tweaked the Washington Consensus', *Dissent*, Fall, pp. 24–9.
Brown, C. (1997) *Understanding international relations*. London: Macmillan.
Browning, C. (1999) 'Coming home or moving home? "Westernizing" narratives in Finnish foreign policy and the reinterpretation of past identities', Ulkopoliittinen Instituutti (UPI) (The Finnish Institute of International Affairs) Working Paper 16. Paper delivered to The Human Spatiality and Geohistory Seminar, University of Turku, 3rd–4th June, pp. 1–30.
Brundtland, A. O. (1971) 'The Nordic countries as an area of peace', in Schou, A. and Brundtland, A. O. (eds.) *Small states in international relations*. Uppsala: Almqvist and Wiskell, pp. 129–46.
Brzozowska, A. (2003) 'Symbols, myths, and metaphors: The discursive battle over the "true" Belarusian narrative', *Slovo* 15 (1):49–58.
Buehrig, E. H. (1950) 'Wilson's neutrality re-examined', *World Politics* 3 (1):1–19.
Bukovansky, M. (1997) 'American identity and neutral rights from independence to the war of 1812', *International Organization* 51 (2):209–43.
Bull, H. (1983) 'Civilian power Europe: A contradiction in terms?', *Journal of Common Market Studies* 21 (2–3):149–70.
Bull, H. (1995) 'Society and anarchy in international relations', in Der Derian, J. (ed.) *International theory. Critical investigations*. Basingstoke: Macmillan, pp. 75–93.
Burgess, J. P. (2000) 'Coal, steel and spirit. The double reading of European unity (1948–51)', in Stråth, B. (ed.) *Europe and the other and Europe as the other*. Brussels: P.I.E.-Peter Lang. Series Multiple Europes, No. 10, pp. 421–55.
Burke, A. (2001) 'Collateral damage: Sweden's legacy of peace.' <www.nnn.se/n-model/foreign/damage.htm>
Bush, G. W. (2001) 'No nation can be neutral in this conflict', Remarks by the President To the Warsaw Conference on Combatting Terrorism. 6th November. <www.whitehouse.gov/news/releases/2001/11/20011106-2.html>
Bush, G. W. (2002) 'President thanks world coalition for anti-terrorism efforts', Remarks by the President on the six-month anniversary of the September 11th attacks. <www.whitehouse.gov/news/releases/2002/03/20020311-1.html>
Bush, G. W. (2003) Remarks by President Bush in his radio address to the nation, 27th September. <www.whitehouse.gov/news/releases/2003/09/20030930.html>
Calleya, S. (2002) 'Malta's foreign policy in an enlarged European Union', Paper presented at the European Documentation and Research Centre conference, Malta, 25th April.

Bibliography

Camilleri, J. and Falk, J. (1992) *The end of sovereignty? The politics of a shrinking and fragmenting world.* Aldershot: Edward Elgar.

Carlsnaes, W. (1993) 'Are the EFTA neutrals *qua* neutrals comparable?', Paper presented to the planning session on: 'The EFTA neutrals and the EC: Foreign policy implications of membership', European Consortium for Political Research (ECPR) joint sessions of workshops. Leiden, 2nd–8th April.

Carlsson, I. (1990) *Statement of government policy.* Ministry for Foreign Affairs. Press and Information Department, 7th March. Unofficial translation.

Carlsson, I. (1991) Statement to the *Riksdag* on Sweden's application for membership of the EC, 14th June. Unofficial translation.

Carr, E. H. (1946) *The twenty years' crisis. 1919–1939. An introduction to the study of international relations.* London: Macmillan.

Cartledge, P. (1986) 'Might and right: Thucydides and the Melos massacre', *History Today* 36 (5):11–15.

Chadwick, A. (2000) 'Studying political ideas: A public political discourse approach', *Political Studies* 48 (2):283–301.

Checkel, J. T. (1999) 'Why comply? Constructivism, social norms and the study of international institutions', Arena Working Paper 99/24, pp. 1–50. <www.sv.uio.no/arena/publications/wp99_24.htm>

Childs, M. W. (1936) *Sweden: The middle way.* Newhaven: Yale University Press.

Churchill, W. S. [1936] (1974) *Speech on Belgian neutrality.* Constituency meeting, Aldersbrook, October 16, 1936, in James, R. R. (ed.) *Winston Churchill: His complete speeches, 1897–1963,* Volume 6, 1935–1942. London, New York: Chelsea House Publishers and R. R. Bowker Company, pp. 5795–6.

Churchill, W. S. [1940] (1974) *A hideous state of alarm and menace.* London broadcast, 30th March 1949, in James, R. R. (ed.) *Winston Churchill: His complete speeches, 1897–1963,* Volume 6, 1935–1942. London, New York: Chelsea House Publishers and R. R. Bowker Company, pp. 6199–200.

Coates, D. (2000) *Models of capitalism. Growth and stagnation in the modern era.* Cambridge: Polity Press.

Cole, Robert. (2001) 'Anglo-American anti-fascist film propaganda in a time of neutrality: The Great Dictator, 1940', *Historical Journal of Film, Radio and Television* 21 (2):137–52.

Collin, F. (1997) *Social reality.* London: Routledge.

Commission of the European Communities (1991) *Austria's application for membership. Commission Opinion,* 1st August. Brussels.

Commission of the European Communities (1992) *Finland's application for membership. Opinion of the Commission* SEC (92) 2048, 4th November, Brussels.

Commission of the European Communities (1993a) Bulletin of the European Communities, Supplement 4/92. *The challenge of enlargement. Commission opinion on Austria's application for membership.* Luxembourg: Office of the Official Publications of the European Communities (OOPEC).

Commission of the European Communities (1993b) Bulletin of the European Communities, Supplement 5/92. *The challenge of enlargement. Commission opinion on Sweden's application for membership.* Luxembourg: Office of the Official Publications of the European Communities (OOPEC).

Commission of the European Communities (1993c) Bulletin of the European Communities, Supplement 6/92. *The challenge of enlargement. Commission opinion on Finland's application for membership.* Luxembourg: Office of the Official Publications of the European Communities (OOPEC).

Commission of the European Communities (1995) Background Report. *Impact of the three new member states of the European Union.* B/06/95. 15th June.

Commission of the European Communities (1995) *Standard Eurobarometer Report No. 43.* Autumn. Brussels.

Commission of the European Communities (1996) *Standard Eurobarometer Report No. 45.* December. Brussels.

Commission of the European Communities (1997) *Standard Eurobarometer Report No. 47.* November. Brussels.

Commission of the European Communities (1998) *Standard Eurobarometer Report No. 49.* September. Brussels.

Commission of the European Communities (1999) *Standard Eurobarometer Report No. 51.* July. Brussels.

Commission of the European Communities (2000) *Standard Eurobarometer Report No. 53.* October. Brussels.

Commission of the European Communities (2001) *Standard Eurobarometer Report No. 55.* October. Brussels.

Commission of the European Communities (2002) *Standard Eurobarometer Report No. 57.* October. Brussels.

Commission of the European Communities (2003) *Standard Eurobarometer Report No. 59.* July. Brussels.

Commission of the European Communities (2004) *Standard Eurobarometer Report No. 61.* July. Brussels.

Copeland, D. C. (2000) 'The constructivist challenge to structural realism', *International Security* 25 (2):187–212.

Council of the European Communities, Commission of the European Communities (1992) *Treaty on European Union.* Luxembourg: Office of the Official Publications of the European Communities (OOPEC). Text of the TEU as signed in Maastricht on 7th February.

Covenant of the League of Nations (1924) (including amendments adopted to December 1924). <www.yale.edu/lawweb/avalon/leagcov.htm>

Cox, M. and MacGinty, R. (1996) 'Farewell to a beautiful idea: The end of neutrality in the post-Cold War world', in Bauwens, W., Clesse, A. and Knudsen, O. (eds.) *Small states and the security challenge in the new Europe.* Brassey's Atlantic Commentaries, No. 8, pp. 122–34.

Cox, R. W. (1993) 'Gramsci, hegemony and international relations: An essay in method', in Gill, S. (ed.) *Gramsci, historical materialism and international relations.* Cambridge: Cambridge University Press, pp. 49–66.

Cramér, P. (1989) *Neutralitets begreppet – den permanenta neutralitetens utveckling* [The idea of neutrality – the development of permanent neutrality]. Stockholm: Norstedts Förlag.

Croft, S., Howorth, J., Terriff, T. and Webber, M. (2000) 'NATO's triple challenge', *International Affairs* 76 (3):495–518.

Bibliography

Dahl, A.-S. (1997) 'Not if but how: Sweden's future relations with NATO', *NATO Review* 45 (3):19–22.

Dahl, A.-S. (2002) 'Activist Sweden: The last defender of non-alignment', in Dahl, A.-S. and Hillmer, N. (eds.) *Activism and (non) alignment*, Conference Papers 31. Stockhom: UI, pp. 139–50.

Dahlsson, H. (1996) 'Creating a world of mutual security. The balance of terror no longer applies'. <www.stationen.com/centernej/e56.html> (accessed 23/06/98).

de Marco, G. (2001) Speech by the President of Malta during the state dinner at Schloss Belleveue, Berlin, 8th November. <www.doi.gov.mt/EN/press_releases/2001/11/pr1662.asp>

de Vylder, S. (1996) 'The rise and fall of the Swedish Model', United Nations Development Programme. Human Development Report Office (HDRO), Occasional Paper 26. <http://hdr.undp.org/docs/publications/ocational_papers/oc26a.htm>

Delanty, G. (1995) *Inventing Europe: Idea, identity, reality*. Basingstoke: Macmillan.

Delanty, G. (1997) *Social science. Beyond constructivism and realism*. Buckingham: Open University Press.

Delsen, L. and Van Veem, T. (1992) 'The Swedish Model: Relevant for other countries?', *British Journal of Industrial Relations* 30 (1):83–105.

Dessler, D. (1999) 'Constructivism within a positivist social science', *Review of International Studies* 25(1):123–37.

Deutsch, K. (1957) *Political community and the North Atlantic area. International organization in the light of historical experience*. New York: Greenwood Press.

Devetak, R. (1995) 'Incomplete states: Theories and practices of statecraft', in Macmillan, J. and Linklater, A. (eds.) *Boundaries in question. New directions in international relations*. London: Pinter, pp. 19–39.

DFA/DEA Integration Office (Swiss Federal Department of Foreign Affairs and the Swiss Federal Department of Economic Affairs) (2000) 'The bilateral agreements between Switzerland and the European Union. Report on the agreements and companion measures, with explanations', Berne, pp. 1–58.

Dickson, P. (1972) 'Sweden's quest for equality', *The Progressive*. November, pp. 23–5.

Diez, T. (1999) 'Speaking "Europe": The politics of integration discourse', *Journal of European Public Policy* 6 (4):598–613.

Divine, R. A. (1962) *The illusion of neutrality*. Chicago: The University of Chicago Press.

Donaldson, T. (1992) 'Kant's global rationalism', in Nardin, T. and Mapel, D. R. (eds.) *Traditions of international ethics*. Cambridge: Cambridge University Press, pp. 136–57.

Dörfer, I. (1987) 'The European neutrals in the strategy of the Reagan administration', in Sundelius, B. (ed.) *The neutral democracies and the new Cold War*. Boulder, Colorado: Westview Press, pp. 182–97.

Dougherty, J. E. and Pfaltzgraff Jr., R. L. (1981) *Contending theories of international relations*. Second Edition. New York: Harper and Row Publishers.

Duchêne, F. (1973) 'The European Community and the uncertainties of interdependence', in Kohnstamm, M. and Hager, W. (eds.) *A nation writ large? Foreign policy problems before the European Community*. London: Macmillan, pp. 1–21.

Dulles, J. F. (1956) 'The cost of peace. Our peace insurance policy', Secretary of State's speech to Iowa State College, Ames, Iowa, 9th June. *Vital Speeches of the Day* 22 (15):549–52.

Dunne, T. (2003) 'Society and hierarchy in international relations', *International Relations* 17 (3):303–20.

Dunne, T., Cox, M. and Booth, K. (1998) 'Introduction: The eighty years' crisis', *Review of International Studies*, December 24:v–xii.

Eddie, G. D. (1993) 'Sweden: Krona crisis stalls "New Start"', *The World Today* 49 (1):9–12.

Eddie, G. D. (1994) 'Sweden: Into Europe with the Social Democrats?', *The World Today* 50 (11):203–5.

Edlund, J. (2000) 'Public attitudes towards taxation: Sweden 1981–1997', *Scandinavian Political Studies* 23 (1):37–65.

EFTA Barometer Autumn (1992) Austria, Finland and Sweden. Gallup Europe. Swedish Social Science Data Service, Göteborg <http://idun.ssd.gu.se/kid/engframe.html> (accessed 29/10/99).

Einhorn, E. S. and Logue, J. (1989) *Modern welfare states. Politics and policies in social democratic Scandinavia*. New York: Praeger.

Ekengren, M., and Sundelius, B. (1998) 'Sweden: The state joins the European Union', in Hanf, K. and Soetendorp, B. (eds.) *Adapting to European integration: Small states and the European Union*. London: Addison Wesley Longman Ltd, pp. 131–48.

Eknes, Å. and Eide, E. B. (1994) 'Peacekeeping: Past experience and new challenges. Lessons from the EFTA countries' experience with peacekeeping', Norwegian Institute of International Affairs (NUPI), Working Papers, No. 516, pp. 1–13.

Eldridge, T. (1997) 'Religion, values and Scandinavian social problems as reflected in film', *Nordic Notes* Vol. 1. <www.ssn.flinders.edu.au/scanlink/nornotes/vol1/articles/te2.html>

Elgström, O. (2000) 'Do images matter? The making of Swedish neutrality: 1834 and 1853', *Cooperation and Conflict* 35 (3):243–67.

Eliæson, S. (2000) 'Gunnar Myrdal: A theorist of modernity', *Acta Sociologica* 43:331–41.

Eliasson, J. (1989) *Sweden and international mediation*. Ministry for Foreign Affairs. Unofficial Translation. Stockholm, 1989:2, pp. 1–21.

Enzensberger, H. M. (1989) 'Swedish Autumn', in Enzensberger, H. M., *Europe, Europe. Forays into a continent*. Translated by M. Chalmers. London: Picador, pp. 3–35.

Erlander, T. [1961] (1997) 'Speech at the congress of the Swedish Steel and Metalworkers' Union', August. Reproduced in Salmon, T. and Nicoll, W. (eds.) *Building European Union. A documentary history and analysis*. Manchester: Manchester University Press, p. 78.

Esping-Andersen, G. (1990) *The three worlds of welfare capitalism*. Cambridge: Polity Press.

European Commission (2003) *Flash Eurobarometer Iraq and peace in the world*, No. 151, November.

European Council (1999) Tampere European Council. Presidency conclusions, 15–16 October. <www.europarl.eu.int/summits/tam_en.htm>

European Council (2001) Extraordinary Council meeting. *Justice, Home Affairs and civil protection*. Brussels, 12019/01, 20 September.

Bibliography

European Council (2003) *A secure Europe in a better world. European security strategy.* Brussels, 12 December.

European Parliament (1983) *Committee on institutional affairs. Selection of texts concerning institutional matters of the Community from 1950-1982.* Luxembourg: Office of the Official Publications of the European Communities (OOPEC).

European Union (1997a) *Consolidated Treaties, Treaty on European Union, Treaty establishing the European Community.* Luxembourg: Office of the Official Publications of the European Communities (OOPEC).

European Union (1997b) Chapter 12. The Common Foreign and Security Policy [Amsterdam Treaty, Section III: An effective and coherent external policy]. Amend Article C, second subparagraph, of the TEU <http://europa.eu.int/eur-lex/lex/en/treaties/dat/11997D/htm/11997D.html>

European Union (2001) *Treaty of Nice.* Official Journal of the European Communities, 10th March. <http://europa.eu.int/eur-lex/lex/en/treaties/dat/12001C/pdf/12001C_EN.pdf>

Fanning, R. (1996) 'Neutrality, identity and security: The example of Ireland', in Bauwens, W., Cleese, A. and Knudsen, O. (eds.) *Small states and the security challenge in the new Europe.* Brasseys Atlantic Commentaries, No. 8, pp. 137–49.

Farrell, M. (1995) 'Developing policy in a post-neutral world – the case of Ireland', in Lovenduski, J. and Stayner, J. (eds.) *Contemporary Political Studies UK,* Vol. 1. Belfast: Political Studies Association, UK, pp. 371–7.

Federal Chancellery (Austria) (2003) 'Overflights ruled out: Schüssel'. 18th March.

Fenech-Adami, E. (2000) Address at the Swedish Institute of International Affairs, Stockholm, 15th February. <www.foreign.gov.mt/stockholm/doc/embassy-23.htm>

Ferrero-Waldner, B. (2001) 'In EU foreign policy there is no neutrality but solidarity', Statement, 18th January.

Finnemore, M. and Sikkink, K. (1998) 'International norm dynamics and political change', *International Organization* 52 (4):887–917.

Fitzmaurice, J. (1995) 'The 1994 referenda on EU membership in Austria and Scandinavia: A comparative analysis', *Electoral Studies* 14 (2):226–32.

Forsberg, T. (2002) 'September 11 as a challenge to understanding transatlantic relations: The case of Sweden and Finland', in Sundelius, B. (ed) *The consequences of September 11,* Conference Papers 30. Stockholm: UI, pp. 151–62.

Freivalds, L. (2004) Statement at the conference on international law and terrorism in Stockholm, 1st October. <www.sweden.gov.se/sb/d/1288/a/30880>

Freymond, J. F. (1990) 'Neutrality and security policy as components of the Swiss model', in Milivojević, M. and Maurer, P. (eds.) *Swiss neutrality and security. Armed forces, national defence and foreign policy.* New York: Berg Publishers, pp. 175–93.

Fukuyama, F. (1992) *The end of history and the last man.* London: Hamish Hamilton, pp. 39–51.

Fukuyama, F. (2004) 'Bring back the state', *The Guardian* 4th July <www.guardian.co.uk/globalisation/story/0,7369,1253605,00.html>

Galbraith, J. K. (1952) *American capitalism. The concept of countervailing power.* Middlesex: Penguin Books.

Gärtner, H. (1996) 'Models of European security and options for the new "neutral"

members in the European Union – the Austrian example', *European Security* 5 (4):604–13.
Gasteyger, C. (1989) 'NATO in the wider world. A neutral state's perspective', *NATO Review* 37 (1):29–33.
Geier, J. (1999) 'Marxism and war', *Internationalist Socialist Review*, Summer, pp. 25–32.
George, J. (1994) *Discourses of global politics: A critical (re)introduction to international relations.* Boulder, Colorado: Lynne Rienner.
George, J. (1996) 'Understanding international relations after the Cold War: Probing beyond the realist legacy', in Shapiro, M. J. and Alker, H. R. (eds.) *Challenging boundaries. Global flows, territorial identities.* Minneapolis: University of Minnesota Press, pp. 33–79.
Gerber, G. (2000) 'Doing Christianity and Europe: An inquiry into memory, boundary and truth practices in Malta' in Stråth, B. (ed.) *Europe and the other and Europe as the other.* Brussels: P.I.E.-Peter Lang. Series Multiple Europes, No, 10. pp. 229–77.
Giordano, B. (2000) 'Italian regionalism or "Padanian" nationalism – the political project of the Lega Nord in Italian politics', *Political Geography* 19 (4):445–71.
Glans, K. (2003) *Sweden's orderly young.* <www.axess.se/english/archive/2003/nr3/currentissue/swedens_orderly_young.php>
Glarbo, K. (1999) 'Wide-awake diplomacy: Reconstructing the Common Foreign and Security Policy of the European Union', *Journal of European Public Policy* 6 (4):634–51.
Goetschel, L. (1999) 'Neutrality, a really dead concept?', *Cooperation and Conflict* 34 (2):115–39.
Goetschel, L. (2000) 'Globalisation and security: The challenge of collective action in a politically fragmented world', *Global Society* 14 (2):259–77.
Goldmann, K. (1991) 'The Swedish Model of security policy', *West European Politics* 14 (3):122–43.
Goldmann, K. (1994) *The logic of internationalism. Coercion and accommodation.* London: Routledge.
Gould, A. (1995) 'The Swedish system in turmoil: Debate, conflict and change', in Brunsdon, E. and May, M. (eds.) *Swedish welfare: Policy and provision.* London: Social Policy Association, pp. 1–22.
Gould, A. (1999) 'The erosion of the welfare state: Swedish social policy and the EU', *Journal of European Social Policy* 9 (2):165–74.
Grant-Bailey, S. N. (1944). *The law of neutrality. Notes and analysis.* London: Stevens and Sons, Ltd.
Gray, C. (2002) 'Realism vindicated? World politics as usual after September 11', in Booth, K. and Dunne, T. (eds.) *Worlds in collision.* London: Palgrave Macmillan, pp. 226–34.
Grotius, H. (1957) *Prolegomena to the law of war and peace.* New York: Liberal Arts Press Inc.
Gustenau, G. (1999) 'Towards a common European policy on security and defence: An Austrian view of challenges for the "post-neutrals"', Institute for Security Studies. Western European Union, Occasional Papers 9, October. <www.iss-eu.org/occasion/occ09.html>

Bibliography

Gyllenhammar, P. (1996) 'Political, industrial and monetary issues – Scandinavia and Europe', address to the European-Atlantic Group, 17th December.
Haas, P. M. (1992) 'Epistemic communities and international policy coordination', *International Organization* 46 (1):1–36.
Hadenius, S. (1997) *Swedish politics during the 20th century: Conflict and consensus.* Stockholm: The Swedish Institute.
Hägglöf, G. (1960) 'A test of neutrality: Sweden in the Second World War', *International Affairs* 36 (2):153–67.
Hagstrom, J. (2001) *To be, not be be seen. The mystery of Swedish business.* Middleburg, VA: The George Washington University School of Business and Public Management.
The Hague Convention (1907) 'Hague Convention (V) Respecting the Rights and Duties of Neutral Powers and Persons in case of War on Land', Bevans 654, signed October 18, 1907, The Hague, reproduced in Reisman, W. M. and Antoniou, C. T. (eds.) (1994) *The laws of war. A comprehensive collection of primary documents on international laws governing armed conflict.* New York: Vintage Books, pp. 134–43.
Hakovirta, H. (1987a) 'The Nordic neutrals in Western European integration: Current pressures, restraints and options', *Cooperation and Conflict* 22 (4):265–73.
Hakovirta, H. (1987b) 'East–West tensions and Soviet policies on European neutrals', in Sundelius, B. (ed.) *The neutral democracies and the new Cold War.* Boulder, Colorado: Westview Press, pp. 198–217.
Hakovirta, H. (1988) *East–West conflict and European neutrality.* Oxford: Clarendon Press.
Hallendorff, C. and Schück, A. (1929) *History of Sweden.* London: Cassell and Co. Ltd.
Halliday, F. and Rosenberg, J. (1998) Interview with Kenneth Waltz, London School of Economics, 7th May 1993. *Review of International Studies* 24 (3):371–86.
Halonen, T. (1998) 'Finland in the EU – perspectives of a small member state', remarks at the European Institute, Nicosia, 12th October. <www.virtual.finland.fi/finfo/english/otkaneng_frame.html> (accessed 15/05/00).
Halonen, T. and Hjelm-Wallén, L. (1997) 'Finland and Sweden on the approaching enlargement of NATO', <www.ud.se/english/press/speformi/970315_0.htm> (accessed 27/02/98).
Hammar, T. (1991) '"Cradle of freedom on Earth": Refugee immigration and ethnic pluralism', *West European Politics* 14 (3):182–97.
Hampden-Turner, C. and Trompenaars, F. (1994) 'Sweden's social individualism: Between raging horses', in Hampden-Turner, C. and Trompenaars, F. (eds.) *The seven cultures of capitalism.* London: Piatheus, pp. 237–64.
Handel, M. (1981) *Weak states in the international system.* London: Frank Cass.
Hansen, F. B. (1996) 'Norden – from consensus to cracks', *NORD REVY* 5:31–3.
Hansen, L. (1995) 'NATO's new discourse', in Hansen, B. (ed.) *European security – 2000.* Copenhagen: Copenhagen Political Studies Press, pp. 117–34.
Hay, C. and Watson, M. (2003) 'Rendering the contingent necessary: New Labour's neo-liberal conversion and the discourse of globalisation', *Policy and Politics* 31 (3):289–305.
Heclo, H. and Madsen, H. (1987) *Politics and policy in Sweden. Principled pragmatism.* Philadelphia: Temple University Press.

Hedin, N. (1943) 'Sweden: The dilemma of a neutral', *Foreign Policy Reports*, 15th May, 19 (5):50–63.

Henkin, L. et al., (eds.) (1987) *International law. Cases and materials.* Second Edition. Minnesota: West Publishing Company.

Henrekson, M., Jonung, L. and Stymne, J. (1996) 'Economic growth and the Swedish Model', in Crafts, N. and Toniolo, G. (eds.) *Economic growth in Europe since 1945.* Cambridge: Cambridge University Press, pp. 240–87.

Henrekson, M., and Jakobsson, U. (2003) 'The transformation of ownership policy and structure in Sweden: Convergence towards the Anglo-Saxon model?', *New Political Economy* 8 (1):73–102.

Herman, S. R. (1998) 'The woman inside the negotiations: Alva Myrdal's campaign for nuclear disarmament, 1961–1982', *Peace and Change* 23 (4):514–30.

Hill, C. (2004) 'Renationalizing or regrouping? EU foreign policy since 11 September 2001', *Journal of Common Market Studies* 42 (1):143–63.

Hinteregger, G. (1989) 'Some misconceptions about Austrian neutrality', in Kruzel, J. and Haltzel, M. H. (eds.) *Between the blocs. Problems and prospects for Europe's neutral and nonaligned states.* Woodrow Wilson International Centre for Scholars and Cambridge: Cambridge University Press, pp. 269–76

Hirsh, M. (2002) 'Bush and the world', *Foreign Affairs* 81 (5):18–43.

Hjelm-Wallén, L. (1996) 'Common security in the post-Cold War era – a challenge for the non-aligned nations in the EU', Institute of European Affairs in Dublin, 8th May.

Hjelm-Wallén, L. (1997a) Article, 'Green light for enlargement', 14th July. <www.ud.se/english/press/speformi/970714_1.htm> (accessed 17/12/98).

Hjelm-Wallén, L. (1997b) Address to the think-tank seminar on hard and soft security in the Baltic Sea region, The Åland Island Peace Institute, 29th August. <www.ud.se/english/press/speformi/970829_0.htm> (accessed 17/12/98).

Holkeri, H. (1990) Prime Minister Harri Holkeri's speech during the parliamentary debate on integration, 4th December 1989, in *Yearbook of Finnish Foreign Policy.* Helsinki: Finnish Institute of International Affairs, p. 50.

Holmes, R. L. (1989) *On war and morality.* Princeton, NJ, Guildford: Princeton University Press.

Hooghe, L. and Marks, G. (1997) 'The making of a polity: The struggle over European integration', European Integration Online Papers (EIOP) 1 (4):1–29. <http://eiop.or.at/eiop/texte/1997-004a.htm>

Hopf, T. (1998) 'The promise of constructivism in international relations theory', *International Security* 23 (1):171–200.

Hopper, B. (1945) 'Sweden: A case study in neutrality', *Foreign Affairs* 23 (3):435–49.

House of Lords (1993) *Enlargement of the Community.* First Report. Select committee on the European Communities.

Huldt, B. (1988) 'Swedish security in the 1980s and 1990s – between the Arctic and Europe', in Möttölä, K. (ed.) *The Arctic challenge. Nordic and Canadian approaches to security and cooperation in an emerging international region.* Boulder, Colorado: Westview Press, pp. 317–29.

Huldt, B. (1995) 'New thinking in Sweden? The public debate on security and defense, 1979–1995', in Lindahl, R. and Sjöstedt, G. (ed.) *New thinking in international rela-*

tions: Swedish perspectives. Stockholm: Yearbook of the Swedish Institute of International Affairs.

Huldt, B. (1996) '*NATO's Northern Dimension. Prospects of Finland and Sweden: Geopolitics in the North*', Paper presented to the Finnish Institute of International Affairs, 2nd–3rd October.

Huldt, B. (1998) 'Nordic security – a historical perspective', in Jopp, M. and Warjovaara, R. (eds.) *Approaching the Northern Dimension of the CFSP: Challenges and opportunities for the EU in the emerging European security order*. Programme on the Northern Dimension of the CFSP, Volume 1. Ulkopoliittinen Instituutti & Institut für Europäische Politik, pp. 37–49.

Huntington, S. (1993) 'The clash of civilizations?', *Foreign Affairs* 72 (3):22–49.

Ingebritsen, C. (1997) 'Redefining national security: Scandinavia comes out of the cold', *Journal of Strategic Studies* 20 (3):27–44.

Jackson, R. H. (1997) 'The evolution of international society', in Baylis, J. and Smith, S. (eds.) *The globalization of world politics*. Oxford: Oxford University Press, pp. 33–48.

Jackson, R. (1999) 'Sovereignty in world politics: A glance at the conceptual and historical landscape', in Jackson, R. (ed.) *Sovereignty at the millennium*. Oxford: Blackwell, pp. 9–34.

Jackson, R. (2005) *Writing the war on terrorism. Language, politics and counter-terrorism*. Manchester: Manchester University Press.

Jahn, D. and Storsved, A. S. (1995) 'Legitimacy through referendum? The nearly successful domino-strategy of the EU referendums in Austria, Finland, Sweden and Norway'. *West European Politics* 18 (4):18–37.

Jakobson, M. (1962) 'Finland's foreign policy', *International Affairs* 38 (2):196–202.

Jenson, J. and Mahon, R. (1993) 'Representing solidarity: Class, gender and the crisis in Social Democratic Sweden', *New Left Review* September–October 201:76–100.

Jepperson, R. L., Wendt, A. and Katzenstein, P. J. (1996) 'Norms, identity and culture in national security', in Katzenstein, P. J. (ed.) *The culture of national security. Norms and identity in world politics*. New York: Columbia University Press, pp. 33–75.

Jervas, G. (1986) *Sweden between the power blocs. A new strategic position?* Stockholm: The Swedish Institute, pp. 1–48.

Jessup, P. C., and Deák, F. (1935) *Neutrality. Volume one. The origins*. New York: Columbia University Press.

Joenniemi, P. (1988) 'Models of neutrality: The traditional and modern', *Cooperation and Conflict*. 23 (2):53–67.

Joenniemi, P. (1989a) 'The underlying assumptions of Finnish neutrality', in Kruzel, J. and Haltzel, M. H. (eds.) *Between the blocs. Problems and prospects for Europe's neutral and nonaligned states*. Woodrow Wilson International Centre for Scholars and Cambridge: Cambridge University Press, pp. 49–60.

Joenniemi, P. (1989b) 'The peace potential of neutrality: A discursive approach', *Bulletin of Peace Proposals* 20 (2):175–82.

Joenniemi, P. (1990) 'Europe changes: The Nordic system remains?', *Bulletin of Peace Proposals* 21 (2):205–17.

Joenniemi, P. (1993) 'Neutrality beyond the Cold War', *Review of International Studies* 19 (3):289–304.

Joenniemi, P. (1999) *The North meets Europe: On the European Union's Northern Dimension*, Copenhagen: Copenhagen Peace Research Institute (COPRI), pp. 1–33.
Joesten, J. (1945) 'Phases in Swedish neutrality', *Foreign Affairs* 23 (2):324–9.
Johnson, R. (2002) 'Defending ways of life. The (anti-) terrorist rhetorics of Bush and Blair', *Theory, Culture and Society* 19 (4):211–31.
Kaldor, M. (1999) *Old and new wars: Organized violence in a global era*. Cambridge: Polity.
Kant, I. [1795] (1996) 'Perpetual peace. A philosophical sketch', in Reiss, H. (ed.) *Kant. Political writings*. Translated by H. B. Nisbet. Second Edition. Cambridge: Cambridge University Press, pp. 93–130.
Kant, I. [1797] (1996) 'The metaphysics of morals', in Reiss, H. (ed.) *Kant. Political writings*. Translated by H. B. Nisbet. Second Edition. Cambridge: Cambridge University Press, pp. 131–75.
Karlsson, B. (1995) 'Neutrality and economy: The redefining of Swedish neutrality, 1946–52', *Journal of Peace Research* 32 (1):37–48.
Kärre, B. and Svensson, B. (1989) 'The determinants of Swedish aid policy', in Stokke, O. (ed.) *Western middle powers and global poverty*. Uppsala: Scandinavian Institute of African Studies, pp. 231–74.
Karsh, E. (1986a) 'Finland: Adaptation and conflict', *International Affairs* 62 (2):265–78.
Karsh, E. (1986b) 'Geographical determinism: Finnish neutrality revisited', *Cooperation and Conflict* 21 (1):43–57.
Karsh, E. (1988) *Neutrality and small states*. London: Routledge.
Katzenstein, P. J. (ed.) (1996) 'Introduction', in Katzenstein, P. J. (ed.) *The culture of national security. Norms and identity in world politics*. New York: Columbia University Press, pp. 1–32.
Keatinge, P. (1987) 'Ireland: A case apart', in Sundelius, B. (ed.) *The neutral democracies and the new Cold War*. Boulder, Colorado: Westview Press, pp. 75–94.
Kekkonen, U. [1967] (1970) 'Finland's path in a world of tensions', Speech to the general church meeting in Vaasa, Finland, 6th January, 1967, in Kekkonen, U. (1970) *Neutrality: The Finnish position*. Speeches by Dr Urho Kekkonen, Translated by Ojansuu, P. and Keyworth, L. E. London: Heinemann, pp. 191–203.
Kellogg-Briand Pact (1928) Reproduced in the *United States statutes at large*, Vol. 46 (2):2343 <www.yale.edu/lawweb/avalon/imt/kbpact.htm>
Keohane, D. (2001) 'Realigning neutrality? Irish defence policy and the EU', Institute for Security Studies. Western European Union, Occasional Papers No. 24, pp. 1–38.
Keohane, R. O. (1989) *International institutions and state power: Essays in International relations theory*. Boulder, CO: Westview Press.
Kleberg, O. (1977) 'De stora och de små – Olof Palmes syn på supermakter och småstater' ['The big and the small – Olof Palme's vision of the superpowers and the small states'], in Dunér, B. et al. *Är svensk neutralitet möjlig?* [*Is Swedish neutrality possible?*]. Stockholm: Liber Förlag, pp. 61–87.
Klowert, P. and Legro, J. (1996) 'Norms, identity, and their limits: A theoretical reprise', in Katzenstein, P. J. (ed.) *The culture of national security. Norms and identity in world politics*. New York: Columbia University Press, pp. 451–72.

Bibliography

Knudsen, O. F. (1998) 'Nordic security: Challenges and responses', in Jopp, M., and Warjovaara, R. (eds.) *Approaching the Northern Dimension of the CFSP: Challenges and opportunities for the EU in the emerging European security order.* Programme on the Northern Dimension of the CFSP, Volume 1. Helsinki: Ulkopoliittinen Instituutti & Institut für Europäische Politik, pp. 25–36.

Korpi, W. (1982) 'The historical compromise and its dissolution', in Rydén, B. and Bergström, V. (eds.) *Sweden: Choices for economic and social policy in the 1980s.* London: George Allen and Unwin, pp. 124–41.

Korpi, W. (1996) 'Eurosclerosis and the sclerosis of objectivity: On the role of values among economic policy experts', *The Economic Journal* 106 (439):1727–46.

Krause, K. and Williams, M. C. (eds.) (1997) *Critical security studies.* Minneapolis: University of Minnesota Press.

Kreisky, B. (1959) 'Austria draws the balance', *Foreign Affairs* 37 (2):269–80.

Kremenyuk, V. A. (1984) 'The European neutrals and Soviet-American relations', in Neuhold, H. and Thalberg, H. (eds.) *The European neutrals in international affairs.* The Laxenburg Papers No. 7. Vienna: Austrian Institute of International Affairs, Wilhelm Braumüller, pp. 93–103.

Kronvall, O., Petersson, M., Silva, C. and Skogrand, K. (2000) 'Comments on Ola Tunander's article "The uneasy imbrication of nation-state and NATO: The case of Sweden"', *Cooperation and Conflict* 35 (4):417–29.

Kruzel, J. (1988) 'New challenges for Swedish security policy', *Survival* 30 (6):529–43.

Kruzel, J. (1989a) 'The European neutrals, national defense, and international security', in Kruzel, J. and Haltzel, M. H. (eds.) *Between the blocs. Problems and prospects for Europe's neutral and nonaligned states.* Woodrow Wilson International Centre for Scholars and Cambridge: Cambridge University Press, pp. 133–60.

Kruzel, J. (1989b) 'The future of European neutrality', in Kruzel, J. and Haltzel, M. H. (eds.) *Between the blocs. Problems and prospects for Europe's neutral and nonaligned states.* Woodrow Wilson International Centre for Scholars and Cambridge: Cambridge University Press, pp. 295–311.

Kruzel, J. and Haltzel, M. H. (eds.) *Between the blocs. Problems and prospects for Europe's neutral and nonaligned states.* Woodrow Wilson International Centre for Scholars and Cambridge: Cambridge University Press.

Kulick, D. (2003) 'Sex in the new Europe: The criminalization of clients and Swedish fear of penetration', *Anthropological Theory* 3 (2):199–218.

Kurunmäki, J. (2000) 'National representation in Sweden in the early 19th century: Erik Gustaf Geijer's two conceptions of "national representation"', Paper presented to Workshop 2, 'The history of political concepts', ECPR Joint Sessions, Copenhagen, 14th–19th April, pp. 1–32.

Kurzer, P. (2001) 'Cultural diversity in post-Maastricht Europe', *Journal of European Public Policy* 8 (1):144–61.

Labs, E. J. (1992) 'Do weak states bandwagon?', *Security Studies* 1 (3):383–416.

Laclau, E. (ed.) (1994) *The making of political identities.* London: Verso.

Laffan, B. (1994) 'Nations and regions in Western Europe', Paper presented to the second ECSA-World conference: *Federalism, subsidiarity and democracy in the European Union*, 5th–6th May, Brussels.

Laffan, B. and Tannam, E. (1998) 'Ireland: The rewards of pragmatism', in Hanf, K.

225

and Soetendorp, B. (eds.) *Adapting to European integration. Small states and the EU.* London: Longman, pp. 69–83.

Lahodynsky, O. (1992) 'The changing face of Austrian neutrality', *NATO Review* December 40 (6):24–8.

Lane, J.-E. (1991a) 'Interpretations of the Swedish Model', *West European Politics* 14 (3):1–7.

Lane, J.-.E. (1991b) 'The Swedish power investigation: The prince without his Machiavelli', *West European Politics* 14 (3):221–7.

Lane, J.-E. (1993) 'The twilight of the Scandinavian Model', *Political Studies* 41 (2):315–24.

Larsen, H. (2000) 'Danish CFSP policy in the post-Cold War period', *Cooperation and Conflict* 35 (1):37–63.

Laursen, F. (1997) *'The EU "neutrals", the CFSP and defence policy'*, Paper presented to the 5th biennial international conference on the European Community Studies Association (ECSA), Seattle, Washington, 29th May–1st June.

Laursen, J. N. and Olesen, T. B. (2000) 'A Nordic alternative to Europe? The interdependence of Denmark's Nordic and European policies, 1945–1998', *Contemporary European History* 9 (1):59–92.

Lawler, P. (1997) 'Scandinavian exceptionalism and European Union', *Journal of Common Market Studies* 35 (4):565–94.

Lawler, P. (2002) 'The "good war" after September 11', *Government and Opposition* 37 (2):151–72.

League of Nations Documents [1923] and Records [1930] (1994). Reproduced in Chatfield, C. and Ilukhina, R. (eds.) *Peace/Mir. An anthology of historic alternatives to war.* New York: Syracuse University Press.

Lebow, R. N. (1994) 'The long peace, the end of the Cold War, and the failure of realism', *International Organization* 48 (2):249–77.

Lega Nord (1996) Padania, Provisional Constitution, 15 September 1996. <www.seveso.org/English_version/constitution_150996.htm>

Lega Nord (2000) 'Fighting for the freedom of North-Italy: Introduction to the Lega Nord (Northern League)'. <www.seveso.org/English_version/Introduction.htm>

Leitz, C. (2000) *Nazi Germany and neutral Europe during the Second World War.* Manchester: Manchester University Press.

Leonard, A. T. (1988) 'Introduction', in Leonard, A. T. (ed.) *Neutrality. Changing concepts and practices.* New Orleans: University Press of America. Institute for the Comparative Study of Public Policy, University of New Orleans, pp. 1–8.

Levinger, M. and Lytle, P. F. (2001) 'Myth and mobilisation: The triadic structure of nationalist rhetoric', *Nations and Nationalism* 7 (2):175–94.

Lewin, L. (1988) *Ideology and strategy. A century of Swedish politics.* Cambridge: Cambridge University Press.

Lindbeck, A. et al. (1994) *Turning Sweden around.* Cambridge, Massachusetts: MIT Press.

Lindbeck, A. (1997) *The Swedish experiment.* Stockholm: SNS Förlag.

Lindbom, A. (2001) 'Dismantling the Social Democratic welfare model? Has the Swedish welfare state lost its defining characteristics?', *Scandinavian Political Studies* 24 (3):171–93.

Lindell, U. and Persson, S. (1986) 'The paradox of weak state power: A research and literature overview', *Cooperation and Conflict* 21 (1):79–98.

Lindh, A. (1998) 'Sweden in Europe', Address to the Swedish Institute of International Affairs, Stockholm, 16th December.

Lindh, A. (1999) *Statement of government policy in the parliamentary debate on foreign affairs*, 10th February.

Lindh, A. and Cook, R. (1999) 'We must be ready to react' (joint article by Anna Lindh and Foreign Secretary Robin Cook, published in *The Scotsman*, 22nd September).

Lindh, A. and Halonen, T. (1998) Article by the Swedish and Finnish Foreign Ministers regarding the EU and European crisis management, published in *Dagens Nyheter* and *Helsingin Sanomat*, 5th December.

Lindmarker, I. (1991) 'Election year '91. How Sweden's political parties view Europe and possible EC membership', *Current Sweden* June, No. 382.

Lindström, G. (1997) 'Sweden's security policy: Engagement – the middle way', Institute for Security Studies. Western European Union, Occasional Paper No. 2, October, pp. 1–46.

Lipschutz, R. D. (1995) 'Negotiating the boundaries of differences and security at millennium's end', in Lipschutz, R. D. (ed.) *On security*. New York: Columbia University Press, pp. 212–28.

Logue, J. (1989) 'The legacy of Swedish neutrality', in Sundelius, B. (ed.) *The committed neutral*. Boulder, Colorado: Westview Press, pp. 35–65.

Logue, J. (1999) 'The Swedish Model: Visions of Sweden in American politics and political science', *Swedish-American Historical Quarterly* 50 (3):162–72.

Long, D. (1991) 'J. A. Hobson and idealism in international relations', *Review of International Studies* 17:285–304.

Løvbræk, A. (1990) 'International reform and the like-minded countries in the North–South dialogue 1975–1985', in Pratt, C. (ed.) *Middle power internationalism. The North-South dimension*. Kingston and Montreal: McGill-Queen's University Press, pp. 25–68.

Loy, P. R. (2003) 'Soldiers in stetsons', *Journal of Popular Film and Television* 30 (4):197–206.

Luif, P. (1986) 'Strategic embargoes and European neutrals: The cases of Austria and Sweden', in Harle, V. (ed.) *Challenges and responses in European security*. Tampere: Tampere Peace Research Institute (TAPRI) Yearbook. Research Reports. No. 30, pp. 174–88.

Luif, P. (1990) 'Austria's application for EC membership: Historical background, reasons and possible results', in Laursen, F. (ed.) *EFTA and the EC. Implications of 1992*. Netherlands: European Institute of Public Administration, pp. 177–206.

Luif, P. (1998) 'Austria: Adaptation through anticipation', in Hanf, K. and Soetendorp, B. (eds.) *Adapting to European integration. Small states and the EU*. London: Longman, pp. 116–30.

Lukas, J. (1992) 'Finland vindicated', *Foreign Affairs* (70th anniversary Issue), Fall:50–63.

Luke, T. W. (1993) 'Discourses of disintegration, texts of transformation: Re-reading realism in the new world order', *Alternatives* 18:229–58.

Bibliography

Lundberg, E. (1985) 'The rise and fall of the Swedish Model', *Journal of Economic Literature* 23 (1):1–36.

Lundkvist, S. (1973) 'The experience of empire: Sweden as a great power', in Roberts, M. (ed.) *Sweden's age of greatness, 1632–1718.* London: Macmillan, pp. 20–57.

Lyon, P. (1963) *Neutralism.* Leicester: Leicester University Press.

Machiavelli, N. (1995) *The prince.* Translated by George Bull. London: Penguin Books.

Maigaard, J. (1996) 'Norden and the second European revolution', *NORD REVY* No. 4, September, pp. 13–18.

Malmborg, af M. (1994) 'The steadfast nation-state. Sweden and West European integration, 1945–59' [Summary of dissertation, *Den ståndaktiga nationalstaten. Sverige och den Västeuropeiska integrationen 1945–1950*]. Bibliotheca Historica Lundensis 80, Lund, pp. 427–38 <www.lustorfs.ldc.lu.se/hist/library /thesis.htm> (accessed 19/08/01), pp. 1–19.

Malmborg, af M. (2001) *Neutrality and state-building in Sweden.* Houndmills: Palgrave.

Marcussen, M. and Roscher, R. (2000) 'The social construction of "Europe": Life cycles of nation-state identities in France, Germany and Great Britain', in Stråth, B. (ed.) *Europe and the other and Europe as the other.* Brussels: P.I.E.-Peter Lang. Series Multiple Europes, No. 10, pp. 325–57.

Martin, L. W. (ed.) (1962) *Neutralism and nonalignment. The new states in world affairs.* New York: Frederick A. Praeger Inc.

Martinsson, E. (2000) *Attentatet på Dramaten. En studie av Alf Sjöbergs uppsättning av Marika Stiernstedts drama* [*The outrage at the Royal Dramatic Theatre in Stockholm. A study of Alf Sjöberg's staging of Marika Stiernstedt's drama*]. Summary of dissertation/monograph. Department of Comparative Literature, Lund University <www.lub.lu.se/cgi-bin/show_diss.pl?db=global&fname=hum_116.html> (accessed 24/09/01).

Masker, J. S. (1995) 'Towards an understanding of small states in security regimes', in Masker, J. S. (ed.) *Small states and security regimes.* New Orleans: University Press of America, Inc, pp. 8–22.

Maude, G. (1982) 'The further shores of Finlandization', *Cooperation and Conflict* 17 (1):3–16.

McInnes, C. (1993) 'The military security agenda', in Rees, G. W. (ed.) *International politics in Europe: The new agenda.* London: Routledge. pp. 71–86.

McSweeney, B. (1998) 'Policy of neutrality no longer exists', *The Irish Times* 21st May.

Mearsheimer, J. J. (1990) 'Back to the future', *International Security* 15 (1):5–56.

Mediterranean Academy of Diplomatic Studies and the Graduate Institute of International Studies, Geneva. (1991) *Colloquium on neutrality and non-alignment.* Opening session, 4th–8th November <http://conf.diplomacy.edu/conf/neutrali /open.htm>

Meidner, R. (1992) 'The rise and fall of the Swedish Model', *Studies in Political Economy* 39:159–71.

Memorandum from Finland and Sweden (1996) *The IGC and the security and defence dimension: Towards an enhanced EU role in crisis management.* 25th April.

MFA (Ministry for Foreign Affairs) (1997a) *Preventing violent conflict.* Stockholm, Ds 1997:18.

MFA (1997b) 'The rights of the poor – our common responsibility. Combating poverty

in Sweden's development cooperation', Government Report 1996/97:169, pp. 1–96.
MFA (1998) *An enlarged EU – opportunities and problems. A summary of the reports on the consequences of enlargement of the EU*, pp. 1–36.
MFA (1999) Extract from the Swedish Government Bill 1998/99:1. Expenditure Category 7. International Development Cooperation, Stockholm, pp. 1–20.
MFA (2000) *Sweden's International Development Cooperation Yearbook 2000*. Stockholm.
MFA (2001) Statement of government policy in the parliamentary debate on foreign affairs, 7th February. <www.ud.se/english/policy/statements/index.htm> (accessed 15/02/01), pp. 1–10.
MFA (2002) Statement of government policy in the parliamentary debate on foreign affairs, 13th February <www.utrikes.regeringen.se/inenglish/policy/statements/index.htm> (accessed 13/02/02).
MFA (2004) 'Making it happen. Sweden's report on the millennium development goals 2004. <www.undp.org/mdg/sweden.pdf>
MFA (2005) Budget bill, presented to the Riksdag September 20. <www.sweden.gov.se/content/1/c6/03/01/22/bb1242a0.pdf>
MFA (Finland) (1986) Concluding remarks of the working group appointed by the Ministry for Foreign Affairs, 'Nordic Nuclear Weapon-Free Zone'. *Yearbook of Finnish Foreign Policy*. Helsinki: Finnish Institute of International Affairs, pp. 3–4.
MFA/SIDA (Ministry for Foreign Affairs and Swedish International Development Cooperation Agency) (1997) *Swedish International Development Cooperation 1997*. Fiscal Year 1995/6.
Miles, L. (1994) *Sweden, security and accession to the European Union*. Nordic Studies Occasional Papers. University of Humberside School of Economics and European Studies, pp. 1–38.
Miles, L. (2000) 'Making peace with the Union? The Swedish Social Democratic Party and European integration', in Geyer, R., Ingebritsen, C. and Moses, J. W. (eds.) *Globalization, Europeanization and the end of Scandinavian Social Democracy?* Basingstoke: Macmillan, pp. 218–39.
Ministry of Defence (Sweden) (1998) Swedish security policy in the light of international change. The concluding chapter of a review by the Swedish Defence Commission. Regeringskansliet. Ministry of Defence, Sweden, 20th February, pp. 1–28.
Ministry of Defence (Sweden) (2005) Memorandum of understanding (Nordic Battle Group). 23rd May <www.sweden.gov.se/content/1/c6/04/49/86/98e7f099.pdf>
Missiroli, A. (1994) 'Austria before and after 1989: Neutrality versus European integration', The Johns Hopkins University. Bologna Centre Research Institute, No. 76.
Missiroli, A. (1999) 'Towards a European security and defense identity? Record – state of play – prospects', in Jopp, M. and Ojanen, H. (eds.) *European security integration: implications for non-alignment and alliances*. Programme on the Northern Dimension of the CFSP, Vol. 3. Helsinki: Ulkopoliittinen Instituutti & Institut für Europäische Politik, pp. 21–56.
Mjøset, L. (1987) 'Nordic economic policies in the 1970s and 1980s', *International Organization* 41 (3):403–56.

Mock, A. (1990) 'Austria in a changing Europe', *The World Today* 46 (3):37–8.
Moerk, E. L. (1998) 'From war-hero to villain: Reversal of the symbolic value of war and a warrior-king', *Journal of Peace Research* 35 (4):453–70.
Møller, B. (1999) The Kosovo crisis and the northern tier: Denmark, Norway, Iceland, Sweden and Finland. For *Kosovo and the international community: Selective indignation, collective intervention, and the changing contours of world politics* (United Nations University) and for presentation at the author workshop, Budapest, 18th–22nd September and to the seminar on the Lessons of Kosovo, Copenhagen, 13th September, pp. 1–25.
Möller, T. (1999) 'The Swedish election 1998: A protest vote and the birth of a new political landscape?', *Scandinavian Political Studies* 22 (3):261–76
Montin, S. and Elander, I. (1995) 'Citizenship, consumerism and local government in Sweden', *Scandinavian Political Studies* 18 (1):25–51.
Moran, M. (1988) 'Crises of the welfare state', *British Journal of Political Science* 18:394–414.
Morgenthau, H. J. (1939) 'International affairs: The resurrection of neutrality in Europe', *The American Political Science Review* 33 (3):473–86.
Morgenthau, H. J. (1958) *Dilemmas of politics*. Chicago: University of Chicago Press.
Morgenthau, H. J. (1993) *Politics among nations*. Boston: McGraw Hill.
Mörth, U. and Sundelius, B. (1995) 'Sweden and the United Nations', in Krause, K. and Knight. W. A. (eds.) *State, society, and the United Nations system: Changing perspectives on multilateralism*. Tokyo: UN University Press. pp. 101–31.
Möttölä, K. (1988) (ed.) *The Arctic challenge. Nordic and Canadian approaches to security and cooperation in an emerging international region*. Boulder, Colorado: Westview Press.
Möttölä, K. (1989) 'Commentary', in Kruzel, J. and Haltzel, M. H. (eds.) *Between the blocs. Problems and prospects for Europe's neutral and nonaligned states*. Woodrow Wilson International Centre for Scholars and Cambridge: Cambridge University Press, pp. 222–7.
Mourtizen, H. (1988) *Finlandization: Towards a general theory of adaptive politics*. Avebury: Gower Publishing Co. Ltd.
Mourtizen, H. (1995) 'The Nordic Model as a foreign policy instrument: Its rise and fall', *Journal of Peace Research* 32 (1):9–21.
Mouritzen, H. (1998) 'A fragmented North', in Jopp, M. and Warjovaara, R. (eds.) *approaching the Northern Dimension of the CFSP: Challenges and opportunities for the EU in the emerging European security order*. Programme on the Northern Dimension of the CFSP, Volume 1. Helsinki: Ulkopoliittinen Instituutti & Institut für Europäische Politik, pp. 55–8.
National Security Council (1948) 28/1 1948. Policies of the government of the United States of America relating to the national security, Volume 1, 1947–48. Position of the United States with respect to Scandinavia. Reproduced in SOU (Statens Offentliga Utredningar) (1994) *Had there been a war . . . preparations for the reception of military assistance 1949–1969*. Report of the Commission on Neutrality Policy, Stockholm, 1994. SOU 1994:11 (Appendix).
National Security Council (1952) A report to the National Security Council by the Executive Secretary on the position of the United States with respect to

Scandinavia and Finland, January 8, 1952. Statement of Policy proposed by the NSC with respect to Scandinavia and Finland. Reproduced in SOU (Statens Offentliga Utredningar) (1994) *Had there been a war . . . preparations for the reception of military assistance 1949–1969*. Report of the Commission on Neutrality Policy, Stockholm, 1994. SOU 1994:11 (Appendix).
NATO (2004) 'September 11 – one year on. NATO's contribution to the fight against terrorism'. 20th January. <www.nato.int/terrorism/index.htm>
NATO (Slovenia) (04/11/01) 'Schüssel says Austria should consider NATO entry'. <http://nato.gov.si/slo/novinarsko-sredisce/clanki/nevtralne-drzave/2001-11-04–reuters/>
NATO (Slovenia) (14/11/01) 'Austrian official advocates country's NATO membership'. <http://nato.gov.si/slo/novinarsko-sredisce/clanki/nevtralne-drzave/2001-11-14-die-presse/>
Neuhold, H. and Thalberg, H. (eds.) (1984) *The European neutrals in international affairs*. The Laxenburg Papers No. 7. Vienna: Austrian Institute of International Affairs. Wilhelm Braumüller.
Neuhold, H. (1994a) 'Security challenges and institutional responses: An Austrian perspective', *The International Spectator* 29 (3):21–36.
Neuhold H. (1994b) 'Perspectives of Austria's membership in the European Union', *German Yearbook of Internaitonal Law* (37): 9–39.
Neuhold, H. (1996) 'Austria on the threshold of the twenty-first century. Another change of international status?', *Europa-Programmet*, Norway, No. 10, pp. 5–32.
Neuhold, H. (2003) 'Comments on the Austrian position', in Ojanen, H. (ed.) *Neutrality and non-alignment in Europe today*. FIIA Report 2003/6, pp. 14–18.
Neumann, I. B. (1999) *Uses of the other. 'The East' in European identity formation*. Manchester: Manchester University Press.
Newby, A. and Titley, G. (2003) 'The "war on terror" and non-alignment', *Peace Review* 15 (4):483–9.
Newell, J. L. (1994) 'The Scottish National Party and the Italian *Lega Nord*', *European Journal of Political Research* 26 (2):135–53.
Nicholson, M. (1998) 'Realism and utopianism revisited', *Review of International Studies* December 24:65–82.
Noël, A. and Thérien, J.-P. (1995) 'From domestic to international justice: The welfare state and foreign aid', *International Organization* 49 (3):523–53.
Norberg, J. (2001) *In defence of global capitalism*. Stockholm: Timbro.
Nordic Council of Ministers (2000) *Finland's programme for the Nordic chairmanship in 2001 – Nordic citizen*. Copenhagen. TemaNord 2000:563.
Nordic Reach (2001) 'On history and heroes: A conversation with Göran Persson'. <www.nordicreach.com/content_sample_gpersson.html>
Nordlund, A. (2000) 'Social policy in harsh times. Social security development in Denmark, Finland, Norway and Sweden during the 1980s and 1990s', *International Journal of Social Welfare* 9:31–42.
Nordstedts Stora Svensk-Engelska Ordbok [Nordstedt's large Swedish-English dictionary] (1993). Second Edition. Stockholm: Nordstedts.
Noreen, E. (1989) 'Perspectives on the Swedish debate: With particular reference to the new Cold War debate between Social Democrats and conservatives in the early

1980s', in Waever, O., Lemaitre, P. and Tromer, E. (eds.) *European polyphony: Perspectives beyond East–West confrontation.* London: Macmillan Press, pp. 250–64.

Norman, T. (1993) 'Stages in Swedish neutrality', in Nevakivi, J. (ed.) *Neutrality in history.* Proceedings of the conference on the History of Neutrality, Helsinki, 9th–12th September, 1992. Helsinki: Commission of the History of International Relations/Finnish Historical Society, pp. 303–12.

Norrback, O. (1998) 'Small states and European security', Opening address to the nineteenth annual conference of the Irish National Committee for the Study of International Affairs, 20 November, 1997. *Irish Studies in International Affairs* 9:5–9.

Notermans, T. (2000) 'Europeanization and the crisis of Scandinavian Social Democracy', in Geyer, R., Ingebritsen, C. and Moses, J. W. (eds.) *Globalization, Europeanization and the end of Scandinavian Social Democracy?* Basingstoke: Macmillan, pp. 23–44.

Nyberg, M. (1996) 'The rise and fall of the Swedish Model', *Clarté.* <www.algonet.se/~clarte/cl_e_0.html>

Nye, J. (2002–3) 'Limits of American power', *Political Science Quarterly* 117 (4):545–59.

Oberg, J. (2000) 'Sweden in the new militarisation of the European Union', Transnational Foundation for Peace and Future Research (TFF), Press Info. No. 109, 12th December. <www.transnational.org/pressinf/2000/pf109 _SwedenEUmilit.html> (accessed 13/07/01).

Oberg, J. (2001) 'The acquiescing, commonplace Sweden', Transnational Foundation for Peace and Future Research (TFF), Press Info. No. 133, 4th October. <www.transnational.org/pressinf/2001/pf133_SwedenAcques.html> (accessed 21/12/01).

Official Journal of the European Communities (OJE) (2001a) *Proposal for a Council Framework Decision on combating terrorism* (2001/C 332 E/17), 19th September.

Official Journal of the European Communities (OJE) (2001b) *Proposal for a Council Framework Decision on the European arrest warrant and the surrender procedures between the Member States* (2001/C 332 E/18), 19th September.

Ogley, R. (1970) *The theory and practice of neutrality in the twentieth century.* London: Routledge and Kegan Paul.

Ojanen, H., Herolf, G. and Lindahl, R. (2000) *Non-alignment and European security policy: Ambiguity at work.* Helsinki: Ulkopoliittinen Instituutti & Institut für Europäische Politik. Programme of the Northern Dimension of the CFSP, No. 6.

Ojanen, H. (2000a) *Participation and influence: Finland, Sweden and the post-Amsterdam development of the CFSP*, Institute for Security Studies. Western European Union Occasional Papers 11, pp. 1–30.

Ojanen, H. (2000b) 'The Common Foreign and Security Policy', in Ojanen, H., Herolf, G. and Lindahl, R., *Non-alignment and European security policy: Ambiguity at work.* Ulkopoliittinen Instituutti & Institut für Europäische Politik. Programme of the Northern Dimension of the CFSP, No. 6.

Ojanen, H. (2002) 'Sweden and Finland: What difference does it make to be non-aligned?' in Græger, N., Larsen, H. and Ojanen, H. (eds.) *The ESDP and the Nordic*

Bibliography

countries: Four variations of a theme. Helsinki: Ulkopoliittinen instituutti. Programme of the Northern Dimension of the CFSP, pp. 154–217.

Olsen, G. M. (1992) *The struggle for economic democracy in Sweden.* Aldershot: Avebury.

Ørvik, N. (1953) *The decline of neutrality. 1914–1941.* Oslo: Johan Grundt Tanum Forlag.

Østergaard, U. (1997) 'The long road to peaceful Nordic relations', *Eagle Street. Newsletter of the Finnish Institute in London.* Issue No. 4, June, pp. 1–2.

Paasio, P. (1990) Speech to the Finnish Parliament, 29th November, 1989, in *Yearbook of Finnish Foreign Policy.* Helsinki: Finnish Institute of International Affairs, p. 58.

Padgett, S. and Paterson, W. E. (1991) *A history of Social Democracy in postwar Europe.* London: Longman.

Pagrotsky, L. (1997) 'Social Democracy towards the 21st century', Speech given in Tel Aviv, 4th October. <www.sb.gov.se/databas/tal-861198907.html> (accessed 17/12/98).

Pagrotsky, L. (2000) 'Globalization with a human face – the role of the unions', Speech at the International Metalworkers Federation central committee meeting, Birmingham, 22nd June.

Pagrotsky, L. (2001) 'Instruments to shape globalization'. *Journal of Human Development* 2(1):53–8.

Palan, R. (2000) 'A world of their making: an evaluation of the contructivist critique in international relations', *Review of International Studies* 26(4):575–98.

Palme, O. (1972) *Democratic socialism means solidarity.* Social Democratic Party of Sweden. Translated by Roger G. Tanner. Borås, Sweden: Socialdemokraterna.

Palme, O. (1982) 'Sweden's role in the world', in Rydén, B. and Bergström, V. (eds.) *Sweden: Choices for economic and social policy in the 1980s.* London: George Allen and Unwin, pp. 234–53.

Parmar, I. (2005) 'Catalysing events, think tanks and American foreign policy shifts: A comparative analysis of the impacts of Pearl Harbor 1941 and 11 September 2001', *Government and Opposition* 40 (1):1–25.

Pedersen, F. S. (1995) 'Nordic cooperation and the EU', in Lovenduski, J. and Stayner, J. (eds.) *Contemporary Political Studies UK,* Vol. 3. Belfast: Political Studies Association, United Kingdom, pp. 1195–202.

Persson, G. (1999) 'Security in a changing world', Speech to the Swedish Institute of International Affairs and the Central Defence and Society Federation, 10th March. <www.utrikes.regeringen.se/inenglish/pressinfo/speeches_other.htm> (accessed 15/03/99).

Persson, G. (2000) Speech by the Swedish Prime Minister at the debate in parliament about the EU, 10th May. <www.regeringen.se/inenglish/speeches.htm> (accessed 20/05/00).

Persson, G. (2001a) *Congress opening speech,* SAP Party congress, 5th November. <www.sap.se>

Persson, G. (2001b) *Speech on a new party programme,* SAP Party congress, 6th November. <www.sap.se/start.nsf> (accessed 19/12/01).

Pestoff, V. A. (2001) 'Globalization, business interest associations and Swedish exceptionalism in the 21st century', Paper presented at the Centre for European Studies,

233

University of North Carolina at Chapel Hill. <www.unc.edu/depts/europe/papers/010319pestoff.pdf>

Petersson, O. (2000) *The European debate in Sweden*. Groupement d'études et de recherches. Notre Europe. Research Policy Paper No. 12, December, pp. 1–41.

Pfaller, A., Gough, I. and Therborn, G. (1994) 'Welfare statism and international competition: The lessons of the cases studies', in Pfaller, A. et al. *Can welfare states compete?* Basingstoke: Macmillan, pp. 271–97.

Phinnemore, D. (1995) 'Austria in the European Union – saying farewell to neutrality', in Lovenduski, J. and Stayner, J. (eds.) *Contemporary Political Studies UK* Vol. 1. Belfast: Political Studies Association, United Kingdom, pp. 363–70.

Politis, N. (1935) *Neutrality and peace*. Translated by Francis Crane Macken. Pamphlet Series of the Carnegie Endowment for International Peace. Division of International Law No. 55.

Pontusson, J. (1992) 'At the end of the third road: Swedish Social Democracy in crisis', *Politics and Society* 20 (3):305–32.

Powell, C. (2002) Statement upon the release of 'Patterns of Global Terrorism', Washington, DC, 21st May 2002. US Department of State May 2002 Patterns of Global Terrorism 2001 (iii). <www.state.gov/secretary/rm/2002/10350.htm>

Pratt, C. (1989a) 'Humane internationalism: Its significance and its variants', in Pratt, C. (ed.) *Internationalism under strain. The North–South policies of Canada, the Netherlands, Norway and Sweden*. Toronto: University of Toronto Press, pp. 3–23.

Pratt, C. (1989b) 'Middle power internationalism and north–south issues: Comparisons and prognosis' in Pratt, C. (ed.) *Internationalism under strain. The North–South policies of Canada, the Netherlands, Norway and Sweden*. Toronto: University of Toronto Press, pp. 193–220.

Pratt, C. (1989c) 'Canada: An eroding and limited internationalism', in Pratt, C. (ed.) *Internationalism under strain. The North–South policies of Canada, the Netherlands, Norway and Sweden*. Toronto: University of Toronto Press, pp. 24–69.

Pratt, C. (1990) *Middle power internationalism. The North–South dimension*. Kingston and Montreal: McGill-Queen's University Press.

Prawitz, J. (1994) *Non-nuclear is beautiful or why and how Sweden went non-nuclear*, Karlskrona: Kungl Krigsvetenskapsakademiens Handlingar och Tidskrift, No. 6, pp. 49–113.

Pred, A. (1995) *Recognizing European modernities. A montage of the present*. London: Routledge.

Pred, A. (2000) *Even in Sweden: Racisms, racialized spaces, and the popular geographical imagination*. Berkely: University of California Press.

Price, R. and Reus-Smit, C. (1998) 'Dangerous liaisons: Critical international theory and constructivism', *European Journal of International Relations* 4 (3):259–94.

Prodi, R. (2001) 'Europe one month after 11th September: Challenges and reactions to the European Trade Union Confederation', Brussels, 11th October.

Quester, G. H. (1990) 'Finlandization as a problem or an opportunity?', *The Annals of the American Academy*. AAPSS 512:33–45.

Radaelli, C. M. and Bruni, M. G. (1998) 'Beyond Charlemagne's Europe: A sub-national examination of Italy within the EMU', *Regional and Federal Studies* 8 (2):34–51.

Ramachandaran, S. (2001) 'Swedish dilemma', *The Times of India*, 30th October. <www.timesofindia.com> (accessed 06/01/02).
Rasmussen, A. F. (2002) 'Nytårstale 2002' (New Years' Eve Speech), 1st January. <www.statsministeriet.dk/taler/tale116%20-%0nytaar.htm> (accessed 30/04/02).
Rasmussen, M. V. (2004) '"A parallel globalization of terror": 9-11, security and globalization', *Cooperation and Conflict* 37 (3):323-49.
Raymond, G. A. (1997) 'Neutrality norms and the balance of power', *Cooperation and Conflict* 32 (2):123-46.
Reus-Smit, C. (1996) *The constructivist turn: Critical theory after the Cold War*. Research School of Pacific and Asian Studies. Australian National University Department of International Relations: Canberra. Working Paper No. 4.
Rhee, S. (1912) *Neutrality as influenced by the United States*. Princeton, NJ: Princeton University Press.
Rice, C. (2000) 'Promoting the national interest', *Foreign Affairs* 79 (1):45-62.
Ringmar, E. (1996) *Identity, interest and action. A cultural explanation of Sweden's intervention in the Thirty Years War*. Cambridge: Cambridge University Press.
Risse-Kappen, T. (ed.) (1995) *Bringing transnational relations back in. Non-state actors, domestic structures and international institutions*, Cambridge: Cambridge University Press.
Rojas, M. (2001) *Beyond the welfare state. Sweden and the quest for a post-industrial welfare model*. Stockholm: Timbro.
Rokkan, S. (1981) 'The growth and structuring of mass politics', in Allardt, E. et al. *Nordic democracy. Ideas, issues and institutions in politics, economy, education, social and cultural affairs of Denmark, Finland, Iceland, Norway and Sweden*. Copenhagen: Det Danske Selskab, pp. 53-79.
Roosevelt, F. D. (1937) 'Quarantine speech', Chicago, 5th October <gopher://wiretap.spies.com:70/00/Gov/US-Speech/quarant.fdr> (accessed 06/03/98).
Rosamond, B. (1999) 'Discourses of globalization and the social construction of European identities', *Journal of European Public Policy* 6 (4):652-68.
Rösch, M. (1993) 'Switzerland's security policy in transition', *NATO Review* 41 (6):19-25 <http://nato.int/docu/review/articles/9306-5.htm> (accessed 23/09/00).
Ross, J. F. L. (1989) *Neutrality and international sanctions. Sweden, Switzerland and collective security*. New York: Praeger.
Ross, J. F. L. (1991) 'Sweden, the European Community, and the politics of economic realism', *Cooperation and Conflict* 26 (3):117-28.
Roth, K. (2004) 'The law of war in the war on terror', *Foreign Affairs* January/February 83 (1):2-7.
Rubin, A. P. (1988) 'The concept of neutrality in international law', in Leonard, A. T. (ed.) *Neutrality. Changing concepts and practices*. New Orleans: University Press of America. Institute for the Comparative Study of Public Policy, University of New Orleans. pp. 9-34.
Ruddy, T. M. (2000) 'US foreign policy, the "Third Force", and European Union: Eisenhower and Europe's neutrals', *Midwest Quarterly* 42:67-80.
Ruggie, J. G. (1998) *Constructing the world polity. Essays on international institutionalization*. London: Routledge.

Ruin, O. (1991) 'Three Swedish Prime Ministers: Tage Erlander, Olof Palme and Ingvar Carlsson', *West European Politics* 14 (3):58–82.
Rusi, A. (1987) 'Finlandization without Finland?', *Yearbook of Finnish Foreign Policy, 1987*. Helsinki: Finnish Institute of International Affairs, pp. 13–16.
Ruth, A. (1984) 'The second new nation: The mythology of modern Sweden', *Daedalus* 113:53–96.
Rydén, B., and Bergström, V. (1982) 'Sweden in the 1980s: How gloomy are the prospects?', in Rydén, B., and Bergström, V. (eds.) *Sweden: Choices for economic and social policy in the 1980s*. London: George Allen and Unwin, pp. 1–8.
Ryner, M. (1994) 'Assessing SAP's economic policy in the 1980s: The "Third Way", the Swedish Model and the transition from Fordism to post-Fordism', *Economic and Industrial Democracy* 15:385–428.
Ryner, M. (2002) *Capitalist restructuring, globalisation and the Third Way: Lessons from the Swedish Model*. London and New York: Routledge.
Ryner, M. (2004) 'Neoliberalization of Social Democracy: The Swedish case', *Comparative European Politics* 2 (1):97–119.
Saeter, M. (1993) 'The Nordic countries and European integration', in Tiilikainen, T. and Petersen, D. (eds.) *The Nordic countries and the EC*. Copenhagen: Copenhagen Political Studies Press, pp. 8–22.
SAF (2000) *Facts about the Swedish economy 2000*. Lund: Swedish Employers' Confederation.
Sainsbury, D. (1991) 'Swedish Social Democracy in transition: The party's record in the 1980s and the challenge of the 1990s', *West European Politics* 14 (3):31–57.
Salmon, P. (1993) 'British attitudes towards neutrality in the twentieth century', in Nevakivi, J. (ed.) *Neutrality in history*. Proceedings of the conference on the History of Neutrality, Helsinki, 9th–12th September, 1992. Helsinki: Commission of the History of International Relations/Finnish Historical Society, pp. 117–32.
Salmon, T. (1992) 'Testing times for EPC: The Gulf and Yugoslavia 1990–1992', *International Affairs* 68 (2):233–53.
Sandomirskaja, I. (1999) 'After the wall. Art and culture in post-communist Europe'. Moderna Museet, Stockholm, 16th October 1999–16th January 2001. <www.artmargins.com/content/review/sandomirskajareview.html> (accessed 16/12/01).
SAP (Social Democratic Party) (Sweden) (2001) Text of the SAP programme approved by the congress, 6th November, SAP Party congress, Vasteras <www.sap.se/start.nsf> (accessed 19/11/01).
Sarbin, T. R. (2003) 'The metaphor-to-myth transformation with special reference to the "war on terrorism"', *Peace and Conflict* 9 (2): 149–57.
Schindler, D. (1991) 'The concepts of neutrality and non-alignment', Mediterranean Academy of Diplomatic Studies and the Graduate Institute of International Studies, Geneva. *Colloquium on neutrality and non-alignment*, 4th–8th November. <http://diplomacy.edu/Publishing/neutrality/schinde.htm> (accessed 28/04/98).
Schlesinger, T. O. (1991) *The United States and the European neutrals*. Vienna: Herausgegeben von Anton Pelinka. Studien zur politischen wirklichkeit, Braumüller.
Schori, P. (1997) 'Globalization on human terms', Speech at the Parliamentary

Bibliography

Debate, 10th December. Ministry for Foreign Affairs, Stockholm, pp. 1–10.

Schultz, D. M. (1992) 'Austria in the international arena: Neutrality, European integration and consociationalism', *West European Politics* (Special Issue: Politics in Austria, January) 15 (1):173–200.

Schüssel, W. (1997) 'Enlarging NATO: The political, economic and cultural Dimensions', conference of the New Atlantic Initiative and the European Forum, Alpbach, 17th October. <www.bmaa.gv.at/presseservice/presseaussendungen/reden/bm/red_bm10.html> (accessed 21/10/00).

Schüssel, W. (2000) Statement by the Austrian Federal Government to the Nationalrat. Vienna: Federal Press Service, 9th February, pp. 1–18.

Schwartz, H. (1994) 'Small states in big trouble: State reorganization in Australia, Denmark, New Zealand, and Sweden in the 1980s', *World Politics* 46 (4):527–55.

Schwok, R. (1991) 'EC-EFTA relations', in Hurwitz, L. and Lequesne, C. (eds.) *The state of the European Community*, Vol. 1, Policies, Institutions, and Debates in the Transition Years. Boulder, Colorado; Harlow: Rienner: Longman, pp. 329–41.

Shapiro, M. J. (1992) 'That obscure object of violence: Logistics, desire, war', *Alternatives* 17:453–77.

SIDA (2003) Budget appropriations, 2003. <www.sida.se/Sida/jsp/polopoly.jsp?d=3170&a=22956>

Skidelsky, R. (2004) 'The just war tradition', *Prospect* December, pp. 28–33.

Smith, A. and Wallace, H. (1994) 'The European Union: Towards a policy for Europe', *International Affairs* 70 (3):429–44.

Smith, S. (1999) 'Social constructivisms and European studies: A reflectivist critique', *Journal of European Public Policy* 6 (4):682–91.

Södersten, B. (1989) 'Sweden: Towards a realistic internationalism', in Pratt, C. (ed.) *Internationalism under strain. The North–South policies of Canada, the Netherlands, Norway, and Sweden*, Toronto: University of Toronto Press, pp. 155–92.

Sofka, J. R. (1997) 'The Jeffersonian idea of national security', *Diplomatic History* 21 (4):519–44.

Sørensen, G. (1998) 'IR theory after the Cold War', *Review of International Studies* 24. Special Issue, December, pp. 83–100.

SOU (*Statens Offentliga Utredningar*) (1994) *Had there been a war ... preparations for the reception of military assistance 1949–1969*. Report of the Commission on Neutrality Policy. Stockholm: SOU 1994:11.

SOU (*Statens Offentliga Utredningar*) (1997) *A larger EU – a more secure Europe. Study of the consequences for security of EU enlargement.* Stockholm: SOU 1997:143.

Sparks, C. and Cockerill, S. (1991) 'Goodbye to the Swedish miracle', *International Socialism* 51:91–103.

Specter, M. (1998) 'Letter from Stockholm', *The New Yorker*, 5th October. <www.michaelspecter.com/ny/1998/1998_10_05_nobel.html> (accessed 16/10/01).

Spielberg, S. (1998) 'Of guts and glory', *Newsweek*, 22/06/98 Supplement, Vol. 131, Issue 25.

Sperling, J. and Kirchner, E. (1998) 'Economic security and the problem of cooperation in post-Cold War Europe', *Review of International Studies* 24 (2):221–37.

Spinelli, A. and Rossi, E. (1985) 'The Ventotene Manifesto', reproduced in Lipgens, W.

(ed.) *Documents on the history of European integration. Vol. 1. Continental plans for European Union, 1939–45*. Berlin: Walter de Gruyter, pp. 471–84.

Stålvant, C.-E. (1990) 'Rather a market than a home, but preferably a home market: Swedish policies facing changes in Europe', in Laursen, F. (ed.) *EFTA and the EC: Implications of 1992*. Netherlands: European Institute of Public Administration (EIPA), pp. 135–62.

Steene, M. S. (1989) 'Role model or power pawn? The changing image of Swedish foreign policy, 1929–1987', in Sundelius, B. (ed.) *The committed neutral*. Boulder, Colorado: Westview Press, pp. 167–94.

Stein, P. (1991) 'Sweden: From capitalist success to welfare state sclerosis', *Policy Analysis* No. 160, 10th September <www.cato.org/pubs/pas/pa-160.html> (accessed 27/09/99).

Steinmo, S. (2002) 'Globalization and taxation: Challenges to the Swedish welfare state', *Comparative Political Studies* 35 (7):839–62.

Stenbäck, P. (1995) 'Nordic cooperation and EU membership of Finland and Sweden', *Yearbook of Finnish Foreign Policy*. Helsinki: Finnish Institute of International Affairs, pp. 23–8.

Stenius, H. (1996) 'Investing in civil society as security policy: An old Finnish strategy'. *Eagle Street. Newsletter of the Finnish Institute in London*, Issue No. 2, December. <www.finnish-institute.org.uk/articles/es_2/editor.htm> (accessed 21/06/98).

Stern, M. (1991) *Security policy in transition – Sweden after the Cold War*. Padrigu Thesis Series. Padrigu Papers. M. A. Dissertation, University of Gothenburg.

Stiernlöf, S. (ed.) (1989) 'Is neutrality necessary?', *Facts about peace (FredsFakta)*. Peace Forum of the Swedish Labour Movement, Special Issue.

Stokke, O. (1989) 'The determinants of aid policies: General introduction', in Stokke, O. (ed.) *Western middle powers and global poverty*. Uppsala: Scandinavian Institute of African Studies, pp. 9–23.

Stråth, B. (2000a) 'The Swedish image of Europe as the other', in Stråth, B. (ed.) *Europe and the other and Europe as the other*. Brussels: P.I.E.-Peter Lang. Series Multiple Europes, No. 10, pp. 359–83.

Stråth, B. (2000b) 'Europe as a discourse', in Stråth, B. (ed.) *Europe and the other and Europe as the other*. Brussels: P.I.E.-Peter Lang. Series Multiple Europes, No. 10, pp. 13–44.

Stråth, B. (2000c) 'Multiple Europes: Integration, identity and demarcation to the other', in Stråth, B. (ed.) *Europe and the other and Europe as the other*. Brussels: P.I.E.-Peter Lang. Series Multiple Europes, No. 10, pp. 385–420.

Stromberg, P. G. (1986) *Symbols of community. The cultural system of a Swedish Church*. Tuscon: University of Arizona Press.

Sundelius, B. (1987) 'Dilemmas and strategies for the neutral democracies', in Sundelius, B. (ed.) *The neutral democracies and the new Cold War*. Boulder, Colorado: Westview Press, pp. 11–32.

Sundelius, B. (1989) 'National security dilemmas and strategies for the European neutrals', in Kruzel, J. and Haltzel, M. H. (eds.) *Between the blocs. Problems and prospects for Europe's neutral and nonaligned states*. Woodrow Wilson International Centre for Scholars and Cambridge: Cambridge University Press, pp. 98–121.

Bibliography

Sundelius, B. (1990) 'Sweden: Secure neutrality', *ANNALS, AAPSS*, 512 November: 116–24.
Sundelius, B. (1994) 'Changing course: When neutral Sweden chose to join the European Community', in Carlsnaes, W. and Smith, S. (eds.) *European foreign policy: the EC and changing perspectives in Europe*. London: Sage, pp. 177–201.
Suominen, I. (1994) 'Finland, the EU and Russia', *The World Today* 50 (1):12–14.
Svanström, R., and Palmstierna, C. F. (1934) *A short history of Sweden*. London: Oxford University Press.
Svensson, S. (1994) 'Sweden votes yes to membership in the EU', *Current Sweden* No. 408.
Svensson, T. (2002) 'Globalisation, marketisation and power: The Swedish case of institutional change', *Scandinavian Political Studies* 25 (3):197–229.
Svensson, T. and Öberg, P. (2002) 'Labour market organisations' participation in Swedish public policy-making', *Scandinavian Political Studies* 25 (4):295–315.
Swank, D. (1999) 'Social Democratic welfare states in a global economy: Scandinavia in comparative perspective', in Geyer, R., Ingebritsen, C. and Moses, J. W. (eds.) *Globalization, Europeanization and the end of Scandinavian Social Democracy?* Basingstoke: Macmillan, pp. 85–139.
Swartz, D. (1996) 'Swedish neutrality and the Second World War'. <http://en.wikipedia.org/wiki/Swedish_Neutrality_During_World_War_Two>
Swiss Government (2000) *Foreign policy report 2000. Presence and cooperation: Safeguarding Switzerland's interests in an integrating world*, 15th November.
Swedish Parliament (2000a) Excerpts from the Riksdag's preliminary record 2000/01:86, *Debate on the European Union*, 27th March. <www.riksdagen.se/english/work/prot/0001/86/index.asp> (accessed 10/11/01).
Swedish Parliament (2000b) Excerpts from the Riksdag's preliminary record 2000/01: 24, *Debate on the European Union*, 9th November. <www.riksdagen.se/english/work/prot/0001/24/index.asp> (accessed 24/11/00).
Swedish Parliament (2004) Press Release, 'Riksdag to have permanent delegation at NATO Assembly', 3rd March. <www.riksdagen.se/english/work/press/200304/permanent_delegation.asp>
Sztucki, J. (1991) 'Sweden', Paper on Swedish neutrality presented to the Colloquium on Neutrality and Non-alignment, Mediterranean Academy of Diplomatic Studies/Graduate Institute of International Studies, Geneva, 4th–8th November. <http://conf.diplomacy.edu/conf/neutrali/sweden.htm>
Thalberg, H. (1989) 'The role of public opinion in neutral policy', in Kruzel, J. and Haltzel, M. H. (eds.) *Between the blocs. Problems and prospects for Europe's neutral and nonaligned states*. Woodrow Wilson International Centre for Scholars and Cambridge: Cambridge University Press, pp. 231–40.
Thompson, P. and Sederblad, P. (1994) 'The Swedish Model of work organization in transition', in Elgar, T., and Smith, C. (eds.) *Global Japanization? The transnational transformation of the labour process*. London: Routledge, pp. 238–65.
Thucydides (1951) *The Peloponnesian war*. Introduction by John H. Finley, Jr. New York: Random House.
Tilton, T. (1990) *The political theory of Swedish Social Democracy. Through the welfare state to socialism*. Oxford: Clarendon Press.

Tingsten, H. (1959) 'Issues in Swedish foreign policy', *Foreign Affairs* 37 (3):474–85.
Tonra, B. (2000) 'Constructing narratives in Irish foreign policy', Paper presented to the panel 'Ireland on the international stage', American Conference for Irish Studies (ACIS), University of Limerick, 27th June, pp. 1–16.
Tooke, J. D. (1965) *The just war in Aquinas and Grotius*. SPCK, Holy Trinity Church, London: William Clowes and Sons, Ltd.
Touraine, A. (1988) *Return of the actor. Social theory in postindustrial society*. University of Minnesota Press: Minneapolis.
Tunander, O. (1999) 'The uneasy imbrication of nation-state and NATO: The case of Sweden', *Cooperation and Conflict* 34 (2):169–203.
Tunander, O. (2001) 'Swedish-German geopolitics for a new century. Rudolph Kjellén's "The state as living organism"', *Review of International Studies* 27 (3):451–63.
UN Peacekeeping website: www.un.org/Depts/dpko/dpko/contributors/index.htm
United States Embassy, Stockholm, Sweden (1998) Holocaust assets. U.S. allied wartime and postwar relations and negotiations with Argentina, Portugal, Spain, Sweden, and Turkey on looted gold and German external assets and U.S. concerns about the fate of the wartime Ustasha treasury, 2nd June <www.usis.usemb.se/nazigold.sweden.html> (accessed 27/10/00).
US State Department (1998) Eizenstat special briefing on Nazi gold. On-the-record briefing upon the release of the report, U. S. and allied wartime and postwar relations and negotiations with Argentina, Portugal, Spain, Sweden, and Turkey on looted gold and German external assets and U. S. concerns about the fate of the wartime Ustasha treasury. Washington DC, 2nd June. <www.state.gov/www/policy_remarks/1998/980602_eizenstat_nazigld.html> (accessed 27/10/00), pp. 1–19.
Vaahtoranta, T. and Forsberg, T. (2000) *Post-neutral or pre-allied? Finnish and Swedish policies on the EU and NATO as security organisations*. UPI Working Paper 29. Helsinki: Ulkopoliittinen Instituutti (The Finnish Institute of International Affairs), pp. 1–43.
Valtasaari, J. (1999) 'A Finnish perspective on the changing Europe', The SASS, Shanghai, 10th February. <www.virtual.finland.fi/finfo/english/otkaneng_frame.html> (accessed 09/05/00).
Van Ekecrantz (1997) 'Journalism's "discursive events" and sociopolitical change in Sweden', *Media, Culture and Society* 19 (3):393–412.
Van Staden, A. (1994) 'After Maastricht: Explaining the movement towards a common European defence policy', in Carlsnaes, W. and Smith, S. (eds.) *European foreign policy: The EC and changing perspectives in Europe*. London: Sage, pp. 138–55.
Vasquez, J. A. (1997) 'The realist paradigm and degenerative versus progressive research programs: An appraisal of neotraditional research on Waltz's balancing proposition', *The American Political Science Review* 91 (4):899–912.
Väyrynen, R. (1989a) 'Commentary', in Kruzel, J. and Haltzel, M. H. (eds.) *Between the blocs. Problems and prospects for Europe's neutral and nonaligned states*. Woodrow Wilson International Centre for Scholars and Cambridge: Cambridge University Press, pp. 122–9.

Väyrynen, R. (1989b) 'Constraints and opportunities in the foreign policies of small states', in Heurlin, B. and Thine, C. (eds.) *Danmark og det internationale system.* Copenhagen: Politiske Studier, Kobenhaven, pp. 52–62.
Venn, C. (2002) 'World dis/order. On some fundamental questions', *Theory, Culture and Society* 19 (4): 121–36.
Von Altenbockum. (2002) 'Neutralized', *Franfurter Algemeine Zeitung* 19/02/02. <www.vrede.be/nl/europa/eudef5.html#1>
Von Clausewitz, C. (1911) 'War as an instrument of policy' [*On war*], reproduced in Williams, P., Goldstein, D. M. and Shafritz, J. M. (eds.) *Classic readings of international relations.* Belmont, California: Wadsworth. pp. 336–41.
Wahlbäck, K. (1986) *The roots of Swedish neutrality.* Stockholm: Swedish Institute, pp. 1–80.
Wahlbäck, K. (1992) 'Swedish security in a changing Europe', *Current Sweden* No. 391, pp. 1–6.
Wahlbäck, K. (1994) 'Nordic and Baltic Security in the 1990s', *European security after the Cold War*, part 2. Papers from the 35th Annual Conference of the International Institute for Security Studies (IISS), Brussels, Belgium, 9th–12th September 1992. Adelphi Paper 285 (February 1994), pp. 47–59.
Walker, D. (1998) 'Tony's ology for sceptics', *The Guardian* 22nd September.
Wallace, H. (1997) 'At odds with Europe', *Political Studies* 45 (4):677–88.
Wallace, W. (1991) 'Foreign policy and national identity in the United Kingdom', *International Affairs* 67 (1):65–80.
Walt, S. (1997) 'The progressive power of realism', *The American Political Science Review* 91 (4):931–5.
Waltz, K. N. (1954) *Man, the state, and war.* New York: Columbia University Press.
Waltz, K. N. (1979) *Theory of international politics.* Reading, Massachusetts: Addison-Wesley.
Waltz, K. N. (1993) 'The emerging structure of international politics', *International Security* 18 (2):44–79.
Waltz, K. N. (1995) 'The United States and the new world order', in Hansen, B. (ed.) *European security – 2000.* Copenhagen: Copenhagen Political Studies Press, pp. 13–25.
Walzer, M. (1992) *Just and unjust wars. A moral argument with historical illustrations.* Second Edition. New York: Basic Books.
Weber, C. (2002) 'Flying planes can be dangerous', *Millennium* 31 (1):129–47.
Weiss, L. (1998) 'Limits of the distributive state: Swedish Model or global economy?', in Weiss, L. (ed.). *The myth of the powerless state. Governing the economy in a global era.* Cambridge: Blackwell Press, pp. 83–115.
Weldes, J. (1996) 'Constructing national interests', *European Journal of International Relations* 2 (3):275–318.
Wendt, A. (1992) 'Anarchy is what states make of it: The social construction of power politics', *International Organization* 46 (2):391–425.
Wendt, A. (1995) 'Constructing international politics', *International Security* 20 (1):71–81.
Wendt, A. (1999) *Social theory of international politics.* Cambridge: Cambridge University Press.

Bibliography

Wendt, F. (1981) *Cooperation in the Nordic countries. Achievements and obstacles.* Stockholm: Almqvist and Wiksell International.

Werner, W. G. and de Wilde, J. H. (2001) 'The endurance of sovereignty', *European Journal of International Relations* 7 (3):283–313.

Widfeldt, A. (1995) 'The Swedish parliamentary elections of 1994', *Electoral Studies* 14 (2):206–12.

Widmer, S. (1989) 'Forms of neutrality', in Kruzel, J. and Haltzel, M. H. (eds.) *Between the blocs. Problems and prospects for Europe's neutral and nonaligned states.* Woodrow Wilson International Centre for Scholars and Cambridge: Cambridge University Press, pp. 17–28.

Wilks, S. (1996) 'Class compromise and the international economy: The rise and fall of Swedish Social Democracy', *Capital and Class* 58:89–111.

Wilson, P. (1998) 'The myth of the "first great debate"', *Review of International Studies* December 24:1–26.

Wilson, W. (1914) *Message to Congress,* 63rd Congress, 2nd Session, Senate Document. No. 566 (Washington, 1914), pp. 3–4. <www.lib.byu.edu/~rdh/wwi/1914/wilsonneut.html> (accessed 06/03/98).

Wilson, W. (1917) 'Wilson's speech for declaration of war against Germany', address delivered at Joint Session of Congress, 2nd April. <www.nv.cc.va.us/~nvsageh/WWwarMessage.htm> (accessed 06/03/98).

Wilson, W. [1918] (1994) 'The fourteen points', reproduced in Williams, P., Goldstein, D. M. and Shafritz, J. M. (eds.) *Classic readings of international relations.* Belmont, California: Wadsworth.

Windsor, P. (1989) 'Neutral states in historical perspective', in Kruzel, J. and Haltzel, M. H. (eds.) *Between the blocs. Problems and prospects for Europe's neutral and non-aligned states.* Woodrow Wilson International Centre for Scholars and Cambridge: Cambridge University Press, pp. 3–9.

Wörlund, I. (1995) 'The Swedish parliamentary election of September 1994', *Scandinavian Political Studies* 18 (4):285–91.

Zakheim, D. S. (1998) 'The United States and the Nordic countries during the Cold War', *Cooperation and Conflict* 33 (2):115–29.

Zehfuss, M. (2001) 'Constructivism and identity: A dangerous liaison', *European Journal of International Relations* 7 (3):315–48.

Zetterberg, H. L. (1982) 'The political values of the 1980s', in Rydén, B. and Bergström, V. (eds.) *Sweden: Choices for economic and social policy in the 1980s.* London: George Allen and Unwin, pp. 36–50.

Zetterberg, H. L. (1984) Vår tids opinionsströmningar. *Två uppsatser* [our current opinions. Two articles] presented to the SAF Congress at Gothenburg 23rd–24th November 1984, pp 13–27. <http://zetterberg.org/Papers/ppr1984c.htm>

Newspaper/Internet articles

Agence France Presse (29/01/03) 'Nordic defense forces to cooperate on Artic civilian rescue missions'.

Bibliography

Agence France Presse (28/04/03) 'Irish court rejects challenge to US use of airport'.
BBC News (08/02/01) '"Stay neutral" Putin urges Austria'. <www.bbc.co.uk/hi/english/world/europe/newsid_1160000/1160048.stm>
BBC News (19/09/01) 'Germans torn by dilemma'. <http://news.bbc.co.uk/hi/english/world/europe/newsid_1553000/1553152.stm>
BBC News (21/11/01) 'Analysis: Denmark's shift to the right'. <http://news.bbc.co.uk/hi/english/world/europe/newid_1668000/1668439.stm>
BBC News (11/03/02) '"No neutrality", warns Bush'. <http://news.bbc.co.uk/1/hi/world/americas/1867101.stm>
BBC News (17/02/03) 'Millions join global anti-war protest'. <http://news.bbc.co.uk/2/hi/europe/2765215.stm>
BBC News (11/05/05) 'An Anglo-Saxon takeover of the EU?'. <http://news.bbc.co.uk/go/pr/fr/-/1/hi/uk_politics/4538249.htm>
CNN (06/11/01) 'You are either with us or against US'. <www.cnn.com/2001/US/11/06/gen.attack.on.terror>
CNN (29/10/04) 'Bin Laden: "Your security is in your own hands"'. <www.cnn.com/2004/WORLD/meast/10/29/bin.laden.transcript/>
Dagens Nyheter (21/10/97) 'Suppressing the memory of recent events: Interview with Maria-Pia Boëthius'. <www.dn.se/DNet/departments/172-static/english/eboethius.html>
Dagens Nyheter (22/11/00) 'Freedom from alliances is no longer valid'.
Dagens Nyheter (11/02/02) 'Swedish party leaders comment on the new security policy doctrine'.
Dagens Nyheter (12/02/02) 'Sweden scraps neutrality'.
Detroit Free Press (06/03/99) 'High-revving Ford worries smooth-running Volvo'. <http://vh1380.infi.net/business/qvolvo6.htm>
Eagle Street, Newsletter of the Finnish Institute in London (1998) Seminar Report: 'Small states and European security', Dublin, 20–22/11/97. <www.polarities.net/articles/es_7/smallstates.htm>
EU Business (10/12/03) 'EU constitution leads Austria to question its neutrality'. <www.eubusiness.com/afp/031210143420.lb6tbtb4>
EU Observer (22/11/00) 'Sweden no longer a non-aligned country'. <www.euobserver.com/index.phtml?selected_topic=none&action=view&article_id=896>
EU Observer (14/12/00) 'Swedish neutrality hardly viable in the EU'. <www.euobserver.com/index.phtml?selected_topic=none&action=view&article_id=1168>
EU Observer (19/01/01) 'No solidarity with neutral countries'. <www.euobserver.com/?aid=1314>
EU Observer (17/01/01) 'Solana: Neutrality is a concept of the past'. <www.euobserver.com/index.phtml?selected_topic=13&action=view&article_id=1291>
EU Observer (26/04/01) 'When Switzerland do as the Danes did'. <www.euobserver.com/index.phtml?selected_topic=none&action=view&article_id=2084>

EU Observer (11/12/01) 'Finns and Austrians prefer neutrality'. <www.euobserver.com/index.phtml?selected_topic=13&action=view&article_id=4503>
EU Observer (17/05/02) 'Social Democracy in Europe is dead'. <www.euobserver.com/index.phtml?aid=6161>
EU Observer (14/03/03) 'Austria blocks transit of US troops'. <www.euobserver.com/?aid=9379>
EU Observer (09/09/03) 'Yes camp "spending more than Bush"'. <www.euobserver.com/?aid=12609>
EU Observer (21/10/03) 'Swedish business spent €55m on euro campaign'. <www.euobserver.com/?aid=13119>
EU Observer (16/02/04) 'No EU army, say the Finns'. <www.euobserver.com/?sid=13&aid=14502>
EU Observer (20/02/04) 'Majority of Austrians in favour of EU army'. <www.euobserver.com/?sid=13&aid=14560>
EU Observer (09/11/04) 'Austrian Greens in heated discussion over neutrality'. <www.euobserver.com/?aid=17718>
Europe (1995) Interview with Peter Wallenberg. September, Issue 349, p. 16.
The European (08–10/02/91) 'The Austrians raise their EC game'.
The European (17–20/12/92) '"Black day" widens Swiss rift'.
The European (24–30/12/93) 'Impatient young tussle with elders over Swiss neutrality'.
The European (18–24/01/96) 'How a financial wizard cast a spell over Finland'.
The European (19–25/08/94) 'Sweden's free-market flirtation cools'.
Financial Times (29/01/99) 'Ireland seeks to join NATO's Partnership for Peace'.
Financial Times (28/11/00) 'Sweden moots ending neutrality'.
Financial Times (09/11/01) 'Persson moving faster than his party'.
Financial Times (20/04/03) 'So who's neutral now?'.
The Guardian (16/06/01) 'EU leaders fear wrath of the people'.
The Guardian (05/11/01) 'Vienna prepares to ditch neutrality'.
The Guardian (04/03/02) 'Switzerland decides to join UN'.
Helsingin Sanomat (31/10/00) 'Nordic countries have different viewpoints in the EU'.
Helsingin Sanomat (20/01/04) 'Finnish defence minister disagrees with General Hägglund on combining EU and NATO'. <www2.helsinginsanomat.fi/english/archive/news.asp?id=20040420IE11>
Helsingin Sanomat (27/09/04) 'French defence minister: Non-alignment means nothing in EU'. <http://helsinginsanomat.fi/english/article/print/1076154060161>
Helsingin Sanomat (09/03/05). 'Finnish MEPs clash over Northern Dimension'.
The Irish Independent (19/04/04) 'Forget neutrality – it's time for us to take sides'.
The Irish Independent (30/05/03) 'We must move away from our neutrality, says FG'.
The Irish Times (05/10/96) 'Solid majority favours neutrality'.
The Irish Times (19/10/96) 'Neutrality concept potent yet ambiguous'.
The Irish Times (31/05/01) 'Former Maltese PM urges no vote'. <www.ireland.com/special/nice/news/3105/news1.htm>
The Irish Times (11/06/01) 'Neutrality may be the key to solving Nice impasse'. <www.ireland.com/newspaper/ireland/2001/0611/hom.28.htm>

Bibliography

The Irish Times (11/06/01) 'Results of the Nice referendum'. <www.ireland.com/special/nice/news/results.htm>

The Irish Times (07/07/03) 'Former UN inspector criticises Irish war role'.

The Irish Times (16/01/04) 'State not neutral by any credible definition'.

The Irish Times (30/07/04) 'Neutrality – nothing but a "group think" mantra?'.

The Irish Times (29/01/05) 'Wartime neutrality theoretical rather than real'.

The Malta Business Weekly (28/06–04/07/01) 'La Salle controversy'. Issue No. 349.

Malta Star (08/03/02) 'Malta: A neutral state?'. <www.maltastar.com/news.asp?newsitemid=2348>

MOMA (Museum of Modern Art) New York (2000) Film and video programme, programme summary, *The imaginary war*, 14th September–12th October. <www.moma.org/about_moma/press/2000/imag_war_10_09_00.html>

The New Yorker (21/07/03) 'Blackballed by Bush'. <www.newyorker.com/printables/talk/030728ta_talk_mcgrath>

Nordic Reach (2001) 'On history and heroes: A conversation with Göran Persson'. November. <www.nordicreach.com/content_samples_gpersson.html>

Radio Free Europe/Radio Liberty (20/12/99) '1999 in review: New challenges as NATO moves East'. <www.rferl.org/nca/features/1999/12/F.RU.991220150049.html>

Radio Sweden (15/11/99) 'Persson Says yes to EMU'. <www.sr.se/rs/red/ind_eng.html>

Radio Sweden (05/03/02) 'Swedes remain opposed to NATO membership'. <www.sr.se/rs/red/ind_eng.html>

Radio Sweden (27/12/02) 'US nuclear-armed submarines violated Swedish waters in the 60s'. <www.sr.se/rs/red/ind_eng.html>

Radio Sweden (30/01/03) 'Denmark signs solidarity statement'. <www.sr.se/rs/red/ind_eng.html>

Radio Sweden (26/03/03) 'Persson says US out of step with rest of the world'. <www.sr.se/rs/red/ind_eng.html>

Radio Sweden (09/05/03) 'Danish PM tells Bush to ignore UN'. <www.sr.se/rs/red/ind_eng.html>

Radio Sweden (22/05/03) 'Norwegians puzzled over Al-Qaeda threat'. <www.sr.se/rs/red/ind_eng.html>

Radio Sweden (14/11/03) 'Persson says welfare costs too much'. <www.sr.se/rs/red/ind_eng.html>

Radio Sweden (01/11/04) 'Bin Laden: Sweden not a target'. <www.sr.se/rs/red/ind_eng.html>

Radio Sweden (25/02/05) 'European Social Democrats meet in Stockholm'. <www.sr.se/rs/red/ind_eng.html>

Reuters Press (05/01/98) 'Was Sweden really on Germany's side in WWII?'. <www.vho.org/GBNews/SRN1_05_98.html#World War Two>

Statewatch (23/03/02) 'EU proposal on European arrest warrant: Swedish parliament votes in favour'. <www.statewatch.org/>

Sunday Mirror (12/10/03) 'US planes earn Aer Rianta €11m'.

Svenska Dagbladet (25/11/91) 'Gamla etiketterna bort' [The old etiquettes go].

Svenska Dagbladet (15/02/96) 'Svensk utrikespolitik har bytt skepnad' [Swedish

foreign policy has changed shape].
Svenska Dagbladet (05/02/97) 'Minskat motstånd mot NATO' [Less resistance towards NATO].
The Times of India (16/10/01) 'Stockholm syndrome'. <http://timesofindia.indiatimes.com>
The Times of India (13/02/02) 'Sweden scraps neutrality, opening to NATO seen'. <http://timesofindia.indiatimes.com/articleshow.asp?art_id=807863>
USA Today (13/02/02) 'Sweden announces new security doctrine'. <www.usatoday.com/news/world/2002/02/13/Sweden.htm>
Wired from Sweden (17/01/97) 'Opposition leader endorses membership of "new NATO", but government cautious'. No. 21. <www.si.se/wired21.html>
Wired from Sweden (09/02/98) 'NATO Membership Debate "Dangerous"'. No. 43. <www.si.se/wired43.html>

Interviews

Hans Arvidsson, *Left Party*. Advisor to Eva Zetterberg, 11th August 1998.
Sverker Åström, Former diplomat, *Department of Foreign Affairs*. 13th August 1998.
Britt Bohlin, *Social Democratic Party*. Member of the Advisory Committee on Foreign Affairs, 13th August 1998.
Viola Furubjelke. *Social Democratic Party*. Chairperson of the Committee on Foreign Affairs; Member of the Advisory Council on Foreign Affairs; Member of the War Delegation, 18th August 1998.
Jesper Haglund, *Christian Democratic Party*. Political Advisor on EU and International Affairs, 13th August 1998.
Anders Hall, *Moderate Party*. Advisor to Göran Lennmarker, spokesperson for foreign and security issues, 11th August 1998.
Colonel Bo Hugemark, *Royal War College*, 26th August 1998.
Henrik Landerholm, *Moderate Party*. Member of the Committee on Defence; Deputy to the Swedish Delegation to the Parliamentary Assembly of the Council of Europe (Committee on Foreign Affairs), 25th August 1998.
Göran Lennmarker, *Moderate Party*. Spokesperson on foreign and security issues. Deputy Member Advisory Council on Foreign Affairs; Advisory Committee on EU Affairs; War Delegation; Deputy Swedish Delegation to the Nordic Council, 18th August 1998.
Helena Nilsson, *Centre Party*. Member of the Committee on Foreign Affairs, War Delegation, and Committee on European Affairs, 13th August 1998.
Annika Nordgren, *Green Party*. Spokesperson on defence and security issues, Member of the Committee on Defence, 13th August 1998.
Lennart Rohdin, *Liberal Party*. Deputy Member of the Committee on Foreign Affairs, spokesperson for Defence, Member of the Committee of Defence, 12th August 1998.
Lars Tobisson, *Moderate Party*. Deputy Member, Parliamentary Assembly of the Council of Europe (Advisory Council on Foreign Affairs); Deputy Chairman, Advisory Committee on European Affairs, 18th August 1998.
Dr Krister Wahlbäck, Ministry for Foreign Affairs, 17th August 1998.

INDEX

abstention from warfare 1–15, 18, 36, 44
acquis communautaire 153, 166, 193
active labour market policy 92–6, 129
Adler, E. 42–7 *passim*, 54–6, 169
Ahern, Bertie 177, 194–5
Al Qaeda 196
Åland Islands 51, 70
alcohol consumption and taxation 175, 200
Amsterdam Treaty (1997) 167–8, 193, 207
anarchy in international relations 37–41, 44–5, 48–51, 55, 73, 77, 90
Anderson, Benedict 169
Andrén, N. 5, 7, 72, 155, 182
Anschluß, 27, 71
armed neutrality 15–17, 28, 37–9, 50, 54, 61, 72, 105
arms control 28, 55, 156
Åström, Sverker 82–3, 101, 106, 115, 134, 151, 158, 181, 191
Athenian politics 12, 37
Austria 6, 25, 27, 41, 49–50, 100, 151–3, 176–7, 192–5, 198

balance of power, international 16, 21–7, 38, 40, 50, 52, 101–2, 107, 206
within Sweden 64
Barkin, J.S. 34, 40
Bartelson, J. 40, 55
Belgium 17, 38, 41, 105, 190
Berger, P.L. 43, 47–8, 99, 160
Bergman, Ingmar 83
Bernadotte, F. 80, 108–9
Bildt, Carl 109, 121, 128, 138, 142–3, 147–61 *passim*, 165–7, 172–3, 180, 183, 199–200, 207
Bin Laden, Osama 196
Binter, B. 32, 35
Blair, Tony 46, 179, 195, 197
third way 174–5
Blyth, M. 123, 127–8, 132, 159, 161
Bohlin, Britt 151, 159, 181
Branting, Hjalmar 67, 69–70
Britain 41, 45–7, 56, 69, 84, 125, 131, 135, 171, 179
Bukovansky, M. 52, 105
Bush, George W. 2, 189–203 *passim*, 206
business interests 128–9, 132, 134, 138, 149, 152, 159, 174, 207

Carlsson, Ingvar 35, 112, 130, 146, 148, 165, 173, 191–2
Carr, E.H. 18–19, 21
censorship 80, 84
Childs, Marquis 73–4
Christianity 12–13, 29
Churchill, Winston 19, 22, 69, 79, 81
Clinton, Bill 202
co-determination 123, 126
'cognitive evolution' 43, 54
'cognitive frames' 159
'cognitive regions' 169
Cold War 25, 28–9, 90, 102, 104, 107–11, 120
ending of 1, 32–5, 50, 56, 143 146, 206
collective security 19–20, 25, 54, 71
Commission on Neutrality Policy 151
Common Foreign and Security Policy (CFSP) 7, 36, 142–5, 152–4, 166–71, 176, 192, 197, 207
Conference on Security and Cooperation in Europe (CSCE)

Index

28, 106, 111, 154
conflict resolution 35, 51, 92, 110, 115, 128, 203
consensualism 75, 92, 97, 121, 137, 203
constructivism *see* social constructivism
Cook, Robin 179
Council of Europe 154, 167
Cox, M. 24, 35, 153
Cronin, B. 34, 40
cruise missiles 28, 111
culture, definition and production of 43
Czech Republic 170–1
Czechoslovakia 102

Dagens Nyheter 128, 172
Davignon Report 135–6
December Compromise (1906) 67–8
decommodification 95, 98, 175
Delanty, G. 100, 170–1
Delors, Jacques 136
democratic deficit 170
Denmark 15, 22, 26, 40, 63, 102–4, 107, 124, 132, 175, 179–80, 195
Deutsch, K. 55, 107, 170
devaluation 130
direct democracy 53
disarmament 70, 110–12, 115–16
Dulles, John Foster 25
Dunne, T. 146, 190, 202–3
Dürrenmatt, Friedrich 4

Economic and Monetary Union (EMU) 40, 174, 200
Eisenhower, Dwight D. 25
epistemic communities 55–6
Erlander, Tage 92, 94–5, 109, 113, 135
Esping-Andersen, G. 95, 132, 137
Estonia 175
Ethiopia 19, 71
ethnic conflicts 33, 189
Eurobarometer surveys 174, 202

European arrest warrant 196–7
European Free Trade Association (EFTA) 106, 136, 145, 153
European identity 169–71, 174–6, 181
European Rapid Reaction Force 168
European Trade Union Confederation 125
European Union (EU) 2, 7, 27, 33, 36, 40, 45–7, 55–6, 106, 134–6, 139, 142–60, 165–81, 188–203, 207
proposed constitution 93–4, 198, 200

Fälldin, Thorbjorn 124, 129, 135, 158
film industry 83
Finland 6, 26, 28, 41, 49, 51, 62, 69, 76–80, 100–4 *passim*, 151–4, 160, 167–8, 171, 175–6, 179, 182, 194–5, 198
Finnemore, M. 43, 159
First World War 17, 20, 28–9, 68–9
FitzGerald, Garret 177
folkhem (People's Home) 7, 47–8, 60, 65, 73–6, 82–3, 94–5, 98–9, 106, 113–14, 120–2, 129, 139, 147, 155, 207
France 41, 125, 198–201
full employment 93, 145
Furubjelke, Viola 151, 158

de Gaulle, Charles 135
Germany 17, 19, 27, 69–72, 78–81, 84–5, 125
globalisation 7, 33, 41, 125, 137–9, 157–8, 172, 179–80, 188–9, 198–201, 208
Gothic Society 63
Greece, Ancient 11–12
Grotius, Hugo 14–15, 18, 22
Group of 21 156
Gustav V, King 69, 81
Gustavus Adolphus, King 10, 54

248

Index

Hägglöf, Gunnar 23, 82, 101–2
Hague Conventions 16, 19, 24, 29, 78–9, 84, 155
Hakovirta, H. 29–30, 49–50
Hall, Anders 147, 154
Hammarskjöld, Dag 108–9, 115
Hampden-Turner, C., 73–4, 99–100
Hansson, Albin 73–6, 82, 92, 97–8
'harmony of interests' doctrine 18–19
Heclo, H. 67, 73–5, 91, 93
Hedin, N. 80, 82
Herodotus 12
Himmler, Heinrich 80
'historical continuity' of Swedish neutrality 60
Hitler, Adolf 23, 72, 82
Hjelm-Wallén, L. 173, 180, 199
Home Guard 71, 82
Huldt, B. 35, 106, 154, 192
human rights 115, 144, 196–7
humanitarian interventions 33, 112–13, 167–8, 189, 202
Hungary 144
Huntington, S. 34, 189
Hussein, Saddam 196

Iceland 104, 107
idealism in international relations 3–4, 17–18, 21, 39
impartiality between bellligerents 16, 23
India 108
individualism 199–200
industrial policy 123
insularity 61–2
'integral neutrality' 79
International Criminal Court 196
international institutions 33, 54, 105
international law 14, 16, 20, 24, 29, 39, 41, 72, 107–10, 115, 155, 189, 196–7, 202
International Monetary Fund 103
international relations (IR) theory 3–4, 10, 20–1, 24, 30, 34, 41–2, 55–7, 208
internationalism 6, 19–20, 53, 70, 72, 85, 91, 101, 107–10, 114–15, 120, 155–8, 195–8, 202–3
radical 113
Iran 109
Iraq 109, 196–8, 202
Ireland 22, 45, 50, 152, 76–7, 194–5
isolationism 20, 32, 41, 52, 61–2, 73, 81, 85, 103, 120, 190, 206–8
Israeli-Palestinian conflict 109, 190
Italy 19, 46, 71

Jackson, R. 37, 40
Jakobson, Max 49, 176
Japan 19
Jefferson, Thomas 52
Jenson, J. 122, 138
Joenniemi, P. 5, 36–8, 50–1, 107, 179–80
Joesten, J. 77–8, 81, 84
'just war' doctrine 14–15, 18–19, 29, 190

Kant, Immanuel 18, 170
Karl VII, King 64
Karl Johan, King 60–3, 85, 108–9
Karlsson, B. 84, 103
Karsh, E. 16, 19, 23, 45
Katzenstein, P.J. 43, 52
Kellogg-Briand Pact 53
Keynesian economics 92–3, 124–5, 130–1
Khrushchev, Nikita 26–7
Klestil, Thomas 153, 176–7
Korean War 107–8
Korpi, W. 77, 92, 132, 137
Kreisky, Bruno 49–50, 74

lagom idea 100, 122
Landsorganisationen Sverige (LO) 67–8, 77, 121–3, 126, 130–3, 138, 145, 175
language 47
Latvia 175
Lawler, P. 76, 98, 160
League of Nations 17–21, 24, 51, 70–2, 101

Index

Leagues of Armed Neutrality 15–16, 61
Lebanon 109
Lindbeck, A. 93, 132, 137
Lindbeck Commission 122, 148–9
Lindh, Anna 171, 173, 179, 181, 191–2, 196–7, 200
Lloyd George, David 69
Logue, J. 70, 74, 81
Luckmann, T. 43, 47–8, 99, 160
Luxembourg 22

Maastricht Treaty 40, 144, 152, 167
McCracken Report 125
MacDougall Report 125
MacGinty, R. 24, 35, 153
Machiavelli, Niccolò 13, 21
Madsen, H. 67, 73–5, 91
Mahon, R. 122, 138
Malmborg, af M. 62–3
Malta 178, 195
Marcussen, M. 149, 160–1
Marshall Plan 102
Marxism 67
means-testing 95
mediation 110, 116, 157, 167, 182–3
Meidner, Rudolph 73, 92–6, 121, 130, 159
Melian Dialogue 11–12, 17, 22, 37
metaphors 47–8, 98, 129
Mintoff, Dom 178, 195
monetarism 132
Morgenthau, H.J. 17, 20–3, 26
Mouritzen, H. 49, 65, 180
Myrdal, Alva 92, 98–9
Myrdal, Gunnar 74, 92, 98–9, 113
myths 47–8, 90, 160, 182, 207

national identity 5, 45, 57, 101, 156
  Swedish 7, 63, 85, 166, 184, 207
national interests 44, 152, 167
nationalism 134, 139
nation-states, building of 51, 61
Nazism 84
neoclassical economics 132, 138

neoliberalism 114, 124–8, 132–3, 136–9, 158, 161, 165, 199–200, 207
neo-realism 27–8, 34, 52, 54
Netherlands, the 22
Neuhold, H. 27, 49
Neumann, Iver B. 47, 134
neutralism as distinct from neutrality 25
neutrality, active form of 105, 108–9
  challenges to 1–2, 41
  common perceptions of 1, 4, 10
  consensus of 110, 150, 155
  definition of 50
  diminishing use of phrase 151
  of European countries 176–8, 193–6
  as an issue of identity 48
  literature on 2–5, 12, 72–3, 82–3
  obsolescence of 183, 188, 208
  positive and *negative* 3
  problem with the concept of 2, 37–8
  public support for 105
  status of 22, 35–9
  Swedish variety of 6–8, 18, 35, 90, 101, 116, 201, 207
  symbolism of 183
new international economic order 114
New Zealand 132
Nixon, Richard 115–16
non-alignment policy 24, 26, 35, 111, 150–1, 169, 173, 176–8, 191–5
Nordic cooperation 106–7, 134, 178–83, 195
norms 42–4, 48, 52–4, 107, 110–11, 115–16, 139, 161, 165, 175, 181–4, 196–203 *passim*, 206–9
North Atlantic Treaty Organisation (NATO) 7, 28, 33–5, 102–4, 107–11, 135, 143–3, 154–6, 160, 166, 171–3, 176–7, 182, 189–98
Northern Dimension project 179
Norway 17, 22, 26, 62, 68, 76, 79, 102–7, 124, 166, 180, 183, 190, 195–8

nuclear technology 28, 102, 110
nuclear test bans 110–12

Oberg, J. 192, 201
oil crises 124, 130, 133
overseas development assistance 112–13, 116

Pakistan 108
Palm, August 66
Palme, Olof 82, 90, 92, 99, 101, 109–12, 115–16, 120, 122, 135, 178
Palme Commission 112
Palme Doctrine 28
pan-Scandinavianism 63, 107
peace research 109
'peaceful coexistence' doctrine 26
peacekeeping operations 109–10, 116, 154, 167–9, 173, 178, 194
Peloponnesian War 11, 29, 41
Persson, Göran 171–5, 179, 181, 184, 188, 191–2, 196–200, 207
Pestoff, V.A. 125, 148
Petersberg tasks 167–9, 183, 193, 207
Poland 77
Portugal 22, 199
positivism 15–17
postmodernism 189
power relations, international 21, 202–3
  see also balance of power
Press Council 80
privatisation 134, 147–8
proclamations of Swedish neutrality 61–2, 69, 77
Prodi, Romano 189
public sector employment 129
Pufendorf, Samuel 15, 18
Putin, Vladimir 190

quasi-neutralism 25

Rasmussen, Anders Fogh 180, 195
rationalism 50

Reagan, Ronald 28, 125, 130
realism in international relations 3–4, 12, 17–18, 21–4, 28, 34–41, 44, 48–52 *passim*, 55, 71–3, 90, 112, 142, 150
referenda 165–6, 194, 200–1
Reformation, the 14, 54
regions within nation-states 46
Rehn, Gösta 92–6, 121, 130, 159
Rice, Condoleeza 202
rights of neutrals 15–18, 22, 29, 37, 83
Riksdag, the 64, 66, 71, 75–7, 91, 101, 104, 112, 122, 136, 146–7, 150, 181–2, 190, 192, 196
Romanticism 63
Roosevelt, F.D. 20, 74
Roscher, R. 149, 160–1
Ross, J.F.L. 36, 135
rule of law 18, 70, 144
Russia 63, 69, 78, 84, 154
  see also Soviet Union
Ruth, A. 63–5, 68, 71, 84, 100, 160, 180
Rydén, B. 131, 137
Ryner, M. 95, 127–8, 132, 149

Sainsbury, D. 92, 97
Salmon, P. 20, 39
Saltsjöbaden Agreement 77, 92, 123, 126
sanctions 19, 24
Scandinavian Defence Union, planned 102–4
Scandinavian Movement 63
Schengen Information System 197
Schori, P. 192, 196, 199
Schüssel, W. 176, 192
sclerosis thesis 132
Scotland 47
Second World War 21–4, 29, 77–85, 177
self-interest of neutral states 23, 120, 206
September 11, 2001 attacks 2, 188–91, 194, 201

Index

Sikkink, K. 43, 159
Single European Act 136
Skandia (company) 159
social constructivism 5–7, 30, 32–3, 41–8, 54, 57, 90, 121, 159, 166, 181, 183, 207
   thick and *thin* varieties of 42
Social Democracy 48, 66–70, 73, 82, 85, 90–2, 97, 100, 108, 112–16, 122–6, 130–9, 142, 145, 148–51, 154–61, 165–6, 172–5, 179, 183, 191, 198–9, 207
   definition of 74
   Swedish variety of 74–5
   see also Socialdemokratiska Arbetarepartiet
social stratification 95
Socialdemokratiska Arbetarepartiet (SAP) 6, 60–1, 66–9, 73–7, 90–101, 105–6, 114–15, 120–35, 138–9, 145–7, 150–1, 156–61, 165–6, 173–5, 180–1, 191–2, 200, 207
   hegemony of 91, 142, 145, 181
   Third Way Policy 121, 129–32
socialisation 45
socialism 66–7, 73–5, 93–4, 112–13
Södersten, B. 114, 157
'soft' security 144, 168–9, 202
Solana, Javier 188, 195, 197
solidarity, 6, 7, 35, 48, 60–1, 72, 76, 77, 82–3, 90, 92, 94, 98–9, 101, 104, 106–7, 108, 111, 113, 115, 116, 121, 183, 198, 199
sovereignty 14–17, 27, 35–41, 44, 81–4, 104, 106, 135, 145, 188, 199, 203, 208
Soviet Union (USSR) 19, 25–7, 49, 56, 102–3, 111, 143, 151–2
   see also Russia
Spain 22, 199–200
Spanish Civil War 71
Stalin, Joseph 82–3
Stern, M. 3, 70, 102, 116
Stockholm Conference (1938) 78
Stockholm Exhibition (1897) 98–9

Stråth, B. 60, 65, 125, 170–1
strike action 122–3, 131, 146
Strindberg, A. 64
Stromberg, P.G. 64–6
Sundelius, B. 28, 62, 70, 113, 150
Svenska Arbetsgivareföreningen (SAF) 67, 123, 127–9, 133, 148
Svenska Dagbladet 128
Swedish Model 6, 66, 74, 90, 92–8, 100–1, 105, 120–2, 129, 131–8 *passim*, 145–9 *passim*, 161, 174, 198, 200
Switzerland 4, 18–28 *passim*, 41, 44, 47, 53–4, 177–8, 193

Tegnér, Esaias 62, 76
terrorism and the 'war on terror' 2, 188–98, 201–2, 206, 208
Thatcher, Margaret 125, 130, 136, 149
Thirty Years War 54, 61
Thucydides 10–12
Tilton, T. 92, 94, 137
Touraine, A. 43, 199
trade, neutrality in 13–16, 61, 68–9, 78, 84
trade unions 131, 199
Transito affair 69
Trompenaars, F. 73–4, 99–100
Truman, Harry 25
Trumam Doctrine 102

Undén, Östen 70, 82, 101–2, 105, 110, 115, 151
   'Third Way' 105, 110
United Kingdom *see* Britain
United Nations 28, 54, 70, 90, 101–15, 154–8, 167, 171, 173, 178–9, 191–3, 197, 202
   Charter 24, 108, 198
   Conference on Trade and Development 114
   General Assembly 25, 107–8, 115, 156
   Security Council 24, 101, 103, 107–8

Index

United States 17, 19, 25–8, 46, 52, 56, 69, 74, 83, 103–4, 115, 125, 196–8, 202–3
  National Security Council 25
  War of Independence 16
universalism, 6, 7, 20, 66, 76, 91, 92, 94–6, 97, 98, 99, 111, 112–14, 116, 175

Vattel, Emmerich de 15, 18
Väyrynen, R. 24, 39–40, 51
Versailles Treaty 52
Vienna, Congress of 16
Vietnam War 83, 115–16

wage earner funds 123–30
wages policy 96, 130
Wahlbäck, K. 62, 157
Wallace, W. 45–6, 57

Waltz, K.N. 21, 27–9, 54, 143
war, causes of 21, 110
Warsaw Pact 33, 102
Washington Treaty 189
Weiss, L. 121–2, 137
welfare state 47, 66, 75, 94–5, 98, 100, 113–14, 121–2, 129, 131–8 *passim*, 145–9 *passim*, 161, 174, 198, 200
Wendt, A. 42–4, 48–51, 63, 85, 156
Werner Report 135–6
Western European Union (WEU) 144, 153–4, 166–71, 177
Westphalian state system 10, 15
Wigforss, Ernst 76, 92, 96, 123
Wilson, Woodrow 17–18, 22, 52, 69
Wolff, Christian 15, 36

Zetterberg, H.L. 128–9

EU authorised representative for GPSR:
Easy Access System Europe, Mustamäe tee 50,
10621 Tallinn, Estonia
gpsr.requests@easproject.com

www.ingramcontent.com/pod-product-compliance
Ingram Content Group UK Ltd.
Pitfield, Milton Keynes, MK11 3LW, UK
UKHW021835140426
5217IPUK00021B/1473